CORPORATE

DECISION

MAKING

in the World Economy

—

COMPANY
CASE
STUDIES

CORPORATE

DECISION

MAKING

in the World Economy

—

COMPANY
CASE
STUDIES

MICHAEL G. RUKSTAD
Harvard University

The Dryden Press
Harcourt Brace Jovanovich College Publishers
Fort Worth Philadelphia San Diego New York Orlando Austin San Antonio
Toronto Montreal London Sydney Tokyo

Acquisitions Editor: Jan Richardson/Rick Hammonds
Project Editor: Kelly Spiller
Production Manager: Barb Bahnsen
Permissions Editor: Doris Milligan
Director of Editing, Design, and Production: Jane Perkins

Text and Cover Designer: Melissa Morgan
Copy Editor: Nancy Shanahan
Indexer: Leoni McVey
Compositor: Impressions, Inc.
Text Type: 10/12 Times Roman

Library of Congress Cataloging-in-Publication Data

Rukstad, Michael G.
    Corporate decision making in the world economy : company case studies
/ Michael G. Rukstad.
        p.   cm.
    Includes bibliographical references and index.
    ISBN 0-03-076526-9
    1. Managerial economics—Case studies. 2. Decision-making—
Case studies. 3. Macroeconomics—Case studies.   I. Title.
HD30.22.R84   1992   91-38381
658.4′03—dc20

Printed in the United States of America
234-090-987654321

Acknowledgment for Cases

Address orders:
The Dryden Press
6277 Sea Harbor Drive
Orlando, Florida 32887
1-800-782-4479, or 1-800-433-0001 (in Florida)

Address editorial correspondence:
The Dryden Press
301 Commerce Street, Suite 3700
Fort Worth, TX 76102

The Dryden Press
Harcourt Brace Jovanovich

To my first and finest mentor, Professor William O. Farber

The Dryden Press Series in Economics

NEW IN 1992

James Gwartney
Richard Stroup
Economics: Private and Public Choice
Sixth Edition
Also Available in Split Volumes

Steven E. Landsburg
Price Theory and Applications
Second Edition

Michael B. Ormiston
Intermediate Microeconomics

Patrick J. Welch
Gerry F. Welch
Economics: Theory and Practice
Fourth Edition

William F. Lott
Subhash C. Ray
Applied Econometrics: Problems with Data Sets

Barry Keating
J. Holton Wilson
Managerial Economics
Second Edition

Walter Nicholson
Microeconomic Theory: Basic Principles and Extensions
Fifth Edition

Ramu Ramanathan
Introductory Econometrics with Applications
Second Edition

Mark Hirschey
James L. Pappas
Fundamentals of Managerial Economics
Fourth Edition

William Samuelson
Stephen Marks
Managerial Economics

Michael G. Rukstad
Macroeconomic Decision Making in the World Economy: Text and Cases
Third Edition

Michael G. Rukstad
Corporate Decision Making in the World Economy: Company Case Studies

SELECTED OTHER TEXTS

William J. Baumol
Alan S. Blinder
Economics: Principles and Policy
Fifth Edition

Edwin G. Dolan
David E. Lindsey
Economics
Sixth Edition
Also Available in Split Volumes

Meir Kohn
Money, Banking, and Financial Markets

Michael R. Edgmand
Ronald L. Moomaw
Kent W. Olson
Economics and Contemporary Issues

Beth V. Yarbrough
Robert M. Yarbrough
The World Economy: Trade and Finance
Second Edition

Mordechai E. Kreinin
International Economics: A Policy Approach
Sixth Edition

Henry Demmert
Economics: Understanding the Market Process

Howard Wachtel
Labor and the Economy
Second Edition

Gary Walton
Hugh Rockoff
History of the American Economy
Sixth Edition

PREFACE

The Impact of Macroeconomics on Business

The purpose of this book is to illustrate how macroeconomics affects the business decisions of corporations and, in so doing, to gain an understanding of how managers may best respond to their macroeconomic environment. It is designed for students of business, public policy, and applied economics, as well as managers and policy makers who are grappling daily with experiences such as those described in this book. The seed for this book was planted ten years ago as a result of conversations with Professors Tom McCraw, David Yoffie, and especially John Lintner, who were all colleagues of mine at the Harvard Business School. Many decades before, when John first arrived at the Business School, he had taught a course with cases similar in spirit to those in this casebook. Those early discussions with him encouraged me and helped shape this project.

A central premise of the pedagogy embodied in this casebook is that the best method for understanding the impact of the macroeconomic environment on a business is in two stages: first one must analyze the environment and then one must analyze the firm operating in that environment. Business managers and public policy makers will gain an understanding of how the macroeconomic environment affects business decisions by studying the channels through which a macroeconomic change is transmitted to the firm, and how managers react. Through the use of relevant applied case studies, students can learn to identify these *channels* and *responses*. Macroeconomic signals and incentives are often distorted in the decision-making process within a firm because of organizational and strategic constraints, as we will see in a later section.

A Companion Volume

This book is a companion to my other book with The Dryden Press, *Macroeconomic Decision Making in the World Economy*, Third Edition (1992). However, neither book is dependent on the other. Rather they are complementary and discuss interrelated themes. Whereas *Macroeconomic Decision Making* analyzes macroeconomic events through the eyes of policy makers, *Corporate Decision Making in the World Economy: Company Case Studies* analyzes business problems caused by macroeconomic events through the eyes of business managers. The development of the two books fits the pedagogical premise discussed above—the first casebook analyzes the marcoeconomic environment and the second casebook analyzes business managers making decisions in that environment. Both books share the feature that all cases are self-contained and can be taught in any order to a variety of audiences. The level of analysis in the class discussion will depend on the students' previous experience.

Uses of This Book

Over the past three years at Harvard, I designed, developed, and taught a second-year elective MBA course, Economic Policy and Business Decisions, which was based on these cases. During that time, I taught the cases in this book to almost 500 MBA students at the Harvard Business School, to the participants of the Advanced Management Program at Oxford University, and to executives of a number of corporate training programs, such as Alcan and IBM. In these forums, the cases were taught either as a self-contained course without a supplementary text, or in conjunction with related cases from *Macroeconomic Decision Making*.

Many of the case studies in this volume directly follow events described in *Macroeconomic Decision Making*. The following table shows some of the more obvious pairings:

Macroeconomic Decision Making	*Corporate Decision Making*
Paul Volcker and the Federal Reserve: 1979–1982	Franklin Savings Association
	Financial Swaps
	RJR/Nabisco and Leveraged Buyouts
	The General Aviation Industry in 1982
The United Kingdom under Thatcher	Massey–Ferguson, 1980
The Reagan Plan	Honeywell's Investment Decisions
	Ryder System
Deficit Reduction under President Bush	Martin Marietta
	Saab-Scania: The Car Division
Privatization in the United Kingdom	Privatization of British Airways
The Decline of the Dollar: 1978	General Motors and the Dollar
Mexico: Crisis of Confidence	Colgate-Palmolive in Mexico

The class discussions of the cases in this book are enriched by a deeper understanding of the contextual setting, which is, after all, the purpose of teaching the above paired cases as a conceptual module. The cumulative effect is to make macroeconomic concepts and events relevant to the next generation of business leaders and policy makers.

Even though the previous suggestions are my preferred method of teaching this material, there are alternatives which may be attractive to some instructors. *Corporate Decision Making*, which emphasizes macroeconomics, could be paired with a conceptually similar macroeconomics textbook that emphasizes international trade. Both books should take the perspective of a firm reacting to its economic environment. A final alternative is to use these cases to illustrate concepts taught in standard macroeconomics texts. For example, one could use the General Motors and the Dollar case to illustrate exchange rate pass-through, hysteresis in exchange rate movements, or the J-curve in payments adjustments, or use the Saab-Scania case to illustrate tax incidence of the social welfare taxes.

Organization of the Book

This casebook is organized into three parts. The parts focus on issues in the corporate management of various business problems initiated by changes in the business cycle, monetary policy, and fiscal policy. We will use the term *business cycle* in the broadest sense of the word to mean the rise and fall of economic activity encompassing aggregate real spending and all its associated output and price relationships. These cycles could be caused on the demand side of the economy by a change in consumer preferences or spending propensities, "animal spirits" affecting business investment, foreign spending on domestic products, or government policy including both monetary and fiscal policies. Alternatively, the cycles could be initiated on the supply side by a change in technology, production capability, productivity, or resources. The central issue unifying the cases in Part I is how firms cope with the cycle, rather than its specific cause.

The cases in Parts II and III, however, are unified by a specific cause: either monetary policy (in Part II) or fiscal policy (in Part III). Monetary policy exerts its influence on the economy through interest rates and exchange rates. Fiscal policy exerts its influence through spending and taxes. All four of these variables can directly affect a business decision, even though they may also affect a business indirectly through a change in the aggregate demand of the economy, and thus the demand for a business' products or services. The indirect channel is (arbitrarily) a concern of Part I of this book.

Grouping cases into topics such as business cycles, monetary policy, and fiscal policy will allow students to recognize issues and options associated with future macroeconomic events in the same format as they will read about the issue in *The Wall Street Journal* or *Business Week*, for example. The business media are more likely to present issues in terms of business cycles or monetary and fiscal policy changes than aggregate demand and aggregate supply, IS-LM curves, or rational expectations, even though the event could be described either way. Moreover, it is my hope that by the end of the course students will recognize common themes among the various macroeconomic influences on a business' behavior. To get students started in their thinking, the next section will identify common issues that span all the cases in this book.

A Framework for Analyzing the Cases

Most texts on business–government relations concentrate on a government policy maker who intervenes in the decision-making process of business managers by telling them what they can or cannot produce, where and how to produce it, where it can be sold, and at what price. This describes most cases of regulation and many cases of international trade. These nonmarket (or administrative) interventions in the private sector are only one method by which the government intervenes in the affairs of the private sector to accomplish public aims. The government also uses market interventions to accomplish its goals, such as when it attempts to influence the financial markets and business investment behavior by changing the money supply in order to change interest rates. These interventions are no less important to the understanding of business–government relations and business competition than is the study of regulation or trade, but they are often neglected.

Macroeconomic events and policies change market incentives. For example, if an interest rate is lowered or an investment tax credit offered, the firm can take advantage of these market incentives by making a new investment. Managers are not forced to make this investment by the regulator; they are only offered an incentive that must fit with the other business considerations for making that investment. These market incentives, in turn, create competitive opportunities and threats, which a business executive must learn to identify. Identifying these opportunities and threats will be the primary challenge for students using this casebook.

There are five issues common to all cases in this book. The first issue is to identify the change in incentives as a result of the macroeconomic event. In some cases, such as RJR/Nabisco, it is not immediately clear what the relevant change in market incentives would be, whereas in other cases, such as Colgate-Palmolive in Mexico, it is obvious that a significant devaluation has occurred, which affects the relative competitiveness of imported and exported products (among other consequences). A second issue is how an organization recognizes and communicates changes in the macroeconomic environment. In the Honeywell, Colgate-Palmolive, and Martin Marietta cases we provide some detail on this monitoring function of the organization. A third issue is to identify the cause, magnitude, and duration of the economic change. In the General Aviation case, for example, this task is central to the understanding of the business problem facing those manufacturers. A fourth issue is the effect the change will have on the firm's business. This linking of the macroeconomic environment and the business decision is the unique feature of these cases. Finally, a closely related issue, often overlooked, is the effect the change will have on the firm's competitors. For example, Ryder and Leaseway were affected quite differently by the tax changes of the early 1980s.

Unfortunately for our purposes, differential responses by rival firms are not a common feature of standard economic models, certainly not those of the macroeconomy. Usually they feature a representative firm, often operating in a relatively efficient, competitive market. In reality, firms differ greatly in their internal goals, strategies, and structures, and markets suffer from numerous rigidities and imperfections. Both realities interfere with the efficient "market response" to macroeconomic events and present *opportunities to gain competitive advantage.*

Differential responses by rival firms is the heart of competitive analysis. Different responses could arise for one of two reasons: (1) the rival firms are located in different geopolitical environments with different macroeconomic events and policies influencing them, or (2) the rival firms face the same macroeconomic incentives but respond differently because of different strategic or organizational considerations within the firm. The first reason is generally mentioned when discussing the rising or declining international competitiveness of firms from a particular nation. It is also featured prominently in the General Motors and Saab-Scania cases in this book. The second reason is more pervasively illustrated in this casebook. We see examples of different business strategies (General Aviation), different corporate strategies (RTZ), different organizational structures (Honeywell), and different managerial attitudes (Ryder).

Market rigidities is a term I use to describe the governmental, technological, institutional, organizational, and managerial constraints influencing the degree to which a firm responds to macroeconomic incentives. Governmental rigidities include trade and capital barriers, and regulations. Technological rigidities arise from construction and delivery lags in the acquisition of tangible capital assets, innovations in information processing, and irreversibility of capital investments. Institutional constraints may be placed on a manager's "free market" decision by legal rules (such as antitrust prohibitions against joint research and development), bargaining and work arrangements, or explicit and implicit contractual arrangements. Finally, organizational and managerial rigidities keeping managers from "optimal" (i.e., unconstrained) decisions would include any lack of skills or resources within the organization, such as a shortage of capital, information, or human talents, and organizational problems, such as lags or gaps in internal communications, organizational slack, or an inefficient internal reward system for workers or management.

Rival firms will almost certainly face a different set of market rigidities when trying to respond to the same macroeconomic incentive (such as a tax cut). This will lead to different responses and the resulting opportunities to gain competitive market position over rivals.

How, then, should a firm respond to a changing macroeconomic environment? First, one should realize that a firm does not have a "macroeconomic problem" per se—it has a business problem that may be caused by some macroeconomic event. Therefore, fundamentally the same analytical tools of strategy and of the other functional areas are still relevant. We must learn to fine-tune those tools and the resulting decisions in order to incorporate our understanding of the macroeconomic environment.

One might make an analogy to driving an automobile in adverse weather, such as in an ice storm. The basic principles of driving still work in those conditions, and that realization should be our starting point in the analysis of how to drive on ice. For example, our standard brakes are still designed to stop the car, but we should exercise great caution when we use them in order to prevent locking up the wheels. (Readers will undoubtedly be able to extend this analogy themselves to the use of chains, low-beam headlights in fog, and other tools and techniques for foul weather driving.) The analogy would be even richer for other means of transportation that are even more weather dependent, such as sailing or flying. In these cases, which start to replicate the complexity of the business environment, we have more options to position ourselves against the weather (and against rivals).

A firm has only a few generic responses to a changing macroeconomic environment. First, and most frequently, the firm can adapt its existing business strategy to the new environment. Second, it can adapt its corporate strategy as well. Finally, in some instances it can try to adopt a political strategy to change the environment. During the course, we will try to refine the generic options and develop specific actions based on the case studies.

Acknowledgments

Foremost, I would like to acknowledge the invaluable assistance of my research associate, Julia Horn, who had worked with me for four years on this and other projects. Her hard work, resourcefulness, perseverance, organizational skills, and encouragement are much appreciated. Julia's many talents were evident in all aspects of this project—the library research, the company interviews, the case writing, and the classroom. Without her assistance, this project would not have been completed.

Among my other friends and colleagues, a special thanks goes to Professors Carliss Baldwin and Scott Mason of the Harvard Business School for the use of their case study on Massey-Ferguson and to Professor Mark Wolfson of Stanford Business School for his collaboration in the writing of the Schlumberger case. In addition, I have received valuable comments and suggestions on many of these cases from David Collis (Harvard Business School), Stephen Marks (Boston University Law School), Glenn Woroch (GTE Labs), and David Yoffie (Harvard Business School). Dean John McArthur and Professor Mike Yoshino of the Division of Research at the Harvard Business School were very generous with funding and encouragement.

All the cases benefited tremendously from interviews with managers in the company under study and with other close observers. Even though the list of all interviewees is too numerous to mention here in its entirety, I want to acknowledge some executives who were extremely helpful in the case studies on their respective companies: Derek Birkin, Guy Elliott, and Ian Strachan of RTZ; Max Bleck of Beechcraft and Bruce Peterman of Cessna; Bob Clos and Frank Shrontz of Boeing; Ernie Fleischer of Franklin Savings; Mike Tangney and Rod Turner of Colgate-Palmolive; Jim Grierson, Bill Mackey, and Jerry Wohler of Honeywell; Sir Colin Marshall of British Airways; Norm Augustine of Martin Marietta; and Bengt Ödmann, Lars Ohlsson-Leijon, and Peter Salzer of Saab-Scania. All these individuals helped through their candid insights, generous sharing of their time, superb access to company information, detailed reading of drafts of cases, and/or visits to the MBA classroom discussions at Harvard. In all instances, the cases were greatly enhanced by their cooperation, and in some cases, the cases could not have been written otherwise. It should be noted, however, that these cases do not necessarily reflect the views or opinions of these individuals or their companies. These executives cooperated in the research, but the case studies with any inadvertent errors and biases are mine.

Finally, I enjoyed excellent administrative support from my secretaries, Cathyjean Gustafson and Margo McCool, and from the Dryden staff, including Jan Richardson, Kelly Spiller, Nancy Shanahan, Wendy Kemp, and Melissa Morgan. Once again, the cheerful, professional Dryden staff has made working on the details of book production a genuine pleasure.

Michael G. Rukstad
Boston, Massachusetts
January 1992

CONTENTS

PART I

CORPORATE MANAGEMENT OF THE BUSINESS CYCLE

Economists use the term "business cycles" to describe the cyclic rise and fall of economic activity. The term encompasses many related economic phenomena, but generally it reflects a rise and fall in the broadest measure of economic activity, gross national product (GNP), which is the total value of all final goods and services produced by a country within a given year. Almost all other economic variables are related directly or indirectly to GNP. It is not surprising, for example, that the sales of most industries and firms are positively correlated with GNP. However, other economic variables, such as industrial production, employment, productivity, inflation, and interest rates, are also positively correlated with GNP to various degrees. Consequently, cyclic behavior in sales and production is usually related to cyclic behavior in prices as well.

Most attention in business cycles has been focused on the trough of the cycle. To qualify as an official downturn (a recession), the economic growth must satisfy the "Three D's": depth, duration, and dispersion. Since World War II, the United States has had eight official recessions—in 1946, 1953–54, 1958, 1970, 1974–75, 1980, 1981–82, and most recently since 1990.

Perhaps because of the difficulty that economists and policymakers have had in explaining and controlling business cycles, business managers have often resigned themselves to accepting the consequences of the cycles on their business. It is certainly true that managers of any one business will be unable to affect the course of the business cycle for a nation as a whole—in that sense, it must be taken as a given feature of the business environment. However, managers can undertake actions that will leave their firm more or less affected by the business cycles. In other words, business cycles can create opportunities for a change in competitive advantage.

The following four cases explore only selected core issues of the corporate management of business cycles.

The first case, RTZ, examines a classic example of an industry affected by business cycles. The management has designed a diversified corporate strategy designed to minimize the impact of the business cycle on its earnings.

The next two cases, The General Aviation Industry in 1982 and Boeing and McDonnell Douglas, examine the competitive dynamics of a downturn and an expansion in sales, respectively. The issues and responses are not necessarily mirror-images of one another.

The final case, RJR/Nabisco and Leverage Buyouts, serves multiple purposes. Primarily it is designed to explore the issue of what makes a company vulnerable to the business cycle. In the process, we gain some insights into leveraged buyouts, as well. In addition, the case serves as a bridge to the other two parts of the book because both interest rates and taxes have important effects on leveraged buyouts.

CASE 1
RTZ

The central issue for managers regarding business cycles is the cyclicality of the company's revenues and earnings as a result of cyclic economic events beyond their direct control. Downturns reflect poorly on managers regardless of the direct blame they may have had in these results. Compensation packages and promotions are often tied to such results. Bankrupcies are certainly more prevalent in economic downturns. Not surprisingly, managers are eager to smooth the fluctuations in reported revenues, and especially in reported profits.

One method available to managers to smooth fluctuations in revenues and profits is diversification. Finance theory indicates that an investor can achieve higher average returns with lower variability among those returns over time through diversification. However, stockholders will not reward managers for diversification that the stockholders could have performed themselves in their own investment portfolio, according to the theory. Therefore, we must decide the proper role for diversification as a tool for managers to combat economic business cycles.

RTZ is competing in the mining business, which is among the most cyclical of all industries. Other industries, besides mining, that are characterized by prominent business cycles include construction-related businesses, heavy industrial equipment such as machine tools, and durable consumer goods such as automobiles. All these cyclical industries have the feature that the good they produce is used as an input in the production process of other goods and/or the good is a long-lived asset.

The RTZ case examines how the world's largest mining company sets its corporate strategy to manage the cyclicality of its industry. RTZ attempts to manage cyclicality predominately at the corporate strategy level through diversification, rather than manage it at the business strategy level through production, marketing, or other functional policies. The critical issue for RTZ will be how they can manage cyclicality in order to gain a competitive advantage over other rivals in the industry.

RTZ (formerly Rio Tinto-Zinc), based in London, England, was the world's largest mining company in 1989 in terms of market capitalization and the market leader in many of the metals it mined. RTZ's net profits had grown at a compounded annual rate of over 20 percent from 1975 to 1988. In the volatile mining industry, RTZ achieved the highest returns of all major mining companies and the lowest variability in those returns. Indeed, their profitability was even superior to companies in traditional, less volatile industries. This was a remarkable record when compared to most other mining companies, such as AMAX, Phelps Dodge, INCO, and ASARCO, which had suffered severe losses during the worldwide economic recession in the early 1980s. That recession coincided with the mining industry's worst slump in more than fifty years.

In the early 1980s, RTZ intensified its long-established corporate strategy of diversifying across many different minerals and into related industrial activities outside of mining. From 1985, RTZ's new Chief Executive, Derek Birkin, reexamined the company's corporate strategy. He recommitted the company to the mining business while ensuring that it had a firm basis for dealing with the industry's volatility over the coming decades. In 1989, as part of that recommitment to mining, RTZ expanded its diversification efforts within the minerals industry by acquiring BP Minerals from British Petroleum for $3.7 billion, the largest private acquisition ever of a British company by another British company.

The Mining Industry

The mining industry included the discovery, extraction, and processing of (1) energy minerals, (2) refined and processed metals, and (3) nonmetals. Energy minerals included coal, petroleum, uranium, and natural gas. Refined and processed metals included ferrous metals and ferroalloys, such as iron ore, nickel, manganese, and molybdenum; nonferrous metals, such as aluminum, copper, lead, zinc, and tin; and precious metals, such as gold and silver. A wide range of nonmetallic minerals included industrial diamonds, borax, titanium dioxide, and phosphate. RTZ was involved in all three areas of the mining business.

Mined products were primarily consumed by the industrial sector. For example, over 85 percent of copper production was used by wire-rod and brass mills. Almost 75 percent of aluminum production was consumed by the packaging, construction, and transportation industries. The majority of lead was used for batteries, whereas nickel was used

This case was prepared by Research Associate Julia Horn under the supervision of Professor Michael G. Rukstad. Copyright © 1989 by the President and Fellows of Harvard College. Harvard Business School case 9-389-093.

primarily in making stainless steel products. Nearly 30 percent of industrial diamonds were used for machinery.

Pricing for mined products varied depending on whether the product was traded on a terminal market or not. Prices for some base metals,
such as copper, lead, aluminum, nickel, tin, and zinc, whose demand was
closely tied to industrial uses, were determined by trading activity on
terminal markets such as the London Metals Exchange. Prices for precious metals, such as gold, silver, and platinum, that were not as closely
tied to industrial uses but were recognized as a store of value, were determined by the daily fixing. Other minerals, such as borax, titanium
dioxide, industrial diamonds, iron ore, coal, uranium, and bauxite, were
sold by straightforward negotiation between buyer and seller often under
medium- or long-term contracts. Freight was an important part of the
price consideration for bulk minerals.

Demand for minerals had changed dramatically since the end of
the second World War. In the 1950s and 1960s, the demand for minerals
grew rapidly and mining companies, which were primarily American and
European and privately held, reaped strong profits. Beginning in the early
1970s, the industries of the world's largest economies started to become
less mineral intensive and more service and technology intensive. Technological progress also resulted in continued savings in the use of metals
for finished goods. Metal demand in developing countries picked up some
of the slack left by the industrialized countries. Their share of total nonferrous metal consumption grew at a compounded annual rate of 3.2
percent from 1964 to 1973. During the early 1970s, when metal prices
and consumption were very strong, mining companies planned large capacity expansions with the expectation that high rates of growth in demand would continue. But, after the first oil shock in October 1973,
demand fell precipitously along with the industry's profits and subsequent
rates of growth were greatly reduced to levels well below expectation.

Most, but not all, mineral prices continued to fall in real terms from
1973 to 1986 with the exception of a general upward blip during the
1979–1980 boom in mineral demand. See Exhibit 1 for trends in prices.
Within this general pattern, prices of individual metals reacted to their
specific supply and demand circumstances. For example, tin prices fell
79 percent between 1985 and 1986 following a collapse of the International Tin Agreement, after a long period of real increases. The price of
copper fluctuated, falling 33 percent from a high of 102 cents per pound
in 1980 to 68 cents per pound in 1986. Despite the falling prices which
began in late 1973, mining companies continued to make investments
in additional capacity that continued to 1986. "It took the industry until
1976 to perceive that the disappointing consumption figures that began
after 1973 were not a temporary aberration, but constituted the beginning
of a new trend. At that time, so much money had already been invested
in many of the projects in the pipeline, that completion was more economical than abandonment or deferral, even if an extended period of

Exhibit 1 Mineral Price Index (Current and Constant Dollars)

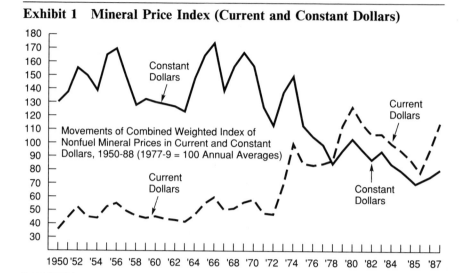

Note: The commodities in the index weighted by 1977–1979 export values are: copper, tin, nickel, bauxite, aluminum, iron ore, manganese ore, lead, zinc, and phosphate rock.

Source: World Bank, *Half-Yearly Revision of Commodity Price Forecasts* and *Quarterly Review of Commodity Markets for December 1988.*

Exhibit 2 Capacity Utilization

	1973	1986
Aluminum smelting	93	84
Copper mining	94	82
Lead mining	95	79
Nickel mining	99	70
Zinc mining	95	82
Steel mills	90	66

Source: Marian Radetzki, "Structural Changes and Depression in World Metal Industries," *Selected Readings in Mineral Economics.* (New York: Pergamon Press, 1987).

depressed price levels was taken into account."[1] In fact, capacity utilization in the mining industry was significantly depressed for the entire decade. See Exhibit 2 for capacity utilization. A shift in minerals demand also occurred in the 1980s. Whereas demand was primarily in North America and Europe in the 1960s, 25 percent of demand was in Third World countries and 10 percent was in Japan by the mid-1980s. Developing countries' share of total nonferrous metal consumption grew at a compounded annual growth rate of 6.4 percent from 1973 to 1984. See Exhibit 3 for mineral demand and Exhibit 4 for industrial production.

[1]Marian Radetzki, "Structural Changes and Depression in World Metal Industries," *Selected Readings in Economics.* (New York: Pergamon Press, 1987), p. 280.

Exhibit 3   Growth in Mineral Demand

Industrialized Countries	1964–1973	1973–1984	1980–1995[a]
Copper	3.8	0.2	
Nickel	6.1	0.1	
Lead	3.3	1.1	
Zinc	4.1	(1.3)	
Aluminum	9.2	0.1	
Developing Countries			
Copper	5.9	7.3	
Nickel	17.1	11.6	
Lead	3.3	1.1	
Zinc	8.4	6.0	
Aluminum	13.2	9.0	
Projected—Free World Countries			
Copper			2.6
Nickel			2.4
Lead			3.2
Zinc			3.1
Aluminum			3.9

[a]World Bank projection.

Source: Marian Radetzki, "Structural Changes and Depression in the World Metal Industries," *Selected Readings in Mineral Economics.* (New York: Pergamon Press, 1987).

The mining industry could be segmented into companies that diversified across many minerals and those that specialized primarily in a single mineral. The multi-mineral companies were not necessarily the largest in the mining industry. See Exhibits 5 and 6 for financial comparisons of representative mining firms. Among the multi-mineral companies were large, multinational corporations, ranked in descending order, such as RTZ (U.K.), Anglo American/DeBeers (South Africa), Broken Hill Proprietary (Australia), Noranda (Canada), AMAX (U.S.), ASARCO (U.S.), and Metallgesellschaft (West Germany). A few of these companies, including RTZ and Broken Hill Proprietary (BHP), were also diversified extensively into other non-mining businesses. Among those mining companies that specialized primarily in a single mineral were Alcoa (U.S., aluminum), Alcan (Canada, aluminum), Inco (Canada, nickel), Placer Dome (Canada, silver), Newmont Mining (U.S., gold), Phelps Dodge (U.S., copper). In addition to the larger companies, there were hundreds of small single-mineral mining companies, primarily specializing in gold.

Beginning in the 1960s, three trends affected mining company ownership. First, state-owned enterprises (SOEs) became heavily involved in the production of metals during that period. Most SOEs focused on a single mineral, typically copper. Among the largest copper-producing SOEs were CODELCO (Chile), ZCCM (Zambia), and Gecamines (Zaire). CVRD (Brazil) was the major iron ore producer. By the 1980s, SOEs

Exhibit 4   Index of Industrial Production

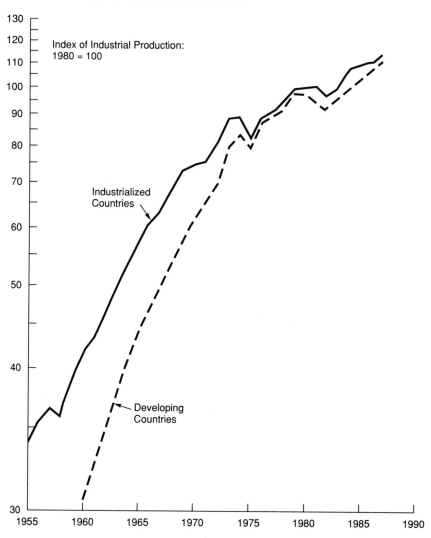

Source: Marian Radetzki, "Structural Changes and Depression in World Metal Industries," *Selected Readings in Mineral Economics.* (New York: Pergamon Press, 1987).

were responsible for almost one-third of mineral production. Even in the developed world, countries were concerned about resource ownership. For example, in the early 1970s, the Foreign Investment Review Act (FIRA) and the Foreign Acquisitions and Takeover Act were passed in Canada and Australia, respectively, to increase local ownership of companies and decrease the number of foreign takeovers of those companies, marking a second ownership trend. In 1979, for example, the Australian government and RTZ agreed that RTZ would progressively reduce its

Exhibit 5   Mean and Variability of Returns: RTZ and Sample Competitors, 1973–1988

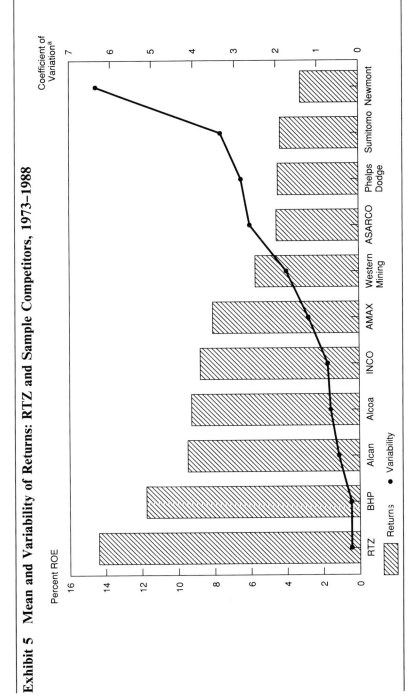

[a]The coefficient of variation is equal to the standard deviation divided by the mean.

Source: Annual Reports

Exhibit 6A   Comparison of Capital Expenditures: RTZ and Other Mining Companies, 1974–1988

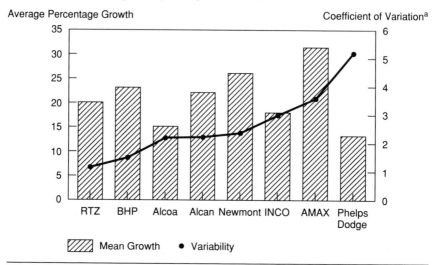

aThe coefficient of variation is equal to the standard deviation divided by the mean.

Exhibit 6B   Correlation of Capital Expenditure With World GNP Growth, 1974–1988

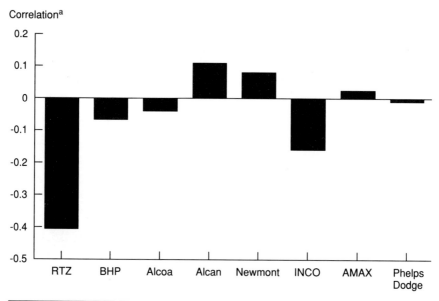

aThe correlation coefficient indicates the association between two variables. It ranges between a positive one (which means the variables move completely together) to zero (no relationship) to negative one (variables move in the opposite direction).

Source: Company Annual Reports

share in Conzinc Rio Tinto of Australia (CRA) to below 50 percent, a process which was completed in 1986, since which time the sharcholding had been 49 percent. By the late 1970s and early 1980s, a third trend emerged as some large petroleum companies began acquiring mining affiliates, such as Shell (Billiton), British Petroleum (Kennecott Copper and Selection Trust), McMoRan (Freeport Minerals), Standard Oil of Indiana (Amoco Minerals), and Atlantic Richfield (Anaconda). The petroleum companies sought diversification opportunities in activities that they thought would be similar to their own business. However, as Phillip Crowson, RTZ's chief economist explained, "The oil business requires an immediate cash input and yields a continuous cash flow output, whereas the mining business requires a longer-term investment and yields a slower cash output."

From the 1982 recession onward, mining companies were forced to cut costs and reduce their capacity in order to survive. Demand started to increase beginning in 1983, but it was initially met by a rundown in the excess inventories that had been built up during the recession. Meanwhile, exchange rate effects, particularly a strong U.S. dollar, held back recovery for U.S. companies. Not until late 1986 were supply and demand balances sufficiently tight and stocks low enough, to cause an increase in prices. By 1988, steel, aluminum, and copper producers were operating at 90 percent of capacity. In 1989, the mining industry's profits continued to rise, aided by both higher prices and previous cost reductions. The profits for U.S. mining companies alone exceeded $2.0 billion in 1989 compared to a $500 million loss in 1984. With metal prices in mid-1989 up tremendously over mid-1986 levels, mining experts believed that the plummeting prices that the industry witnessed before 1986 were not likely to return. Demand was still firm and likely to grow further, thereby absorbing probable increases in capacity.

The Economics of a Mining Project

The total costs for a mining project could be divided into two stages: the cost of preparing a mine for production and the cost of operating a mine. There were three steps involved in the preparation of a new mine for mineral production: exploration, feasibility, and construction. See Exhibit 7 for a mine development and funds deployment chart. In the exploration step, companies drilled to identify the existence of mineral deposits. In the second step, the feasibility study determined whether or not those deposits could be mined profitably. Given the intense global competition, it was crucial for companies to identify low cost sources of ore. Typically, those two steps cost a mining company at least $50 million. The third step was the construction of the mine by open-pit or underground mining, and the construction of a supporting infrastructure, including railroads, electricity, and environmental compliance facilities. Open-pit mining was mainly used to extract minerals such as iron, bauxite, and copper, while

Exhibit 7   Mine Development and Funds Deployment Chart

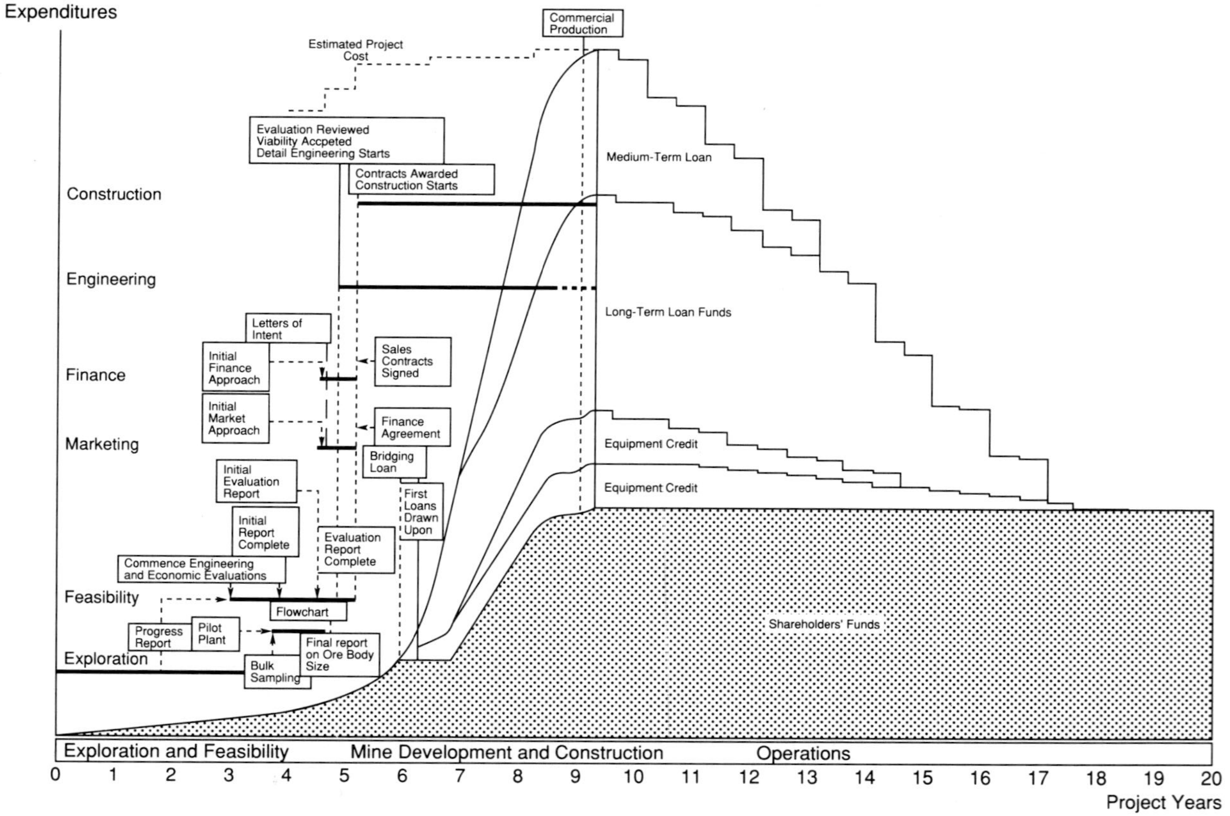

Expenditures

Construction

Engineering

Finance

Marketing

Feasibility

Exploration

Estimated Project Cost

Commercial Production

Evaluation Reviewed
Viability Accepted
Detail Engineering Starts

Contracts Awarded
Construction Starts

Medium-Term Loan

Long-Term Loan Funds

Equipment Credit

Equipment Credit

Shareholders' Funds

Letters of Intent

Initial Finance Approach

Initial Market Approach

Sales Contracts Signed

Finance Agreement

Bridging Loan

First Loans Drawn Upon

Initial Evaluation Report

Initial Report Complete

Commence Engineering and Economic Evaluations

Evaluation Report Complete

Flowchart

Progress Report

Pilot Plant

Bulk Sampling

Final report on Ore Body Size

Exploration and Feasibility   Mine Development and Construction   Operations

Project Years

0   1   2   3   4   5   6   7   8   9   10   11   12   13   14   15   16   17   18   19   20

other minerals such as lead, zinc, silver, and gold were primarily extracted by underground mining methods. The mineral industry had approximately 1,250 metal mining operations around the world producing in excess of 150 kilotons per year of ore divided about equally between underground and open-pit mines. By comparison, the coal industry had a similar number of operations at a production rate of 450 kilotons per year.

A key factor when constructing the mine was cost control. In an effort to keep costs low, some mining companies had practiced "cherry picking," the process of only mining a relatively small amount of choice ore from a mine. Though this was economically viable in the short-term, costs escalated tremendously if future expansion was desired. Therefore, a mining company was better off planning the profitability over the long-term if it could afford to do so. Typically, a mining plan for an open-pit mine was established which involved decisions on the parameters of the pit, the steepness of the slopes within the pit, the disposal of pit waste, and the disposal of the tailings that remained after the ore was processed. The plan also involved the design of the mill, decisions regarding the type of equipment to be used, the rate of metal recovery, the methods of transporting the product from the mine to the port of shipment, and the infrastructure needed to support the mine. After the mine was operating, the primary costs arose from the equipment's utilization, maintenance, and repair. After the useful life of the mine was over, there were also large costs involved in returning the mine to an environmentally acceptable state.

The whole process of setting up and running a world-class mining complex in 1989 required capital outlays of $1 billion or more and at least five years from the exploration step to the construction step. Annual capital expenditure needs for the mining industry were estimated to be $10 to $15 billion. Though that was a small percentage of world industrial requirements, the issue for mining companies was the availability and cost of those funds over the course of the business cycle. The initial financing, typically in the form of bank loans and parent financing, covered the expenses of bringing a mine through the preparation stage. If a major upgrading were needed later, financing took the form of intracompany debt or equity, or local bank loans, rather than renegotiating the initial financing. Thus typically a mine would be highly leveraged at start-up and then progressively reduced to zero leverage. The leverage of the mining company (as distinct from the mine itself) differed depending on its strategy, the number of mines in operation, and the balance between new and old mines. RTZ's own leverage during the 1970s and 1980s fluctuated widely depending on particular circumstances, but was within a range near its long-term average of approximately a 40:60 debt to equity ratio. Debt was supplied primarily from banks and supranational agencies such as the export-import banks of various countries. However, those sources were curtailed after the debt crisis of the early 1980s.

Prior to the early 1960s, most mining projects were financed with foreign private equity capital (supplied by the large mining companies themselves), supplemented by internally generated cash flow from the project. By the early 1960s, however, an important new technique called project financing was born for funding mining projects in developing countries. Project financing emerged because capital costs for new projects were growing beyond the internal cash generation and borrowing capacity of existing mining firms. The term project financing described a loan to a new mining project that relied upon the anticipated cash flow of the project itself to repay the loan in contrast to relying on the overall creditworthiness of the project sponsor.

The lenders in a project financing bore the political, commercial, and mineral reserve risk after project completion. Therefore, they attempted to share the risks by syndicating the loan as broadly as possible. The political risk arose from the possibility that the host government might not provide a suitable environment for investment, including the possibility that a company might be deprived of its property rights through expropriation. The commercial risk occurred because of the uncertainty of prices and demand in the metals markets. The mineral reserve risk included the risk of exhaustion of the mine before the loan had been repaid, and unforeseen metallurgical difficulties. Because the lending banks assumed these risks, the financing was often termed "non-recourse" to the parent mining company. Only a few of the largest banks played a leading role in structuring project financing, including Bank of America, Citibank, Chase Manhattan, and Bankers Trust in the United States, and Lloyds Bank in the U.K. Project financing loans were structured on a floating-rate basis at a premium of 0.5 percent to 2.5 percent above the London Interbank Offer Rate (LIBOR). Supranational agencies, such as the International Financial Corporation of the World Bank or the Export Import Bank of Japan, tended to lend long-term, fixed-rate funds.

In return for the risk that was borne by the syndicated banks, the parent mining company provided guarantees that the proposed mine and supporting facilities would be brought onstream at a specified time and level of production. Until that level was reached, the parent was still liable for the debts incurred in the project financing. Project financing was typically more expensive for a mining project than direct borrowing from the parent by approximately 1 percent per year. However, it had a number of advantages as well. For example, project financing could be carried off the balance sheet in which the mine was not consolidated in the parent company's balance sheet as a subsidiary. In such cases, where the mining company was in a minority position, the financing would not impair the parent company's general credit standing.

Strategies of Mining Companies

The mining industry's competitive structure had changed by the mid-1980s as the demand for minerals and their prices continued their decade-long decline. "In response to the recession and global competition of the early 1980s, many companies were forced to improve their cost positions."[2] Many companies closed high cost inefficient mines, and cut maintenance, repair, and labor costs. From 1980 to 1987, the industry cut unit costs by 40 percent in real terms. Beginning in 1980, for example, ASARCO and INCO chopped their payrolls and postponed expansion plans. ASARCO reduced its capital expenditures and cash requirements for operations to equal its limited internally generated cash flow. Phelps-Dodge took more severe steps, closing some of its mines and smelters for more than a year and slashing its workforce by 56 percent. The company also took on nearly a dozen labor unions, demanding the elimination of the cost-of-living adjustment—a move that resulted in violent strikes against the company that dragged on for more than two years. Numerous companies took a more short-sighted approach to cost cutting by "cherry picking" their mines.

To respond to the volatile economic environment of the 1980s, mining companies had tried almost all variations of corporate strategy. While some companies were divesting their non-minerals businesses, others were diversifying into such businesses. In the U.S., oil companies, with the exception of Shell and Exxon, sold off their mining businesses, as did a number of conglomerates, including Fluor (St. Joe Minerals), and General Electric (Utah Minerals). Some mining companies such as Phelps-Dodge tried to strengthen their competitive position by diversifying into non-minerals businesses. Phelps-Dodge bought Columbian Chemicals in 1986, the world's second largest producer of carbon black (used in tires) and Accuride Corporation in 1987, a maker of truck wheels. Together the two companies contributed 25 percent to Phelps Dodge's sales. In 1988, the company formed a distinct non-mining group, which also included wire and cable products.

Unlike those companies that diversified into or out of non-minerals, some companies chose to narrow the scope of their minerals business and their geographic exposure, while other companies were diversifying into a broader base of minerals and geographic locations. AMAX and Newmont Mining, for example, sold off some of their minerals businesses to focus on a narrower range of products. In 1985, AMAX refocused its strategy on three core businesses: aluminum, coal, and gold, selling off operations in copper mining, nickel refining, and iron ore. AMAX turned a large part of its attention to gold, amassing nearly 3 million ounces of reserves in the U.S., including the lowest cost gold mine in the U.S. in Nevada. Newmont Mining followed a similar path. In 1986, it sold off its copper assets, the Foote Mineral Company (diversified minerals), and its oil and gas interests, so that it too could focus on gold. Anglo Amer-

---

[2]William Potter and Roger Pyle, "The Impact of a Recessionary Environment on Private Company Finance," in Tinsley, Emerson, and Eppler, eds., *Finance for the Minerals Industry.* (New York: Society of Mining Engineers, 1985), p. 810.

ican/DeBeers, on the other hand, had broadened its scope and diversified geographically, primarily because the majority of its assets were in South Africa. In their eagerness to accomplish this diversification, Anglo American/DeBeers typically acquired a minority interest in existing mining firms. After it formed a mining affiliate, it generally sold most of the remaining shares to the public. Anglo American/DeBeers provided both management and administrative services to its affiliates with little direct management control. However, the company did exercise considerable influence over affiliates' policies and financing.

Other companies, such as Alcoa and Alcan, had diversified into related businesses. Alcan was the world's second largest aluminum producer after Alcoa and was vertically integrated throughout all stages of the industry from bauxite mining to aluminum smelting and fabricating. As demand for aluminum products began to increase again in 1988 after years of depressed prices, Alcan renewed its commitment to establish an array of aluminum-related businesses.

Finally, some mining companies, had made efforts to become either more or less vertically-integrated. When commodity prices did rebound slightly, such as the firming zinc prices in mid-1984, companies such as Union Miniére S.A. of Belgium seized the opportunity to begin to integrate their smelting capacity and cut investment significantly in less viable subsidiaries. Metallgesellschaft diversified from smelting operations to mining activities, a similar route to the one ASARCO chose. For nearly 100 years, ASARCO had focused on smelting and refining lead and copper from ore mined by other companies. In the mid-1980s, when its suppliers closed mines, the company ran short of products and closed mines, losing $442 million in four years. Shortly after that, ASARCO bought 49.9 percent of Montana Resources, Inc., which owned Anaconda's former Montana copper properties. As a result, ASARCO mined 67 percent of the copper ore it processed in 1989 and 55 percent of the lead, up from 25 percent and 5 percent in 1985. The company's goal was to produce 100 percent of the copper ore it used.

Nonetheless, some companies had not made any major strategic changes. BHP continued to divide its operations into three distinct groups: petroleum, minerals, and steel. Both petroleum and minerals accounted for close to 30 percent of sales, with steel comprising the remainder. Within its minerals group, BHP concentrated on three products (copper, coal, and iron ore) in two broad geographical areas (Australia and the Americas). Beginning in 1989, a new copper deposit at Escondida in Chile, in which BHP owned a 57.5 percent stake,[3] was ready to begin a three-year construction phase. Escondida was expected to be the second largest copper producer in the world. CODELCO, a Chilean SOE, had not made any major strategic changes either. SOEs typically had not

[3]RTZ owned a 30 percent interest in the Escondida copper project.

diversified during this period. However, during the early 1980s, many
SOEs were often forced to produce at any price in order to meet their
countries' debt service payments.

RTZ's Position in the World Mining Industry

History of RTZ

The RTZ Corporation traced its origins back to the 1870s, when the Rio
Tinto Company was formed with Rothschild family financial backing to
acquire the Rio Tinto mine in Spain. In 1955, General Franco partly
nationalized the mine, leaving the company with a small stake and interests in Northern Rhodesian copper. The company then developed substantial interests in Canadian uranium and mounted a large international
exploration program. At that time, Sir Val Duncan, Sir Mark Turner,
and Roy Wright took control of RTZ. Sir Val was known as the entrepreneur of the group and was often said to have carried the company
around in his head. Sir Mark was the financial genius of the group, and
Wright was credited with being the "ideas man." In 1962 the company
merged with Consolidated Zinc Corporation of Australia to form Rio
Tinto-Zinc. By the mid-1960s, RTZ was widely recognized as having
built an organization of autonomous companies with some of the highest
quality mineral assets in the world.

Later in 1968, RTZ acquired U.S. Borax, which operated the world's
largest borax mine in Mojave Desert, California. Borax was used primarily in laundry, home improvement, and ceramic products. Though
U.S. Borax was not very profitable in the 1960s, sales had increased
significantly beginning in the 1970s, after the first oil price shock, when
the home insulation market grew and flame-proof borax was used in
cellulose insulation. In 1970, RTZ purchased Pillar Aluminum. At that
time, Pillar supplied non-electrical products, primarily to the construction
markets in the U.K. and Europe. RTZ hoped that an aluminum company
such as Pillar could be easily integrated into RTZ's prospective U.K.
smelter operations. Since RTZ's plans for an integrated smelting operation were never realized because of government involvement, Pillar was
never integrated in that regard. Nevertheless, it became a very profitable
operation for RTZ.

In the early 1970s, when competitors were adding mining capacity,
Sir Val Duncan spoke about designing low-cost mines that would be
robust enough to weather a downturn in mineral demand and prices.
Though the company's profitability had increased since the 1960s, and
its mines were widely regarded as high quality, RTZ had grown into a
large company with a number of complex holdings and its management
structure needed pruning.

In 1975, Sir Val Duncan died. He was succeeded as Chairman by
Sir Mark Turner and then, in 1981, by Sir Anthony Tuke, a retired Chair-

man of Barclay's Bank. The tenure of Sir Anthony, and his Chief Executive Sir Alistair Frame, from 1981 to 1985, witnessed the company's first diversification efforts since Pillar and U.S. Borax. In 1982, RTZ acquired T. W. Ward, a cement and engineering group. Later in the year, Tunnel Cement, a leading U.K. industrial firm, was acquired to augment RTZ's growing cement business. The Tunnel Cement acquisition also brought Derek Birkin, Tunnel's chief executive, to RTZ. Birkin saw many similarities between the management styles of Tunnel and RTZ. Though Tunnel was a smaller company, "it put the same value on devolving management control to entrepreneurial attitudes."[4] In 1985, when Sir Anthony retired as chairman, Sir Alistair Frame and Derek Birkin took over the chairman and CEO posts, respectively. Birkin immediately turned his attention to the development of both a more concrete management structure and a more definite corporate strategy.

Management Structure and Corporate Strategy

The three years that followed Derek Birkin's appointment as chief executive at RTZ were spent reshaping RTZ's corporate strategy. The new team's first initiative was to introduce a new management discipline into the company, ensuring that each was made to "row in the same direction." Among the measures adopted was bringing the remaining chairmen of RTZ's largest operating divisions to the company's head office in St. James's Square in London to become members of a CEO committee. Each member brought operating experience to the group and was given collective responsibility, producing a group cohesiveness. Care was taken, however, to maintain a decentralized management structure, allowing each division substantial autonomy in operating areas. Even though the decentralized structure allowed RTZ managers greater flexibility, major investment funding decisions were still made by senior management. However, some funds allocation from one activity to another was allowed, providing those activities were related in their organizational structure. See Exhibit 8 for an organizational chart of RTZ's operations. A number of cost-saving measures were instituted. The number of directors on the company's board, previously somewhat extended, was reduced to 13, and the company's head office staff was lowered substantially to approximately 200. In keeping with the goal of decentralized management, Birkin also reduced the number of people reporting to him from 19 to 6.

While making the changes at the management level, Birkin also focused heavily on strategy formulation at RTZ. Previously, the firm had not announced a cohesive strategy. As a temporary measure, a strategy was devised that focused the company on metals, energy, and industrial businesses. The RTZ board also reexamined the company's major

[4]Stefan Wagstyl, "How RTZ Reshaped Itself for a New Era." *Financial Times,* April 3, 1987.

Exhibit 8   Schematic Postacquisition Structure

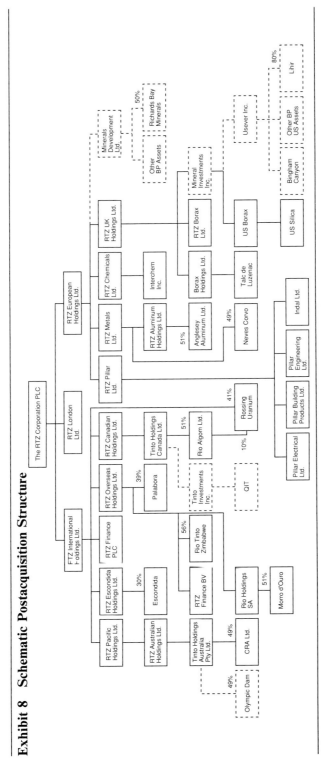

All holdings 100% unless indicated. The chart represents organizational, rather than managerial structure.

strengths. They identified those overall strengths as being among the best miners in the world while having the project management and financing abilities that allowed them to add value to the minerals business, and being able to successfully run non-minerals businesses as well, such as RTZ Pillar. Birkin explained those strengths in relation to corporate strategy, "We made a conscious decision to be mine operators and not just investors. Therefore, in areas where we had no operating skills, such as in our oil and gas business, we decided to exit the market." As part of the company's attention to strategic issues, there was a change in the nature of the presentations made to the head office by each operation from around the world on a biannual basis. The presentations became strategic rather than budget-oriented. Each operation outlined its strategy, including its own strengths and weaknesses, for the senior managers.

By 1987, RTZ had articulated its corporate objective: to maximize shareholders' return by operating only in extractive and related industrial areas of proven expertise. The corporate strategy to achieve this revolved around four elements: (1) to operate mines in the lowest cost quartile, (2) to ensure a diverse natural resources portfolio, (3) to maintain a broad geographic spread of assets, and (4) to develop related industrial activities (primarily Pillar) in growth sectors where competitive advantage could be sustained. RTZ's senior managers believed that disposing of businesses that did not adhere to that strategy would help the company focus on what businesses it knew best, increase the company's share price, and help to avoid the possibility of a takeover. Within a short time, RTZ sold off its cement, oil and gas, and double-glazing operations, and in 1989, its chemicals business.

Business Segments

RTZ's activities were segmented into natural resources (mining) and related industries. In 1988, RTZ's natural resources segment was the largest group within the company comprising 74 percent of total assets and contributing 73 percent to total profits. The segment included metals: aluminum, copper, gold, iron ore, lead, zinc, steel, tin; industrial minerals (primarily RTZ Borax); and energy minerals. See Exhibit 9 for RTZ financial information by business segment and Exhibit 10 for earnings by sector. Within natural resources, aluminum accounted for the largest percentage of profits (22 percent). The largest of the RTZ's mines were located primarily in North America, Australia, and Southern Africa. See Exhibit 11 for mine locations. The company supplied 17 percent of the free-world's uranium, 11 percent of its aluminum, 8 percent of its copper, and 8 percent of its iron ore in 1988. As with other minerals that it mined, RTZ boasted some of the lowest cash breakeven costs in the industry. See Exhibit 12 for an example of copper cash breakeven costs. In the first half of 1989, higher production levels were achieved at all of RTZ's principal mines and smelters, except the Bougainville Copper mine in Papua, New Guinea.

Exhibit 9   Mean and Variability of RTZ Segments Return on Sales, 1973–1988

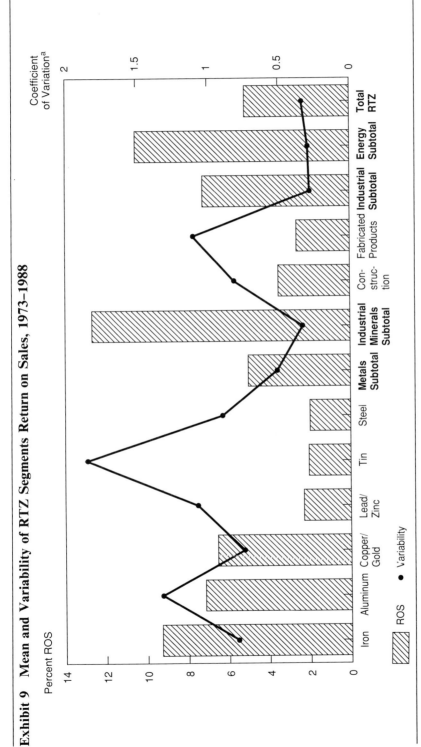

[a]The coefficient of variation is equal to the standard deviation divided by the mean.

Source: RTZ

Exhibit 10   RTZ Earnings by Sector, 1975–1989

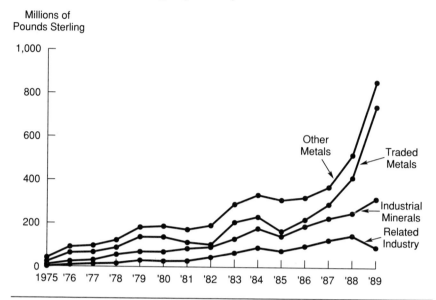

Millions of
Pounds Sterling

Source: RTZ

The largest of RTZ's industrial minerals operations was RTZ Borax, which accounted for 21 percent of RTZ's total net profits in 1988. RTZ Borax, through its subsidiary, U.S. Borax, accounted for 54 percent of world borate sales in 1988. Turkish mines, the second largest producers of borax, accounted for 35 percent. There were a wide variety of uses for borates in 1989. In the U.S. domestic market, where U.S. Borax held a high market share, the largest use was in glass and fiberglass, including glass wool, high temperature glasses, and enamels. Detergents, electronic equipment, flame retardants, and abrasives were other important uses. The sale of borax for the detergent market was the largest use for the product in Europe. The U.S. Bureau of Mines forecasted borax demand to grow at a rate of 3.2 percent in the United States, and 2.4 percent worldwide, throughout the 1990s. The natural resources segment contributed £253 million to net earnings in the first half of 1989, or a 148 percent increase over the same period in 1988.

Outside of the natural resources business, RTZ's most profitable segments were: RTZ Pillar, and RTZ Chemical, a specialty chemical producer with interests ranging from agrochemicals to biotechnology. RTZ had a 100 percent interest in both subsidiaries.

RTZ Pillar, in 1988, had seventy principal operating subsidiaries primarily in the United Kingdom and North America. The group's principal activities were the manufacture and distribution of a wide range of specialized products for the building and construction industries; the manufacture of electrical products and systems for buildings; the manufacture and distribution of engineered products; and the provision of

Exhibit 11   RTZ's Natural Resources

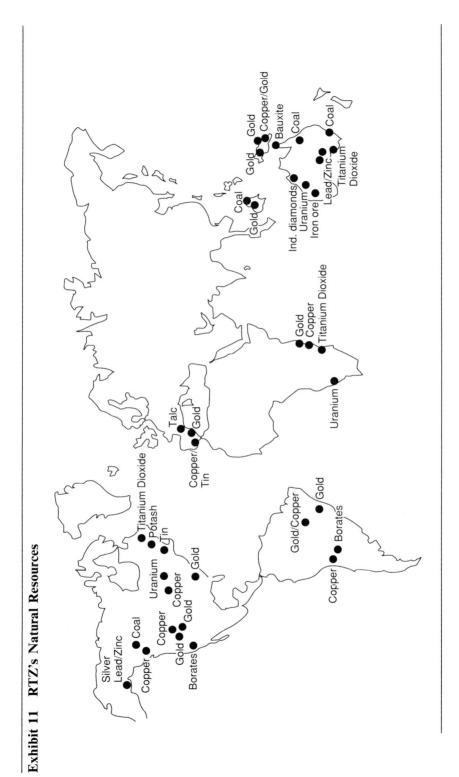

Exhibit 12   Copper Cash Breakeven Costs (1988 Terms): Cumulative Industry Production, Million Tons

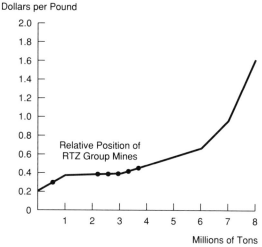

Source: RTZ

engineering support to the aviation industry. Pillar contributed £90 million or 21 percent to net profit at RTZ in 1988 on revenues of almost £1.5 billion. If Pillar were included in the Fortune 500 for U.S. companies it would, in its own right rank near number 150, alongside companies such as Ingersoll-Rand and Kerr-McGee.

RTZ Chemicals held interests in the manufacture and supply of chemicals for a wide range of applications and was one of the largest U.K.-based specialty chemical companies. The subsidiary's revenues were £462 million in 1988 and it contributed £23 million or 5.4 percent to net profit at RTZ. RTZ Chemical's businesses ranged from mineral acids and organic fluorine chemicals for use as pharmaceutical intermediates and coolants to performance chemicals for use in the tire, paper, and paint industries. It was also the only U.K. producer of citric acid and its derivatives for the food, soft drink, and pharmaceutical industries. The division was sold in its entirety in 1989.

Mine Financing at RTZ

RTZ's financial policies, particularly with regard to operating leverage, had remained conservative under the new management team. As RTZ's Director of Finance, Ian Strachan, explained, "Our operating leverage is based on high quality, low cost mines that are able to ride out the storms. We believe we have limited our exposure to individual product cycles because of the diversification in our mining portfolio." In addition, RTZ proceeded only with those projects where they were able to see long-term prospects of added value. "That criterion," explained Phillip Crowson, "together with RTZ's conservative price forecasts (based on the marginal costs of production of existing rather than new mines) for evaluating new projects had saved the company from investing in over-priced zinc assets in the late 1970s and gold assets in the mid-1980s. We do not bid based upon high prices just to get involved in a new project." For example, though consultants predicted a $0.55 price for zinc in the late 1970s, RTZ evaluated new projects on the basis of a $0.30 price for zinc. As a result, RTZ did not invest in a zinc operation in Northern Canada at that time, which Cyprus Dome quickly bought on the basis of a $0.55 zinc price. On the contrary, RTZ made the decision to invest $185 million in the Neves Corvo mine in Portugal in 1985, and $375 million in the Escondida mine in Chile in the same year. In both those cases, the decision to proceed was taken at a period of copper price weakness. Another example was the Rossing mine in Namibia, developed in the early 1970s, in a weak uranium market.

In addition to being a world leader in terms of the size and quality of its assets, RTZ led the industry in being able to obtain and negotiate project financing. The Palabora copper project in South Africa was the first modern example of project financing pioneered by RTZ. A later example was the Bougainville copper project in Papua, New Guinea. Bougainville was 53.6 percent owned by CRA, an Australian company, and was one of the largest single copper mines in the world. In 1973, when Bougainville reached full production, RTZ had an 80.7 percent interest in CRA. Because of the cyclical nature of the copper business coupled with the fact that Bougainville was the first major investment project in New Guinea, there were particularly high risks associated with the project from the banks' point of view. However, RTZ was able to negotiate for non-recourse project financing to fund Bougainville, and the mine was up and running by 1972.

Throughout the 1970s and 1980s, RTZ continued to build its reputation for completing projects on schedule and within budget constraints. Both Strachan and Robert Wilson, RTZ's Director of Mining and Minerals, emphasized the importance of reputation. "RTZ has built up a proven track record in problem-free project completions," said Strachan. "As a result, when a new project opportunity arises, the banks are eager to lend to our projects because of our project management capabilities. In addition, RTZ is often invited to participate in a project because of these special capabilities, such as when BHP invited us into the Escondida copper project." RTZ signed onto the Escondida project in 1986 when copper prices were at an all time low of $0.63 and Chile's political climate was tenuous. However, the firms' negotiating skills and financing history helped arrange $1.14 billion in financing, of which 40 percent was equity and 60 percent was debt in loans from a whole range of lenders in different countries. The Escondida copper project was also unusual because the political risk both pre- and post-completion was negotiated prior to the project's completion. Other measures protecting the investment were also included in the package.

In addition to project financing, RTZ had designed its currency exposure management policy to mitigate the adverse effects of cyclicality. The prices for RTZ's major products were largely determined by economic activity in the United States, Europe, and Japan. However, the costs of the company's major operations were largely determined in local currencies, such as the Australian dollar or the Chilean escudo. RTZ measured the effect of changing exchange rates on the economic value of its business and not the effect on the company's accounts. Strachan explained RTZ's currency management strategy as, "sharing the exposure amongst a widely diversified range of different currencies so that no one currency carried sufficient weight to represent a cause for concern. The very wide spread of RTZ's activities, both geographically and by product, naturally results in a reasonably well-diversified currency exposure profile. Therefore, we do not engage in short-term currency speculation." Fundamentally, however, the company had to decide in which currencies to borrow. The bulk of RTZ's borrowing was in U.S. dollars, which approximately matched RTZ's U.S.-dollar revenues. "Our borrowing policy represents, in effect, our currency exposure management program," Strachan added.

RTZ Purchases the Mining Operations of British Petroleum

In keeping with its commitment to diversify cyclical risk within the mining industry, RTZ announced its plans to purchase BP Minerals America from British Petroleum for $3.7 billion in January 1989. RTZ first became aware of the possibility of a BP Minerals sale in May 1988. BP was under pressure at the time from the U.K. government to reach an agreement about a stock buy-back program after having been forced to buy back a large portion of its stock from a large Kuwaiti shareholder. However, BP could not announce a financing plan within the short specified time horizon. Having just sold off their cement, and oil and gas assets, RTZ was in a unique position to consider purchasing BP's mineral division in 1988, and was able to do so quickly despite the fact that the industry was just beginning to recover. However, BP's initial offer was for a minority ownership stake, which RTZ rejected. Robert Wilson explained, "We weren't interested in a passive investment. We wanted to acquire 100 percent of the assets. We also insisted that we be the sole buyer of the division to avoid a competitive bidding war." BP complied with RTZ's criteria, and the deal was finalized.

With the purchase, RTZ gained a number of low cost mines. BP Mineral's assets were comprised primarily of copper (Kennecott), gold (Bingham Canyon), and titanium dioxide slag (QIT, Richards Bay). See Exhibit 13 for RTZ's share of mineral production including BP. Bingham Canyon belonged to Kennecott Copper, which BP acquired in 1981 for $1.8 billion. It was the oldest open pit copper mine in the world, and

Exhibit 13   RTZ Net Share of Western World Mineral Production

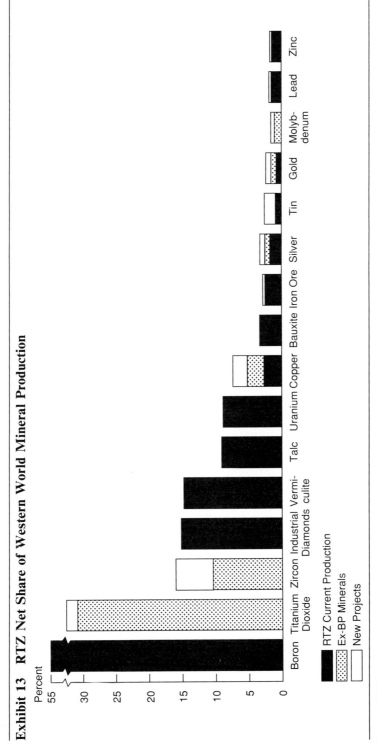

Source: RTZ

had undergone a $375 million modernization program. The mine was also among the lowest cost copper producers with some of the highest quality copper assets in the world, with gold as a by-product. BP's gold assets, especially Bingham Canyon, made RTZ one of the bigger gold players outside of South Africa. BP also had a number of new exploration projects in the pipeline, including a major gold project at Lihir in Papua, New Guinea.

RTZ quickly integrated BP Mineral's operations with its own. Kennecott Copper was given back its name, with the BP America name maintained for the entire operation. Birkin explained, "We want to maintain our commitment to an indigenous management structure so that the former BP operators see themselves as independents, much like private companies, but with all of the benefits that a strong parent can provide. In addition, we reduced many of the layers of management which had existed at BP. For example, the president of Kennecott reports directly to the corresponding managing director at RTZ."

RTZ in the 1990s

In 1989, following the acquisition of BP Minerals and the sale of $2.6 billion in cement, oil, gas, and chemical assets, some observers wondered if RTZ, now more reliant upon mining activities, was still in a strong position to earn the high returns to which it had grown accustomed and if it would be able to weather future volatility in the mining industry. Derek Birkin was faced with the formidable task of integrating BP's worldwide mining operations into the RTZ organization.

Questions

1. How vulnerable is the mining business to the macroeconomic environment? Why?
2. How well has RTZ managed the economic cycles of the mining industry?
3. How would you evaluate RTZ's diversification strategy?
4. Under what conditions should RTZ pursue additional diversification? Does RTZ's acquisition of BP Minerals fit with those conditions?

CASE 2

The General Aviation Industry in 1982

A sharp, sustained decline in revenues and earnings is perhaps one of the most difficult situations a manager may ever face. The continued viability of the company may be jeopardized as competitors adopt more aggressive strategies to cope with the collapsing market. However, the actions taken by managers in response to the collapsing market may, in turn, influence the pace and depth of the decline.

This is particularly apparent in industries in which there are relatively few competitors with significant market power, as in the general aviation industry. Therefore, managers must be aware of the long-term consequences of their decisions on the future structure of their industry.

The recession of 1982 provides the setting for the decline in the general aviation industry sales described in this case. Many other industries experienced declines of similar magnitudes during this period, thus the generic problem described in this case is not unique. The persistent problem for managers in these situations is that they must decide whether the decline is a transient cyclical decline or long-term structural decline. After they correctly diagnose the causes of the problem, they are better able to design a strategy to counter the consequences of the downturn and position themselves against the competition.

Typically, not all segments of the industry will respond similarly to a given decline in sales. This case allows one to identify differences among the segments that account for the differences in performance. The correct segmentation of the industry is another key decision facing managers in these situations.

The general aviation industry included all civil aviation except large commercial airlines. The industry manufactured airplanes ranging from single-engine aircraft to multimillion-dollar business jets. General aviation served a wide range of uses such as air taxi (charter), commuter, agricultural, business, instructional, and sport flying. With over 75 percent of all non-commercial aircraft sales, the United States made up most of the world's general aviation market.

Throughout the 1970s, the industry in the U.S. had enjoyed continuous growth in both total factory unit shipments and total dollar billings. However, in 1980 and 1981 unit shipments declined by 50 percent to 9,457, even though billings continued to rise over those two years, reaching $2.9 billion in 1981. Moreover, in 1982, not only did shipments fall an additional 55 percent, but billings also declined by a record 46 percent—the first decline since 1971. (See Exhibit 1.) Manufacturers of general aviation aircraft wondered if the industry was a victim of the longest and deepest economic recession since the Great Depression of the 1930s or if the downturn in aircraft demand would persist even after the economy recovered.

The Product

General aviation sales consisted of four categories of aircraft: single-engine piston, twin-engine piston, turboprops, and small jets. Exhibit 2 shows the distribution of unit sales and dollar sales between 1976 and

Exhibit 1.   Unit Shipments of U.S. General Aviation Aircraft

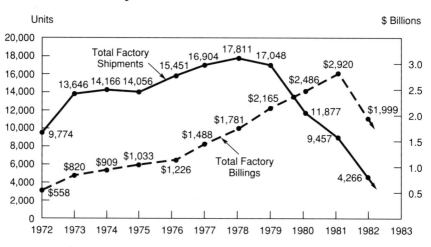

This case was prepared by Research Associate Julia L. Horn under the supervision of Professor Michael G. Rukstad. Copyright © 1989 by the President and Fellows of Harvard College. Harvard Business School case 9-389-088.

Exhibit 2A.   U.S. General Aviation Shipments by Type of Aircraft

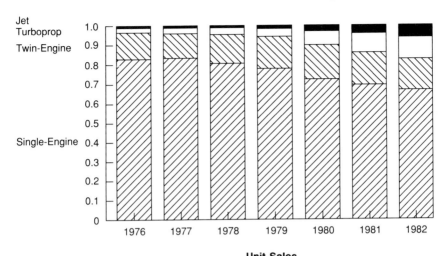

Unit Sales							
	1976	**1977**	**1978**	**1979**	**1980**	**1981**	**1982**
Single-engine	$12,785	$14,054	$14,398	$13,286	$ 8,640	$6,608	$2,871
Twin-engine	2,120	2,195	2,634	2,843	2,116	1,542	678
Turboprop	359	428	548	639	778	918	458
Jet	187	227	231	282	326	389	259
Total	15,451	16,904	17,811	17,048	11,877	9,457	4,266

Source: General Aviation Manufacturers' Association Statistical Database, 1987.

1982 among the four categories of aircraft. The largest category, in units shipped, was the single-engine category, including both light single-engine and high performance single-engine planes. A single-engine plane was powered by one piston engine driving a propeller. Light single-engine planes were most often used by the personal and flight school markets and ranged in price from $17,000 to $60,000. High performance single-engine planes were used for both personal and business purposes, and typically ranged in price from $60,000 to $120,000. The primary differences among single engine aircraft were cruising speeds, fuel efficiency, and horsepower. Cruising speeds ranged from 105 mph for the slowest single-engine planes to 205 mph for the fastest high performance singles. Fuel efficiency, measured by seat-miles-per-gallon of fuel, varied from 28 to 92.[1] Horsepower, which constrained the useful load of the aircraft, ranged from 110 to 310. The largest manufacturers of single-engine aircraft were Cessna, Piper, Beech, and Mooney.

The second category was twin-engine piston aircraft, which were

---

[1] Generally seating was provided for two to four passengers but a few models afforded seating for six. By comparison, a Boeing 747 and other large commercial aircraft had a seat-miles-per-gallon rating in the mid-40s.

Exhibit 2B.   Value of U.S. General Aviation Shipments by Type of Aircraft

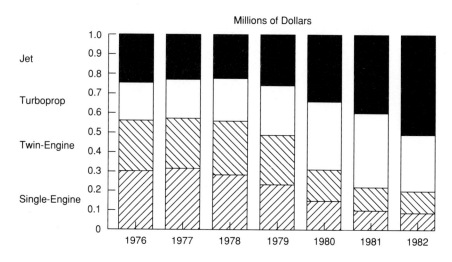

	1976	1977	1978	1979	1980	1981	1982
	Dollar Sales (Millions)						
Single-engine	$ 376	$ 473	$ 516	$ 523	$ 391	$ 327	$ 200
Twin-engine	320	390	493	555	403	348	220
Turboprop	238	296	394	548	875	1,120	590
Jet	293	329	378	540	816	1,125	990
Total[a]	1,225.5	1,448.1	1,781.2	2,165.0	2,486.2	2,919.9	1,999.5

[a]Breakdown by type of aircraft may not be added to total due to independent rounding.

Source: General Aviation Manufacturers' Association Statistical Databook, 1987.

used by businesses, air taxi services, and commuter airlines for both passenger and cargo transportation. They accommodated from 4 to 10 passengers and their prices ranged from $10ʿ,000 to $375,000. Cruising speeds varied from 195 to 225 mph and seat miles per gallon of fuel ranged from 40 to 70. Cessna, Piper, and Beech were the largest manufacturers of twin-engine piston aircraft.

The third category was twin-engine turboprop aircraft in which a jet turbine engine drove the propeller. Turboprops were primarily used for business and commuter purposes and ranged in price from $1 million to $2 million. These aircraft had the advantage of higher fuel efficiency and better performance on short runways than a jet aircraft. Turboprops typically carried 7 to 15 passengers. Their cruising speeds ranged from 225 to 360 mph, and horsepower per engine ranged from 450 to 900. The largest U.S. manufacturers of turboprops were Beech, Piper, Cessna, and Fairchild/Swearingen, and the largest foreign manufacturers included Saab-Scania (Sweden), deHavilland (Canada), and Mitsubishi (Japan).

The fourth category of general aviation aircraft was small jets. Like turboprops, jets were used by corporations and commuter airlines. Jets were driven by the thrust from two engines, either turbojet or turbofan engines. In a turbofan engine, the jet was in the center of the engine and the fan circulated air past the engine to give it additional thrust. Jets had even higher cruising speeds than turboprops, ranging from 400 to 530 mph, and accommodated more passengers with seating capacities from 8 to 28 passengers. Prices on the bottom end of the small jet line started at $1.5 million, while models at the top end of the line were priced as high as $10 million. The largest U.S. manufacturers of business jets were Cessna, Gulfstream, Gates-Learjet, and Rockwell. Foreign manufacturers, including Dassault (France), British Aerospace, Canadair, and Israel Aircraft, and Mitsubishi (Japan), were the most competitive with the United States in the jet category.

Sales and Marketing

Aircraft were sold to a variety of users, including individuals and flight schools, and commuter, charter, and business aircraft users. Each of these markets had different requirements in terms of the size of aircraft, price, fuel capacity, and cruising speed. Exhibit 3 shows the distribution of all active aircraft in 1982 among various uses.

Manufacturers of smaller single and twin-engine aircraft sold their planes through dealer networks much like those used for automobiles. Piper Aircraft used distributors to distribute piston aircraft from the factory to the dealer. Its distributors typically bought aircraft at a fixed price, receiving discounts of 25 percent off the list price and sold to dealers at 20 percent off the list price. In contrast, Cessna had a few distributors, but sold primarily through dealers, and Beech sold exclusively through dealers. Piper, Cessna, and Beech all produced piston aircraft for inventory.

The dealer's function was to place orders from the factory based on the number of aircraft he or she planned to sell, arrange customer financing, stock spare parts, and display aircraft. Typically, the dealer also provided maintenance and repair facilities at airports, similar to an automobile dealer's service department. Dealers shared this responsibility with fixed base operators (FBOs) which also provided aircraft service and support as well as some used aircraft sales from airport locations. FBO's operated much like automobile repair shops did. Most piston aircraft purchasers made a downpayment to the dealer of 10 to 25 percent of the aircraft's price. The remainder of the aircraft's cost was usually covered by a finance agreement. Most large aircraft manufacturers including Cessna, Piper, Beech, and Fairchild/Swearingen had in-house financing agencies.

The purchase decision for piston aircraft involved substantially more than the initial cost of the aircraft, though price was often a primary factor in deciding between similar models of aircraft. (The price elasticity for single-engine aircraft had been estimated to be 6.) Piston aircraft

Exhibit 3.   Type and Primary Use of Active General Aviation Aircraft in 1982

Aircraft Type	Active GA Aircraft	Executive	Business	Personal	Instructional	Aerial Application	Aerial Observation	Other Work	Commuter Air Carrier	Air Taxi	Rentals
Total All Aircraft	209,799	15,739	47,873	94,820	14,708	7,155	4,164	1,733	1,070	8,122	9,844
Piston-Total	189,195	8,115	46,707	90,882	13,634	6,261	3,324	1,256	711	5,932	9,401
One-Engine	154,173	2,731	36,857	87,305	13,083	5,943	3,003	1,187	212	2,819	9,062
Two-Engine	24,882	5,380	9,847	3,573	551	267	315	66	477	3,109	326
Other Piston	140	4	2	4	0	50	5	2	22	4	13
Turboprop-Total	5,186	3,327	570	32	0	101	26	6	296	499	34
Two-Engine	5,037	3,322	570	29	0	0	24	0	294	493	34
Other Turboprop	149	5	0	3	0	101	3	6	3	6	0
Turbojet-Total	3,996	3,054	231	47	0	0	0	0	63	393	0
Two-Engine	3,309	2,477	222	47	0	0	0	0	24	393	0
Other Turboprop	687	577	8	0	0	0	0	0	39	0	0
Rotorcraft-Total	6,169	1,238	352	486	457	793	715	300	0	1,227	29
Piston	2,419	190	201	356	379	677	352	51	0	43	3
Turbine	3,749	1,048	151	130	78	116	364	249	0	1,184	26
Other-Total	5,233	4	13	3,373	616	0	98	172	0	71	380

NOTE: Row and column summation may differ from printed totals due to estimation procedures.

Source: General Aviation Manufacturers' Association Statistical Databook, 1984.

buyers also evaluated the insurance, maintenance, and fuel costs required to keep the aircraft flying. Maintenance, on average, was performed every 100 hours, including a major engine overhaul about every 2000 hours, which cost approximately $6,400 per piston engine. After making the decision to purchase a piston aircraft, it took approximately five months between the time an aircraft order was placed and the aircraft was delivered to the customer.

In the turboprop and turbojet markets, manufacturers' selling efforts began with advertisements and articles in trade publications. Of the 1,000 largest corporations in the United States, 514 already owned and operated at least one business jet in 1979. In 1980, oil companies accounted for 20 percent of all new business jet unit sales. At both Beech and Piper, all turboprop and turbojets were sold exclusively through dealers. As with piston aircraft, Cessna maintained a few distributors, but sold primarily through dealers. Unlike Beech and Piper, which produced turboprop and turbojet aircraft against firm product orders, Cessna produced for inventory. Dealers arranged ground and air demonstrations of the aircraft at the buyer's expense, though the cost was often refundable upon purchase.

The purchase decision for turboprop and turbojet aircraft involved the evaluation of costs such as pilot salaries, cost per seat mile, aircraft storage, insurance, maintenance, fuel, and landing fees as well as the resale value of the plane. Major engine overhauls, performed about every 3,000 hours, cost $24,000 per engine. The choice of types and brands of avionics equipment (the flight instruments and electronics) was one of the most important made by the purchaser of turboprop and turbojet aircraft. Optional avionics equipment could cost as much as between $800,000 and $1.6 million, particularly for business turbojets.

In the turboprop and turbojet markets, it took approximately six months from the initial contact with a potential buyer before an actual purchase contract was signed. Beyond that, delivery positions for turboprops and business jets often required substantial downpayments and a waiting period of up to three years on some models. In 1980, for example, an order for a Citation II, Cessna's largest corporate jet, required a down payment of $200,000 with the initial order, followed by a 10 percent payment two years prior to delivery, 20 percent one year before delivery, 20 percent at the six-month mark, and another 20 percent three months before delivery. The total purchase price was approximately $2.5 million. Because of delivery waiting periods, it was not uncommon for some purchasers of turboprops and turbojets to merely "take a position" in the delivery line for an airplane, hoping later to sell that position to a buyer who did not want to wait the necessary two to three years.

Used Aircraft Sales

Buyers of piston, turboprop, and turbojet aircraft sometimes chose to buy a used plane rather than a new one. Because aircraft maintenance requirements were heavily regulated, there was a higher safety margin in buying a used aircraft than in buying, for example, a used automobile. The average useful life of an airplane was approximately 25 years in 1982, depending on utilization. Turboprop and jet aircraft typically retained most of their original value, in real terms, at resale. Business and personal aircraft utilization was very low relative to that of commuter airlines which often operated five or more flights per aircraft per day. Used aircraft for sale ranged in value from 40-year-old single-engine planes to one-year-old business jets. In the early 1980s, as many as 60,000 used general aviation aircraft were sold each year.

The importance of used aircraft had forced many aircraft manufacturers to accept used planes as trade-ins in order to sell new aircraft. Several U.S. manufacturers, including Cessna and Beech, had established used aircraft divisions within their sales departments. Used aircraft, if sold through a manufacturer's dealer network, were financed in much the same manner as new aircraft. Some airplanes were sold through independent aircraft brokers, which handled numerous types of aircraft from different manufacturers and often advertised in the newspaper. Financing for aircraft sold through brokers was typically arranged through bank loans.

Manufacturing

The manufacturing of general aviation aircraft was a custom job shop production process. For a short period during the 1960s, as unit sales volume continued to increase, some progress was made toward "mass production" on a few models. For example, because of the immense popularity and relatively simple design of its Skyhawk 172 (the trainer aircraft sold over 30,000 units from its first year of production in 1955 to 1982), Cessna was able to step up production and achieve some economies of scale. However, because of the low volume sales and design complexity for the majority of airplane models, production by a batch process remained the rule, with workers moving from one plane's work station to the next, and with little automation. Similarities among aircraft allowed some common parts to be used. However, the Skyhawk 172, for example, was not intentionally designed with common parts in mind. Production periods varied by type of aircraft. In 1982, Cessna had eight piston production lines, each of which produced one aircraft per day; one turboprop line that produced one aircraft per week; and two Citation jet lines that each produced one aircraft per month.

The primary production-related assets used in aircraft manufacturing were jigs used for fabrication and assembly. Though manufacturers typically built their own aircraft-specific machine tools, capital requirements for tooling, engineering and development were often less than 5 percent of sales. In 1982, the average utilization of production capacity for aircraft manufacturers was 39 percent compared to 83 percent in 1980.

The general aviation industry in the early 1980s was not characterized by a high degree of technological innovation. The majority of manufacturers introduced adaptations of older models rather than all-new aircraft, though incremental improvements were made with each adaptation. Aircraft engine manufacturers had not produced many major innovations outside of increased reliability, less noise, and better fuel efficiency. The airframe had not changed much either, though some manufacturers were experimenting with new composite materials. It was estimated that from $200 million to $500 million was required in nonrecurring costs alone to design, produce, certify, and market an all-new aircraft model. The majority of the expenditures were made early in the program before any appraisal of the success of the product could be made. Three to five years were generally required for a manufacturer to perform all of the required steps to deliver a new business or commuter aircraft. As a general rule, a new turbine-powered business or commuter aircraft had a break-even production level of 200 units before non-recurring costs (primarily retooling) could be paid. The smaller piston-powered aircraft had a break-even level of approximately 100 units.

Average product costs varied by manufacturer and by type of aircraft produced. A representative breakdown of average costs for the industry would be:

	Single Engine	Jet
Marketing	25%	5%
Labor	5	5
Overhead	10	10
Materials:		
Engine(s)	20	20
Avionics	15	15
Other	10	20
Total materials	45	55
Capital	15%	25%
Total	100%	100%

Manufacturers' pre-tax profit margins averaged 10 percent to 13 percent through the early 1980s though they had fallen slightly in 1982.

Increasing product liability costs posed a significant problem for aircraft manufacturers just as they did for manufacturers of nearly all types of consumer goods. A recent survey by the General Aviation Manufacturer's Association (GAMA) revealed that product liability costs to general aviation manufacturers were $50,000 if averaged on a per airplane basis across all aircraft types in 1982, compared with $2,111 per airplane in 1972 and $51 in 1962. Rising and unlimited product liability costs were often blamed for increasingly higher prices for aircraft. Each year manufacturers' revenues from airplane sales had to cover the product liability costs for the aircraft produced in that year and for the manufacturer's entire fleet of airplanes still in service, without regard to the number of times engines and parts had been rebuilt, the maintenance that had been performed, and the training level of the pilot. In some cases, manufacturers were purchasing insurance coverage on airplanes produced 40 to 50 years back, long before they were able to forecast the length of time an aircraft could continue to fly.

Insurance companies, primarily based in London, offered aircraft product liability insurance. Companies such as Cessna, Piper, and Beech were required to self-insure the first layer of coverage (typically between $5 to $10 million), which acted much like a deductible did in other insurance policies. The second layer of insurance, ranging from $10 to $40 million, was provided by insurance companies. The third layer of coverage, from $40 to $100 million was self-insured again. The highest layer, which covered catastrophic settlements over $100 million, was provided by insurance companies. Premiums to insure against catastrophic claims alone typically cost aircraft companies from $7 to $9 million per year, but varied from year to year depending on market conditions.

Suppliers

Because of the nature of the batch manufacturing process, approximately one-half of product costs were materials. A jet typically required over 30,000 parts, compared to less than 15,000 for a single-engine aircraft. The engine, avionics, and airframe comprised the majority of materials costs. The airframe components were aluminum, steel, and fiberglass, and were generally considered commodities that a number of different suppliers could provide. Aircraft production executives believed that increased volume of both engine and avionics purchases yielded significant bargaining power with regard to price. The two dominant suppliers of piston engines were Avco-Lycoming and Teledyne/Continental. Both manufactured a competing range of aircraft engines, with horsepower varying from 100 to 400 per engine. Comparably-sized engines from either manufacturer could be substituted for one another, but only after reengineering the airframe. Most aircraft engines were given a suggested lifespan by their manufacturer according to the time interval between overhauls. The time between major overhauls for piston engines ranged from 1,200 to 2,000 hours.

The leading turboprop, turbojet, and turbofan engine manufacturers were General Electric, Pratt and Whitney (a subsidiary of United Technologies), Rolls Royce, and Garrett (a subsidiary of Signal Corporation). Each manufactured engines that had horsepower ranges of 450 to 1500 on turboprops, and 4,000 to 25,000 pounds of thrust on turbojet or turbofan engines, though not all companies had a full range of engines for each type of aircraft. Like piston engines, comparably-sized engines from those manufacturers could be substituted for one another with reengineering. Because turbine engines had a simpler construction and fewer moving parts than piston engines, their time between overhauls averaged 3,000 hours. Engine overhaul and spare parts revenue averaged approximately a third of an engine manufacturer's business. Aircraft manufacturers often experienced significant lead times for some raw materials such as engines, landing gear, or forgings and castings, and typically signed contracts with suppliers one to two years in advance.

Avionics were a key component in the manufacture of aircraft. They included communication, navigation, instrument landing, and flight control products and systems. The four largest suppliers of a full line of avionics were: Cessna, Collins, Bendix/King, and Narco. Cessna's avionics were standard or optional equipment on various Cessna models, though buyers could usually choose any type of equipment they wanted. Cessna also marketed all of its avionics products, except radios, to other aircraft manufacturers, and was active in the large avionics aftermarket as well. Collins, a subsidiary of Rockwell International, was considered a top-of-the-line avionics manufacturer. Its radios were found in most business jets as well as in most commercial airline jets. The Bendix/King line was the result of a merger of the two companies' avionics lines, which were then refocused on high quality and generally more expensive products. Narco's products were considered the standard in light aircraft avionics. Unlike the other manufacturers, it had never addressed the top end of the aircraft line.

Other aircraft parts suppliers included propeller manufacturers such as Hamilton Standard, a division of United Technologies, McCauley, a division of Cessna Aircraft, and Hartzell Propeller, a division of TRW, Inc. Bendix and Cessna's McCauley division also manufactured wheels and brakes for smaller aircraft.

Historical Overview of the General Aviation Industry

The market for general aviation aircraft was born after World War II. The War was a major catalyst in the development of the industry because it increased the emphasis placed on air transport and introduced an unprecedented number of people to flying. Pilots from the Korean War also provided a ready market for the industry. In 1957, there were 223,297 active student and private pilots. By 1967, that figure had almost doubled to 434,599. Through three decades from the 1950s to the 1970s, the industry's growth seemed unstoppable despite a few cyclical downturns.

In 1973, the first oil price shock caused aviation fuel prices to almost double from mid-1973 to mid-1974. Nonetheless, the general aviation industry's unit shipments and billings continued to climb. By 1978, the total number of aircraft shipped reached an unprecedented 17,811, of which 81 percent were single-engine piston aircraft. Aircraft manufacturers could not build planes fast enough, and backlogs for jet orders climbed to three years.

In 1978, the peak in general aviation unit and dollar sales, the Airline Deregulation Act was passed. Deregulation effectively gave regional and commuter airlines an opportunity to build sales by capturing those routes in low density markets that the larger airlines had dropped because of low profitability. The number of airports served by major carriers dwindled significantly after deregulation, opening the door for smaller airlines that were willing to service less-traveled routes. Following deregulation, subsidies were available for commuter airlines for the first time and the government guaranteed loans to commuter operators for the purchase of aircraft.

In 1979, the second oil price shock caused aviation gasoline and jet fuel prices to nearly double again by early 1980. The industry experienced a 4 percent decline in unit shipments in 1979, the first decline since 1970, though industry billings rose 22 percent. The decline in units was entirely in the light single- and twin-engine piston categories, where the steep rise in the price of fuel was felt the hardest by the individuals, flight schools, and small businesses that operated them. Demand continued to be strong in the turbojet and turboprop categories, accounting for the continued increase in industry billings. (See Exhibit 2.)

At the start of the 1980s, the economy moved into a recession, and the downward trend in single and twin-engine piston units persisted. Interest rates had reached a staggering 22 percent, inflation was creeping up to 13 percent per year, and industrial production had fallen by 16.7 percent early in the year. By the end of 1980, the industry had experienced a 30 percent decline in unit shipments for the year, though billings still rose 15 percent. Despite the drop in shipments, aircraft manufacturers continued current production rates, making small but insufficient cutbacks. Production rates were still beyond what sales could sustain, resulting in large inventories, primarily in the piston-engine category. Most manufacturers believed that, because the industry had experienced occasional periods of slow sales since World War II, sales would pick up again after six months to a year, as they had in the past. In 1981, unit sales fell by 20 percent but billings rose by an additional 18 percent. In 1981, U.S. aircraft manufacturers shipped more turboprop and turbojet business aircraft than in any other year in history, a total of 918 and 389 units respectively, accounting for 77 percent of the industry's total factory billings.

Despite hopes for a recovery, 1982 proved to be the worst year in decades for the general aviation industry. Aircraft manufacturers in all of the aircraft categories, including the once-shielded turboprop and jet makers, were dealt a strong blow as unit shipments dropped by 55 percent to a low not seen since the 1950s, and billings fell 46 percent, the largest one-year drop in 35 years. (Refer again to Exhibit 1.) Aircraft manufacturers were forced to make even sharper cuts in employment and production levels. Another blow to the industry was the 1982 reduction of many of the accelerated depreciation benefits that had been offered in the Economic Recovery Tax Act (ERTA) of 1981.

While unit shipments and finally billings suffered, the number of active student and private pilots also fell between 1979 and 1982. Student pilots declined by 26 percent and the number of private pilots dropped by 10 percent. The average purchase price for a single-engine aircraft grew from $38,604 in 1979 to $67,853 in 1982, while the average income in the U.S. grew from $7,671 to $9,710.

One encouraging statistic for the industry was the decline in the accident rate for general aviation aircraft. The total accidents per 100,000 hours flown had fallen every year from 1972 to 1981, rising only slightly in 1982. The number of fatal accidents showed the same declining pattern. The industry's improved safety record had been attributed to better pilot education and improved aircraft design. (See Exhibit 4 for trends in flying activity, flying costs and macroeconomic activity.)

Competition in 1982

U.S. Competition

The U.S. general aviation aircraft industry was dominated by seven companies: Cessna, Beech, Piper, Gates Learjet, Gulfstream, Fairchild/Swearingen, and Mooney. Exhibit 5 summarizes their relative market shares.

Cessna.   Cessna was founded in 1911 by aviation pioneer Clyde Cessna. It was the largest manufacturer of general aviation aircraft in the world. The company manufactured the most complete line of aircraft of any company. Cessna's product line included the 172 Skyhawk trainer, the 182 Skylane high performance single, the 210 Centurion, the world's only pressurized single, the 310 twin-engine aircraft, the Conquest turboprop, and the largest-selling business jet, the Citation. The Citation I and II models had been developed by the company in the late 1960s. See Exhibit 6 for representative brands of the seven largest U.S. manufacturers in each category. The company's products catered to the lower end of the market in each category, and its planes had mass market appeal. Approximately 50 percent of Cessna's unit sales were of single-engine aircraft in 1982. For Cessna, like Beech and Piper, approximately 20 percent to 25 percent of the company's total sales were overseas.

Cessna was headquartered in Wichita, Kansas, often called the general aviation capital of the world because of the number of manufacturers with production facilities located there. In 1982, approximately 25 percent of all jobs in Wichita were directly related to aircraft manufacturing. Cessna's manufacturing facilities were also located in Wichita, in the original plant built in 1929 and another plant built in the 1950s. Cessna maintained additional facilities outside of Kansas for the manufacture of aviation parts. The company also leased office, hanger and aircraft tie-down space, primarily at airports, for use as regional sales facilities. Cessna was the most vertically integrated of all aircraft manufacturers,

Exhibit 4   Trends in Flying Activity and Costs

	1975	1976	1977	1978	1979	1980	1981	1982	Compounded Annual Growth Rate (%) 1975–1982
Flying activity:									
Total active U.S. pilots (in thousands)	728	744	783	798	814	827	764	733	0.1%
U.S. student pilot applications (in thousands)	127	129	138	137	139	102	117	84	−5.7%
General aviation hours flown (in millions)	31.7	33.0	35.3	37.1	39.0	41.6	41.1	37.8	2.5%
Flying costs:									
Unit value of a single-engine airplane	$24,117	$30,840	$33,037	$35,602	$38,604	$44,066	$50,255	$67,853	15.9%
Base price of a Cessna Skyhawk 172	$17,890	$20,750	$22,300	$23,495	$25,950	$30,735	$37,810	$38,450	11.5%
Aircraft operating costs (per hour)[a]	$9.29	$10.41	$11.95	$13.34	$15.50	$19.63	$22.54	$23.76	14.4%
Fuel costs (per hour)[a]	$7.04	$7.67	$8.96	$10.23	$12.24	$16.15	$18.86	$19.66	15.8%
Maintenance costs (per hour)[a]	$2.25	$2.74	$2.99	$3.11	$3.26	$3.48	$3.68	$4.10	9.0%
Insurance cost index	100	129	144	148	157	170	178	189	9.5%
Total accidents per 100,000 hours flown	13.9	13.2	12.9	12.1	9.9	9.9	9.5	10.1	−4.5%
Fatal accidents per 100,000 hours flown	2.20	2.16	2.09	2.06	1.63	1.69	1.78	1.84	−2.5%

(Continued)

Exhibit 4 Continued

	1975	1976	1977	1978	1979	1980	1981	1982	Compounded Annual Growth Rate (%) 1975–1982
Macroeconomic Activity:									
Real GNP (% change)	−1.3%	4.9%	4.7%	5.3%	2.5%	−0.2%	1.9%	−2.5%	2.3%
Real after-tax personal income per capita (% change)	0.9	2.6	2.2	3.8	1.0	−1.1%	0.5%	−0.5	1.2%
Corporate profits after tax (% change)	33.7	21.4	25.7	11.7	−1.4	−17.6	15.6	−18.6	3.9%
Industrial production index (% change)	−8.8	9.2	8.0	6.5	3.9	−1.9	2.2	−7.1	2.8%
Consumer price index (% change)	9.1	5.8	6.5	7.7	11.3	13.5	10.4	6.1	8.7%
Prime interest rate	7.9	6.8	6.8	9.1	12.7	15.3	18.9	14.9	9.5%

aFor single-engine piston airplanes.

Exhibit 5A.   Aircraft Sales of U.S. General Aviation Aircraft Manufacturers

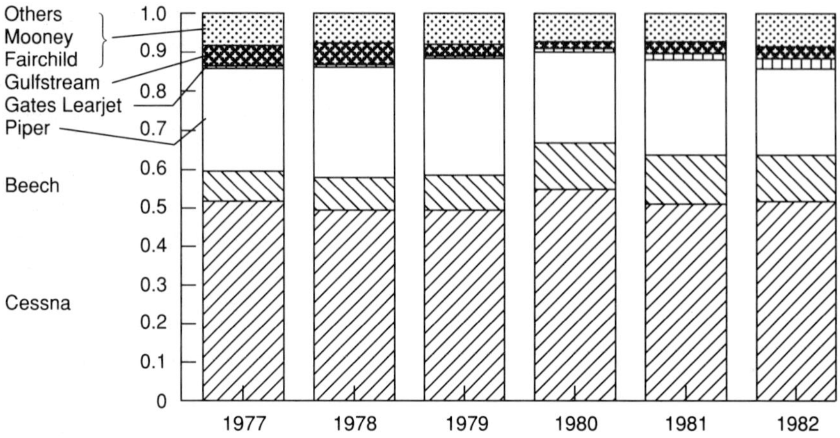

Unit Sales						
	1977	**1978**	**1979**	**1980**	**1981**	**1982**
Cessna	8,839	8,770	8,400	6,393	4,680	2,140
Beech	1,203	1,367	1,508	1,394	1,242	526
Piper	4,499	5,276	5,255	2,954	2,495	1,048
Gates Learjet	105	102	107	120	138	99
Gulfstream[a]	866	933	400	167	248	96
Fairchild/Shearingen[b]	39	51	70	86	85	49
Mooney	362	379	439	332	330	188
Total Industry Units	16,904	17,811	17,048	11,877	9,457	4,266

[a]Grumman American became Gulfstream Aerospace in 1978.

[b]Fairchild Industries acquired Swearingen in 1979.

Source: General Aviation Manufacturers' Association.

producing avionics equipment, propellers, aircraft wheels, and brakes for use in its own aircraft as well as for sale to other manufacturers. In 1982, its sales of aircraft, parts, and avionics were $832 million on assets of $528 million. Net earnings for 1982 were $18.1 million.

From 1978 to 1982, Cessna accounted for 51 percent of the industry's total unit output and 29 percent of the industry's dollar volume. When it introduced its Citation I business jet in 1972, Cessna's first entry into the business jet category, the company was behind competitor Learjet, the market share leader. In 1978, Cessna introduced a second generation model, the Citation II. Four years later, in 1982, Cessna edged out Learjet with lower prices to command a leading unit market share of 35 percent of the business jet market.

As early as 1979, Cessna was the first in the industry to cut back production and lay off employees in response to the drop in unit shipments, especially in the light single- and twin-engine aircraft categories.

Exhibit 5B.   Value of Aircraft Sales of U.S. General Aviation Aircraft Manufacturers

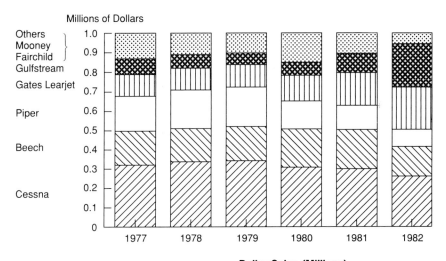

	Dollar Sales (Millions)					
	1977	**1978**	**1979**	**1980**	**1981**	**1982**
Cessna	$ 483.0	$ 612.7	$ 755.0	$ 783.5	$ 895.7	$ 531.9
Beech	262.7	310.5	402.1	514.6	619.7	320.2
Piper	259.2	341.8	419.0	335.5	368.9	179.0
Gates Learjet	168.6	193.2	226.0	298.5	436.1	423.1
Gulfstream	119.1	125.6	138.7	156.0	303.8	446.4
Fairchild/Swearingen	35.4	52.3	80.0	108.7	129.8	87.6
Mooney[a]	22.9	25.2	30.7	24.4	25.5	15.2
Total Industry Billings	1,488.1	1,781.2	2,165.0	2,486.2	2,929.9	1,999.5

[a]Mooney's dollar sales were estimated based on a $63,125 average selling price per plane in 1977 and a 5% increase in the average selling price per year.

Source: General Aviation Manufacturers' Association.

Between 1980 and 1982, the company cut back total unit production by two-thirds and reduced employment in its Wichita operations from 11,000 to 3,000. At the same time, its remaining distributors were eliminated and Cessna's dealers relied even more heavily on price cutting strategies. In 1982, total deliveries of small planes by Cessna were down 60 percent, while deliveries of the company's turboprops and Citation jets, cushioned by a 19-month order backlog going into the recession, were down 20 percent. In addition, in 1982, Cessna continued to make sizable investments in the development of a larger business jet, the Citation III, and a new turboprop model, the Conquest I. Business jets and turboprops typically had a higher safety record than piston aircraft, which helped partially to shield the company from skyrocketing product liability premium costs. However, the number of settlements against the products of single- and twin-engine manufacturers raised both premium and deductible costs at Cessna.

Exhibit 6. Representative Products of U.S. General Aviation Manufacturers in 1982 (Ranked by Increasing Performance within Each Category)

	Cessna	Beech	Piper	Gates Learjet	Gulfstream	Fairchild Swearingen	Mooney
Single-engine piston (standard)	152 Skyhawk 172 Cutlass	Skipper Sundowner Sierra	Super Cub Tomahawk Warrior Archer Arrow				201 231
Single-engine piston (high performance)	Skylane 182 Stationair Centurion 210	Bonanza	Dakota Saratoga Malibu				
Twin-engine piston	Crusader 303 Skymaster 337 Tital 404 Chancellor 444 Golden Eagle 421	Duchess Baron Duke	Seminole Seneca Aztec Navajo Chieftain Aerostar				
Turboprop	Conquest 425 Conquest 441	King Air Super King Air	Cheyenne I Cheyenne II Cheyenne III		Commander	Metro II Merlin IIIA Merlin IVA	
Business jet	Citation I Citation II			Learjet 25 Learjet 35 Learjet 36	Gulfstream II Gulfstream III		

Source: Compiled by author from General Aviation Manufacturers' Association data.

Cessna had been the industry leader in designing innovative sales and pricing programs since the 1960s, and in 1982, Cessna introduced two new marketing programs to try to recover sales and provide outlets for future sales. To help dealers, Cessna offered one-year, zero-interest loans to purchasers of piston aircraft, reduced dealer inventory requirements, and initiated a learn-to-fly program. "Other general aviation manufacturers have steered clear of such deals because they smack of rebates, which have been an anathema to the industry."[2] The company also offered a new leasing program to create new business for its turboprops and business jets. Cessna's Senior Vice President of Marketing, Brian Barents, summed up the industry's prospects, "It's not a question of when the industry will pick up, but how quickly. 1983 will be a flat year, and then we're looking for a dramatic upturn in late 1984 that will be the beginning of strong performance for the rest of the decade."[3] Cessna planned to produce just one twin-engine aircraft as a 1983 model and was not expected to start production of four 1984 models until the end of 1983, such that only a few would actually be ready soon enough to become 1983 deliveries.

Beechcraft.   Beech was founded jointly in 1932 by Olive Ann Beech and Walter Beech, pioneer builders and designers of light airplanes in the United States. The company was formed for the purpose of designing and building the first four-seat enclosed cabin byplane. This first Beechcraft model, called the Staggerwing, set dependability and performance standards for the industry. Throughout the decades that followed, Beech had maintained the high quality standards begun with the Staggerwing.

In 1982, Beech manufactured products in all but the jet category, though its primary products were twin-engine planes specifically targeted to the business, air-taxi, and commuter airline markets. Its aircraft line included the Skipper, a single-engine piston trainer, the Bonanza, a high performance single-engine piston, the Baron twin-engine piston, and the King Air turboprop. The company was considered to have the highest quality products in each of the categories in which it competed. The King Air and Beech's other turboprop models, including its C-99 commuter turboprop introduced in late 1981, accounted for the largest portion of company sales in 1982. Beech was also the most active of its competitors in the military market, manufacturing variations of its King Air and Bonanza models with military specifications, as well as missile targets, and missile components. In 1982, military sales accounted for 25 percent of sales at Beech and 20 percent of profits. In February 1980, Beechcraft became a wholly-owned subsidiary of Raytheon Corporation, accounting for 16 percent of Raytheon's sales and 22 percent of profits in 1981 and 10 percent of sales and 9 percent of profits in 1982.

[2]*Business Week.* October 11, 1982.
[3]*Barron's.* April 11, 1983.

Beech's complete aircraft manufacturing facility was also located in Wichita. In addition, Beech had five smaller facilities, primarily in Kansas, that manufactured light aircraft assemblies and subassemblies, and shipped spare parts to customers. Beech owned 20 fixed base operations at airports, under the name Hanger One, which provided general aviation sales and service and distributed Beechcraft products.

Beech was especially hurt by the slump in business and commuter aircraft purchases in 1982, because it was almost totally dependent on them for sales of its KingAir turboprops, the company's mainstay. At the beginning of 1982, Beech had 10,700 employees, but that figure had dropped to 7,500 by mid-year. Beech had also planned to curtail production of twin-engine piston aircraft in 1983 to match depressed order levels. GAMA President Edward Stimpson expected 1983 to be different for Beech. "Not only should sales of the company's 'Cadillacs of the turboprops' (King Air) pick up, but Beech will also enjoy an extra boost from the military contracts that it won in 1982. Most importantly is an $82.3 million award to supply trainer aircraft to the U.S. Navy, the largest single order in Beech's history." The company had also developed another turboprop commuter aircraft model scheduled to begin delivery in 1983.

Piper Aircraft.   Founded in 1930 in Vero Beach, Florida, Piper's first aircraft was the Cub, a name which had become synonymous with single-engine aircraft in America. Piper manufactured general aviation aircraft in every category except jets. Its products included the single-engine Warrior, the high performance single-engine Saratoga, the Aerostar twin-engine piston, and the Cheyenne turboprop. In trying to emulate Cessna's broad-line product strategy, Piper was adding new models to make up for any gaps in its existing line. For example, it offered up to three different models of both the Cheyenne and the Warrior alone. Piper concentrated on general aviation aircraft sales, and though willing to sell standard aircraft to the military, the company did not want to modify its aircraft designs to cater to military sales. Piper was the market share leader (11 percent) in the commuter aircraft market. Even though Piper designed and produced the lowest priced model of any major manufacturer in each segment of the market in which it competed, it also had products in the high performance, high-priced categories. The company sold spare parts for all of its airplanes as well.

In 1978, Piper was acquired by Bangor Punta Corporation after a nine-year bitter takeover struggle with Chris Craft that was eventually settled by the Supreme Court. Bangor Punta was the product of the merger between a Maine potato railroad and a Cuban sugar refinery, whose other business holdings included everything from Smith and Wesson firearms, to ovens and conveyor belts. In 1979, following Cessna's lead, Piper laid off 400 employees, due to a lack of sales in the bottom end of its product line. By 1981, Piper accounted for 51 percent and 30 percent of Bangor

Punta's sales and profits, respectively. In 1982 Piper's sales were 16 percent of corporate sales but Piper's 1982 net loss of $22.4 million lowered Bangor Punta's profits to $3.1 million.

Piper's manufactured aircraft in Vero Beach, Florida, Lakeland, Florida, and in Lock Haven, Pennsylvania. Between mid-1981 and mid-1982 when industry shipments and billings lagged, Piper laid off approximately 35 percent of its workforce and shut down its single and twin-engine piston aircraft production facility in Vero Beach for one month. In 1979, Piper had a 33.3 percent market share of single-engine aircraft deliveries. By 1982, it had fallen to 21.4 percent. At the same time, the company's two-tier distributor/dealer network, which it used to sell piston aircraft, collapsed as dealers faced rising inflation. The resulting network was significantly smaller and was modeled after its turboprop system, which had eliminated the wholesaler function. Bangor Punta President David Wallace, though he had not completely ruled out the possibility of manufacturing a jet to round out their product line, believed that, "It's unlikely to me that we would develop a jet on our own. However, we could be very interested in acquiring a jet manufacturer."[4]

Gates Learjet.   Learjet was founded in 1960 as the Swiss American Aviation Company by William Lear. Lear, an entrepreneur, had dreamed about designing and producing a high-speed, twin-engine executive jet, a product without a market at that time. Contrary to popular opinion which said that a business jet could not be produced efficiently and would never sell, Lear succeeded in selling the first Learjet Model 23 in 1961. That year the company's name was changed to Learjet Industries. Most of the tooling for the Learjet 23 was done in Europe, but in 1962, all production facilities were relocated to Wichita.

In 1967, Mr. Lear's 60 percent interest in the company was acquired by the Gates Rubber Company and the company's name was changed to Gates Learjet. The company continued to produce aircraft in the jet category only and catered primarily to the top end of the business market. By 1982, the company manufactured five models of the Learjet with prices ranging from $2.2 for the Model 24F to $5.0 million for the Model 36A. Learjets carried between 8 and 12 passengers and their cruising speeds ranged from 500 to 510 mph. Learjets were sold primarily to large corporations and commuter airlines with some models tailored to military specifications as well.

Gates Learjet's manufacturing took place at the company's facilities in Wichita and in Tucson, Arizona. Gates Learjet typically produced 12 aircraft per month, and customers often waited up to three years on orders. Since 1971, Gates Learjet had been streamlined into three clearly-defined, aviation-oriented operations: Learjet manufacturing, Combs-

[4]*New York Times.* August 5, 1979.

Gates fixed base operations at five airports in the United States, and Jet Electronics and Technology (JET), a small manufacturer of avionics in Grand Rapids, Michigan. In 1982, most of total company sales were from Learjet aircraft. Combs-Gates offered aircraft support for the large commercial and regional carriers in addition to general aviation aircraft, was a wholesaler of aircraft parts, sold fuel, and sold used high performance business planes, including those not manufactured by Gates.

In 1980, Gates Learjet commanded a 26 percent unit share of the worldwide business jet market. Both 1981 and 1982 were record year's in the company's history as it delivered 120 and 138 Learjets respectively. However, in 1982, the company felt the downturn in the economy as unit shipments fell to 99, the lowest in four years. To match decreased orders and production rates in 1981 and 1982, Gates instituted employee layoffs. In 1982, Gates cut its employment level by more than 60 percent, stopped production of two of its aircraft models, and reduced production of a third model of aircraft.

By the end of 1982, Gates announced that it was expanding its product line to include more special mission aircraft (maritime surveillance, photographic reconnaissance, etc.) and more subcontract work. Previously, Gates had limited itself to delivering fully completed aircraft to the corporate market. However, the downturn in corporate aircraft sales and the unused manufacturing facilities prompted Gates to look outside of its traditional markets. As for the near future of the business jet market, Anthony Hain, Learjet's controller said, "Companies are going to find it harder and harder to go to their boards for capital appropriations (for purchasing business jets) when their earnings are so low."[5]

Gulfstream Aerospace.   Gulfstream's business jets were the largest and most expensive business jets in the world, catering to the upscale end of the business jet category. They accommodated from 10 to 16 passengers and cost from $8 to $12 million.

The Gulfstream name was first used in 1958 when Grumann American Aviation, the general aviation division of Grumann Corporation, decided to produce a turboprop aircraft. Production of the first Gulfstream turboprop ended in the 1960s in favor of production of a large model corporate jet. The first Gulfstream corporate jet, the turbofan Gulfstream II, was produced in 1966. In 1978, American Jet Industries acquired Grumann's general aviation subsidiary, Grumann American Aviation and changed its name to Gulfstream Aerospace. American Jet Industries was a holding company formed in 1976 by Allen E. Paulson (now chairman, and chief executive officer of Gulfstream). In 1980, Paulson recapitalized the company, bringing his personal stake in it to 95.6 percent. In 1981, Gulfstream acquired the turboprop business of Rockwell

[5]*New York Times.* March 22, 1982.

International. Because of the acquisition, the company also manufactured four smaller turboprop corporate aircraft models that were considerably less expensive.

Compared with other manufacturers of general aviation aircraft, Gulfstream did not suffer as much from the effects of the economy in the early 1980s. The company's earnings, despite industry declines, more than tripled from 1980 to 1982. The company did not have to impose any layoffs and demand for its high-end corporate jet models remained strong. However, orders for its top-of-the-line Gulfstream III, which had the largest cabin, fastest cruising speed, and longest range of any business jet, dropped from 32 in 1981 to 15 in 1982. To stimulate sales of its turboprop line, Gulfstream instituted a new marketing policy in 1982 that offered lower interest rates and smaller downpayments.

Fairchild-Swearingen.   Swearingen Aircraft, located in San Antonio, Texas, was founded in the 1950s by aircraft designer, Ed Swearingen. Among its varied activities during the company's early years, it built prototypes for other companies and marketed improved versions of two Beech models. The improved models had larger engines, revised exhaust systems, and increased total fuel capacity. In 1966, Swearingen began delivery of a new brand of turboprop aircraft, its first, the Merlin IIA. In 1979, Swearingen became a subsidiary of Fairchild Industries, which was a spinoff from Fairchild Aviation Corporation, founded by Sherman Fairchild in the 1920s after he founded the Fairchild Camera Corporation. Mr. Fairchild had produced the first successful enclosed-cabin monoplane as a means to use the automatic aerial camera he had invented. In 1982, Fairchild Industries produced military and commercial aircraft, domestic satellite communications, and commercial and industrial products. In 1982, Swearingen accounted for 8 percent of Fairchild's total sales.

In 1982, Swearingen's business continued to be the manufacture of fuel efficient turboprop aircraft for the commuter and business market-places. Its commuter line was made up of the Metro 19 passenger aircraft, and its business line consisted of the Merlin 12 to 15 passenger aircraft. In 1979, the Metro had a 61 percent market share of the 15 to 19 passenger commuter turboprop sales. Both unit shipments and dollar sales continued to grow at Swearingen through the 1979 to 1981 period. However, in 1982, unit shipments fell by 46 percent and dollar sales fell by 35 percent. Fairchild's chairman, Edward Uhl, remarked on Swearingen's hopes for recovery in 1983: "A resurgence in Merlin and Metro turboprop aircraft sales after the sharp decline in 1982 is dependent upon the recovery of the commuter airline industry and the corporate aircraft segment. Both of these markets are expected to improve only after a solid economic upturn. The current low level of order backlogs for these aircraft makes a sharp recovery in 1983 unlikely."

Mooney Aircraft Company.   Mooney was formed in June 1948 in Wichita by two former executives of Culver Aircraft Company, Charles Yankey and Al W. Mooney. The first product of the new company was the Mooney M-18 single-seat, single-engine plane, designed for extremely economical operation. The M-18 incorporated many innovative systems including automatically proper settings for take-off, climb, approach, and landing. In 1953, Mooney moved to its present location in Kerrville, Texas. In 1967 the company merged with Alon Inc. of Kansas, a tool and machine company that was dissolved after the merger. Later, in 1969, Butler Aviation International, the country's largest fixed base operator, acquired the company and changed its name to Aerostar Aircraft in 1970. In October 1973, Republic Steel bought the the company and changed its name back to Mooney. In 1981 and 1982, Mooney's sales were less than 1 percent of Republic's total sales.

Mooney manufactured aircraft in the high performance single-engine category only. It produced two high performance models, the 201 and the 231. Both were among the fastest and most fuel efficient single-engine planes manufactured anywhere. Mooney continued to be the innovator that it was in its earliest days, and was the only U.S. manufacturer to make technological inroads in the development of high performance singles. The company was the fourth largest producer of single-engine aircraft in units behind Cessna, Beech, and Piper.

Mooney's manufacturing facilities were located in a single factory in Kerrville, built in 1953. In 1982 Mooney's production of its two models of single-engine aircraft dropped to 188 from 330 in 1981 and 332 in 1980, as that category became the hardest hit by the slump in the industry's sales. Mooney President, Tom Smith, said, "From 1976 to 1979, Mooney could sell all it could produce. In early 1980, for the first time, we had some unsold planes. Price ($75,000 to $90,000) is not the issue. Buyers are waiting for interest rates to come down."[6] By the end of 1982, Mooney had begun development of a new high-performance single called the 252, which they planned to begin delivering in 1985. The 252 was going to be a replacement for the 231, offering greater horsepower and better fuel efficiency, again setting the standard for the industry. In addition, of all the U.S. aircraft manufacturers, Mooney was expected to be the first to offer substantial price reductions on its models in order to boost sales, particularly because of its complete reliance on single-engine piston aircraft at a time when that category's sales were consistently declining.

Foreign Competition

Since World War II, foreign governments had been very involved in their aerospace industries. In the general aviation industry, however, there was little foreign competition until the late 1970s. In 1982 there were ap-

---

[6]*The New York Times.* April 9, 1980.

proximately 18 foreign-based manufacturers that were in direct competition with the U.S. industry. A number of foreign firms also competed in the general aviation industry in the United States. At one time, some U.S. operators shied away from aircraft manufactured by companies outside the United States because their service was not supported at the same level as domestic aircraft. However, the larger firms quickly set up supply depots in the United States and now offered the same level of support and service as domestic manufacturers did.

Competition was most intense in the jet category. Companies such as British Aerospace, Canadair, deHavilland, Dassault-Breguet, Mitsubishi Aircraft International, and Israel Aircraft Industries were the largest foreign competitors in the turbofan/turbojet aircraft category. Many foreign aircraft manufacturers were either government-owned or subsidized, assuring the availability of funds for capital improvements and for research and development. Third world, government-owned manufacturers were also involved including Embraer, the 51 percent government-owned Brazilian manufacturer of commuter airplanes. In 1982, approximately 40 percent of all business jets sold in the United States were manufactured by non-U.S. firms. Total world jet shipments peaked at 555 in 1981, falling to 444 in 1982. The United States had a 70 percent share of world jet shipments in 1981, and a 58 percent share in 1982.

Questions

1. What are the most important factors causing the decline in general air-craft sales from 1979 to 1982?
2. How well did each of the manufacturers respond to the recession of the early 1980s? Which competitor is best positioned in 1982?
3. What should Cessna do in 1982? Piper? Mooney?
4. Based on the evidence in the case, make some rough estimates of where industry shipments and billings will be in 1988. What are your assumptions? Do you anticipate any major changes in market share of any of the competitors? Why?

CASE 3
Boeing and McDonnell Douglas

Generally when one thinks of business cycles, one is most concerned with the trough of the cycle when sales and production are low, such as in the general aviation industry discussed in the last chapter. However, the peak in the cycle, when sales and production are booming, presents managers with a new set of problems and opportunities that are not the mirror-image of those during a trough.

In 1989 all three commercial jet manufacturers were confronted with a worldwide record-setting boom in new jet orders. In this case we will be focusing on the two American manufacturers, Boeing and Mc-Donnell Douglas, since they were pursuing different strategies yielding different results. As in the previous chapter, one of the first issues confronting a manager was the nature of the business cycle and its causes. The premise implicit in this statement is that one can develop a better strategy if the strategy is tailored to the conditions causing the boom.

A boom in sales will have implications for all functional policies in the firm. Managers must plan human resources to ensure an adequate supply of workers and skills needed for the boom, as well as the timing and incentives for those resources. Production and capacity management may need to be reevaluated, since temporary surges in sales may not justify permanent additions to capacity or permanent changes in production techniques. The finance department must consider the additional demands that the boom will place on working capital and whether long-term additions to capital assets require a reevaluation of the capital structure. The aggressiveness of the marketing campaign ought to be coordinated with the company's ability to supply the products and to service the customers after the sale. Also, the company must determine how much managerial time and corporate resources should be devoted to research and development of new products, since these new efforts may overextend the capacity of the company to supply the current booming market. The strategies of Boeing and McDonnell Douglas differed along all these dimensions, which provides us with an opportunity for identifying the components of the more successful policies for dealing with a boom in sales.

Commercial jet aircraft manufacturers had a record boom in new orders in the late 1980s, unlike anything that the industry had seen in the two previous decades. Orders totaled almost 5,000 planes between 1985 and 1989, far surpassing the record set before the arrival of jumbo jets in the late 1960s. In 1989, the world's airlines ordered more large commercial aircraft than ever before in the 31-year history of commercial jet aviation. In that year alone, orders had reached a staggering $95 billion, a 75 percent increase over record 1988 levels.

The two American jet manufacturers, Boeing and McDonnell Douglas, sought to gain market share and profits from the record boom in new aircraft orders during the late 1980s. However, each company's response to the surge in new orders differed—a difference that was reflected in their profits. For example, Boeing's net earnings in 1989 were $973 million, while McDonnell Douglas lost $224 million. Over the past five years of the boom, Boeing's return on sales of commercial aircraft was more than double that of McDonnell Douglas over the same period. Though both companies faced problems in 1990, particularly in expanding production levels to meet the unprecedented rise in orders, Boeing management was generally cited as having responded more successfully to the boom in demand.

The Structure of the Commercial Jet Aircraft Industry

Aircraft companies manufactured jet airplanes that fell into three broad categories: short-range, medium-range, and long-range, with further breakdowns by the number of seats in the aircraft. See Exhibits 1A–1C for the types of aircraft in each category. Since the 1970s, three aircraft companies had dominated the jet aircraft industry in the free world, Boeing and McDonnell Douglas in the United States, Airbus Industrie in Europe. Airbus, a competitor since the 1970s, was a consortium of Europe's leading aircraft manufacturers, and was heavily subsidized by their governments.[1] In addition to the consortium, several European companies produced short-range commercial jet aircraft themselves, including British Aerospace, Fokker, and Aerospatiale. For a short time, beginning in the 1970s, U.S.-based Lockheed also produced a commercial jet model. However, because of cost overruns that threatened the company's existence, Lockheed exited the commercial market in 1984. In

This case was prepared by Research Associate Julia Horn under the supervision of Professor Michael G. Rukstad. Copyright © 1990 by the President and Fellows of Harvard College. Harvard Business School case 9-390-141.

[1]The consortium members were Aerospatiale of France, Messerschmitt Bolkow-Blohm of West Germany, British Aerospace of Great Britain, CASA of Spain, Fokker of the Netherlands, and Belairbus of Belgium. The U.S. Commerce Department estimated that the European governments provided one-fourth of Airbus Industrie's cash flow of $35 to $40 billion between 1974 and 1987.

Exhibit 1A Aircraft Model Categories

Category	Historical 1952–1989					Forecast 1990–2005				
	Models	1990 Dollars (Billions)	Share %	Units	Share %	Models	1990 Dollars (Billions)	Share %	Units	Share %
Short/Medium Range <120 Seats	727-100 737-100/-200 DC-9 MD-87 BAe 146 Caravelle Trident-1/2 F-28 F-100 880 BAC 1-11	66.8	18	3,812	36	737-500 MD-87 MD-90-10 BAe 146 F-100 BAC 1-11	20.3	3	808	8
Short/Medium Range 120–170 Seats	727-200 737-300/-400 707-120/220 720 MD-81/-82/-83/-88 DC-8-10/-20 Trident-3 Mercure A320	83.0	22	3,033	28	737-300/-400 MD-81/-82/-83/-88 MD-90-20 A320	108.7	17	3,230	32
Short/Medium Range 171–240 Seats	757 767-200 A310-200 DC-8-61	26.6	7	548	5	757 767-200 A310 A321 MD-90-30	90.9	15	1,955	20
Short/Medium Range 241–350 Seats	767-300 A300 L-1011-1 DC-10-10/-15	41.1	11	657	6	767-300 767-X A300-600	49.6	8	556	6
Short/Medium Range >350 Seats	747	2.9	1	33	—	747SR MD-11 STR 767 STR A330	80.0	13	798	8

(Continued)

Exhibit 1A (Continued)

Category	Models	Historical 1952–1989					Forecast 1990–2005				
		1990 Dollars (Billions)	Share %	Units	Share %	Models	Models	1990 Dollars (Billions)	Share %	Units	Share %
Long Range <240 Seats	767-200 707-320/-420 A310-300 DC-8-62/-63 DC-8-30/-40/-50	53.2	14	1,461	14	Concorde VC-10 990 Comet	767-200 A310	8.2	1	126	1
Long Range 241–350 Seats	L-1011-100/-200/-500 DC-10-30/-40 747SP	37.3	10	492	5	767-300	767-300 767-X 747 A330 A340 MD-11	63.2	10	770	8
Long Range >350 Seats	747	62.0	17	677	6	747	747 MD-11 767-X A340	205.0	33	1,692	17
		Total 372.9	100	10,713	100			Total 625.9	100	9,935	100

Note: The 700 series is manufactured by Boeing. The DC and MD series are manufactured by McDonnell Douglas. The A300 series is manufactured by Airbus. The L-1011 series is manufactured by Lockheed. The BAe series is manufactured by British Aerospace. The F series is manufactured by Fokker.

Source: Boeing.

Exhibit 1.   Current and Commited Programs: Boeing Airplane Family 1A, McDonnell Douglas Family 1B, and Airbus Family 1C.

Boeing Airplane Family

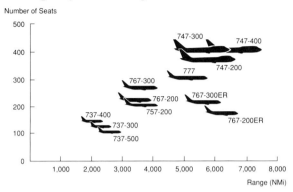

McDonnell Douglas Family

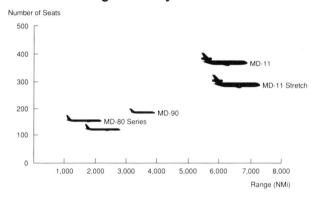

Airbus Family

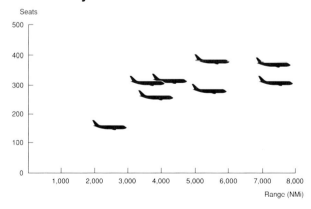

Source: Boeing.

addition to the free world manufacturers, two Soviet companies, Ilyushin and Tupolev, produced commercial jet aircraft in large numbers, which they sold to Communist-bloc countries.

Commercial airlines, both United States and foreign, accounted for approximately three-quarters of new industry sales, with the rest going to cargo operators and leasing companies. Typically, the largest dozen airline customers accounted for over one-half of a manufacturer's sales. Most cargo operators bought used aircraft, and consequently accounted for only a small portion of new aircraft sales. Leasing companies, such as International Lease Finance Corporation and GPA, bought aircraft for lease to some airlines, particularly smaller airlines and third world governments. During the 1980s, however, leasing companies expanded their purchase of aircraft. "In 1988, more than 20 percent of large aircraft deliveries were made to leasing companies compared to less than 5 percent in 1985."[2] Customers wanted aircraft as closely tailored to their anticipated load and flying requirements as possible. Other aircraft could be used, but would be more costly. Approximately one-third of the cost of the aircraft was paid by customers after their order, with the remainder paid at delivery. Though customers could cancel or delay delivery of their ordered aircraft, it was seldom done because of the financial cost and the potential damage to their long-term relationship with the manufacturer. On the other hand, if manufacturers missed their contracted delivery date, they too faced similar costs.

Sales to commercial airlines depended on a number of factors, including airline company profits and world travel demand. In the late 1980s, airlines had reached record profits after a dismal performance following the airline deregulation and recession years of the early 1980s. See Exhibits 2 and 3 for airline company revenues and profits. The industry standard for measuring travel demand was a revenue passenger mile (RPM), defined as one paying passenger flown one mile. Travel demand was closely related to the level of economic activity. See Exhibits 4 and 5 for world travel demand and jet orders. Airlines could accommodate the growth in travel by either buying new aircraft or expanding the utilization of existing aircraft. They could utilize the aircraft more intensively by increasing the load factor (i.e., the percentage of seats filled), by putting in more seats, or by flying the aircraft more often or over longer distances during the year. See Exhibit 6 for the accommodation of traffic growth. Some industry analysts observed that the recent surge in aircraft orders indicated that airlines were replacing that portion of their fleets that they purchased in the late 1960s, since the average useful life of an aircraft was now 25 years. See Exhibit 7 for the world airline jet fleet age. The average age of the world jet aircraft fleet had been rising steadily since the 1970s, a trend which was expected to continue.

[2]U.S. Department of Commerce, *The U.S. Industrial Outlook for 1989-Aerospace* (U.S. Department of Commerce: Washington), 1989.

Exhibit 2 The World's Ten Largest Airlines

Billions of Revenue Passenger Miles (1988)[a]

Airline	
1. Aeroflot	136.6
2. United	69.1
3. American	64.7
4. Delta	51.7
5. Continental	40.7
6. Northwest	40.6
7. British Airways	35.5
8. TWA	34.8
9. JAL (Japan Airlines)	30.1
10. Pan Am	29.6

[a]A revenue passenger mile is equal to one paying passenger flown one mile.

Source: *Airline Business Magazine*, cited in *The New York Times*, May 7, 1989.

Exhibit 3 Airline Industry Operating Profits

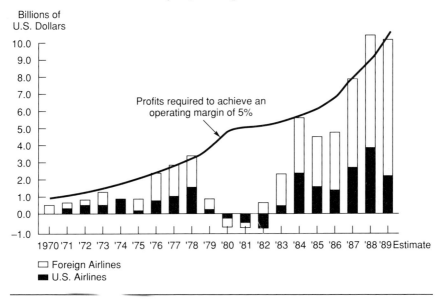

Source: Boeing.

In the late 1960s, commercial jet aircraft deliveries reached an all-time peak. Airplane deliveries fell after the recessions of 1970 and 1974-1975. See Exhibit 8 for airplane deliveries. By the late 1970s, aircraft deliveries rose sharply for two reasons. First, airlines were purchasing the more fuel-efficient and labor-efficient aircraft recently developed by the manufacturers.[3] On average, almost one-half of an airline's total operating

---

[3]Labor efficiency was achieved by reducing the required cockpit crew from three to two people.

Exhibit 4   Travel Growth and Economic Activity

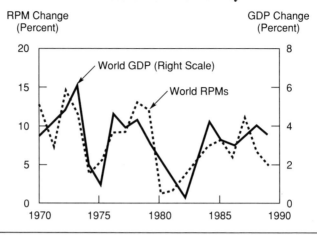

Source: Boeing.

Exhibit 5   Airplane Orders vs. Travel Demand

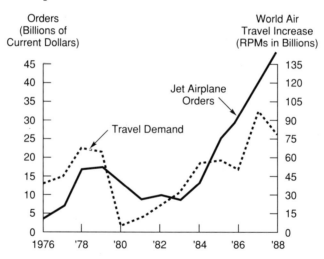

Source: Boeing.

costs were related to the aircraft, such as fuel (15 percent), flight operations (12 percent), maintenance (12 percent), and depreciation (8 percent). Second, the Airline Deregulation Act of 1978 created a need for more shorter-range aircraft capable of carrying more passengers to newly created hubs. See Exhibit 9 for seats delivered by airplane size category. By the early 1980s, airplane deliveries fell once again as the recession dampened travel demand. Despite the severity of the recession, deliveries were on the rebound by the mid-1980s, and had surpassed all previous records by the end of the decade.

Exhibit 6   Accommodation of Traffic Growth

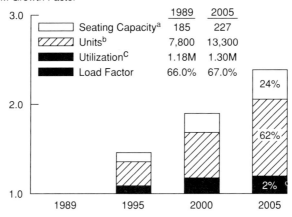

RPM Growth Factor

	1989	2005
Seating Capacity[a]	185	227
Units[b]	7,800	13,300
Utilization[c]	1.18M	1.30M
Load Factor	66.0%	67.0%

[a]Seats per mile basis.
[b]Mid-year passenger jet fleet.
[c]Revenue airplane miles per year per airplane (millions).
Source: Boeing.

Exhibit 7   World Airline Jet Fleet Age

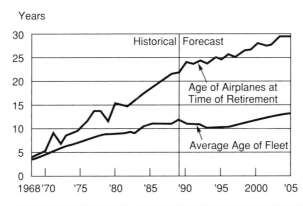

Source: Boeing.

The boom in orders that occurred after 1985 wreaked havoc on the production operations of aircraft manufacturers. Those manufacturers typically risked between $2 and $5 billion to design and produce a new product, with a high probability that even a successful venture would not break even in terms of cash flow for 10 to 15 years. Launch costs could be as high as $20 million per aircraft seat. By 1989, the lead time between order and delivery of an aircraft was approximately four to five years. Because of the average expected lifespan of an aircraft, the market at which the product was aimed could be 5 to 30 years in the future. "Cus-

Exhibit 8   World Annual Commercial Airplane Deliveries

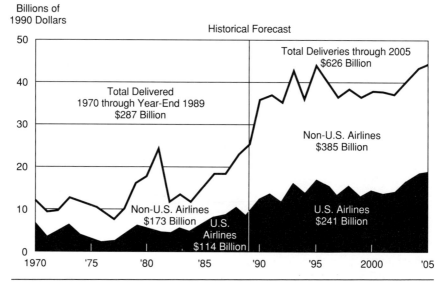

Source: Boeing.

Exhibit 9   Seats Delivered by Airplane Size Category

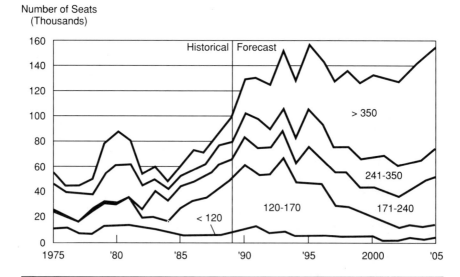

Source: Boeing.

tomer airlines play a major role in establishing performance character-istics (based on fleet needs). Airline advance orders, therefore, are essen-tial for undertaking production, engineering, and aircraft assembly."[4] The production of aircraft was a very labor-intensive process that required highly-skilled engineers and production workers. Production workers in the aircraft industry were unionized, with the majority belonging to the International Association of Machinists and Aerospace Workers (IAM). Unlike the auto industry, for example, where workers at all three man-ufacturers signed similar pacts based on contract negotiations with just one of the three producers, production workers at Boeing and McDonnell Douglas operated under separate contracts.

Typically, half of the cost of an aircraft was purchased parts. Spe-cialty parts supplied by outside manufacturers included engines, landing gear, brakes, wheels, tires, and auxiliary power units as well as structural units for the fuselage and wings. For many of those parts, there were very few qualified suppliers who could provide parts for all three of the major jet manufacturers. Engines, which ranged in cost from $4 to $10 million per engine, comprised the largest portion of purchased parts. The largest jet engine suppliers were General Electric and Pratt and Whitney in the United States, and Rolls-Royce in the United Kingdom. Another example of an important part supplied by a limited number of vendors was landing gear, which was manufactured by only two companies, Menasco and Cleveland Pneumatic.

The Boeing Company

The Boeing Company was founded in 1916 in Seattle, Washington by a wealthy timberman's son, William E. Boeing. Boeing's prowess began during World War II with the renowned B-17 Flying Fortress and the B-29 Superfortress, the biggest bomber of its time. In 1952, Boeing "bet the company" by gambling $16 million, the majority of its net worth, on a prototype passenger jet, at a time when the market was dominated by Douglas Aircraft's propeller-driven DC (Douglas Commercial) series of aircraft. The resulting Boeing 707 commercial model introduced in 1958, made propeller planes obsolete.

The 707 model marked the beginning of Boeing's long-term com-mercial aircraft strategy, which focused on the manufacture of a family of aircraft to service the entire range of customer needs. In 1964, the Boeing 727 entered commercial service, selling over 1,800 planes before production ended in 1984. Later in 1967, Boeing rolled out the 737 model, which was to become the company's most popular model and the highest selling commercial jet in aviation history. By the end of the 1960s, a

---

[4]*A Competitive Assessment of the U.S. Civil Aircraft Industry* (Washington: U.S. Department of Commerce, 1984).

worldwide recession brought a 17-month halt to commercial aircraft orders from domestic manufacturers and a slackening of military contracts. At the same time, Boeing's workforce surged to 104,000, and the company was nearly pushed into bankruptcy while developing the 747 model for the long-range, intercontinental market. As a result of that experience, Boeing learned important lessons about parts scheduling and labor force training. Following initial deliveries of the 747 in December of 1969, the workforce dropped to 38,000. Throughout the 1970s, Boeing worked on developing more fuel-efficient and labor-efficient aircraft. In 1982, the company began delivery of both the 757 and the larger 767, which were more efficient and aimed at the medium- and long-range domestic markets. In early 1988, Boeing rolled out the 747-400 model, which extended the range of the base 747 model by 33 percent and offered even more seating capacity.

In 1988, Boeing dominated the industry and was the third largest exporter in the United States, after GM and Ford, accounting for 2 percent of the nation's export revenue, primarily from overseas sales of its commercial aircraft. Exports accounted for $7.9 billion in sales in 1988, or 46 percent of the company's total. The company's backlog of commercial orders jumped 70 percent between 1984 and 1987, and then surged another 70 percent in 1988 alone. During the boom in 1988, the company's profits jumped by 66 percent over 1987, while the company remained virtually free of debt. Boeing had built more than 60 percent of all commercial jets flying in 1989. See Exhibit 10 for market shares and Exhibit 11 for financial information.

At the end of 1989, Boeing's order backlog, for customers ranging from American Airlines to Air Zimbabwe, had reached $85 billion or 1,718 aircraft. Currently, Boeing was producing its popular 737 family at a rate of 14 per month and producing the total of its other models at the rate of 14 per month. The company planned to raise production rates for all aircraft from its 1989 total of 28 planes per month to a 1990 total of 34 planes per month, namely seventeen 737s, seven 757s, five 767s, and five 747s. By 1992, the total production rate was planned to increase to 41 planes per month. The slow increase initially would allow Boeing to train its workers and allow suppliers to schedule parts production.

The order boom together with a dearth of experienced production workers had resulted in production problems. As employment at Boeing rose 86 percent to 157,000 workers from 1984 to 1989 and firm orders at the company quadrupled over the same period, nearly 60 percent of the 1989 workforce had less than two years of experience. The production problems in 1989 were worsened by a 48-day worker strike, which began on October 4, and was the longest strike against Boeing since 1948. During the strike, supervisors were able to complete some finishing work and delivered 23 planes, however, new production came to a virtual halt. "Stock analysts say that the effects of the strike that cost workers more than $4 million per day in wages, and put the company's delivery schedule in disarray, will be slight over the long-term, though it will dampen fourth

Exhibit 10   Historical Manufacturers' Market Shares Jet Airplane Orders (Announced Basis)

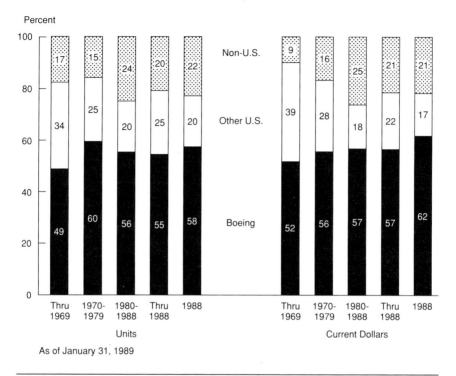

Percent

As of January 31, 1989

Source: Boeing.

quarter results for 1989."[5] Rather than accelerate its production rates to compensate for time lost during the strike, Boeing pushed back its production schedule by seven weeks.

In response to the order boom, Boeing tried to balance its appetite for sales with its production constraints. To deal with the problems created by inexperienced workers and an overambitious production schedule, Boeing's Chairman and Chief Executive Officer, Frank Shrontz, and his colleagues devised a workforce training strategy. That strategy focused on training new workers for six to eight weeks before sending them to the factory floor, rather than having experienced workers spend time away from their work to provide on-the-job training. Ideally, Boeing hoped to encourage possible new recruits to obtain training on their own before they were hired. "In the long run, Boeing executives figure time is on their side. They will raise production rates steadily but gingerly in order to give workers a chance to learn their jobs and do them better. Says

[5]Polly Lane, "Approval Expected," *The Seattle Times*, November 20, 1989.

Exhibit 11   Boeing: Selected Financial Data (in Millions)

	1988	1987	1986	1985	1984	1983	1982	1981	1980	1979	1978	1977
Revenues by Industry Segment												
Commercial transport	11,369	9,827	9,820	8,024	5,457	6,998	5,135	7,004	7,665	6,395	3,827	2,459
Military transport	3,668	3,979	4,852	3,973	3,103	2,617	2,372	1,687	923	804	811	964
Space systems and missiles	1,457	1,063	1,126	1,219	1,366	1,047	938	667	509	667	592	446
Other	468	636	616	529	516	569	682	525	431	339	294	208
Total operating revenues	16,962	15,505	16,444	13,745	10,442	11,231	9,127	9,883	9,528	8,205	5,524	4,077
Operating Profit by Segment												
Commercial transport	585	352	411	376	17	98	16	308	678	611	417	196
Military transport	(95)	60	367	317	346	289	269	223	78	49	55	73
Space systems and missiles	124	119	55	68	131	95	96	39	26	7	34	40
Other	(28)	(34)	(9)	3	15	8	3	10	16	14	11	5
Total operating profit	586	497	824	764	509	490	384	580	798	681	517	314
Net Income	614	480	665	566	787	355	292	473	600	505	323	180

(Continued)

Exhibit 11 (Continued)

Capital Expenditures by Segment

Commercial	326	286	332	191	112	104	204	329	463	426	185	56
Military	241	316	356	236	144	65	77	100	91	87	36	21
Space systems and missiles	62	72	82	45	33	21	17	51	41	29	25	10
Total	629	674	770	472	289	190	298	480	595	542	246	87
Total assets	12,608	12,566	10,910	9,153	8,423	7,471	7,593	6,954	5,931	4,897	3,573	2,440
Firm backlog	53,601	33,204	26,388	24,724	21,511	18,043	19,025	19,389	20,032	18,011	11,154	5,917
Employees	147,300	136,100	118,500	98,700	86,600	84,600	95,700	105,300	106,300	98,300	81,200	66,900

Jet airplane deliveries by model:

707-A(a)	—	9	4	3	8	8	8	2	3	6	11	7
727	—	—	—	—	8	11	26	94	131	136	118	67
737	165	161	141	115	67	82	95	108	92	77	40	25
747	24	23	35	24	16	23	25	53	73	67	32	20
757	48	40	35	36	18	25	2	—	—	—	—	—
767	53	37	27	25	29	55	20	—	—	—	—	—
Total	290	270	242	203	146	204	176	257	299	286	201	119

Philip Condit, executive vice president of the commercial airplane group, 'We just want people to settle down.' "[6]

In the production of all of its aircraft models, Boeing relied heavily on alliances with outside suppliers. Because Boeing was the largest manufacturer in the industry, suppliers were eager to contract with the company. Outside suppliers provided Boeing with subcontracting services, particularly in the development of the 747 model, in which one-half of the jet's value came from outside suppliers. Because the company was "reluctant to expand capacity in case of a sudden downturn, and with little spare labor in the Seattle area, Boeing's only option is to subcontract still more of its manufacturing."[7] Three of the company's larger subcontractors were Mitsubishi Heavy Industries, Kawasaki Heavy Industries, and Fuji Heavy Industries, all of Japan, which had supplied flaps, wing ribs, and fuselage panels. For some other models, as much as 15 percent came from overseas suppliers.[8] The company believed that it could, "earn more money as a designer, assembler, and marketer of aircraft than as an integrated manufacturer producing all the parts. Just like American carmakers, Boeing had to forge close alliances with component suppliers that could be trusted not only to manufacture parts and subassemblies, but also to do the R&D needed to ensure that their components get better and cheaper."[9] Boeing, however, would not share any of the final assembly work with the suppliers because that was the point at which the company tailored its aircraft to customers' needs, established important marketing ties, and stamped its name on the aircraft.

Although production was strained for all models, the problems were particularly acute with the company's largest and newest model, the 747-400. The employment situation got so desperate that Boeing contracted with Lockheed's Georgia plant to borrow 544 skilled workers each averaging ten years of experience—a move that was estimated to cost $25 million. Boeing also brought in approximately 300 people from its various divisions, including its military airplane and helicopter divisions.

During the surge in demand for its largest aircraft, Boeing's nearly 3,000 subcontractors for the 747-400 were having problems meeting deadlines. Boeing assumed that suppliers who had performed well in the past would continue to do so. However, that was not always the case. For example, Jamco, a Japanese manufacturer of aircraft lavatories was critically behind schedule. Because the lavatories had to go into the aircraft before the seats, the plane would be late if they were. Having delivered only twelve of the 747-400s in the first six months of 1989, Boeing had to deliver forty-five by the end of 1989 to fulfill its contracts for 57 aircraft.

[6]Anthony Ramirez, "Boeing's Happy, Harrowing Times," *Fortune*, July 17, 1989.

[7]The Sincerest Form of Flattery," *The Economist*, November 11, 1989.

[8]Louis Uchitelle, "A Japanese Strategy for Boeing," *The New York Times*, November 3, 1989.

[9]*The Economist*, November 11, 1989.

"What I don't want," Shrontz said, "is to have management attention and resources we need to get the 747-400 job done diverted to a new airplane."[10] Industry observers believed that the 747 program was the one the company needed to monitor most closely. "Because of penalties to be paid for late delivery and the extra costs of pushing production, gross margins on the new 747-400s will initially be 20 percent compared with 30 percent for previous 747 models."[11] By the end of 1989, Boeing had delivered 41 new 747-400 aircraft, sixteen fewer than it needed to fulfill its contracts for that year.

"With this in mind, it is difficult to find a lot of enthusiasm among Boeing executives for developing new programs. Boeing is definitely riding with its family concept of airline transports. It can already cover nearly anything an airline wants to do."[12] Nonetheless, at the end of 1989, Boeing was working on the development of a new airliner, called the 767-X model (later named the 777). The 767-X began as a derivative of the twin-engine 767 model, and would be capable of carrying approximately 350 passengers over distances of 4,600 nautical miles. Eventually, the company planned to extend the range of the 767-X by more than half. Rough estimates by analysts put the cost of the 767-X launch at $2.5 billion. For the new 767-X, Boeing relied even more heavily on alliances with subcontractors, including several from Japan, than it had for the 747-400 model.

In light of the growth the industry was experiencing in the late 1980s, Boeing's objectives were to hold onto its dominant position in the market, and to boost its profits, particularly by improving productivity. To achieve those goals, Boeing planned to continue to maintain and update a range of aircraft that covered the entire market from 100 to 500 seats. "The policy means that Boeing must avoid massive investment by evolving successive derivatives of its existing range of airliners. And, unless the economic situation changes drastically, particularly by a dramatic rise in the price of oil, or unless a major technological breakthrough occurs, Boeing can see no reason to change its strategy. Therefore, it can concentrate on the problem of the moment, the production operation."[13]

For the company's future productivity gains in the 1990s, Boeing was betting heavily on what was referred to as design/build teams." Already in use at Boeing's Renton, Washington commercial aircraft facility, the approach involved gathering together engineers, production people, and support staff. A specific sum of money was allocated to the group. Then the team was directed to come up with a wing, fuselage section, or avionics package that met performance, manufacturing, budgetary, and

[10]*Fortune*, July 17, 1989.

[11]Stewart Toy, "Planemakers Have It So Good It's Bad," *Business Week*, May 8, 1989.

[12]James P. Woolsley, "Boeing's Sales Lead Industry to Record Backlog," *Air Transport World*, November 1988.

[13]Airline Makers Struggle With Growth," *Interavia*, June 1989.

delivery criteria. "We think its going to take cost out of a product," said Shrontz. "We think it has the opportunity to build quality into the product by having the people who have to build it, iterate it. And we think its going to cut flowtime."[14]

McDonnell Douglas

The commercial airline division (Douglas Commercial) of McDonnell Douglas was, in the words of the company's 1988 annual report, "close to extinction six years ago" (during the severe worldwide recession in 1982). In 1989, the company had firm orders for more than 500 commercial aircraft. From 1984 to 1989, firm orders at McDonnell Douglas tripled, while the number of workers rose 60 percent over the same period. The company was the eighth largest exporter in the United States; exports accounted for $3.5 billion or 23 percent of the company's total sales in 1988. However, of the 2,101 total aircraft ordered from the three largest manufacturers at the end of 1988, McDonnell Douglas finished third after Boeing and Airbus. Whatever measure one used (number of seats or value of orders), the placings remained the same. McDonnell Douglas had also posted losses throughout the 1970s and into the 1980s. In the first half of 1989, the company suffered operating losses of $224 million. That loss came at a time when the company had increased its debt load to $2.3 billion in just 18 months with a 53 percent debt to total capitalization, partly to finance the manufacture of a new aircraft, the MD-11. According to one industry observer, the situation could be explained by the fact that, "McDonnell Douglas only offers two families of aircraft to compete with the much broader ranges of the two other manufacturers."[15] See Exhibit 12 for financial information on McDonnell Douglas.

In 1967, the McDonnell Company, a leading combat aircraft producer, purchased the Douglas Aircraft Company, which had just introduced the short-range DC-9 model. Shortly after the acquisition, Douglas brought to market what was to become its last all-new airliner, the DC-10, which would also become the company's longest-running aircraft program. Instead of producing completely new aircraft designs, Douglas's strategy was to earn as much as possible from the DC-9 family, by developing a succession of derivatives, which incorporated some new technology. The MD-80, brought to the market in 1981, was a retooled DC-9, while the three-engine, long-range MD-11, which the company rolled out in late 1989, was a derivative of the DC-10. "Thus, without having to make a number of large investments, McDonnell Douglas had maintained its share of the profitable short-and medium-range airliner

[14]John S. McClenahen, "Boeing's Turbulence," *Industry Week*, April 3, 1989.
[15]*Interavia*, June 1989.

Exhibit 12 McDonnell Douglas: Selected Financial Data (in Millions)

	1988	1987	1986	1985	1984	1983	1982	1981	1980	1979	1978	1977
Revenues by Industry Segment												
Combat aircraft	6,070	5,925	5,888	5,957	5,285	4,385	3,709	3,276	2,639	2,280	2,256	2,090
Transport aircraft	4,877	3,977	3,681	2,896	2,226	1,802	1,810	2,772	2,275	1,989	986	720
Space systems and missiles	2,368	2,146	2,013	1,661	1,420	1,342	1,296	952	830	790	720	596
Information systems and other	1,754	1,625	1,504	1,346	1,084	581	516	385	322	220	169	139
Total operating revenues	15,069	13,673	13,086	11,860	10,015	8,110	7,331	7,385	6,066	5,279	4,131	3,545
Operating Profit by Segment												
Combat aircraft	403	337	389	527	483	373	304	297	198	232	230	212
Transport aircraft	127	108	121	102	57	(52)	(69)	(117)	(144)	(56)	(60)	(50)
Space systems and missiles	177	132	75	74	36	97	86	63	49	55	59	47
Information systems	3	17	(3)	(79)	(5)	5	16	30	14	21	15	6
Total operating profit:	710	594	582	624	571	423	337	273	117	252	244	215
Net Income	347	310	274	346	325	275	215	177	145	199	161	123

(Continued)

Exhibit 12   (Continued)

	1988	1987	1986	1985	1984	1983	1982	1981	1980	1979	1978	1977
Capital Expenditures by Segment												
Combat aircraft	202	223	341	281	176	74	82	79	73	33	14	7
Transport aircraft	219	253	168	53	42	29	33	63	45	29	23	15
Space systems and missles	124	101	86	128	147	96	37	20	32	29	18	16
Information systems	106	95	85	82	109	147	107	68	55	83	82	17
Total	651	672	680	544	474	346	259	230	205	174	137	55
Total assets	11,885	10,624	9,487	8,592	7,313	4,792	4,621	4,364	3,900	3,381	3,098	2,468
Firm backlog	26,351	18,890	16,512	16,585	14,968	10,734	10,185	8,780	8,737	6,909	5,981	4,597
Employees	121,421	112,400	105,696	97,067	88,391	74,466	72,451	74,264	82,550	82,736	70,547	61,577
Jet airplane deliveries by model:												
MD-80	121	95	86	71	44	50	44	—	—	—	—	—
DC-10/KC-10 (a)	10	10	17	11	10	4	5	19	40	36	18	14
DC-9	—	—	—	—	—	—	—	78	23	39	22	22
Total	131	105	103	82	54	54	49	97	63	75	40	36

[a]KC-10 is the cargo version of the DC-10.

Source: Annual reports.

market carrying 110 to 160 passengers."[16] Similarly, McDonnell Douglas waited for the recovery of the long-range market in the early 1980s before beginning work on the MD-11. Throughout the 1970s and early 1980s, McDonnell Douglas was besieged by losses as it grappled with stronger competitors. In addition, the company's commercial division was plagued by a worker slowdown that began in late 1986 when workers rejected a contract offer, and continued through mid-1987. Rather than strike, the company's workers, represented by the IAM and the United Auto Workers (UAW) unions, continued to receive wages during the slowdown, while the company missed delivery dates for its MD-80 jets.

McDonnell Douglas management recently realized that they would have to capitalize on the trend toward larger capacity aircraft. Paine Webber analyst, Jack Modzelewski, believed that the blueprint for Boeing's wider-fuselage, twin-engine 767-X had immediately put Mc-Donnell Douglas on the defensive. "Because the Boeing plane will have a wider fuselage than the MD-11, it may force an already overburdened McDonnell Douglas to come up with a new, bigger offering of its own. There may be no place for them to hide."[17] In 1989, McDonnell Douglas began planning a "Super Stretch" version of the MD-11, with a fuselage 35 feet longer than the standard version, that would be available in 1994. If the Super Stretch could use a modified wing design from the standard model, nonrecurring costs would be $550 million. An all-new wing would bring that figure to $1 billion. Breakeven sales for the Super Stretch were reported to be 110 units and total sales were forecasted to be between 300 and 400. The Super Stretch would compete in the long-range, greater than 400-seat aircraft category directly against some of Boeing's (four-engine) 747 models, and a stretch version of the new (two-engine) 767-X model, but it would have three engines.

Though the MD-11 program was proceeding as planned, development of the MD-80 remained behind schedule in 1989. A customer who wanted to order an MD-80 in 1989 could expect to wait at least four years for delivery. It was widely believed that the MD-80 program needed to be cleaned up before McDonnell Douglas could get back on track. In 1983, James Worsham (who retired in 1989 as President of Douglas) persuaded American Airlines to lease twenty MD-80s and later buy 67 more at very low prices. McDonnell Douglas offered the low prices based on the belief that costs would fall as the learning curve improved. "The learning curve flattened out, however, and so did costs, but prices kept coming down," said Howard Rubel, an analyst at C.J. Lawrence, Morgan Grenfell.[18] McDonnell Douglas's models were typically less expensive

[16]*Interavia*, June 1989.

[17]Rick Wartzman, "Boeing Plans to Develop Passenger Jet in an Effort to Fill Gap in Product Line," *The Wall Street Journal*, December 11, 1989.

[18]Richard W. Stevenson, "At McDonnell, Growing Pains," *The New York Times*, August 15, 1989.

than their Boeing counterparts. The MD-80, rival of the $25 million 737, sold for $24 million. The $100 million MD-11 competed with some series of the 747 model, priced at about $120 million.

Critics of Douglas' pricing practices also pointed to the company's apparent success in capturing $6.4 billion in firm orders and options for MD-80s from Delta in late 1988. "While the large order will help McDonnell Douglas stay in the commercial aircraft business, analysts said the company would not make much money because it gave Delta low prices. They said that Boeing, the industry leader, whose planes are far more in demand, would get a better price for its planes. Philip Friedman, airline analyst for Drexel Burnham Lambert, said that McDonnell Douglas would have to develop new airplanes instead of relying on derivatives."[19] Freidman also believed that, "low-ball pricing tactics have helped produce cumulative losses of over $200 million in the past decade."[20]

At the end of 1989, McDonnell Douglas' order backlog had reached $18 billion. The MD-80, which had been in production for eight years and which analysts believed should have been making a reasonable profit in 1989, lost $34 million in the second quarter of 1989 alone because the company was unable to build planes at the rate it had planned or to keep costs down. Some industry observers believed that the company's woes stemmed from its own success, pointing to the fact that since McDonnell purchased the Douglas Aircraft unit, it has fought desperately to boost orders for Douglas, "a perennial financial laggard and also-ran to Boeing Company."[21] Finally, Worsham had developed such successful, and by then famous, plane-selling ploys as cut-rate leases and promises to deliver faster than Boeing. "Then the world's airlines started buying new equipment en masse. That fat order book suddenly became the source of some big headaches."[22]

The largest problem brought on by the sudden surge in orders at McDonnell Douglas was in the company's production operations. In an effort to prepare for the new orders, McDonnell Douglas needed to expand its operations. "They're expanding to be ten times the size in the early 1990s that they were in the early 1980s, and that's been too much happening too quickly," observed Paul Nisbet, an analyst at Prudential-Bache Securities.[23] After a hiring spree between 1984 and 1988 that more than doubled commercial employment to 44,000, Douglas was handicapped by inexperienced workers who required costly training programs. Because of the boom in orders, new workers went through a shortened training

[19]Agis Salpukas, "Delta Order For Boeing, McDonnell," *The New York Times*, November 15, 1989.

[20]Ronald Henkoff, "Bumpy Flight at McDonnell Douglas," *Fortune*, August 28, 1989.

[21]*Business Week*, May 8, 1989.

[22]*Business Week*, May 8, 1989.

[23]*The New York Times*, August 15, 1989.

period before they hustled to the assembly lines. In addition, the cost of training new production workers escalated. "The fact that Douglas is based in the notoriously high-cost area of California . . . hardly makes things any easier."[24]

To make matters worse, at the end of 1988 until February 1989, managers at the company's plant in Long Beach, California, "tried to keep to the schedule by pushing planes through the giant assembly line even if all the work at one particular station had not been completed. As a result, workers had to leave their stations and catch up with the planes elsewhere, either in other parts of the factory or outside on the tarmac."[25] Though that method had occasionally been used by other aircraft manufacturers, critics charged that production slowdowns would have been preferable. "Initial quality has slipped, forcing expensive and time-consuming repair work. So tangled are the assembly lines that Douglas lost money building the ten-year-old MD-80 in the first half of 1989."[26] Delivery schedules for the MD-80 were pushed back by an additional 30 days in mid-1989. John F. McDonnell observed, "Late deliveries of aircraft had been a source of inconvenience and irritation for military and commercial customers alike."[27] Like Boeing, McDonnell Douglas relied on outside suppliers for approximately 50 percent of its aircraft parts. Many of those suppliers were having trouble shipping parts on time to the company, resulting in even more late deliveries. In an effort to extract some needed profit from Douglas, Mr. McDonnell appointed Robert J. Hood as president of Douglas. As the former head of McDonnell's missile systems group, Hood had a reputation in the industry for high profits and tight cost controls on the assembly line. Mr. McDonnell also farmed out some component work to Douglas' sister company, McDonnell Aircraft, and has leased a plant owned by the U.S. Air Force in Ohio to expand its own aircraft-parts fabrication.

In February 1989, in another effort to fix its factory problems, Douglas underwent a turbulent reorganization of its managerial and production workers at the company's commercial aircraft plant in Long Beach, California. "The aim of the makeover is to streamline decision-making and avert the need for another billion-dollar production facility—a risky move in the cyclical aircraft business."[28] In the process of reorganizing, every one of Douglas' 5,000 managerial and supervisory positions was eliminated. The former occupants of those jobs could apply for just 2,800 newly created posts. Most of the others were stripped of their managerial responsibilities and put to work as technicians on "Japanese-style manufacturing teams" both in design offices and on the production lines.

[24]*Interavia*, June, 1989.

[25]*Business Week*, May 8, 1989.

[26]*Fortune*, August 28, 1989.

[27]*Interavia*, June 1989.

[28]*Business Week*, May 8, 1989.

Douglas also introduced a quality management system that scrapped the old functional setup in which engineers worked on several classes of aircraft and replaced it with a product-oriented system that allowed them to focus on a single plane as was the case at Boeing. In addition, workers were organized into teams, each of which was responsible not just for performing a particular physical function, but also for ensuring that needed supplies were on hand, that quality and schedule concerns were met, and that the work was coordinated with previous and future steps of the plane's assembly. The company also made procedural changes so that planes were not moved on the assembly line until virtually all work was completed at each step. "McDonnell Douglas concedes that the re-organization has cost more money than it has saved so far."[29]

McDonnell Douglas' problems largely reflected the worldwide boom in commercial aircraft orders that had also taxed the production capacity of Boeing. "But Boeing has substantial cash reserves and the security of several highly profitable commercial jetliner programs, advantages that Douglas does not enjoy. Moreover, Boeing has kept its manufacturing costs lower than Douglas has and has been able to afford higher levels of research and development spending," said Lawrence M. Harris, an analyst at Bateman, Eichler, Hill Richards.[30]

CEO McDonnell was convinced that he could put the family-run firm back on course. " 'Our goal,' he asserts 'is to produce higher-quality products at lower cost.' That may seem like an obvious objective, but that is a new tack for an organization where sales have long dominated manufacturing."[31]

[29]*Fortune*, August 28, 1989.
[30]*The New York Times*, August 15, 1989.
[31]*Fortune*, August 28, 1989.

Questions

1. What caused the boom in demand for jet aircraft in the late 1980s? How certain are you that this boom will continue?
2. Compare and evaluate the problems created by this boom for Boeing and McDonnell Douglas.
3. Compare and evaluate the responses of Boeing and McDonnell Douglas to the boom.
4. What lessons from this industry may be applicable to other industries and under what conditions?

CASE 4

RJR/Nabisco and Leveraged Buyouts

A company is always more vulnerable to competitive attack, or even financial insolvency, in the trough of the business cycle, however that vulnerability may be heightened by a company's inherited capital structure. The popularity of leveraged buyouts in the 1980s significantly changed the capital structures of many of America's largest corporations. Even though most of the 1980s were years of high economic growth, the specter of a possible recession and its impact on firms that had undergone a leveraged buyout worried managers and policymakers alike.

In the RJR/Nabisco case we can examine the largest leveraged buyout in corporate history. We want to use this case to refine our understanding of vulnerability. The most obvious notion of vulnerability for a company is that it is unable to make its debt payments and must declare financial insolvency. A broader understanding of vulnerability should include the change in competitive position resulting from changes in the economic environment, including the business cycle. Moreover, the alleged benefits of a leveraged buyout in terms of increased economic efficiency may offset the increased costs, including those associated with the increased risk in the event of an economic recession.

In the process of evaluating the vulnerability of leveraged buyouts, we can also gain a better understanding of the reasons why leveraged buyouts came to be so widespread in the 1980s. Among the proposed economic reasons for leveraged buyouts are changes in interest rates and tax rates during that decade. These issues foreshadow topics that we will be discussing in Parts II and III of this book.

The leveraged buyout (LBO) had undergone phenomenal growth in the
1980s. In the late 1970s, LBO transactions were almost always less than
$100 million. However, by the beginning of the 1980s, transactions of
$3 billion became commonplace. The number and value of LBOs com-
pleted had grown from 75 deals worth a total of $636 million in 1979
(or $1.4 billion in constant 1988 dollars) to 214 deals worth almost $80
billion in 1988. See Exhibit 1 on the growth of LBOs.

In February 1989, RJR Nabisco, whose primary businesses were
tobacco and food, completed a $25.4 billion LBO with the help of Kohl-
berg, Kravis, and Roberts (KKR), the premier LBO firm. The RJR deal
made the headlines as the largest transaction of any kind in the investment banking industry. Its value dwarfed what was previously recorded
as the largest LBO, the $6.2 billion LBO of Beatrice Company in 1986.
In 1989, the total value of new LBOs was expected to top $100 billion.
By early 1990, however, no major LBOs had taken place since the "mini-
crash" of the stock market in October 1989. Consequently, many wondered if the growth of LBOs would continue at its previous pace.

Exhibit 1   The Growth of LBOs: Total Value of Leveraged Buyouts

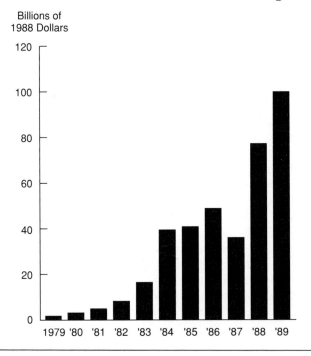

Billions of
1988 Dollars

Source: Michael Jensen, "Eclipse of the Public Corporation," *Harvard Business Review*,
September–October 1989.

How LBO Transactions Work

An LBO was a special type of corporate acquisition that was initiated by a private investor or by management itself and arranged either by an LBO firm or by the mergers and acquisitions department of an investment bank. In an LBO, an outside investor or management would borrow virtually the entire amount of funds necessary to purchase all of the publicly held equity of the target company. The shareholders of the target company would receive premiums that averaged from 40 percent to 55 percent . The resulting capital structure generally was comprised of equity of less than 10 percent, senior debt to banks and bondholders of 50 percent to 65 percent, and subordinated debt (often "junk bonds") of 25 percent to 40 percent. After the LBO, the company would pay down its debt by selling assets and cutting costs. Typically, all LBO-related debt would be eliminated in seven to eight years after the LBO.

The funds borrowed for financing an LBO could either be secured or unsecured. The earliest LBOs relied on borrowing that was secured by the assets of the target company. Since the late 1970s, however, "modern LBOs" had used unsecured borrowing, which relied on the expected cash flows generated by the target company to service the debt. Most of the early companies involved in unsecured LBOs were in the oil and gas, food, or broadcasting businesses.

Financing Sources for LBOs

Much of the money that provided the equity for investing in LBOs during the 1980s came from LBO partnership buyout funds. By 1989, over forty LBO partnership buyout funds had an estimated total capitalization of $25 billion, of which the largest was KKR ($5.6 billion), followed by Forstmann Little ($3 billion), Morgan Stanley Group ($2 billion), and Shearson Lehman ($1.5 billion). "When leveraged at the usual 10-to-1 ratio, the $25 billion in buyout money could fund $250 billion dollars in LBOs."[1] In contrast, at 1988 market prices, all of the equity in public companies in the United States was valued at less than $3 trillion, or just slightly more than ten times the amount of available leveraged buyout money. Buyout firms as a group garnered fees running into the hundreds of millions of dollars. For example, in the $25 billion RJR buyout, KKR received a fee of $75 million. KKR's standard fees included a 1.5 percent management fee for running its buyout funds, plus a percentage of any profits from successful LBOs in which it had an ownership stake.

The primary sources of equity money for the LBO buyout funds were pension funds and private investors (including, possibly, management itself). In addition, the LBO firms and investment banks arranging

[1]John Liscio, "The Buyout Bubble," *Barron's*, October 31, 1988.

the LBO could take an equity position in the transaction. Annualized returns for equity investors usually ranged from 30 percent to over 100 percent. Investors left the choice of the target company to the LBO fund operators. When evaluating and analyzing LBOs, managers of buyout funds compared a target company's market value to its expected cash flows in order to assess if the company was properly valued and if it could service its debt.

Commercial and investment banks arranged the debt financing for an LBO. Commercial banks provided long-term (three to five years) secured senior debt, accounting for 60 percent of total debt on average. Typically, about 75 percent of that senior debt was financed at floating rates ranging from 1.5 to 4 percentage points above the prime lending rate, which, with attractive origination fees of as much as 2.5 percent of the overall deal, made LBO loans more appealing to banks than regular commercial lending. Many LBOs, in an effort to hedge the risk of fluctuating interest rates, purchased interest rate caps to set a ceiling on their interest charges. In addition, commercial banks often made more money by repackaging and selling the LBO loans to smaller, regional banks. A large bank that was active in such secondary sales could have, for example, only $1 billion of LBO loans on its books, but it may have sold off billions of dollars of similar loans. In 1988, commercial banks made leveraged buyout-related loans totaling $54 billion, which was 40 percent of all commercial loans, up from 14 percent in mid-1987. Manufacturers Hanover, Banker's Trust, and Citicorp had the largest amount of LBO loan exposure on their books in 1989 at approximately $5.0 billion each. Investment banks earned fees for arranging LBOs, provided short-term bridge loans, and were underwriters for the high-yield ("junk") bonds that funded the LBOs. In making bridge loans, investment banks used their own capital and were typically repaid within a few months.

The Junk Bond Market

The reemergence of the new-issue junk bond market in 1977 opened up the public credit markets to companies who could not issue investment-grade securities. During most of the postwar years before 1977, these companies could only borrow from banks and insurance companies. Because only 6 percent of the approximately 11,000 public corporations in the United States qualified for investment grade bond ratings, junk bond financing quickly gained popularity. See Exhibit 2. During the 1980s, public junk bonds outstanding averaged over 10 percent of the total corporate bonds outstanding, but the percentage was on the increase. Between 10 percent and 40 percent (depending on the year and source) of the junk bonds issued annually were used to finance merger and acquisition activity. Junk bonds offered fixed-rate financing with fewer restrictive covenants than either bank or private placement debt. The risks to investors in junk bonds were higher than on ordinary corporate bonds.

Exhibit 2   Publicly-Issued Junk Bonds Outstanding

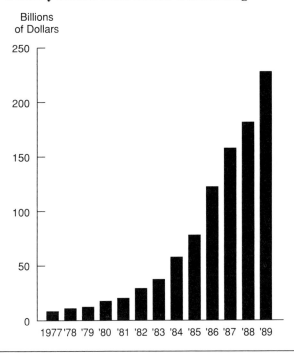

Source: First Boston Corp.

In 1981, investment banking firms such as Drexel Burnham Lambert, the largest junk bond issuer, began selling junk bonds specifically to finance LBOs. Insurance companies and mutual funds were the largest investors in junk bonds, each typically representing 30 percent of all buyers, followed by pension funds (15 percent) and thrifts (8 percent). Firms like Drexel Burnham, with its established network of potential investors and its willingness to provide a liquid secondary market for junk bond investors, encouraged the flow of vast amounts of funds into such instruments.

Junk bonds, however, were not used to finance hostile takeovers until 1983. As a result of the growth in unfriendly acquisitions, some companies considered an LBO as a defense mechanism to avoid a takeover. Other companies, however, had turned the tables and used LBOs as an offensive technique. "Increasingly frustrated by the stock market's undervaluation of their companies, some of the largest U.S. companies are evaluating leveraged buyouts as an offensive mechanism to generate shareholder value," said J. Tomilson Hill, head of the mergers department at Shearson Lehman Hutton.[2]

[2]Sarah Bartlett, "Buyout Proposals Reach a Milestone," *The New York Times*, October 26, 1988.

The Recent Wave of LBOs

In this century there have been four waves of mergers and acquisitions—
at the turn of the century, in the late 1920s, in the late 1960s, and in the
1980s. See Exhibit 3. Unlike earlier acquisition waves, LBOs were a significant portion of all acquisitions during the 1980s. By 1988, LBOs accounted for almost one-third of all mergers and acquisitions in the United
States. However, most mergers and acquisitions in the 1980s did not
involve significant amounts of debt; instead, they were financed by cash
(rather than the exchange of securities that was prevalent in the 1960s).
Other distinguishing characteristics of the merger wave in the 1980s were
that the individual transactions were very large (even in constant dollar
terms); they had premiums almost double those of the previous decade;
and they were more often divestitures (rather than acquisitions as in
previous waves) in which the stock or assets were purchased by other
competitors in that industry.

In the 1970s and into the early 1980s, slow growth caused by
two oil shocks, deregulation in many industries, increased international
competition, and double-digit inflation and interest rates led many companies to dismal returns. See Exhibit 4. LBOs were often used as a method
of "spinning off" underperforming companies or divisions—divisions often
acquired during the "go-go" years of conglomerate mergers in the late
1960s—while allowing the company's management to maintain control.
Corporations were hoping that their new diversification and divestiture
strategies would improve their poor market valuations. See Exhibit 5.

The double-digit inflation rates of the late 1970s raised the nominal

---

Exhibit 3   Annual Number of Mergers and Acquisitions

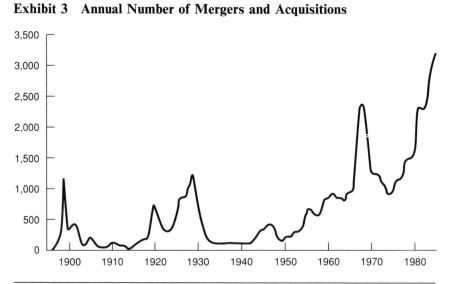

Source: Adapted from Alan Auerbach, ed., *Mergers and Acquisitions* (Chicago: University
of Chicago Press, 1988).

Exhibit 4 Return to Capital and Real Cost of Capital in the Marketing Sector, Twenty Industries, 1949–1987[a]

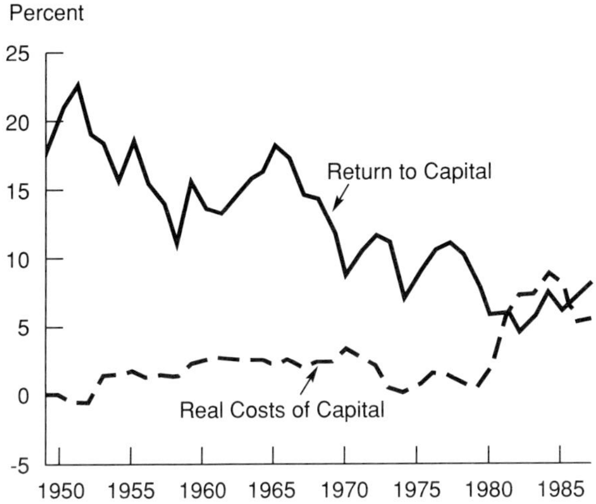

Percent

Source: Return to capital constructed from a Department of Commerce data on capital stocks, inventories, and factor payments, and estimates of land values constructed from Compustat data. Real cost of capital equals nominal rate on Moody's AAA-rated bonds minus three-year moving average of percentage changes in personal consumption expenditure index.

[a]Standard industrial classification 20-39.

value of corporate assets above their historical cost, creating the opportunity to buy used assets and to depreciate them once again from a larger step-up in their basis. In addition, inflation rates altered the liability side of the balance sheet by substantially reducing real corporate debt obligations because the fixed amount of debt could be paid off with inflated dollars. The book value of the average debt-to-equity ratio for U.S. nonfinancial corporations had risen from 50 percent in the early 1980s to approximately 80 percent in the late 1980s. However when measured in terms of market values, the ratio had remained constant at approximately 70 percent over that same period. See Exhibit 6. After 1983, a significant change occurred in the marginal financial decisions of nonfinancial corporations in which large amounts of equity were retired and replaced with debt. See Exhibit 7.

Not only was the balance sheet altered, but so too was the income statement. In most cases, inflation reduced real corporate earnings. Firms could deduct historical depreciation and inventory costs, which were less than their inflation-adjusted value, from their inflated revenues. Consequently their taxable earnings were larger than they would have been with a more accurate accounting for inflation, and thereby real corporate taxes were increased. To worsen matters, any corporate earnings paid to shareholders would be taxed twice—once at the corporate level and once as dividends. On the other hand, interest on debt, which was tax de-

Exhibit 5   Net Worth of Nonfinancial Corporations

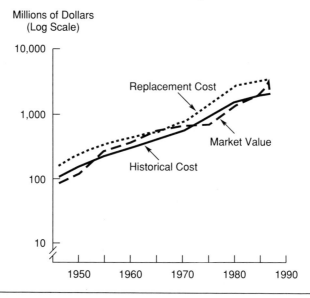

Source: Board of Governors of the Federal Reserve System, 1946–1985; Batterymarch Financial Management estimates, 1986 and 1987.

Exhibit 6a   Debt-to-Equity Ratios for the Nonfinancial Corporate Sector, Book Values, 1949–1988

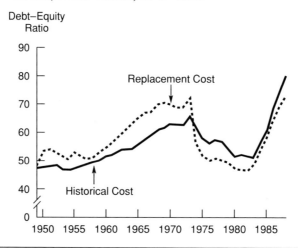

Source: Board of Governors of the Federal Reserve System, "Balance Sheet for U.S. Economy, 1949–1988." Statistical Release C.9 (April 1989).

Exhibit 6b   Debt-to-Equity Ratios for the Nonfinancial Corporate Sector, Market Values, 1949–1988

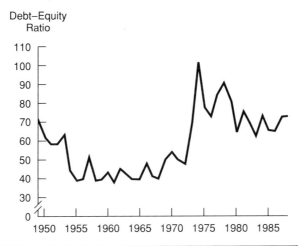

Exhibit 7   Net New Debt and Equity Raised by Nonfinancial Corporations, 1965–1988

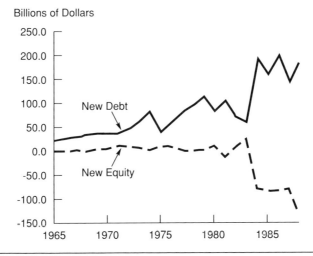

Source: Board of Governors of the Federal Reserve System, "Flow of Funds Accounts," Federal Reserve Bulletin, various issues.

ductible for the corporation, was only taxed once as income for the investor. Interest payments as a percent of cash flow for nonfinancial corporations had risen from 22 percent in the mid-1970s to approximately 35 percent by the late 1980s. See Exhibit 8.

Throughout this period, the U.S. tax law changed significantly on many occasions. Two of the most important changes were the Economic Recovery Tax Act (ERTA) in 1981 and the Tax Reform Act (TRA) in

Exhibit 8   Interest–Cash Flow Ratios for the Nonfinancial Corporate Sector, 1948–1987

Interest–Cash-Flow Ratio

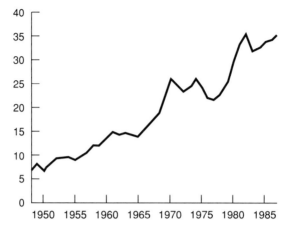

Source: National Income and Product Accounts.

1986. ERTA provided the most accelerated depreciation benefits in the history of U.S. tax law and a very significant reduction in the capital gains tax rate. Five years later, TRA reversed those benefits while offsetting the loss in depreciation benefits with a reduction in the corporate tax rate. At the same time, the capital gains tax increased to a maximum rate of 28 percent.

Financial observers debated whether or not LBOs were able to avoid huge tax payments by relying on the deductibility of interest expenses. Critics charged that interest deductions and foregone dividend payments associated with LBOs would reduce the U.S. Treasury's tax revenues. Supporters countered that LBOs increased revenues from capital gains from shareholders and asset sales, corporate taxes on increased operating income, and capital taxes on increased interest income.[3]

During this same period in the 1980s, the economy reversed its course. Inflation and interest rates fell after 1983, the country witnessed the longest peacetime expansion in its history, and the stock market set record all-time highs (and record lows, such as the crashes in October 1987 and October 1989). These trends also coincided with the relaxation of the antitrust regulations after 1982 under Reagan's Justice Department, which allowed more freedom for companies to engage in horizontal mergers, among other practices. In addition to the shift in policy at the Justice Department, the deregulation activity that continued into the 1980s (in

[3]Michael C. Jensen, Steven Kaplan, and Laura Stiglin, "Effects of LBOs on Tax Revenues of the U.S. Treasury," *Tax Notes*, February 6, 1989.

particular in the banking, broadcasting, communications, transportation, and oil and gas industries) was also significant in restructuring those industries.

Success and Failure in LBOs

Critics charged that LBOs focused on the short term by avoiding capital investment and research and development expenses. Since the mid-1980s, U.S. corporate investment had fallen by 30 percent, and R&D growth had slowed by approximately 10 percentage points. William J. Spencer, executive vice president of research and development at Xerox was one such critic: "We've moved from research and development as being a corporate asset to where it's what a corporate raider looks for first. They can make significant cuts and get cash flow. I haven't seen a takeover yet where they increased research and development activities."[4]

Supporters of LBOs argued that the new private company that emerged after an LBO was a leaner, more profitable structure that was capable of providing greater benefit to the economy. Steven Kaplan of the University of Chicago found that LBOs, "increase operating efficiency without massive layoffs or big cuts in research and development. Average operating earnings increase by 42 percent from the year prior to the buyout to the third year after the buyout. Cash flows increase by 96 percent over this same period."[5] Kaplan's research also found that, "the great concern about the effect of buyouts on R&D and capital investment is unwarranted. The low-growth companies that make the best candidates for LBOs don't invest heavily in R&D to begin with." Of 76 LBO transactions over $50 million that Kaplan studied from 1979 to 1985, only seven companies spent more than 1 percent of sales on R&D before the buyout.

LBOs completed in the 1980s had produced a number of divergent outcomes. Some companies, such as Safeway and Beatrice, had successfully sold off assets and cut operating costs to reduce their debt burdens. Others, such as Fruehauf and Campeau, were saddled with more debt than their cash flow could cover, driving them into bankruptcy. See Exhibits 9 and 10 for comparative statistics on these companies.

Safeway Stores

By most accounts, Safeway Stores, the nation's largest food retailer based in California, became a smaller and more profitable company after its leveraged buyout. To avoid a hostile takeover by the Dart Group in 1986,

---

[4]John Markoff, "A Corporate Lag in Research Funds is Causing Worry," *The New York Times*, January 23, 1990.

[5]Steven Kaplan, "Sources of Value in Management Buyouts," *Journal of Financial Economics*, forthcoming, cited by Michael C. Jensen, "Eclipse of the Public Corporation," *Harvard Business Review* (September–October 1989).

Exhibit 9   Financial Comparisons of Representative Firms (in $ millions)
Results for years preceding black line were unaffected by the LBO

	1977	1978	1979	1980	1981	1982	1983	1984	1985	1986	1987	1988	First half 1989
Beatrice													
Sales[a]													
U.S. Food[b]	5,745	6,522	7,479	8,291	8,773	9,024	9,188	9,327	8,400	8,900	8,926	4,066	
International Food	4,040	4,514	3,200	4,680	4,900	5,170	5,424	5,502	4,493	4,868	4,817	N/A	
Consumer Products	—	—	1,325	1,444	1,749	1,773	1,840	1,788	1,960	2,255	2,866	N/A	
	1,508	1,739	2,029	2,147	2,028	2,069	1,903	1,570	1,053	1,177	1,243	N/A	
Operating Income													
U.S. Food[b]	441	500	617	678	723	723	773	742	199	605	702	N/A	
International Food	265	293	290	339	373	358	411	433	(35)	407	448	N/A	
Consumer Products	—	—	90	99	108	129	129	112	105	109	142	N/A	
	176	207	237	240	242	236	233	197	129	89	112	N/A	
Net Income	206	227	262	290	304	390	43	433	232	(79)	(93)	5	
Interest Expense	34	58	73	91	96	90	114	113	157	446	347	379	
Safeway													
Sales	13,475	13,963	13,718	15,103	16,580	17,632	18,585	19,642	19,650	20,312	18,300	13,612	
Net Income	26	47	(2)	129	109	160	183	185	164	(15)	(488)	32	
Interest Expense	70	74	91	99	121	129	134	151	173	348	576	401	

(continued)

Exhibit 9 (Continued)

Fruehauf

Sales[a]	2,244	2,451	2,082	2,175	1,853	2,129	2,788	2,564	2,684	2,685	1,831	2,077
Trailer operations	882	1,248	1,423	1,184	1,160	951	1,119	1,644	1,384	1,535	969	909
Auto operations[c]	732	751	763	550	628	568	746	917	919	879	810	1,114
Maritime operations	184	243	285	372	436	358	251	251	283	298	67	54
Operating Income	135	177	186	89	101	−1	63	224	173	62	44	23
Trailer operations	54	86	112	48	30	(31)	9	138	74	(3)	–	(31)
Auto operations	61	67	54	21	13	(2)	36	80	91	49	53	60
Maritime operations	20	24	20	20	58	32	18	6	8	16	(9)	(6)
Net Income	61	77	87	32	21	(30)	8	85	71	(61)	(77)	(72)
Interest Expense	21	30	45	53	55	39	92	79	80	19	106	101

Allied Stores

Sales	1,908	2,083	2,210	2,268	2,733	3,216	3,676	3,970	4,135	4,328	3,953	2,978
Net Income	73	82	89	83	88	91	128	141	159	(26)	(169)	51
Interest Expense	27	32	32	33	30	58	86	91	80	153	445	251

RJR/Nabisco

Sales	6,363	6,622	8,935	10,354	11,692	13,075	7,565	8,200	11,622	15,102	15,766	16,956	6,600
Net Income	424	442	585	670	768	870	881	1,210	1,001	1,064	1,209	1,393	(345)
Interest Expense	84	72	126	127	145	186	196	187	356	565	489	579	(1,601)

[a]Total segment sales may not equal total company sales due to the exclusion of intersegment and corporate sales.

[b]In 1977 and 1978, U.S. Food and International Food data were combined.

[c]Consists primarily of Kelsey-Hayes.

Source: Company documents.

Exhibit 10   Financial Comparisons of Representative Firms (in $ millions)

Results for years preceding black line were unaffected by the LBO

	1983	1984	1985	1986	1987	1988	First Half 1989
Beatrice							
Total Assets	4,732	4,464	7,611	7,903	5,551	3,786	
Long Term Debt	772	779	1,241	4,326	3,341	1,252	
Shareholders' Equity	2,215	2,028	2,958	308	489	816	
Safeway							
Total Assets	4,174	4,537	4,840	7,443	4,917	4,372	
Long Term Debt	1,188	1,393	1,315	4,593	3,104	2,769	
Shareholders' Equity	1,390	1,469	1,622	3	(461)	(368)	
Fruehauf							
Total Assets	1,596	1,700	1,803	2,477	1,793	1,584	
Long Term Debt	479	479	544	956	794	709	
Shareholders' Equity	503	570	618	263	180	226	
Allied Stores							
Total Assets	2,530	2,676	5,401	3,924	4,006	3,501	
Long Term Debt	756	753	664	2,867	2,186	1,830	
Shareholders' Equity	964	1,063	1,258	320	184	156	
RJR/Nabisco							
Total Assets	9,217	9,272	16,930	16,701	16,861	17,751	34,629
Long Term Debt	1,420	1,257	4,857	4,833	3,884	4,975	22,279
Shareholders' Equity	5,223	4,796	4,478	5,312	6,038	5,694	1,778

Source: Company documents.

a group comprised of Safeway management and KKR acquired the company in an LBO for $5.8 billion, which included $1.6 billion in assumed debt and only $130 million in equity. Shareholders received an unusually high premium of 69 percent over its predeal level. The deal left Safeway burdened with close to $5.7 billion in debt, making it one of the most highly leveraged deals in history.

In the two years that followed the buyout, Safeway's management, under the direction of KKR, had undergone a dramatic belt tightening. For the most part, Safeway's debt was pruned by selling underperforming stores. Safeway reduced its number of stores from 2,326 to 1,161, and by mid-1988, Safeway had pared its debt load down to $3.4 billion. "By paring back to the most profitable operations, we've ended up with a smaller company, but one that is making more operating income on a $13.5 billion sales base than it was on $20 billion,"[6] said Peter A. Magowan, Safeway's chairman and chief executive officer.

Some observers were dubious of the continued success of Safeway. Profit margins at supermarket chains were often so thin that companies did well just to keep more than a penny of every dollar. Some LBO critics argued that companies invariably cut capital spending and raised prices in an effort to generate additional cash flow after an LBO, but Magowan disagreed. Although Safeway did reduce capital spending in the first year after the buyout, it had increased expenditures steadily in the following years. In 1989, the company planned to add 45 new stores and continued to remodel existing stores. With regard to prices, Magowan argued that Safeway was more competitive than it had ever been. Safeway planned to build even larger stores, called "super stores," which would lower costs and create higher margins without increasing prices. The competition seemed to agree. "In the areas that they have targeted to stay in, they remain awfully tough competitors," said Gary Michael, vice chairman of Albertson's, another supermarket chain.

Beatrice Companies

Before it was dwarfed by the RJR/Nabisco deal, the largest LBO was Beatrice. In 1986, a group of investors, led by KKR, paid a 45 percent premium to acquire the giant conglomerate for a total of $8.2 billion, which included $2 billion in assumed debt and $417 million in equity. The size of such a leveraged deal put the company's debt repayment plan under public scrutiny. After appointing former Esmark chairman, Donald P. Kelly, to the post of chief executive officer, the company embarked on a strategy to reduce the debt that was borrowed to finance the buyout. "Kelly had inherited a daily debt load of about $2.1 million, which was 62 percent more than the company's average daily net income the year before the buyout."[7] Kelly's plan to streamline operations had to comply with Beatrice's borrowing agreements which required the company to sell at least $1.5 billion of assets by mid-1987.

By the end of 1986, Beatrice had sold off its Coca-Cola bottling operations, Avis Rental Car Agency, International Playtex, Americold refrigerated warehouses, and Webcraft Technologies for a total of $3.5 billion, of which $3.2 billion was used to repay banks. In mid-1987, Beatrice announced a reorganization that involved the creation of a new entity called E-II Holdings, which would house Beatrice's 15 remaining non-food businesses. The food businesses would still be part of Beatrice

[6]Lawrence M. Fisher, "Safeway Buyout: A Success Story," *The New York Times*, October 21, 1988.

[7]Robert Johnson, "Beatrice Faces Tricky Task in Dismantling Its Empire," *The Wall Street Journal*, April 11, 1986.

companies. In early 1988, Kelly sold E-II to American Brands for $1.2 billion. Beatrice's total sales after the E-II deal came to $5.7 billion and its buyout-related debt had been pared to $2.9 billion. Shortly after, Kelly began looking for a suitor for Beatrice, whose major brands then included Hunt-Wesson, Tropicana, and Swift-Eckrich. After months of failed efforts, the company was taken off the auction block at the end of 1988, shortly after Tropicana was sold for $1.2 billion. Industry analysts believed that Kelly had difficulty selling the entire Beatrice entity because of the staggering $1.9 billion of goodwill on its books, the result of the company having been bought and sold three times in less than ten years.

Initially, when the Beatrice LBO was first constructed, "KKR crowed that breaking up the company and selling off the assets would produce a windfall profit of $3.8 billion. However, by the end of 1988, the best estimate of pre-tax investor profit was $383 million. Though that was a respectable return, it was nowhere near the $3.8 billion pre-tax profit that the group had expected, and a disappointment by industry standards."[8]

In 1989, Beatrice announced that after three years of divestitures, it was seeking acquisitions. After selling off a myriad of units, William Carmichael, Beatrice's chief financial officer, said, "We think we're closer to a corporate credit operation than to an LBO. That gives us the ability to finance acquisitions."[9] Beatrice officials said that the company was looking for businesses that would be compatible with operations such as Beatrice's Swift-Eckrich meat division or its Hunt-Wesson food operations.

Fruehauf

In 1985, Fruehauf was the largest U.S. manufacturer of truck trailers. The company was earning record profits and planning massive capacity expansions. In early 1989, however, Fruehauf became the country's largest LBO to date to have filed for bankruptcy. The Detroit-based maker of truck vans and auto parts, had gone private in a $1.8 billion LBO in 1986 to avoid a takeover by corporate raider, Asher Edelman. Shareholders received a 34 percent premium for their stock. The deal included $1 billion in junk bond financing, $260 million in preferred stock, the assumption of $500 million in existing debt, and just $60 million in equity.

Fruehauf's trailer business did not live up to growth expectations of 24 percent between 1987 and 1990. By 1988, the company's revenues were 45 percent below projections. And, although Fruehauf's debt bur-

[8]Bryan Burrough, "Beatrice, Once Hailed Deal of the Century, Proves Disappointing," *The Wall Street Journal*, November 21, 1988.

[9]George Anders, "Beatrice Says It Now Seeks Acquisitions After Three Years of Rapid-Fire Divestitures," *The Wall Street Journal*, April 10, 1989.

den was 12 percent lower than originally anticipated, the company lost $42 million in 1987 compared to a forecasted profit of $240 million. The following year, the company lost $56 million. By 1989, Fruehauf was losing $1 million per week and could not escape its $101 million per year debt payments. Though the company tried to push through a recapitalization plan, it failed to do so in the face of opposition from large bondholders.

In response to mounting debt problems, Fruehauf began a massive restructuring of its unprofitable trailer operations in 1988. However, industry analysts believed that Fruehauf tried to cut operational costs but found that they had to resort to selling assets. As a result, in early 1989, Fruehauf sold its trailer operations to Terex Corporation for $233 million in cash and debt, or about $100 million less than its book value. The cash proceeds, approximately $170 million, allowed Fruehauf's remaining division, Kelsey-Hayes auto parts, to pay off the company's bank debt. Kelsey-Hayes, which had remained consistently profitable, was sold in May 1989 to Varity Corporation, a Canadian farm equipment and auto parts manufacturer, for $655 million in cash and securities.

Allied/Campeau

In 1986, Allied Stores was one of the largest retailing organizations in the United States, operating nearly 700 department and specialty stores. In December of that year, Robert Campeau and the Campeau Corporation, a Canadian-based builder and shopping center developer with revenues of $150 million, bought all of the stock of Allied for a 36 percent premium for a total of $3.6 billion. Campeau also assumed $1.4 billion in Allied debt. Campeau financed the deal with $2.5 billion in bank debt and an $850 million bridge loan. Because of the heavy use of debt for the purchase of all shares, the Allied transaction could be considered an LBO, even though it became a subsidiary of the publicly traded Campeau Corporation.

Almost immediately, Campeau began to sell Allied's less profitable units. By 1988, Campeau refinanced $2.1 billion of its existing Allied bank debt and had shed $2.2 billion of Allied assets (such as Bonwit Teller, Garfinckels, and Brooks Brothers), twice its goal by that time. Concurrent with the sale of its old assets, Campeau was also expanding its department store empire. Campeau acquired Federated Department Stores in 1988 for $6.6 billion, making it the largest merger ever outside of the oil industry. Campeau financed the acquisition with $3.25 billion in bank loans, a $2.1 billion bridge loan, and $1.1 billion in junk bonds. Industry analysts observed that the Federated acquisition put both Campeau and Allied under a crushing burden of debt during a time in which the retail environment was sluggish. As a result, Campeau was forced to suspend payments to suppliers in some cases, forcing suppliers to stall and even cancel shipments to many of the stores. In January 1990, slightly more than one year after the acquisition of Federated, Campeau Corporation filed for protection under Chapter 11 bankruptcy rules, making it the fourth largest bankruptcy in U.S. history. At that time, Allied's outstanding debt totaled close to $2.9 billion, while Federated was saddled with $5.1 billion in debt.

RJR Nabisco

RJR was established as the R.J. Reynolds Tobacco Company in North Carolina in 1875. The company's activities were confined to the tobacco industry until the 1960s, when diversification led to investments in transportation, energy, and food. In 1979, RJR acquired Del Monte and began to concentrate its diversification efforts on consumer products. That strategy led to the acquisition of Heublein, Inc. in 1982, whose primary business was wine and spirits. In 1985, RJR acquired Nabisco for a total cost of $4.9 billion. With its renewed focus on tobacco and food products, the company divested several operations in 1986 and 1987, including Heublein. By 1988, 41 percent of RJR's sales were made up of tobacco products, with food products comprising the remainder. Almost three-quarters of both total sales and tobacco sales from 1985 to 1988 were made in the United States. See Exhibits 11–13 for financial information on RJR/Nabisco.

In the fourth quarter of 1988, RJR entered into an agreement with KKR to become a private company through an LBO transaction. The magnitude of the $25.4 billion LBO of RJR uneased many of the industry's players on Wall Street. More than three times larger than the Beatrice buyout, RJR's transaction had far-reaching effects. To put the size of the RJR deal in perspective, the company's new debt burden was greater than the market value of 90 percent of the companies listed on the New York Stock Exchange.

The RJR buyout had a detrimental effect on the company's bondholders as well as the bond market in general. Prices for the approximately $5 billion of RJR's investment grade bonds plummeted 20 percent on the news that RJR would take on an additional $16 billion in new debt. In response, some bondholders, such as Metropolitan Life Insurance, which sustained a paper loss of $40 million on RJR bonds, filed suit against RJR. Met Life argued that RJR's management violated its fiduciary responsibility to existing bondholders by initiating an LBO. The bond market seemed to feel the effects of the RJR deal as well. During the first ten months of 1988, an average of $8 to $9 billion of long-term corporate debt was sold each month. But, after the chill of the RJR deal set in, debt offerings totaled only $3 billion per month for the remainder of the year.

In addition to the controversy over RJR's bonds, accusations were made that the gains to RJR's shareholders were at the expense of the U.S. Treasury in the form of lost tax revenue. Estimates of the loss to U.S. taxpayers from the RJR deal ranged from $2 to $5 billion over the

**Exhibit 11   RJR Nabisco: Consolidated Statement of Income
(in $ millions)**

	1986	1987	1988	Six months ended June 30, 1989
Net sales	15,102	15,766	16,950	6,600
Cost and Expenses:				
Cost of products sold	7,920	8,221	8,786	3,042
Selling, general, & administrative	4,842	4,991	5,322	2,158
Restructuring expense				236
Operating income	2,340	2,304	2,848	1,164
Interest and debt expense	(565)	(489)	(579)	(1,601)
Other income	7	1	17	113
Income before taxes	1,782	1,816	2,286	(324)
Provision for income taxes	757	735	893	—
Income from continuing operations	1,025	1,081	1,393	(324)
Income from discontinued operations	78	(7)	—	(21)
Gain on sale of discounted operations	(39)	215	—	—
Extraordinary item	—	80	—	—
Net income (loss)	1,064	1,209	1,393	(345)

Source: Company documents.

long term. However, one study indicated that the Treasury was "highly likely to gain rather than lose tax revenues. In present value terms, the increased revenue for the Treasury is $3.8 billion, $3.3 billion of which it will likely gain in the year following the buyout. These payments are more than eight times higher than the approximately $370 million in federal taxes paid by RJR/Nabisco in 1987."[10]

On October 20, 1988, F. Ross Johnson, chief executive officer of RJR/Nabisco, and Shearson Lehman announced that they were considering a leveraged buyout bid of $17.6 billion or $75 per share for the company. The bid was proposed as a way to raise the value of the company's stock, which was trading at $53 per share. Four days later, KKR announced a counter bid for RJR of $20.6 billion or $90 per share. After numerous rounds of bidding, KKR was named the winner on November 29, with a bid of $108 per share or $25.4 billion, topping management's bid of $108 per share because of the higher value of the package in cash, preferred stock, and convertible debt. After all of the refinancings associated with the tender offer, RJR bought out the shares for approximately $5 billion in senior bank debt, $8 billion in various bridge loans, $5 billion in subordinated increasing rate notes, $6 billion in cumulative exchange-

[10]Jensen, Kaplan, and Stiglin, p. 733.

Exhibit 12   RJR Nabisco: Consolidated Balance Sheets (in $ millions)

	1986	1987	1988	June 30, 1989
Assets				
Current Assets:				
Cash and cash equivalents	$ 827	$ 1,088	$ 1,425	$ 902
Accounts and notes receivable	1,675	1,745	1,920	1,332
Inventories	2,620	2,678	2,571	3,418
Prepaid expenses and excise taxes	273	329	265	393
Total current assets	5,395	5,840	6,181	6,045
Property, plant, and equipment, net	5,343	5,847	6,149	5,459
Unallocated excess of purchase cost over net assets acquired	—	—	—	21,238
Goodwill and trademarks	4,603	4,525	4,555	—
Other assets	1,360	649	866	1,887
Total Assets	$16,701	$16,861	$17,751	$34,629
Liabilities				
Current Liabilities:				
Notes payable	$ 518	$ 442	$ 423	$ 378
Accounts payable and accrued accounts	2,923	3,187	3,220	3,036
Current maturities of long-term debt	423	162	337	3,436
Income taxes accrued	202	332	300	526
Total current liabilities	4,066	4,123	4,280	7,378
Long-term debt	4,833	3,884	4,975	22,279
Other noncurrent liabilities	1,448	1,797	1,617	2,065
Deferred income taxes	751	846	1,060	1,129
Redeemable preferred stock	291	173	125	—
Common stockholders' equity:				
Common stock	236	251	229	3
Paid-in-capital	320	312	290	2,186
Cumulative translation adjustments	(76)	86	101	(62)
Retained earnings	4,832	5,548	5,349	(345)
Treasury stock, at cost	—	(159)	(190)	—
Unamortized value of restricted stock	—	—	(85)	(4)
Total common stockholders' equity	$ 5,312	$ 6,038	$ 5,694	$ 1,778
Total Liabilities	$16,701	$16,861	$17,751	$34,629

Source: Company documents.

able preferred stock and senior converting debentures,[11] and finally, $1.5 billion in shareholders' equity. In addition, KKR assumed the $5.2 billion in RJR debt existing before the takeover bid.

[11]The preferred stock and convertible debentures were pay-in-kind (PIK) securities which paid dividends and coupons with additional units of the security instead of cash.

Exhibit 13   Financial Information for RJR by Business Segment (in $ millions)

	1979	1980	1981	1982	1983	1984	1985	1986	1987	1988
Tobacco Products										
Sales	5,032	5,608	6,228	6,804	4,807	5,178	5,422	5,866	6,346	7,068
Operating Income	863	977	1,109	1,188	1,150	1,305	1,483	1,660	1,822	1,924
Assets	2,022	2,211	2,839	3,219	3,378	3,812	4,496	4,882	5,208	5,393
Capital Expenditures	77	121	178	238	383	527	647	613	433	459
Depreciation	53	55	65	81	78	107	146	145	178	205
Food Products										
Sales	1,962	2,265	2,471	3,356	2,759	3,022	6,200	9,236[a]	9,420	9,888
Operating Income	128	94	106	101	129	181	549	944	1,035	1,215
Assets	1,558	1,741	1,775	3,506	1,761	2,212	9,598	9,822	10,117	10,382
Capital Expenditures	71	86	96	123	94	86	279	344	445	621
Depreciation	77	45	38	32	56	68	195	246	260	279

(continued)

Exhibit 13   (Continued)

Spirits and Wines

Sales	—	—	746[b]	703	766	876	—	—
Operating Income	—	—	113	122	131	138	—	—
Assets	—	—	740	815	895	991	—	—
Capital Expenditures	—	—	13	13	26	25	—	—
Depreciation	—	—	24	22	24	30	—	—

Other[c]

Sales	1,227	2,498	—	—	—	—	—	—
Operating Income	124	249	(74)	(74)	(83)	(139)	(182)	(166)
Assets	2,484	2,962	3,197	2,257	1,684	1,281	1,536	1,976
Capital Expenditures	511	659	15	29	20	65	58	62
Depreciation	219	262	16	15	13	11	12	14

[a]RJR acquired Nabisco in 1986.

[b]Heublein was acquired in 1982 and sold in 1986.

[c]In 1979 and 1980, RJR's transportation and energy businesses were included in this segment. Those businesses were sold off in 1981. From 1983 to 1988, the segment primarily consists of corporate sales and income.

Source: Company documents.

The Tobacco Industry

The six companies in the U.S. tobacco industry in 1989 had $35 billion in sales. See Exhibit 14. Cigarette sales accounted for 94 percent of the value of all tobacco shipments, with cigars, chewing and pipe tobacco making up the remainder. Industry sales in the United States, which peaked in 1981, had fallen for eight straight years—a total decline of 11 percent. Since 1988 the industry had faced new challenges. The U.S. Surgeon General declared tobacco a drug as addictive as heroin; U.S. airlines banned smoking on most of their domestic flights; communities passed tough anti-smoking ordinances; and the courts awarded for the first time ever damages to a claimant in a tobacco liability suit. As a result of these actions, total cigarette consumption in the United States

Exhibit 14   U.S. Tobacco Companies: Worldwide Sales and Profits

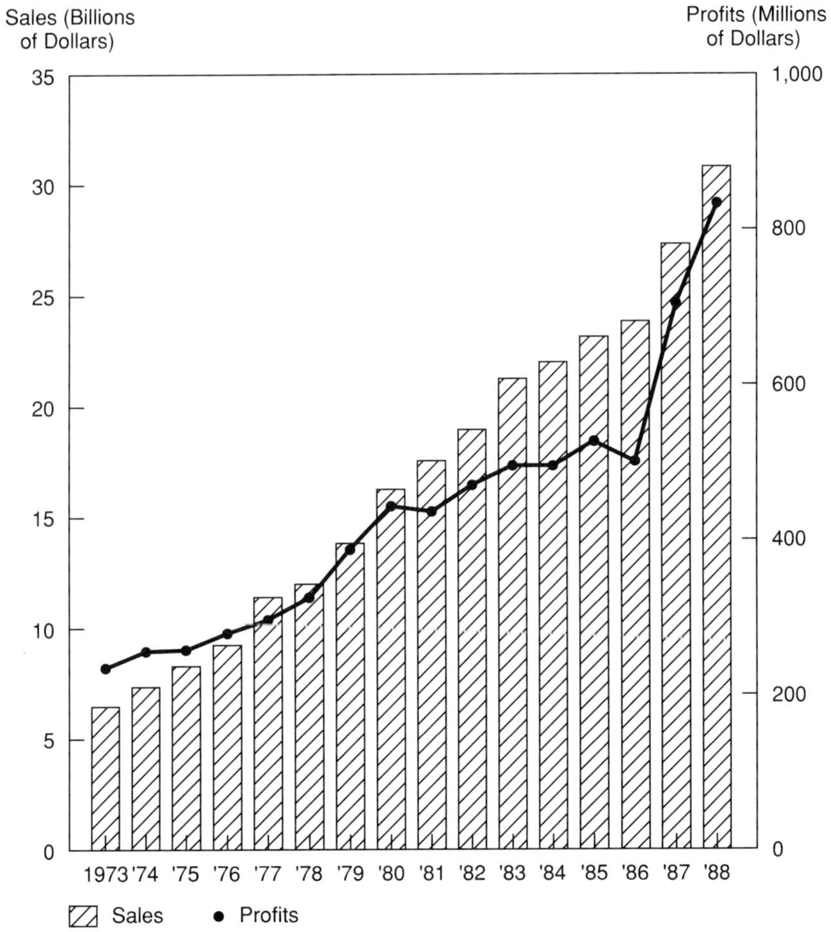

Source: Company Annual Reports

was forecasted to decline by 3 percent per year in 1989 and 1990. The average cost of a package of cigarettes exceeded $1.50 in many markets in 1988, up more than 50 percent from just five years before. While aggressive price hikes had kept cigarettes a very profitable product, companies had to increase spending on packaging, advertising, promotion, and new product development, and to rely more on sales of lower-margin discount cigarettes.

While domestic consumption had declined, U.S. cigarette exports had nearly doubled from 1984 to 1988. Export shipments accounted for 20 percent of all U.S. production in 1988. The growth in exports had been particularly strong in the Far East, where the removal of import barriers had been recently negotiated in Japan, Taiwan, and South Korea. Japan consumed 32 billion American cigarettes in 1988, or 10 percent of that country's total cigarette consumption, making it the largest overseas market for American-made cigarettes.

The tobacco industry was divided into two major segments with advertising and promotion expenditures totaling $587 million in 1988. The largest of the two segments was the full-price segment, dominated by brands such as Marlboro, Winston, and Salem. However, the fastest growing segment was the off-price cigarette market, which represented 11 percent of industry volume. These off-price products required substantial advertising and promotional support, making them only one-third to two-thirds as profitable as the full-price cigarettes.

The six tobacco companies in the United States were Philip Morris (with a 1988 worldwide market share of 39 percent), RJR (32 percent), Brown and Williamson (11 percent), Lorillard (8 percent), American Brands (7 percent), and Liggett Group (3 percent). Philip Morris was the world's largest tobacco company with $14.6 billion in 1988 sales and the manufacturer of the world's most popular cigarette, Marlboro. Philip Morris was the only U.S. cigarette producer whose market share and unit sales rose at the expense of its competitors in 1988. Philip Morris had been increasing its tobacco market share in recent years at the same time that it was diversifying into the food and beverage industry. In addition to its acquisition of Miller Brewing Company in the 1970s, Philip Morris acquired General Foods for $5.6 billion in 1985. In 1988, its $13 billion acquisition of Kraft made the headlines as the year's biggest deal. The strategy of Philip Morris was to expand into businesses that they believed would be more promising in terms of future sales. However, even with the Kraft takeover, Philip Morris's tobacco-derived profits were reduced only to 64 percent from the previous 76 percent.

RJR was the second largest tobacco company with $6.4 billion in world tobacco sales in 1988. RJR's leading brands, Winston and Salem, were the industry's second and third most popular brands. The company's tobacco business accounted for two-thirds of total company profits. RJR's strategy after the LBO was to generate cash for its tobacco business by selling off the non-tobacco parts. For example, RJR invested over $300 million in the "smokeless" Premier-brand cigarette, but after very negative public response in various test markets, it was forced to withdraw the product in mid-1989.

During 1989, Philip Morris had made sizeable gains in market share in the tobacco industry, widening its lead over RJR by almost three percentage points. The results were even worse in the rapidly growing off-price segment in which the gap between Philip Morris and RJR widened by seven percentage points. Nonetheless, RJR continued to do well overseas, with operating profit jumping 17 percent in the first half of 1989. These profits were aided by $500 million in cost cuts following the LBO. At the same time, Philip Morris had initiated successful pricing tactics, and had made inroads into product areas that were previously dominated by RJR, such as very low-nicotine cigarettes. In addition, Philip Morris, led by its Marlboro brand, had captured 67 percent of smokers 25 years old and younger. RJR's customer base, on the other hand, was the older, less-affluent smoker, who was more price sensitive.

The Processed Food Industry

The processed food industry was made up of hundreds of firms, ranging from large multinationals to smaller single-product companies with industry sales of $110 billion. See Exhibit 15. Two of the largest players were the Kraft Foods division of Philip Morris and Nabisco Brands of RJR. Kraft's major brand names included Kraft salad dressings, mayonnaise, Miracle Whip, Velveeta, and Parkay margarine. In 1987, Kraft's sales approached $10 billion and net income was $435 million, representing 27 percent and 11 percent increases over 1986 levels, respectively.

Nabisco's brand names included Del Monte fruits and vegetables, Planters, LifeSavers, Oreo, Grey Poupon, Chips Ahoy!, Premium crackers, and Blue Bonnet. The company's Nabisco Biscuit division was the largest manufacturer of cookies and crackers in the United States with the top five selling brands, each of which had annual sales of over $100 million in 1988. Total company sales in that year were $9.9 billion and operating income was $1.2 billion. In 1989, the company introduced a new product, Teddy Grahams, which become the industry's third largest-selling cookie in less than one year on the market, behind Nabisco's own Oreos and Chips Ahoy! brands. Sales of Teddy Grahams were forecasted to be an unprecedented $150 million in its first year. Nabisco also made a number of aggressive cost cuts in that year, such as deferring plant modernization plans, and eliminating some high-paid research engineers. Nabisco's operating income grew 41 percent in the first six months of 1989.

Asset Sales and Refinancings After the LBO

Shortly after the LBO at RJR was completed in February 1989, KKR announced that Louis V. Gerstner, previously president of American Express, would become the new chief executive officer. Within six

Exhibit 15   U.S. Food Processing Companies: Worldwide Sales and Profits

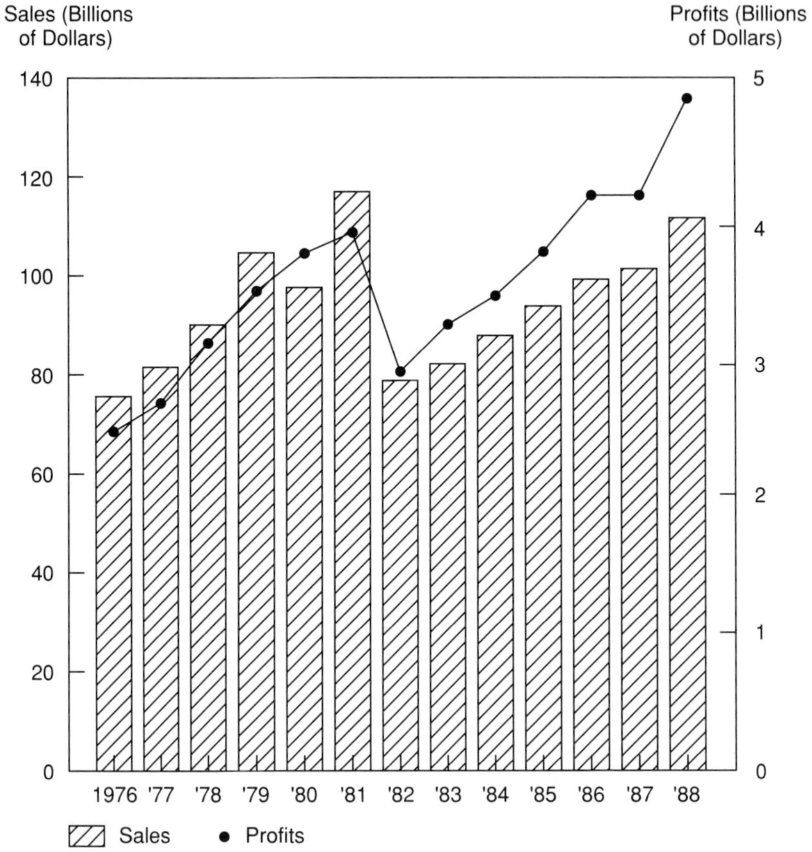

Sales (Billions   Profits (Billions
of Dollars)   of Dollars)

Source: Value Line

months, Gerstner had sold Nabisco's European food units for $2.5 billion, part of the Del Monte subsidiary for $1.5 billion, and various other units for a combined total of nearly $1 billion. He also moved the company's headquarters from Atlanta to New York, shedding almost 2,000 employees. In November 1989, RJR sold its Baby Ruth, Butterfinger, and Pearson candy businesses to Nestle for $370 million. In early 1990 RJR also planned to receive $1.5 billion from the sale of Del Monte's canned food unit to a group led by Merrill Lynch.

RJR used most of the proceeds from the $2.5 billion sale of its European food unit to pay down about $2 billion of a $6 billion bridge loan in June. The company owed another $3 billion on that particular loan in February 1990, which it expected to pay with $1 billion from sales of assorted small assets, including the proceeds from its candy business sales and $2 billion from the two-part sale of most of Del Monte.

By August 1990, RJR had to pay the last $1 billion of its bridge loan. Once that bridge loan had been paid off, the company still owed $19 billion in various types of debt.

RJR's performance in 1989 had pleased analysts. In the first six months of the year, operating profit had soared 21 percent over the year earlier period. Those results led analysts to predict the company's 1989 cash flow to be more than 20 percent ahead of the debt-coverage ratio required by RJR's banks. However, some worried about the $6 billion in payment-in-kind (PIK) debt. "Although RJR is having no trouble meeting cash-interest payments, it is too early to tell just how onerous the high-interest PIK notes will be once they come due." The real test of the success of the deal will come before early 1991. Some time before April of that year, the company "must fix interest rates on $5.8 billion worth of PIK bonds so the notes trade at par, in accordance with the bonds' terms. That means if the notes continue trading below their $100 par value, RJR must boost that bonds' interest rates as high as necessary to drive their market price to $100. That could require fixing the interest rate as high as 20 percent, bankers say, especially if the junk-bond market remains weak or deteriorates further."[12]

There were also worries about RJR's junk bonds, which it had used to finance the LBO. Though asset sales had gone well in 1989, the price of RJR's junior bonds had fallen significantly since the mini-crash of October 1989. "Everything had gone well until the junk bond market went into disarray," said David Goldman, an analyst with Nomura Securities. "But from this point forward, I think the jury is definitely out."[13] On January 26, 1990, Moodys Investor Service unexpectedly downgraded the ratings on $19.5 billion of RJR debt, sending all bond prices plummeting while hitting the junk bond market particularly hard. RJR's PIK debentures were selling at 59-5/8 for a $100 par value. "One reason why RJR's downgrade was so devastating to the junk market is that investors had assumed that the company was virtually immune to the troubles that have hurt other highly leveraged issuers. Until January 26, RJR bonds were considered among the highest quality issues on the market as well as among the easiest bonds to sell."[14]

[12]Peter Waldman, "After RJR's Buy Out: Successes, Worries," *The Wall Street Journal*, October 27, 1989.

[13]Ibid.

[14]Constance Mitchell, "RJR's Bonds Skid Again and Junk Market Falls," *The Wall Street Journal*, January 30, 1990.

Questions

1. Why have LBOs become so popular in the 1980s?
2. How much value is created by LBOs and what is the source of that value in general? In the case of RJR?
3. What are the similarities and differences between the LBO of RJR and LBOs of Safeway, Beatrice, Fruehauf, and Allied.
4. What are the major threats and/or opportunities for RJR after its LBO?
5. What changes in public policy, if any, should be undertaken to correct the possible problems created by LBOs.

PART II
Corporate Management of Monetary Policy Changes

*Monetary policy is the control by the central bank of the money supply
and credit of a nation through the manipulation of short-term interest
rates or bank reserves in order to affect the levels of prices and real production in the economy. Non-bank businesses are not directly concerned
with the money supply or bank reserves per se, but rather with the cost
and availability of credit and the price of financial assets, including the
nation's currency itself. These are directly observed in the numerous interest rates and the exchange rate of the country.*

*During the past three decades in the United States, monetary pol-
icy has had a number of highlights including the credit crunches of
1966, and 1970, the first double-digit peacetime interest rates in 1974–
1975, and the extremely high and volatile interest rates of the 1979–
1982 period. Since the beginning of the 1980s, we have also observed
prolonged periods of appreciation and depreciation of real exchange
rates as well. The monetary policies of other countries have been related
to that of the United States (and vice versa) as a result of the trend
towards deregulation and liberalization of the international and national capital markets around the world. Countries can, to various degrees depending on the openness of their economy, conduct independent
monetary policies, but significant deviations are often reflected in major
exchange rate adjustments.*

*The cases in Part II of this book illustrate the business implica-
tions of monetary policy changes. All these cases begin their stories in
the volatile monetary environment of the early 1980s, since it had such
a profound influence on the economic landscape during the past decade.
The Chapter 5 case, Massey-Ferguson 1980, details the most obvious
channel by which monetary policy can affect a business—financial insolvency because of excessive interest burdens. In the next chapter, Franklin Savings Association considers interest rate movements from the perspective of lenders rather than borrowers. In the process of studying
Franklin's predicament, we also gain a better understanding of the
causes of the savings and loan crisis. The Financial Swaps case in
Chapter 7 examines the causes of financial innovation as financial in-*

stitutions try to develop new instruments, such as swaps, to mitigate some of the effects of monetary policy. The final two cases in Part II of this book focus on exchange rate movements. The case on General Motors and the Dollar demonstrates how managers can react to continuous changes in market exchange rates and affect their competitive standing in their industry. In contrast, Colgate-Palmolive in Mexico illustrates how managers can cope with discrete changes in controlled exchange rates.

CASE 5

Massey-Ferguson, 1980

The classic illustration of the effects of monetary policy on a business is rising interest rates forcing a firm to bankruptcy. Bankruptcies abound during periods of tight money in all countries. In the United States, beginning in the early 1980s, the business failure rate rose to more than 100 per 10,000 businesses. In comparison, during the two previous periods of tight money, 1970 and 1974–1975, the business failure rate peaked slightly more than 40 per 10,000.

The task for managers in this situation is to determine how to set the best financial strategy for the firm in order to raise the funds needed to support the firm's product market strategy and at the same time to avoid running into debt payment constraints. The choice of the firm's capital structure becomes critical. If financial managers place too great a reliance on equity, the firm may dilute the benefits to the shareholders of the product market strategy, which their equity funds are financing. If financial managers place too great a reliance on debt, the firm may not generate the cash needed to meet the interest and principal payments on the debt.

The Massey-Ferguson case in this chapter allows us to investigate the sources of financial distress and its competitive consequences. The story is not simply that tight money causes high interest rates which in turn causes some firms to fail. We need to understand the concomitant factors leading to failure, and more importantly, how the setting of business (and financial) strategies during periods of tight money shape the competitive landscape. The most significant consequences of monetary policy are not the costs associated with the failed firms, but rather the competitive advantage gained and ceded during the period of tight money.

Massey-Ferguson Limited, a multinational producer of farm machinery, industrial machinery, and diesel engines, was founded in 1847 and by 1980 had manufacturing and assembly operations in 31 countries throughout the world. Massey-Ferguson was the West's largest producer of farm tractors and the world's largest supplier of diesel engines to original equipment manufacturers.

In 1978 however, Massey reported an unprecedented year-end loss of U.S. $262.2 million. The new president, Victor A. Rice, pledged to restore Massey to profitability by the end of its 1979 fiscal year. Massey did show a profit of U.S. $37.0 million in 1979, but reported a loss on continuing operations of U.S. $35.4 million (see Exhibit 2). Sales in the first half of fiscal 1980 were up, but earnings remained severely depressed. (Historical financial data are provided in Exhibits 1–4.)

In April of 1980 a preferred share issue of Can. $300 million to $500 million[1] was postponed indefinitely. The postponement was attributed to Massey's operating problems and to the fact that Argus Corporation, Massey's largest shareholder, refused to take a block of the preferreds as a vote of confidence in Massey.

As 1980 progressed, it became apparent that without an equity infusion, Massey would be in default of several loan covenants before the end of the fiscal year (October 31, 1980). Cross-default provisions made substantially all long- and short-term debts callable if any single default occurred. If Massey's lenders then cut off credit and moved to secure their loans, company operations would quickly come to a halt. Plant shutdowns, further worker layoffs, and a liquidation of corporate assets would follow. Creditors and customers around the world wondered if Massey would make it through the looming financial crisis.

Company Background

Massey-Ferguson had been called "the one true multinational." Its products—farm equipment, industrial machinery, and diesel engines—were sold throughout the world by dealers, distributors, and company retail outlets. (Exhibit 5 shows a breakdown of 1980 sales by national markets. Table A summarizes Massey-Ferguson's sales by product line and geographical area.)

Massey's production facilities were also dispersed around the world. (Exhibit 5 shows the distribution of MF capacity by country.) Massey's largest facilities were located in Canada (Brantford and Toronto), France

---

This case was prepared by Professors Carliss Baldwin and Scott Mason. Copyright © 1982 by the President and Fellows of Harvard College. Harvard Business School Case 9-282-043.

[1]In 1980, the Canadian dollar was trading in the range of U.S.$.80–.85.

Exhibit 1   Consolidated Balance Sheet, October 31, 1978–1980 (U.S. $ millions)

	1980	1979	1978
Assets			
Current assets			
Cash	$ 56.2	$ 17.2	$ 23.4
Receivables	968.2	731.1	531.3
Inventories	988.9	1,097.6	1,083.8
Prepaid expenses and other current assets	93.0	89.8	63.8
Total current assets	$2,106.3	$1,935.7	$1,702.3
Investments	205.8	217.1	213.3
Fixed assets, net	488.2	568.7	602.2
Other assets and deferred charges	27.3	24.0	29.3
Total	$2,827.6	$2,745.5	$2,547.1
Liabilities			
Current liabilities			
Bank borrowings	$1,015.1	$ 511.7	$ 362.3
Current portion of LTD	60.2	59.3	115.0
Accounts payable and accrued charges	793.8	907.4	778.7
Other current liabilities	24.5	31.1	16.1
Total current liabilities	$1,893.6	$1,509.5	$1,272.1
Deferred income tax	14.3	13.8	64.3
Long-term debt (less current portion)	562.1	624.8	651.8
Minority interest in subsidiaries	4.5	19.1	18.4
Contingent liabilities and commitments	—	—	—
Shareholders' equity			
Redeemable preferred shares	95.8	95.8	95.8
Common (18,250,350)	176.9	176.9	176.9
Retained earnings	80.4	305.6	267.8
Total	$2,827.6	$2,745.5	$2,547.1

Table A   Breakdown of Massey-Ferguson's 1980 Sales (in U.S. $ millions)

	Farm and Industrial Equipment	Diesel Engines	Percentage of Sales Geographically
Sales	$2,533	$599	
North America			
(U.S., Canada,			
Mexico)			33.2%
Western Europe			35.6%
Rest of world			31.2%

Source: Massey-Ferguson annual report

**Exhibit 2   Consolidated Statements of Income, 1978–1980
(U.S. $ millions)**

	Years Ended October 31		
	1980	1979	1978
Net sales	$3,132.1	$2,973.0	$2,925.5
Costs and expenses			
Cost of goods sold, translated at average exchange rates for the year	2,568.5	2,381.8	2,371.2
Effect of foreign currency exchange rate changes[a]	7.7	18.6	—
	2,576.2	2,400.4	2,371.2
Marketing, general and administrative	404.7	351.9	372.0
Engineering and product development	59.7	58.2	66.0
Interest on long-term debt	71.0	75.7	78.6
Other interest expense	229.9	128.8	108.0[b]
Interest income	(42.0)	(40.3)	—
Exchange adjustments	49.9	(24.9)	90.9
Minority interest	0.2	1.4	(0.8)
Miscellaneous income	(13.5)	(10.3)	(10.6)
Total costs and expenses	3,336.1	2,940.9	3,075.3
Profit (loss) before items shown below	(204.0)	32.1	(149.8)
Provision for reorganization expense	(28.5)	(95.0)	(116.0)
Income tax recovery	10.1	6.3	(11.8)
Equity in net income of finance subsidiaries	22.7	16.6	16.3
Equity in net income of associate companies	—	4.6	4.6
Income (loss) from continuing operations	(199.7)	(35.4)	(256.7)
Loss from discontinued operations	(25.5)	(23.0)	—
Extraordinary item	—	95.4	—
Net income (loss)	(225.2)	37.0	$ (256.7)
Unfavorable (favorable) impact on continuing operations of exchange adjustments and foreign currency exchange rate changes in cost of good sold	$ 57.6	$ (6.3)	—

[a]This item is the difference between cost of goods sold translated to U.S. dollars at average exchange rates and such costs translated at historical rates.

[b]Amount shown is net of interest income.

(Marquette), England (Coventry), and Australia (Melbourne). Diesel en
gine production was concentrated in England (Peterborough).

In certain markets, primarily North America, Massey financed retail
sales of farm and industrial machinery through wholly owned finance
subsidiaries. In Europe and Australia, Massey's finance subsidiaries were
primarily involved in financing sales to distributors, but they could also
finance dealer receivables in their home markets. In October 1980 Massey's finance subsidiaries had assets totaling U.S. $1,130.6 million and
outstanding debts of U.S. $825.6 million. (Massey's finance subsidiaries
are not consolidated in the financial statements of Exhibits 1–4.)

Exhibit 3   Consolidated Statement of Changes in Financial Position (U.S. $ millions)

| | Years Ended October 31 | | |
	1980	1981	1978
Source of funds			
Disposal of investments in associate companies and changes in long-term advances to finance subsidiaries	$ 41.3	$ 29.1	—
Proceeds on disposal of fixed assets	34.1	31.1	11.3
Extraordinary item (less $31.4 million in 1979 not affecting working capital)	—	64.0	—
Proceeds from long-term debt issues	—	35.8	169.0
Total funds provided	$ 75.4	$160.0	$180.3
Use of funds			
Funds used in operations	$168.4	$ 30.0	$176.2
Reductions in long-term debt	67.1	59.0	158.6
Additions in fixed assets	46.2	76.6	99.3
Other (net)	7.2	(0.7)	18.2
Total funds used	$288.9	$164.9	$452.3
Working capital			
At beginning of year	426.2	431.1	703.1
At end of year	212.7	426.2	431.1
Decrease in working capital	(213.5)	(4.9)	(272.0)
Changes in elements of working capital			
Current assets—increase (decrease):			
Cash	39.0	(6.3)	10.8
Receivables	237.1	174.4	(19.9)
Inventories	(108.7)	13.8	(52.1)
Prepaid expenses and other current assets	3.2	26.0	(8.4)
Total	$170.6	$207.9	$(69.6)
Current liabilities—(increase) decrease:			
Bank borrowing and current portion of long-term debt	(504.3)	(93.8)	(132.2)
Accounts payable and accrued charges	54.3	(156.0)	(55.1)
Accrued charges	59.3		
Income, sales and other taxes payable	6.0	33.4	(5.4)
Advance payments from customers	0.6	3.6	(9.7)
	$(384.1)	$(212.8)	$(202.4)
Decrease in working capital	$(213.5)	$ (4.9)	$(272.0)

Massey's Products

Farm and Industrial Machinery

Massey's farm machinery line consisted of tractors, combine harvesters, balers, forage harvesters, cane harvesters, agricultural implements, farmstead equipment, and other equipment for agricultural use. The industrial

Exhibit 4   10-Year Financial Statement (U.S. $ millions)

	1980	%	1979	%	1978	%	1977	%	1976	%
Sales	$3,132	100%	$2,973	100%	$2,631	100%	$2,862	100%	$2,774	100%
Operating profit[a]	(139)	(4)	(30)	(1)	(133)	(5)	77	3	126	5
Net income[b]	(225)	(7)	37	1	(262)	(10)	32	1	108	4
Assets										
Cash	56	2	17	1	23	1	13	—	7	—
Receivables	968	34	731	27	531	21	542	21	558	24
Inventory	989	35	1,098	40	1,084	43	1,136	44	967	42
Other current assets	93	3	90	3	64	2	81	3	83	4
Current assets	$2,106	74%	$1,936	71%	$1,702	67%	$1,772	68%	$1,615	70%
Net property, plant and equipment	488	17	569	21	602	24	594	23	519	23
Other assets and investments	234	9	241	8	243	9	228	9	171	7
Total assets	$2,828	100%	$2,746	100%	$2,547	100%	$2,594	100%	$2,305	100%
Liabilities										
Bank borrowings	$1,015	36%	$ 512	19%	$ 362	14%	$ 249	10%	$ 113	5%
LTD due in one year	60	2	59	2	115	5	96	4	66	3
Other current liabilities	819	29	938	34	795	31	730	28	704	30
Total current liabilities	$1,894	67%	$1,509	55%	$1,272	50%	$1,075	42%	$ 883	38%
Long-term debt	562	20	625	23	652	26	616	24	529	23
Other liabilities	19	1	33	1	82	3	96	3	90	4
Owners' equity	353	12	579	21	541	21	807	31	803	35
Total liabilities and owners' equity	$2,828	100%	$2,746	100%	$2,547	100%	$2,594	100%	$2,305	100%

(continued)

Exhibit 4 (Continued)

	1975	%	1974	%	1973	%	1972	%	1971	%
Sales	$2,554	100%	$1,791	100%	$1,497	100%	$1,190	100%	$1,029	100%
Operating profit[a]	111	4	—	—	—	—	—	—	—	—
Net income[b]	100	4	—	—	—	—	—	—	—	—
Assets										
Cash	20	1	13	1	8	1	10	1	33	3
Receivables	485	24	433	27	417	33	368	35	339	33
Inventory	878	44	711	44	461	37	362	34	335	33
Other current assets	72	4	66	4	53	4	33	3	31	3
Current assets	$1,455	73%	$1,223	76%	$ 939	75%	$ 773	73%	$ 738	72%
Net property, plant and equipment	401	20	278	17	205	16	180	17	186	19
Other assets and investments	141	7	113	7	105	9	104	10	87	9
Total assets	$1,997	100%	$1,614	100%	$1,249	100%	$1,057	100%	$1,011	100%
Liabilities										
Bank borrowings	$ 170	9%	$ 163	10%	$ 81	6%	$ 139	13%	$ 168	17%
LTD due in one year	47	2	16	1	13	1	11	1	10	1
Other current liabilities	613	31	542	34	406	32	251	24	224	22
Total current liabilities	$ 830	42%	$ 721	45%	$ 500	39%	$ 401	38%	$ 402	40%
Long-term debt	452	23	325	20	244	20	196	18	187	18
Other liabilities	63	3	44	3	35	3	16	1	18	2
Owners' equity	652	32	524	32	470	38	444	43	404	40
Total liabilities and owners' equity	$1,997	100%	$1,614	100%	$1,249	100%	$1,057	100%	$1,011	100%

[a]Operating profit (loss) is defined as total revenue less those recurring expenses that are controllable by management. It excludes extraordinary items, net exchange adjustments, and reorganization expense pertaining to continuing operations.

[b]Prior to 1978, results reflect sales from construction machinery businesses. After 1978, construction machinery is treated as a discontinued operation.

Exhibit 5   Massey-Ferguson Worldwide Sales and Distribution of Capacity by Country, 1980

| | 1980 Sales | | Percentage of Capacity | |
	Amount in U.S. $ millions	%	Farm Equipment	Diesel Engines
North America				
Canada	$ 219	7.0%	27.4%	—
United States	819	26.1	14.6	3.4%
Mexico	75	2.4	—	—
	1,113	35.5	42.0	3.4
Western Europe				
United Kingdom	297	9.5	15.6	76.7
France	227	7.2	10.2	1.0
Italy	211	6.7	8.0	—
West Germany	157	5.0	5.5	—
Spain	8	.3	—	—
Benelux	28	.9	—	—
	928	29.6	39.3	77.7
South America				
Brazil	306	9.8	6.4	17.9
Argentina	44	1.4	1.8	—
	350	11.2	8.2	17.9
Ocenia				
Australia	131	4.2	10.5	1.0
Scandinavia	114	3.6	—	—
South Africa	66	2.1	—	---
Iran	31	1.0	—	—
Pakistan	29	.9	—	—
Japan	25	.8	—	—
Turkey	14	.4	—	—
All other	331	10.6	—	—
Total	$3,132	100.0%	100.0%	100.0%

machinery line consisted of industrial tractors, tractor loaders, tractor/loader/backhoes, rough-terrain forklifts, skid steer loaders, utility loaders, and log skidders. In 1980 Massey held 17 percent of the worldwide market for tractors, 14 percent of the market for combines, and 13 percent of the market for industrial machinery.

Massey's competition in farm and industrial machinery included both large, multinational companies with full product lines and medium-to-small companies conducting business locally with a limited range of products. In the large North American farm equipment market, Massey had traditionally ranked third in sales of farm equipment behind Deere & Co. and International Harvester. However, in 1980 it held first or second position in markets for small (30- to 90-HP) tractors and combine harvesters. (Exhibit 6 compares Massey's sales, operating, and financial data with Deere and Harvester for the years 1976–1980.)

Exhibit 6 Comparative Data on Farm Equipment Producers, 1976–1980 (all income, asset, and liability data in U.S. $ millions)

	1980	1979	1978	1977	1976
Massey-Ferguson Limited					
Sales	$3,132	$2,973	$2,925	$2,805	$2,772
Operating profit[a]	(139)	(30)	(133)	77	126
Net income	(225)	37	(257)	33	118
Assets	2,828	2,746	2,547	2,594	2,305
Short-term debt[b]	1,075	571	477	345	180
Long-term debt	415	478	505	469	529
Equity	353	578	541	807	803
Capital expenditures	$46	$77	$99	$147	$175
Operating profit/sales	(4.44%)	(1.01%)	(4.55%)	2.74%	4.55%
Net income/sales	(7.19%)	1.24%	(8.77%)	1.17%	4.25%
STD/capital[c]	58.33%	35.09%	31.35%	21.29%	11.89%
Total debt/capital	80.85%	64.46%	64.50%	50.24%	46.90%
Sales/assets	1.11	1.08	1.15	1.08	1.20
Coverage[d]	0.46	0.82	0.14	1.42	2.10
Market share[e]	28.19%	27.09%	31.03%	32.08%	33.94%
Capital expenditure share[f]	7.43%	17.22%	24.69%	33.10%	47.80%
International Harvester					
Sales	$6,312	$8,392	$6,664	$5,975	$5,488
Agricultural sales	2,507	3,069	2,348	2,334	2,262
Operating profit, firm[a]	(262)	827	610	531	473
Operating profit, agriculture	(1)	442	288	0	0
Net income	(397)	370	187	204	173
Assets	5,843	5,247	4,316	3,788	3,575
Agricultural assets	1,739	1,548	1,385	0	0
Short-term debt[b]	860	442	380	292	302
Long-term debt	1,327	948	933	926	923
Equity	1,896	2,199	1,876	1,734	1,564
Capital expenditures	$ 384	$ 285	$ 210	$ 164	$ 158
Operating profit/sales	(4.15%)	9.85%	9.15%	8.89%	8.61%
Agricultural operating profit/ agricultural sales	(0.04%)	14.40%	12.25%	—	—
Net income/sales	(6.29%)	4.40%	2.80%	3.41%	3.15%
STD/capital[c]	21.07%	12.31%	11.91%	9.90%	10.84%
Total debt/capital	53.56%	38.73%	41.16%	41.28%	43.93%
Sales/assets	1.08	1.60	1.54	1.58	1.54
Agricultural sales/agricultural assets	1.44	1.98	1.70	—	—
Coverage[d]	0.24	4.92	4.21	4.11	3.66
Market share[e]	22.57%	27.96%	24.90%	26.70%	27.70%
Capital expenditures share[f]	24.62%	23.30%	18.45%	14.43%	17.79%
Deere & Company					
Sales	$5,470	$4,933	$4,155	$3,604	$3,134
Operating profit[a]	470	564	537	483	438
Net income	228	311	265	256	242

(continued)

Exhibit 6   (Continued)

	1980	1979	1978	1977	1976
Deere & Company (Continued)					
Assets	5,202	4,179	3,892	3,429	2,944
Short-term debt[b]	742	202	137	242	134
Long-term debt	702	619	637	482	494
Equity	2,141	1,974	1,756	1,571	1,379
Capital expenditures	$ 421	$ 266	$ 228	$ 233	$ 126
Operating profit/sales	8.59%	11.43%	12.92%	13.40%	13.98%
Net income/sales	4.17%	6.30%	6.37%	7.09%	7.71%
STD/capital[c]	20.69%	7.22%	5.43%	10.55%	6.69%
Total debt/capital	40.28%	29.36%	30.61%	31.55%	31.31%
Sales/assets	1.05	1.18	1.07	1.05	1.06
Coverage[d]	3.19	6.32	6.38	6.32	6.15
Market share[e]	49.24%	44.95%	44.07%	41.22%	38.37%
Capital expenditures share[f]	67.96%	59.48%	56.86%	52.47%	34.41%

[a]Casewriter's estimates. Operating profit excludes extraordinary items, foreign exchange gains or losses, and reorganization expense on continuing operations.

[b]Short-term debt equals bank borrowing plus long-term debt due in one year.

[c]Capital equals long- and short-term debt plus equity.

[d]Coverage is here defined as operating profit plus interest and lease rental expense divided by interest and lease rental expense plus preferred dividends. No adjustment for taxes was made because of the unstable tax status of these companies in this period. As a result, Deere's actual coverage is understated relative to Massey's in all years, as is Harvester's in 1980.

[e]For each company, market share is calculated as own sales (agricultural only for Harvester) divided by total (three company) agricultural sales.

[f]For each company, capital expenditure share is calculated as own capital expenditures divided by total (three company) capital expenditures. Harvester's total capital expenditures are adjusted by the ratio of its agricultural sales to total sales.

Historically, Massey's strength had been in markets outside North America and Western Europe. In less-developed countries, Massey had success in dealing directly with governments or public institutions. During the 1970s Massey entered into agreements to supply farm equipment or construct manufacturing facilities in Peru, Pakistan, Egypt, Iran, Libya, Mozambique, Turkey, Saudi Arabia, Sri Lanka, and the Sudan. In 1974 Massey obtained a $360 million contract to modernize and expand Poland's tractor and diesel engine industry.

Diesel Engines

Diesel engines were produced in England by the Perkins Engine Group. Perkins produced 60 basic models of multicylinder diesel engines in the 30- to 300-brake horsepower range. Perkins engines were used in Massey-Ferguson's equipment and were also sold to manufacturers of a wide variety of agricultural, industrial, and construction equipment. In 1980

Perkins exported 86 percent of its product; over 50 percent of its exports were to Massey-Ferguson's subsidiaries and affiliates.

Because of rising gasoline prices, many auto and equipment manufacturers were expanding research and development in diesel engines. The emerging market for small, high-powered engines used in automobiles and light trucks was particularly promising. Perkins's long-range business plan called for it to maintain and increase its market share in areas such as agriculture vehicles, industrial and construction equipment, and marine craft. Perkins also was engaged in research on the dieselization of gasoline engines and the development of engines capable of operating on a variety of fuels.

Massey's Financial Difficulties

During the 1960s and 1970s, Massey-Ferguson was involved in an ambitious program of acquiring assets and expanding operations. The 1970s were years of dramatic growth financed by debt, much of it short term. By 1978 Massey's debt-to-equity ratio stood at 214 percent (see Exhibit 4). In that year, Massey lost U.S. $262 million. Management attributed the massive loss to (1) the imposition of credit and monetary restrictions in Argentina and Brazil, which caused sharp declines in farm machinery sales; (2) the decline in North American farm prices and incomes; (3) poor weather in Western Europe; and (4) high interest rates, which raised the cost of carrying excess inventory.

Between 1978 and 1980, Massey reacted to the loss by cutting its labor force from 68,000 to 47,000 and its manufacturing space from 30 million to 20 million square feet. The company reduced inventories from U.S. $1,083.2 million to U.S. $988.9 million. Unprofitable operations in the manufacture of office furniture, garden tractors, and construction machinery were eliminated, and 24 plants were closed. The divestment program initiated in 1978 resulted in the sale of more than U.S. $300 million in assets by 1980.

Despite these efforts, in fiscal 1979 Massey's loss on continuing operations was U.S. $35.4 million, or U.S. $2.38 per share; losses from discontinued operations amounted to another U.S. $23.0 million. The company showed a positive net income in 1979 only as a result of an extraordinary item reflecting the recovery of previous years' taxes.

In the first three quarters of fiscal 1980, Massey's financial condition deteriorated even further. At the end of the third quarter, year-to-date losses totaled U.S. $62 million, including an unfavorable currency adjustment of U.S. $37 million. Preliminary reports indicated that Massey's fourth-quarter losses would be as high as those of the three previous quarters combined.

Massey's continuing problems were caused by high interest rates, low demand, lack of alignment between products and markets, and failure to penetrate the North American market.

low demand, lack of alignment between products and markets, and failure to penetrate the North American market.

Interest Rates

The high interest rates of 1979 and 1980 had a double negative impact on Massey's performance. First, the cost of Massey's short-term debt rose dramatically. Second, high interest rates depressed markets for farm and industrial machinery and thus hurt company sales. (See Exhibit 10.)

Demand

The North American market for farm machinery crashed in the fall of 1980. The decline in demand was attributed to high interest rates, an economic recession, the Soviet grain embargo, and a severe drought during the summer of 1980. Because of the recession, European and Third World markets were also severely depressed. (See Exhibit 11.)

The recession made 1980 a difficult year for all farm equipment manufacturers. In North America, both Deere and Harvester experienced reduced sales and profits and showed sharp increases in short- and long-term debt. By the end of 1980, International Harvester was in technical violation of debt covenants and was in the process of negotiating a refinancing plan with its bankers.

Product-Market Alignment

Massey's farm equipment production was in rough regional alignment with its sales. At the margin, North America and the United Kingdom were net suppliers to the rest of the world (see Table A and Exhibit 5). Engine production, however, was heavily concentrated in the United Kingdom. In 1980, with the influx of North Sea oil, the pound rose dramatically relative to currencies in which Massey sold its products. The high price of the pound increased Massey's cost of goods sold, reducing margins and thus hurting the competitiveness of Massey's products.

Lack of alignment between production sites and markets meant that currency fluctuations were a recurring problem for Massey-Ferguson. For example, in 1974 Massey purchased Hanomag, a West German construction equipment manufacturer. The venture was unprofitable in part because the strong German mark made its exports too costly in world markets. In 1980 the Hanomag subsidiary was sold to IBH Holdings for an undisclosed amount.

Massey-Ferguson's product-market alignment would continue to have an unfavorable impact on profits as long as the British pound was strong and the company's operations concentrated in the United Kingdom. However, political risk argued against matching production and sales on a country-by-country basis. Although successful in negotiating directly with Third World and Eastern bloc governments, Massey was vulnerable to changing political conditions in these countries. During the 1970s, several governments with whom Massey had dealings—including Iran, Pakistan, Libya, and Poland—were overthrown as a result of coups or civil unrest.

Economies of scale in engine production also made it advisable to concentrate facilities at a few sites. One possibility discussed within Massey was to relocate capacity at the margin in Canada. Concentration of assets in Canada would bring the company closer to North American markets and make its costs similar to those of Deere and Harvester. Massey already had two large Canadian facilities, forming a base on which it could expand.

North American Efforts

In the 1960s Massey concentrated its marketing and product development efforts overseas. As a result, the company lagged in its development of the high-horsepower tractors and combines desired by farmers in the Canadian and U.S. farm belts.

In 1975 Massey turned its attention to the North American market, introducing a new range of 34- to 81-HP tractors as well as an improved baler line. In 1978 Massey introduced large, high-horsepower tractors in Europe and North America. Management claimed in its 1978 annual report:

> These new products will make Massey-Ferguson fully competitive in North American and European markets and will demonstrate the company's ability to design, produce, and market large tractors as successfully as tractors in the 40- to 90-horsepower range.

Unfortunately, Massey's drive into North America coincided with a depressed market and the beginnings of its own financial difficulties. Doubts about the future of the company eroded sales and weakened the distribution network. During 1980 the number of Massey's dealerships in North America fell by 50 percent—from 3,600 to 1,800.

The Future

Despite these problems, and even though in the fall of 1980 worldwide demand for farm equipment stood at depression levels, management continued to be optimistic about the future. In the 1980 annual report, Rice reaffirmed that the cost-cutting efforts initiated in 1978 had made Massey a viable company. As evidence, he pointed to a 1 percent increase in Massey's world-wide tractor sales over the first nine months of 1980—an increase achieved in spite of the collapse of the North American market (Exhibit 2).

However, in order to take advantage of its long-run opportunities,

Massey had to raise capital to finance its investment programs. New funds were needed for (1) ongoing R&D for new-product development; (2) repair and replacement of existing facilities; (3) reallocation of facilities from the United Kingdom to Canada; (4) penetration of the North American market; (5) defense of markets in Europe and the rest of the world; (6) further growth in the Third World; and (7) Perkins' prospective entry into the market for small diesel engines. It was not known for sure how much would be needed for each of these programs, but, in aggregate, they might require U.S. $500–$700 million over the next five years.

A major unresolved question was the future of the Perkins Engine subsidiary. Perkins was Massey's most valuable salable asset, but at the same time, diesel engines were the company's best hope for profitable future growth. Some thought that Massey should seek to cut its currency exchange losses while concurrently pleasing the governments of Canada and Ontario by setting up diesel engine production in Canada. The possibility of selling Perkins to a third party was also discussed; however, some felt that Perkins's future depended on the existence of a healthy Massey-Ferguson that was able to buy Perkins products.

The most immediate problem, however, was to engineer Massey's survival. By mid-1980 all expenditures except those necessary to continue operations had been suspended in an effort to conserve cash. Despite these efforts, the cash continued to flow out; by September, bank lines were nearly exhausted and the company's position became daily more precarious.

A major restructuring of claims on Massey-Ferguson was necessary. However, to achieve a restructuring, Massey's lenders and major shareholders had to consent to a refinancing plan. By September 1980 top management knew that a default on Massey's existing debt was practically inevitable at the fiscal year end (October 31). Once Massey defaulted, any lender could potentially trigger a worldwide scramble for assets that would bring company operations to a halt. For this reason, the economic interest of each category of claimant had to be carefully considered to be sure that any refinancing plan proposed would be acceptable to all.

The Players

The Banks

As of late fiscal 1980 Massey-Ferguson had total debt of U.S. $1.6 billion outstanding with more than 100 banks around the world. Exhibits 7 and 8 provide a breakdown of Massey's short-term lines of credit and long-term debt. Most of the borrowing was unsecured. In addition, Massey's finance company subsidiaries owed another U.S. $825 million worldwide. Finance company debt usually was not guaranteed, but Massey had agreed to maintain assets in the subsidiaries in certain specified relationships to their indebtedness.

Exhibit 7 Summary of Long-Term Debt Outstanding (U.S. $ millions)

	At Year End October 31	
	1980	1979
***Bonds, debentures, notes, and loans*[a]**		
Massey-Ferguson Perkins S.A. (Brazil): Bank loans maturing 1981–1984 repayable in U.S. dollars bearing interest at ¾% to 2½% above Eurodollar interbank rate	$ 14.3	$ 30.9
Massey-Ferguson S.A. (France): Bank loans maturing 1981–1985 bearing interest at 1.95% above base rate	23.4	24.4
Massey-Ferguson S.p.A. (Italy): Bank loans maturing 1981–1982 repayable in U.S. dollars bearing interest at 1.3% above Eurodollar interbank rate	10.0	10.0
Massey-Ferguson Holding Limited (United Kingdom): 7½% Loan Stock maturing 1986–1992	19.4	16.6
Bank loans maturing 1981–1984 bearing interest at various London bank market rates	34.5	38.6
Massey-Ferguson Inc. (U.S.): 8.55% promissory notes maturing 1981–1984	21.6	26.3
5⅞% Subordinated notes maturing 1981–1984	10.4	12.0
Massey-Ferguson (Delaware) Inc. (U.S.): 9% senior notes maturing 1983–1997	150.0	150.0
Perkins Diesel Corporation (U.S.): Capitalized value of property and equipment lease terminating 1993 discounted at 10%	24.5	25.5
General purpose loans (repayable in U.S. dollars): 9½% debentures maturing 1991[b]	61.5	66.0
9¾% Sinking fund debentures maturing 1981-1982	30.0	32.0
Other long-term debt[c]	75.7	104.8
Total unsubordinated long-term debt	$475.3	$537.1
***Convertible subordinated notes*[d]**		
Massey-Ferguson (Delaware) Inc. (U.S.): 10% convertible subordinated notes maturing 1988–1992	147.0	147.0
Total long-term debt	$622.3	$684.1

[a]Debts are repayable in currency of country indicated unless otherwise shown. Current maturities are included in this summary; maturity dates are for fiscal years ending October 31. As of September 1980, the company had met all contractual sinking fund requirements. An additional $800,000 in sinking fund payments was due in October 1980. Sinking fund requirements and debt maturities during the next five years were as follows: 1981, $60.2 million; 1982, $78.5 million; 1983, $46.3 million; 1984, $54.3 million; 1985, $25.9 million.

[b]The company is obligated to purchase for cancellation up to $4.5 million of these debentures each year to 1986 if the market price goes below par value during the period March 1 to May 31.

[c]Other long-term debt includes long-term loans each of which is less than $10.0 million.

[d]These notes are convertible into common shares of Massey-Ferguson Ltd. at an initial price of U.S. $45.00 per share rising to U.S. $55.00 per share in 1982. There is no dilution of 1980 or 1979 annual results per common share as a result of this convertible feature.

Exhibit 8   Short-Term Credit Lines by Banks at June 30, 1980

	Manufacturing Companies										Corporate Companies[b]				
	Brazil	Argentina	Canada	United States	Australia	France	Eicher GmbH		Italy	United Kingdom Total[a]	Corporate Companies[b]	France	Brazil	Other	Total
CIBC			222.9							3.4					229.9
Barclays										133.4					133.4
Midland										36.2					36.2
Lloyds										36.2					36.2
Citibank		0.5		17.5					3.0	1.1					22.1
Societe Generale						50.1									50.1
Deutsche Bank							5.6	26.6							32.2
Chase Manhattan				15.0											15.0
Credit Lyonnais				3.0		33.0						3.3			39.3
Banque National de Paris			15.0			34.6						3.8			53.4
Continental Illinois				21.0											21.0
Bank of America				17.5	3.3										20.8
Dresdner							3.3	33.3							36.6
Commerzbank							3.9	27.8							31.7
Bankers Trust				13.0											13.0
FNB Chicago				15.0											15.0
Chemical				13.0					1.2						14.2
Allied & Associates											5.0				5.0
Banque Francais du Commerce Exterieur						18.3					12.2	3.3			33.8
Royal Bank of Canada				15.0							5.0				20.0
Toronto Dominion				15.0											15.0
Others	31.2	40.1		48.2	25.5	16.1	15.4	28.9	56.3	19.2	51.8	1.0	7.7	7.0	348.4
Total	31.2	40.6	237.9	193.2	28.8	155.7	28.2	116.6	60.5	229.5	74.0	11.4	7.7	7.0	1,222.3

(continued)

Note: Because of sales seasonality, the maximum use of credit lines usually occurs in June or July. By September 1980, borrowing by manufacturing companies had decreased to approximately U.S. $1.0 billion. Borrowing by finance subsidiaries was down to between U.S. $.8 and $.9 billion.

[a]Includes Perkins U.K.

[b]Includes MF, AG, Agrotrac, MF International, and MF Nederland.

Exhibit 8 (Continued)

		Finance Companies								
	Canada	United States	Australia	Germany	Italy	United Kingdom	Finag	Total	Grand Total	Ranking
CIBC	37.8					27.1		64.9	294.8	1
Barclays						42.5		42.5	175.9	2
Midland						54.3		54.3	90.5	3
Lloyds						42.5		42.5	78.7	4
Citibank		17.5						17.5	39.6	11
Societe Generale						9.0		9.0	59.1	7
Deutsche Bank				3.3				3.3	35.5	13
Chase Manhattan		15.0						15.0	30.0	17
Credit Lyonnais						9.0		9.0	48.3	9
Banque National de Paris			7.8			11.3		19.1	72.5	5
Continental Illinois		21.0			3.8	4.5		29.3	50.3	8
Bank of America		17.5						17.5	38.3	12
Dresdner				3.3				3.3	39.9	10
Commerzbank				3.3				3.3	35.0	14
Bankers Trust		13.0						13.0	26.0	20
FNB Chicago		15.0						15.0	30.0	17
Chemical		13.0						13.0	27.2	19
Allied & Associates						18.5	45.0	63.5	68.5	6
Banque Francais du Commerce Exterieur									33.8	15
Royal Bank of Canada						11.3		11.3	31.3	16
Toronto Dominion						6.8		6.8	21.8	21
Others		78.1	23.4	7.8	81.2	50.8		241.3	589.7	
Total	37.8	190.1	31.2	17.7	85.0	287.6	45.0	694.4	1,916.7	

As Exhibits 7 and 8 show, Massey's borrowings were dispersed among lenders in Canada, Great Britain, West Germany, France, Italy, and the United States. Except for a consortium of U.S. banks that had issued a revolving credit, most lenders operated independently of one another. The numerous covenants related to these loans hampered Massey's free access to the capital markets. For example, before Massey could issue new preferred shares (as it had proposed to do in April 1980), it had to pay accumulated preferred dividends, which were U.S. $14 million in arrears as of December 1979. But, since March 1978 when Massey announced first losses, covenants on certain U.S. loans had caused dividends to both preferred and common shares to be suspended.

The Canadian Imperial Bank of Commerce was Massey's largest lender, with an aggregate exposure estimated at between Can. $200 million and $300 million. Commerce had ties not only to Massey-Ferguson but to Massey's largest shareholder, Argus Corporation. Conrad Black, Massey's chairman from 1978 to 1980 and president of Argus from 1978, was made a director of the bank in 1980.

Argus Corporation

Since the 1960s, Argus Corporation, a Canadian holding company, had owned a controlling interest in Massey-Ferguson. Argus's philosophy was to make major investments in a small number of promising enterprises. In 1956, shortly after Massey Harris merged with the Ferguson Company to become Massey-Ferguson, several Argus directors had played a major role in saving the newly formed company from bankruptcy by forcing it to liquidate certain assets and cut its prices on farm equipment. In 1980 Argus held 16.5 percent of the outstanding shares. Six of the eighteen board members were Argus appointees.

In 1978 Conrad Black, age 34, son of one of the founders of Argus, took over as president of Argus and, as a result, became chairman of the board of Massey-Ferguson. Black picked Victor Rice to succeed Albert Thornburgh as Massey's president; two years later in 1980, Black relinquished the chairmanship of Massey to Rice.

Argus was considered by the financial community to be a potential source of equity capital for Massey, but Black's public comments on the company were highly equivocal. In a 1979 interview, Black indicated that Argus was "not interested in putting up a lot of money and staying at 16 percent." He expressed surprise that Massey's lenders kept approaching him for advice when Argus held only 16 percent of the stock and was therefore much less exposed than the major lenders. There were also perennial rumors that "Conrad Black has been trying to peddle Massey-Ferguson's stock."

In April 1980 a preferred stock issue was postponed, in part because Argus was reluctant to take a block of shares. Chairman Black was quoted as saying, "We could finance the company tomorrow. I'm not going to get panicky. We're good for another year." Black also maintained that he was willing to contribute Can. $100 million to $500 million to Massey-Ferguson "on the right terms."

Other Preferred and Common Shareholders

Massey had two issues of preferred stock outstanding—Series A and B. Each had a liquidation value of $25 per share and was entitled to annual cumulative dividends of $2.50 per share. A total of 1,526,300 shares of Series A preferred had been issued in April 1975, followed by 2,298,500 shares of Series B in March of 1976. The purpose of each issue was "to reduce [Massey's] short-term debt." Dividends on the preferred shares were suspended in 1978. Indentures provided that after a failure to pay dividends for eight quarters, shareholders of each class of preferred stock would have the right to elect two members to Massey's board of directors. Board representation was attained by Series B shareholders in March 1980 and by Series A shareholders in April 1980.

Massey's 18,250,000 shares of common stock were listed on the New York, London, Toronto, Montreal, and Vancouver stock exchanges. From January 1976 through July 31, 1980, Massey lost 16⅞ points per share, or 69 percent of market value (see Exhibit 9). Over the same period, the New York Stock Exchange Composite index gained 30 percent.

The Governments of Canada, Ontario, and The United Kingdom

For some time Rice and Black had been trying to convince the governments of Canada, Ontario, and the United Kingdom to intervene on Massey's behalf. Massey had approached the Trudeau and Thatcher governments for aid as early as June 1980. The governments were anxious to avoid a loss of jobs (6,700 in Ontario and 17,000 in the combined Massey and Perkins operations in the United Kingdom); but in both Canada and the United Kingdom, there was strong resistance to bailing out a privately-owned multinational. Talks with the governments were continuing, but very little progress had been made and time was rapidly running out.

The Situation: The Fourth Quarter of 1980

In August 1980 the international financial press reported that the Canadian governments were considering some form of financial assistance for Massey. It was said that Rice hoped to make a positive announcement when Massey released its third-quarter results in September. Black was quoted:

It's fair to assume that if there isn't any indication of possibility of some equity when third-quarter results are released, the situation could be-

Exhibit 9   Financial Markets Data (prices as of last trading day)

	Massey-Ferguson Common	NYSE Composite[a]		Massey-Ferguson Common	NYSE Composite[a]
1980			**1977**		
October	5½	$73.53	December (.25 div)	14½	$52.50
September	6⅓	72.38	November	14½	52.36
August	7⅞	70.53	October	16½	50.65
July	7⅝	69.64	September (.25 div)	17	52.81
June	6¾	65.34	August	16½	52.93
May	7⅜	63.44	July	19⅜	54.12
April	7½	60.36	June (.25 div)	19⅞	55.10
March	8⅜	57.65	May	20⅜	52.56
February	9½	64.95	April	20¼	53.66
January	10⅛	65.91	March (.25 div)	19⅜	53.53
			February	19¼	54.23
1979			January	21	55.48
December	10¼	61.95			
November	9⅛	60.71	**1976**		
October	8⅝	57.71	December (.33 div)	21¾	57.88
September	10½	62.24	November	20	54.80
August	11⅛	62.40	October	23⅛	54.89
July	12	59.14	September (.25 div)	22¾	56.23
June	12⅝	58.38	August	26¼	54.92
May	11	55.99	July	28⅜	55.26
April	11¼	57.36	June (.25 div)	28¾	55.71
March	11¾	57.13	May	27	53.31
February	10⅜	53.93	April	26¾	54.11
January	9⅜	55.99	March (.25 div)	27¾	54.80
			February	27⅞	53.35
1978			January	24½	53.55
December	8¾	53.62			
November	9¼	52.89			
October	9½	51.63			
September	11	57.78			
August	10½	58.35			
July	10⅜	56.59			
June	10½	53.66			
May	11¼	54.52			
April	10½	53.90			
March	9	49.85			
February	9½	48.43			
January[b]	13½	49.41			

[a]NYSE composite does not include dividends.
[b]Dividends omitted after December 1977.

results as talks continued with the Canadian governments. By October, Massey and its finance subsidiaries had debt of U.S. $2.5 billion outstanding to 150 banks worldwide, and speculation on the probability of Massey's survival was rampant.

Only a few weeks remained before the November 1 deadline when Massey would be technically in default on several loans. Cross-default

Exhibit 10   Massey-Ferguson 1980

World Short-Term Interest Rates

	1977	1978	1979	1980	1981	1982
Canada	7.5	8.8	12.1	13.2	18.3	14.2
U.S.	5.3	7.2	10.1	11.4	14.0	10.6
U.K.	8.2	9.2	13.7	16.6	13.9	12.3
France	9.2	8.2	9.5	12.2	15.3	14.7
Germany	4.4	3.7	6.7	9.5	12.1	8.9
Italy	14.9	11.1	13.5	15.9	19.6	19.4

Massey-Ferguson's Estimated Cost of Short-Term Credit*

	1977	1978	1979	1980	1981	1982
M-F	8.0	8.1	11.8	14.0	15.5	13.1

Sources: IMF, *World Economic Outlook*, 1985.

*Author's estimates using weights based on Massey-Ferguson's actual proportions of short-term credit raised in each national market in 1980. Approximate weights are U.K. (27%), U.S. (20%), Canada (15%), France (9%), Germany (8%), Italy (8%), and others (13%).

Exhibit 11   Massey-Ferguson, 1980

World Economic Growth (Real GNP)

	Avg. 1967–76	1977	1978	1979	1980	1981
World	4.5	4.5	4.4	3.5	2.0	1.6
U.S.	2.8	5.5	5.0	2.8	−0.3	2.5
Canada	4.8	2.0	3.6	3.2	1.1	3.3
Europe	6.0	5.4	5.4	3.8	1.6	2.5
U.K.	2.2	3.0	4.0	3.2	−2.6	−1.4
Germany	3.5	2.8	3.4	4.0	1.9	−0.2
France	4.7	3.1	3.8	3.3	1.1	0.2
Italy	4.3	1.9	2.7	4.9	3.9	0.2
Africa	5.0	4.3	1.4	4.2	3.7	0.9
Asia	5.2	7.2	9.4	4.8	4.7	5.8
Mid-East	9.3	6.9	1.9	1.8	−1.8	−0.7

Source: IMF, *World Economic Outlook*, 1985.

provisions made substantially all outstanding loans callable if any single default occurred. Suddenly, on October 2, 1980, Argus donated its 16.5 percent controlling interest to Massey-Ferguson's two pension funds. This move made Massey the world's largest employee-controlled corporation and resulted in a Can. $23 million tax write-off for Argus. On the same day, the government of Canada announced it would "work closely" with Massey to achieve a refinancing.

Two weeks later, on October 20, 1980, the governments of Canada

and resulted in a Can. $23 million tax write-off for Argus. On the same day, the government of Canada announced it would "work closely" with Massey to achieve a refinancing.

Two weeks later, on October 20, 1980, the governments of Canada and Ontario announced they had reached an agreement in principle with Massey and its major lenders:

> The governments are prepared to guarantee the capital risk of a portion of the new equity investment in Massey, providing various conditions are met, including a satisfactory degree of cooperation from the existing lenders.[2]

The press attributed the governments' actions to the upcoming Ontario provincial election and the need to protect jobs. According to the *Economist* (October 26, 1980):

> While the federal government is Liberal, Ontario is still Conservative. . . . It needs both the Massey jobs and Mr. Black, a Conservative supporter, who is in favor of more Massey investment in Canada. . . . Meanwhile, the Trudeau government is trying to use Massey to help its constitutional plans.[3]

However, other press reports indicated that the governments had been forced to act, and "in effect [they are] still supplying only inexpensive moral support for the company at this time."

On October 31 Massey-Ferguson closed its books on fiscal year 1980. The loss for the year (subsequently reported) amounted to U.S. $225.2 million, or $12.79 per share. Scheduled principal repayments were suspended in October; interest payments were suspended on December 1, 1980.

Massey-Ferguson began fiscal year 1981 in default on its $2.5 billion of outstanding debt. The company's future depended on the ability of lenders, the governments of Canada and Ontario, and management to agree on a feasible refinancing plan. In the course of the continuing negotiations, serious questions were raised about Massey's long-term ability to compete in its industry. Persons close to the situation wondered what sort of restructuring would allow the company to survive, and whether Massey would ever regain its status as a self-sufficient corporation.

---

[2] *Wall Street Journal,* October 21, 1980.

[3] The repatriation of the Constitution was a major political issue in Canada in 1980 and 1981.

Questions

1. How would you evaluate Massey-Ferguson's product-market and financial strategy? Is it internally consistent? Did it fit with the external environment?

2. How does Massey-Ferguson's strategy change the competitive environment and the options available to International Harvester and John Deere?

CASE 6
Franklin Savings Association

There are two fundamental issues raised by the Franklin Savings Association case. First, at the firm level, is the issue of interest rate risk and how best to manage it. Second, at the public policy level, is the issue of the savings and loan crisis and how we got into such a mess. As we will see by the end of the case, these two issues are not unrelated.

In the last chapter, interest rates affected Massey-Ferguson most directly through its liabilities, since interest rates are the cost of its debt. When the firm was unable to generate sufficient cash to meet its interest rate obligations, financial insolvency followed. But changes in interest rates will also affect the returns and prices of the asset side of a firm's balance sheet as well, though not necessarily by the same amount as its effect on liabilities. You will remember that an asset's return or its interest rate is inversely related to its price. The most sensitive type of firm to interest rate fluctuations is a financial firm, since financial assets and liabilities comprise the bulk of its balance sheet.

Interest rate risk is the gain or loss resulting from changes in interest rates when a financial firm's assets do not mature at the same time as its liabilities. Since not all interest rates rise and fall by exactly the same amount nor do they change with the same frequency, there is a danger that interest rates will rise faster on liabilities than on assets, thus causing a squeeze on profits. This was the central problem for all financial institutions in the early 1980s, including Franklin Savings. The case discusses different approaches to managing interest rate risk. In the process of evaluating the situation facing Franklin Savings, one can better understand why savings and loan institutions ran up such large losses during the past decade.

Between 1979 and 1982, Franklin Savings Association of Ottawa, Kansas, suffered from rising interest rates. See Exhibit 1 for the pattern of interest rates in the 1980s. Franklin, like all thrifts, funded its asset portfolio of long-term fixed rate mortgages with short-term liabilities, primarily deposits. Consequently, they were vulnerable when rising interest rates squeezed their profit margins. In fiscal 1982, largely as a result of those rising interest rates, Franklin lost $4 million, the biggest loss in the company's 93-year history.

Earlier that year, Franklin's directors, including Ernest Fleischer, a major Association shareholder, adopted a new strategy that would make Franklin one of the most successful thrift institutions in the 1980s, in contrast to the disastrous losses of other thrifts during that time. Fleischer employed hedging techniques that became singularly responsible for Franklin's growth in assets from $402 million in 1982 to over $13 billion in 1988 (a compounded annual growth rate of 79 percent). During that same period, Franklin's return on equity, measured under generally accepted accounting principles (GAAP), had averaged 53 percent compared to the thrift industry's average of just over 3 percent and an 11 percent average for companies in Standard & Poor's top index. See Exhibit 2 for financial ratios of savings institutions in the United States. In 1988, with interest rates rising again, Fleischer was counting on Franklin's continued success at balancing interest rate risk.

Evolution of the Thrift Industry

The structure of the thrift industry was established by Congress in 1932. Patterned after Britain's building societies, thrifts started out as public-spirited local organizations that accepted savings from members and then made mortgage loans to help people in the community buy houses. The thrifts took short-term deposits and used them to make 15-, 20-, and 30-year mortgages. At that time, thrifts were considered the key to the American dream of home ownership. Approximately 80 percent of their assets were mortgage loans and 20 percent were short-term government securities. Liabilities were savings deposits and some debt from loans made by the Federal Home Loan Bank Board (Bank Board), the major regulatory agency governing thrifts. Since 1934, the Federal Savings and Loan Insurance Corporation (FSLIC) had guaranteed deposits in thrift institutions.

From 1935 to 1965, there was little change in the regulatory structure of the industry. However, substantial growth in assets occurred and the industry underwent a wave of consolidation. At the end of 1935, there

This case was prepared by Research Associate Julia Horn under the supervision of Professor Michael G. Rukstad. Copyright © 1989 by the President and Fellows of Harvard College. Harvard Business School Case 9-389-098.

Exhibit 1   U.S. Interest Rates

Money Market Rates
Monthly Averages of Daily Figures

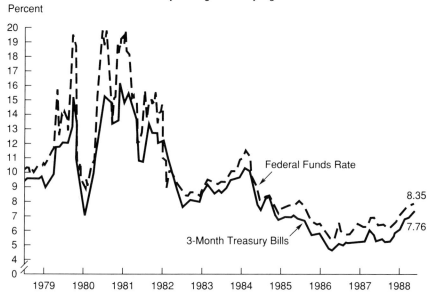

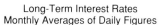

Long-Term Interest Rates
Monthly Averages of Daily Figures

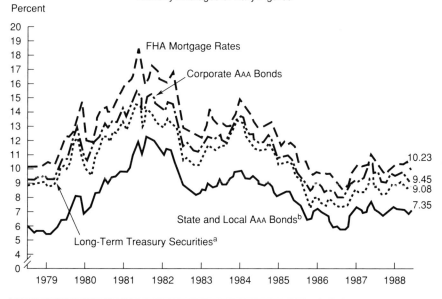

Latest Data Plotted: November

[a]Average of yields on coupon issues due or callable in ten years or more. Excluding issues with federal estate tax privileges; computed by the Federal Reserve Bank of St. Louis.

[b]Monthly averages of Thursday figures.

Exhibit 2   Significant Ratios of Federally Insured Savings Institutions, 1960–1986

Year	Asset Utilization[a]	Profit Margin[b] Percent	Return on Equity[c] Percent	Return on Average Assets[d] Percent
1960	5.55	15.55	12.35	0.86
1965	5.72	11.63	9.83	0.67
1970	6.60	8.56	8.02	0.57
1971	6.93	10.24	10.51	0.71
1972	7.02	11.01	12.14	0.77
1973	7.34	10.31	12.15	0.76
1974	7.63	7.03	8.63	0.54
1975	7.73	6.06	7.82	0.47
1976	8.01	7.87	11.10	0.63
1977	8.23	9.32	13.94	0.77
1978	8.50	9.57	14.84	0.82
1979	9.08	7.37	12.06	0.67
1980	9.60	1.38	2.44	0.13
1981	10.48	−6.96	−15.44	−0.73
1982	11.27	−5.64	−16.13	−0.65
1983	11.20	2.34	6.77	0.27
1984	11.66	1.05	3.15	0.12
1985	11.49	3.27	9.14	0.39
1986	10.70	0.93	2.24	0.09

[a]Total income divided by average assets (net of loans in process or contra-assets).

[b]Net after-tax income divided by total income.

[c]Net after-tax income divided by average net worth.

[d]Net after-tax income divided by average assets (net of loans in process or contra-assets).

Note: Beginning in 1982, average assets exclude certain contra-asset balances that had been reported as liabilities.

Sources: Federal Home Loan Bank Board, United States League of Savings Institutions.

were 10,266 thrifts with combined assets of $6 billion; by the end of 1965, only 6,185 thrifts were in existence with total assets of $130 billion. Congress passed the Interest Rate Adjustment Act in 1966, which gave the Bank Board the power to set ceilings on interest rates for thrifts' deposit accounts (known as Regulation Q), and the ability to grant higher ceilings for thrifts than for commercial banks. The purpose of this act was to prevent competition among thrifts for deposits and to contain the rise in the cost of funds as market interest rates rose. However, the result of the interest rate ceilings was to encourage depositors to withdraw their funds from thrifts offering a ceiling rate of interest and instead to purchase directly primary market securities with their higher interest rates—a process known as disintermediation. Throughout the 1970s, the interest rate ceilings were raised several times, often not enough to cover peaks in market interest rates.

Major changes were occurring on the asset side of thrifts' balance sheets as well. By the 1980s, thrifts held fewer mortgage loans in their portfolios, as they were supplanted by the explosive growth of mortgage-backed securities. See Exhibit 3. A mortgage-backed security was a pool of loans secured by mortgages in which interest and principal on the underlying mortgages were passed through to investors in order to pay principal and interest on the mortgage-backed security itself. A variety of lenders were making loans directly to customers, many of which then in turn sold those loans on a thriving secondary market. The initiators of mortgage loans had changed in the 1980s as shown in Exhibit 4. A second major change, authorized by the Bank Board in 1981, was the approval of adjustable-rate mortgages (ARMs), which were supposed to minimize interest rate risk for lenders.

Exhibit 3   Annual MBS/CMO Issuance, 1970–86 ($ millions)

	GNMA MBS[a]	FHLMC Pcs[b]	FNMA MBS[a]	Agency MBS Total	CMOs Issued[d]	Agency MBS and CMO Total
1970	452	—	—	452	—	452
1971	2,702	65	—	2,767	—	2,767
1972	2,662	494	—	3,156	—	3,156
1973	2,953	323	—	3,276	—	3,276
1974	4,553	46	—	4,599	—	4,599
1975	7,447	450	—	7,897	—	7,897
1976	13,764	960	—	14,724	—	14,724
1977	17,440	4,057	—	21,497	—	21,497
1978	15,358	5,712	—	21,070	—	21,070
1979	24,940	3,796	—	28,736	—	28,736
1980	20,647	2,526	—	23,173	—	23,173
1981	14,257	3,529	717	18,503	—	18,503
1982	16,012	24,169	13,970	54,151	—	54,151
1983	50,496	19,691	13,340	83,527	4,680	88,207
1984	27,857	18,684	13,546	60,087	10,765	70,852
1985	45,868	38,829	23,649	108,346	16,015	124,361
1986	98,169	99,963	60,556	258,698	48,315	307,013
All-time Totals	265,576	223,294	125,788	714,658	79,775	794,433

[a]GNMA is the Government National Mortgage Association (Ginnie Mae). Ginnie Mae carries out Federal government housing policy, administering a special assistance loan program and a mortgage-backed securities (MBS) program backed by a government guarantee.

[b]FHLMC is the Federal Home Loan Mortgage Corp. (Freddie Mac). Freddie Mac is a Congressionally chartered corporation that purchases mortgages in the secondary mortgage market from S&Ls, banks, and mortgage bankers. It sells mortgage participation certificates (PCs) secured by pools of conventional mortgage loans.

[c]FNMA is the Federal National Mortgage Association (Fannie Mae). It is a Congressionallly chartered corporation with private stockholders. It raises funds to purchase residential mortgages through the sale of mortgage-backed securities.

[d]CMOs, or collateralized mortgages, are a type of bond that is backed by mortgages. The first CMO was issued by Freddie Mac in 1983.

Source: Compiled by Financial World Publications.

Exhibit 4   Orginations of Long Term Mortgage Loans: Percentage Originated by Selected Lenders (Percent)

Year	Mortgage Bankers	Savings & Loans	Commercial Banks	Others[a]
1960	19.3	50.9	13.2	16.6
1965	21.3	44.8	21.0	12.9
1970	25.0	41.6	21.9	11.5
1972	17.5	48.4	23.3	10.8
1974	19.3	45.8	23.9	11.0
1976	14.0	54.9	21.7	9.4
1978	18.6	48.6	23.7	9.1
1979	24.2	44.2	22.1	9.5
1980	22.0	45.7	21.5	10.8
1981	24.4	42.7	22.1	10.8
1982	29.4	36.7	24.5	9.4
1983	28.8	42.1	28.7[b]	0.4
1984	22.9	49.4	27.3[b]	0.4
1985	23.5	44.5	20.2	11.8
1986	29.8	39.8	20.5	9.9

[a]Includes mutual savings banks, life insurance companies, and federal, state, and local credit agencies.

[b]Due to lack of detailed information, figures for 1983 and 1984 include mutual savings banks.

Interest Rate Volatility and Deregulation

Many of the structural problems in the thrift industry that had been present since the 1930s began to be generally observed in 1979. Early in that year, some of the tight regulations that had governed the thrift industry were relaxed. The most important change was the relaxation of some of the interest rate ceilings on deposit accounts. Federal regulators authorized market-related interest rates on specific six-month money market certificate accounts. Within a year, this type of account represented 20% of total thrift deposits. With these changes, thrifts became extremely vulnerable to interest rate increases. On October 6, 1979, in an effort to stop the double-digit inflation, Chairman Paul Volcker of the Federal Reserve Board of Governors announced his decision to target the money supply and to allow interest rates to rise to whatever level was necessary to meet his target. Short-term interest rates quickly rose to 20 percent. The rising interest rates increased the cost of savings deposits faster than the thrifts could increase interest rates on their mortgages. Thrifts faced substantial interest rate risk because they were unable to change the rates they offered on fixed-rate mortgages that they then owned to keep up with the rates they had to pay on savings deposits.

    In 1980, Congress passed the Depository Institutions Deregulation and Monetary Control Act (DIDMCA). The landmark legislation dictated three broad provisions that applied to all depository institutions (banks, thrifts, mutual savings banks, and credit unions). One provision applicable to thrifts was that all remaining deposit ceilings (Regulation Q) would be completely phased out by March 1986. A second provision allowed for all depository institutions to offer interest-paying checking accounts (for example, NOW accounts), granting broader fund-raising powers to thrifts. The final provision provided for uniform reserve requirements across all depository institutions. That meant that all would have the same borrowing privileges at the Federal Reserve. In addition to the deregulation efforts on the national level, several states, most notably California, Florida, and Texas, passed their own, even more sweeping, deregulatory provisions in an attempt to protect the interests of their state-chartered thrifts.

Changes in accounting methods were also the result of relaxed Bank Board regulations that began in 1980. Thrifts, like most major public corporations, used Generally Accepted Accounting Principles (GAAP) for accounting purposes. In 1980, however, the Bank Board instituted its own accounting rules called Regulatory Accounting Principles (RAP) to evaluate the net worth positions of thrifts. Though both methods relied on book rather than market values, RAP allowed the financial statement issuer to adopt methods that increase the carrying value of assets and the amount of income. For example, RAP allowed for the continued deferral of losses even after the loss-producing asset was sold, rather than recognizing the loss at the time of the asset's sale as required by GAAP. This encouraged thrifts to dispose of assets created in the 1970s (i.e. mortgages made at low, fixed interest rates) by selling them at a deep discount in order to take advantage of this accounting anomaly.

Consequently, in the early 1980s, RAP net worth figures were always higher as a percentage of assets than GAAP net worth figures. That distinction was important because, beginning in 1980, the Bank Board used RAP net worth figures to judge whether or not a thrift was insolvent. The Bank Board did not close a thrift until its RAP net worth was less than zero. As a result of the Bank Board's accounting regulations, many thrifts that would have been insolvent under GAAP rules were allowed to continue to operate under RAP rules and generate further GAAP losses.

By the end of 1980, the economic effectiveness of regulations governing the thrift industry continued to diminish. Weak thrifts were bidding up savings rates to win deposits, raising the thrift industry's cost of funds, which already exceeded the interest they earned on mortgages. Analysts attributed this move to the relaxation of the deposit insurance ceiling from $40,000, a level which was still subject to Regulation Q interest rate ceilings, to $100,000, a level which had never been subject to Regulation Q. Even if thrifts took big risks and lost large amounts of money, the depositors knew that the government would protect them. Despite the increasingly higher Regulation Q rates permitted for thrifts (before Regulation Q was phased out in 1986), the average market rates paid by money market mutual funds were still three percentage points higher during the early 1980s.

Record Losses for the Thrift Industry in the 1980s

In 1981, the industry had its first year of negative profits, as U.S. thrifts lost over $4 billion (even as measured under RAP) and the industry witnessed the first in a series of thrift crises of the 1980s. The following year was no better for the industry. In 1982, losses exceeded the $4 billion level again as more than 450 thrifts failed or were declared insolvent by the Bank Board. Many analysts cited the rising cost of funds as the leading cause of those failures. The average cost of funds for thrifts had risen from 7 percent in 1978 to more than 11 percent in 1982. See Exhibit 5 for thrift spreads and insolvencies. Congress also passed the Garn-St. Germain Depository Institutions Act in 1982, which further expanded thrifts' asset powers by permitting them to enter new businesses similar to those offered by commercial banks, such as commercial lending. It also allowed all federally-chartered thrifts to operate across all states. The idea was to let the industry diversify its asset portfolio and shore up its finances.

After the two years of record losses, the thrift industry had a positive net income of $2 billion in 1983 as interest rates began to fall. However, the industry's illness was thinly disguised. To counter net operating losses of $11 billion during 1981 and 1982, thrifts sold appreciated assets (resulting from the sharp fall in interest rates from their high 1981 and 1982 levels) that were valued on their balance sheets at original cost and recorded the gains as nonoperating income. Net nonoperating income rose from $957 million in 1981 to over $2.5 billion in both 1982 and 1983. This return to profitability was more of an illusion than a reality for many

Exhibit 5   Thrift Spreads and Insolvencies 1980–1987

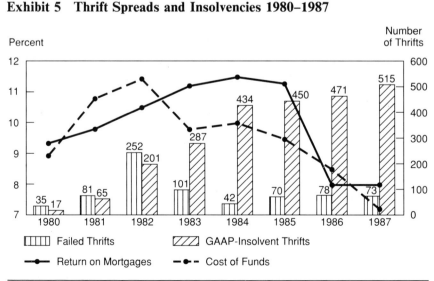

Source: Federal Home Loan Bank Board

thrifts. It reflected the incentives and effects of using not only book value as opposed to market value, but of using RAP instead of GAAP rules.

Despite the fall in interest rates that began after 1982, many insolvent thrifts suffered from the coinciding deflation in real estate, primarily in the Southwest, and particularly in Texas. Because Texas regulators had further broadened the powers of state-chartered thrifts, many had tied up their asset portfolios in local real estate development. At the beginning of 1983, there were enough office buildings planned or underway in Dallas alone to house the entire work force of Minneapolis. Critics also pointed to the influx of newcomers that came to Texas to take advantage of the state's liberalized thrift regulations, often engaging in fraudulent practices. At the same time the recession hit, the Southwest was also buffeted by falling oil prices. In the affected areas, many of the thrifts that had sold assets in 1982 to produce nonoperating income were left with deteriorating assets. Even those thrifts that had survived without asset sales were weakened by deflation and regional recession.

Later in 1983, thrifts' cost of funds fell below the return on their assets for the first time since 1980. Many thrifts took advantage of the recent changes in regulations and restructured their assets and liabilities. They tried to lengthen the maturity of their liabilities by using Bank Board advances and interest rate swaps. On the asset side, they tried to shorten the maturity of their assets. This involved holding a greater percentage of adjustable-rate mortgages, selling off fixed-rate loans, and diversifying into shorter-term assets such as credit card loans or floating-rate assets such as commercial real estate loans. Some thrifts also began to shift their asset mix away from mortgage loans toward investment securities. Restructuring, though it improved interest rate mismatches, created another problem—the quality of assets. "Thrifts with little skill in assessing the risk of such ventures as commercial real estate bet big that the pie in the sky deals on hotels, shopping malls, and office buildings would pay off. Some thrifts, realizing the deals would probably go bad, lent money anyway, hoping that local economic expansion or inflation would bail them out."[1] See Exhibit 6.

In 1984, the condition of the thrift industry continued to weaken. Though the number of failed institutions dropped to 41 in 1984 from 102 in 1983, the number of GAAP insolvent institutions continued to increase. In addition, the number of RAP insolvent thrifts (RAP net worth of less than zero) rose steadily from 80 in 1982 to nearly 250 in 1985. Beginning in 1985, the Bank Board tried to institute regulatory changes to reverse the loose accounting measures that had been permitted in an effort to restore credibility to the industry's balance sheets. It approved regulations that limited the direct investment that thrifts could make in building projects, limited the amount they could grow each year,

---

[1]Jeffrey N. Tuchman, *Latest Innovations in the U.S. Mortgage Market.* (The Economist Intelligence Unit, 1987), p. 93.

Exhibit 6   Risky Loans of GAAP Insolvent S&Ls: Real Estate and Other High Risk Lending

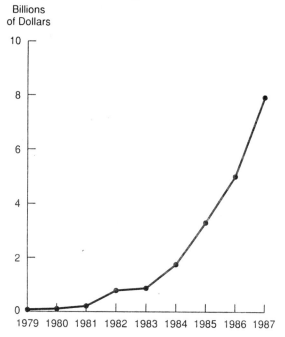

Source: Federal Home Loan Bank Board

phased in increases in capital requirements to 6 percent, phased out RAP accounting principles, and returned to the more stringent GAAP practices. Despite these measures, which many in the industry argued were too few and too late, by 1986, an additional 485 thrifts were GAAP insolvent, and 83 thrifts failed. In total, 33 percent of assets ($381 billion) were in institutions with GAAP net worth of 3 percent or less.

Troubles with the Deposit Insurance System

In 1986, to further weaken the industry's health, FSLIC's net worth plummeted, as the insurance provider also became insolvent. After nearly two years of insolvency, Congress approved legislation in August 1987 that allowed FSLIC to borrow over $10.8 billion from the government over three years to close down thrifts in order to stem mounting losses. By the end of 1987, almost one-third of the country's thrifts were losing money, a staggering total of $6.8 billion in 1987 alone. In that year, 588 thrifts failed or became insolvent. Meanwhile, hundreds of those insolvent thrifts continued to operate while draining the reserves of the healthy thrifts. The industry continued to show signs of deterioration in 1988. With FSLIC's net worth $13.7 billion in the red, it was estimated that it would take at least three years for the Bank Board to close crippled thrifts, providing it had replenished reserves.

To avoid complete collapse, FSLIC continued to tax profitable thrifts with what it called, "special assessments." In 1988 alone, healthy thrifts paid $1.2 billion in extra insurance premiums, or half of their total earnings, driving up their "all-in" cost of funds. Those premiums went to help the 515 thrifts that became insolvent in 1988. Nearly 50 percent of the year's insolvent thrifts were located in California, Florida, and Texas. In Texas alone, it was estimated that it would cost $50 billion to close all of the state's troubled thrifts, which made up nearly 50 percent of the state's total thrift institutions. Though part of the state's failures and insolvencies had their roots in fraud, the majority of problems were the result of large investments in Texas real estate, which plunged in value with the drop in oil prices in 1986.

Because of the number of troubled Texas thrifts, the state served as a model for what the Bank Board called its Southwest Plan. The Plan's goal was to liquidate, sell, or merge more than 100 insolvent Texas thrifts. It offered buyers of failed thrifts a chance to bet on Texas property with no risk of loss. FSLIC not only agreed to pay an exorbitant income on greatly devalued thrift assets for ten years, but agreed to guarantee the principal. McKinsey and Company estimated that the cost to the taxpayer of the guarantees contained in the Plan was, at the very least, between $15 and $30 billion for Texas alone. McKinsey's calculations for the whole thrift industry showed that in 1988, the total assets of unhealthy thrifts grew to $423 billion, or 34 percent of the industry's total assets.

In addition to the benefits offered to thrift buyers under the Southwest Plan, FSLIC began to offer incentives to nonbankers that would encourage purchases. For example, companies as diverse as Ford Motor Company and Kinder-Care Learning Centers, acquired thrifts. In 1987, Ford acquired First Nationwide Bank of San Francisco, the industry's sixth largest thrift. In 1988, billionaire Robert Bass acquired the ailing American Savings and Loan of California, then the nation's second largest thrift. Bass agreed to pump $550 million in new capital into American and acquired the thrift with $2 billion in federal aid. In another case, Trammel Crow Company, a leading Dallas-based real estate company, was part of a team that acquired three Texas thrifts. The team agreed to invest $75 million up front and to raise their investment to $128 million by 1991. FSLIC contributed $1.5 billion in assistance, including a $710 million note, and capital and income guarantees on certain assets.

The Magnitude of the Thrift Crisis

The future of the thrift industry in 1988 was uncertain, but most experts believed that taxpayers faced the largest government bailout of all time. Estimates ranged from $150 to $200 billion, dwarfing the $50 billion (in 1988 dollars) that Americans spent after World War II to rebuild Western

Europe under the Marshall Plan. See Exhibit 7. Experts believed that the most important statistic in measuring the size of the bailout was the difference between the unhealthy thrifts' liabilities and their earning assets. According to McKinsey estimates, that amount had risen from $39 billion in 1987 to $59 billion in 1988, with a strong possibility that the figure could grow to $109 billion by the end of 1989. With the 1988 U.S. federal budget deficit of $155 billion, Washington was not well positioned to pay the industry's bill.

In 1988, there were almost 1000 FSLIC-insured thrifts with GAAP net worth of less than 3 percent. This group consisted of insolvent (one-third of the group) or near-insolvent (two-thirds) thrifts whose performance had declined despite falling interest rates through most of the 1980s. The remaining 2,237 FSLIC-insured thrifts, with assets of approximately $800 billion, were responsible for any profits that the industry had posted since 1982. A number of different investment strategies had contributed to the success of the firms in the second group. One of the most successful was the strategy used by Ernest Fleischer, chairman of Franklin Savings Association.

Franklin Savings Association

Franklin Savings Association, a state-chartered thrift, was formed in Kansas as a small-scale lender to the state's homeowners. In 1972, it was still charting the course of a conventional thrift when Ernest Fleischer made his first investment in Franklin. At that time, Fleischer was a leading tax

---

Exhibit 7   Where the S&L Money Went? Two Estimates (Billions of Dollars Before Interest Costs)

	Ely & Company	Wall Street Journal
Pre-1983 S&L Losses Resulting from Cheap Mortgages to Homeowners	$ 25	$25 to 30
Interest on Pre-1983 Mortgages	43	40
Real Estate Losses	28	40
Excess Operating Costs at Insolvent S&Ls	14	15
Excess Interest Paid on Brokered Deposits of Insolvent S&Ls	14	20
Deterioration of Seized S&Ls Run by Government	7	7
Fraud	5	10 to 20
Excess Cost of 1988 Deals to Sell Insolvent S&Ls	3	4
Losses on Junk Bond Held by Insolvent S&Ls	3	4
Losses on Other Non-Real Estate Investments	3	0
Government and Administrative Costs	0	10 to 15
Total in Billions (Before Interest Costs)	$147	$178 to 200

Sources: *Wall Street Journal*, July 20, 1990, p. 1, and November 5, 1990, p. 1; *Fortune*, September 10, 1990, p. 84.

lawyer in nearby Kansas City and became one of a group of three investors that took control of Franklin for $2 million. Fleischer continued the full time practice of law and relied upon the Association's management to carry out the regulatory imposed business plan of using short-term deposits to make long-term fixed rate loans. At the peak of interest rates in the early 1980s, that regulatory plan led to a thrift industry with only $60.00 in assets to repay each $100.00 in liabilities if both assets and liabilities had been valued at the industry's then all-in cost of funds. As a typical thrift, Franklin was no different.

While Fleischer continued the practice of law, he became more active at Franklin by assisting management in devising a business plan. He worked extensively in 1981 and 1982 with a consultant retained by the Association—Wayne Angell, then an economics professor at Ottawa University (and since 1986, a governor of the Federal Reserve Board). Dr. Angell observed that the thrift industry was the integration of five separate businesses: (1) loan origination; (2) loan servicing; (3) credit underwriting; (4) management of the uncertain cash flow that results from the borrowers' prepayment option; and (5) the intermediation of those cash flows between the borrowers and savers. Dr. Angell further instructed that the Association could only prosper if it could identify and exploit a business in which Franklin had a comparative advantage sufficient to recover the losses then in place. Accordingly, Franklin began to concentrate on the management of cash flows from mortgage prepayments nationally while continuing its other activities locally. A senior Franklin officer was given the responsibility to keep regulators advised of the progress of Franklin's new business plan.

Fleischer's first big challenge in running Franklin came in 1981, when skyrocketing interest rates devastated Franklin's portfolio as well as the portfolios of almost every thrift in the business at that time. Franklin lost $4 million, and, said Fleischer, "We were deeply in the hole; it was only a question of time before accounting realities caught up."[2] He continued, "My background as a tax lawyer taught me long ago that unless a transaction makes economic sense, it should be ignored as a sham." Based upon that criterion, Fleischer believed that traditional thrift portfolio management had always been too dangerous. His solution to the problem at hand was to find a strategy to reduce Franklin's interest rate risk.

Fleischer realized that the process of shortening his thrift's asset maturities and lengthening its liability maturities was not easy and could result in lower profits or the exchange of interest rate risk for another risk, such as credit risk. Because of that situation, Fleischer decided to use a hedging solution to solve the thrift's interest rate risk problem. With interest rate hedging strategies, asset management and liability management were each carried out separately, as required by GAAP. This max-

[2]Jack Willoughby, "The Hedgeaholic," Forbes, November 16, 1987.

imized the net return on assets and minimized the net cost of liabilities, without direct concern for whether the maturity of assets and liabilities actually matched. Once the asset and liability decisions were made, however, any extra imbalance between asset and liability maturities was "sold" to the interest rate hedging markets. Those markets generally included exchanges for interest rate futures, swaps, and options and markets for mortgage-backed securities.

The particular hedging strategy that Franklin used was an asset-purchase and funding technique, sometimes referred to as "risk-controlled arbitrage" by Salomon Brothers, the dominant Wall Street player in the business. It involved matching the duration[3] of assets and liabilities to lock in a profit that was insulated from interest rate risk. Under this strategy, Franklin first borrowed funds through certificates of deposit (CDs) and Bank Board advances. With those funds, Franklin bought mortgage-backed securities.[4] The mortgage-based securities bought by Franklin in the early 1980s (during the period of record high interest rates) were particularly attractive in Franklin's portfolio not only because of the high yields, but also because they were sold at such a deep discount (often around 60 percent of their par value). The deep discounts meant that the MBS was secured by a pool of mortgages made in the previous decades at considerably lower nominal rates of interest. Consequently, Franklin was certain that these homeowners would not prepay their very cheap mortgages, thus virtually eliminating prepayment risk in these securities. Typically, the duration of the mortgage-backed securities might be 4.5 years and the duration of the borrowed funds would often be less than one year. At this point, Franklin was still similar to a traditional thrift in that the duration of its assets exceeded that of its liabilities, though not as much.

In the second stage, the newly purchased mortgage-backed securities could then be used as collateral to borrow additional funds, creating a liability known as a repurchase agreement or "repo," which is a short-term market-rate instrument. Franklin then turned around and used these additional funds to purchase even more mortgage-backed securities (if they were attractive), which again increased Franklin's total assets. By the time the process of borrowing funds to purchase assets was repeated a third time, Franklin was earning a spread on three times the number of its initial assets, providing a high return on equity. Though it was possible to repeat the process a fourth time, Franklin and others believed that the collateral risk was too high.

In the final stage of this risk-controlled arbitrage strategy, Franklin

---

[3]Duration is the weighted measure of the average life of a security.

[4]Mortgage-backed securities (MBSs) were securities that represented a pool of loans secured by mortgages. Principal and interest on the underlying mortgages were typically passed through to investors to pay principal and interest on the mortgage-backed security itself. Examples of mortgage-backed securities are GNMAs, FHLMCs, and FNMAs. See the footnotes to Exhibit 3 for the definitions of these acronyms.

would externally hedge its assets and liabilities to minimize interest rate risks. Franklin would match the duration of its assets with the duration of its liabilities through the use of interest rate futures, swaps, and options, which are financial transactions recorded off the balance sheets. In particular, because the duration of its assets was greater than the duration of its liabilities, Franklin used interest-rate swaps or futures markets to extend the duration of its liabilities. As Fleischer said, "We buy interest rate insurance cheaper then we sell it, and that is our spread."[5]

The strategy was termed "risk-controlled" as opposed to "risk-free" because it did not completely eliminate risk. The largest risk that it could not eliminate was prepayment risk. Homeowners could sell their homes and pay off the mortgage, or they could default, prepay, or refinance their mortgages at any time. Therefore, cash flows from the mortgages that backed the securities that Franklin bought varied considerably. The worst case scenario for risk-controlled arbitrage was one in which interest rates dropped to such an extent that the mortgages underlying the securities were prepaid immediately. The thrift was then left exposed to what had become expensive liabilities without any high-yielding assets to counterbalance them. This was also the only scenario where the traditional unhedged thrift could succeed, because the cost of its variable-rate short-term funds would fall more than its yield on its fixed-rate long-term portfolio of mortgages.

Franklin was often noted as one of the most avid and ambitious thrifts to practice this type of hedging strategy. According to Alden Toevs of Morgan Stanley, "Franklin has enveloped the old, troubled institution with an even more profitable, new institution that is no longer interest rate dependent. Though they are not the only institution to have practiced diligent asset-liability management under this type of strategy, they have adopted a unique, all-encompassing approach." Praise also came from Eric Hemel, a First Boston vice president and former Bank Board official, "Franklin and Fleischer understand prepayment risk and mortgage economies as well as any Wall Street Firm. They are very scientific about minimizing interest rate risk."

Because his particular strategy could be implemented only with the aid of highly sophisticated interest rate sensitivity analysis and portfolio optimization programs, both Franklin's daily trader and Fleischer himself were in constant contact with the consulting firm of Smith Breeden Associates. When Fleischer first went to outside financial consultants in 1982 to glean the financial wizardry needed to develop his strategy, he went to, among others, Gregory Smith and Douglas Breeden. Smith, a futures expert, was a consultant to the Chicago Board of Trade Clearing Corporation, and Breeden was a professor of finance at Stanford University. Later in that year, Fleischer helped the two launch their consulting

---

[5]Barbara Donnelly, "Cashing in on risk-controlled arbitrage," *Institutional Investor,* February 1986, p. 161.

**Exhibit 8   Selected Financial Data for Franklin Savings Association
(dollar in millions)**

(Fiscal Year Ends June 30)	1984	1985	1986	1987	1988
Selected Balance Sheet Data:					
Total Assets	**$1,154**	**$2,014**	**$4,544**	**$9,370**	**$13,419**
Pass-through certificates (including MBS, IO, PO, and CMO)	859	1,701	3,929	7,353	7,292
Mortgage loans	177	166	172	239	415
Cash, trading, and investment securities	62	80	329	550	2,961
Receivable for unsettled sale of loan receivable and investment securities	—	—	—	891	108
Total Liabilities	**1,136**	**1,959**	**4,331**	**9,039**	**13,012**
Savings deposits (including brokered deposits)	686	852	1,380	2,172	3,326
Securities sold under agreements to repurchase (repos) and other short-term borrowings	398	425	1,554	2,668	1,699
Collateralized mortgage obligations	—	—	—	2,195	2,249
Bonds payable and other long-term borrowings, primarily FHLB advances	22	355	458	1,865	3,613
Payable for unsettled purchases of loans receivable and investment securities	—	201	833	—	291
Stockholders' Equity	**18**	**55**	**213**	**331**	**407**

(continued)

business in Kansas City. By 1987, Smith-Breeden helped 16 different thrifts, primarily in the Midwest, manage over $20 billion in assets. Smith argued that the money that Franklin and others practicing risk-controlled arbitrage channelled into the mortgage-backed market helped the mortgage market function more efficiently. "Franklin is a pure mortgage institution—maybe not for Ottawa, Kansas, but for the whole nation," Smith said.[6]

In 1985, Fleischer resigned from his law firm and thereafter devoted additional time to Franklin. Fleischer's long days, beginning each morning at 4:00 a.m., proved profitable for both Fleischer and Franklin. Fleischer and his wife controlled over 50 percent of Franklin's stock. His initial investment of $25,000 was estimated by *Forbes* magazine to be

[6]Donnelly, p. 166.

Exhibit 8 (Continued)

(Fiscal Year Ends June 30)	1984	1985	1986	1987	1988
Selected Operations Data:					
Interest income	$111	$173	$303	$552	$825
Interest expense	91	147	268	489	731
Net interest income before provision for loan loss reserve	19	26	34	63	93
Loan loss reserve	—	—	—	6	3
Net interest income after provision for loan loss reserve	19	26	34	57	90
Capital gains (losses) on:					
Sale of debt and investment securities	(7)	39	13	85	116
Options on financial futures contracts	—	—	141	15	—
Financial futures contracts	—	—	—	8	20
Financial futures contracts hedging terminated liabilities	—	—	—	(13)	(10)
Expenses	12	32	50	64	96
Income before income tax expense	12	56	174	128	137
Net income	**9**	**37**	**112**	**71**	**80**

worth $225 million and his company had assets of $13.4 billion. See Exhibit 8 for selected financial data.

By 1985, interest rates started falling rapidly and there was an increased risk that mortgages might start prepaying more rapidly than in the early 1980s. Franklins' solution was to buy call options on Government securities. For a fee, this would allow them to purchase these securities at a fixed price if interest rates fell (which implies that the price of these securities rose above that fixed price). Consequently Franklin would have a capital gain on the call option which it could use to offset the decline in the expected returns from its asset portfolio resulting from lower interest rates and faster prepayments. If interest rates had risen, Franklin would have gained on its asset portfolio, but it would have lost all of the money it invested in call options. Unfortunately, the cost of externally hedging their returns was not cheap and, by the beginning of 1986, Franklin's margin was being reduced to zero. As measured by the standard industry ratio, net income to operating expenses, Franklin's strategy of risk-controlled arbitrage needed to be revamped in order to find less costly means of hedging.

In 1986, Fleischer began work on a new strategy, which he called "internal hedging." With this technique, he took pieces of mortgage-backed securities that reacted in opposite directions to interest rate fluctuations and patched them together like a quilt, balancing out both prepayment and interest rate risks. By the end of the year, Franklin had invested more than $1.7 billion in that way, internally hedging 60 percent of its portfolio. Two techniques that were used to create an internal hedge were collateralized mortgage obligations (CMOs) and stripped securities. CMOs are bonds with multiple security classes secured by mortgage loans or mortgage-backed securities. See Exhibit 9 for an illustration of the cash flows and duration of a typical CMO. To protect itself from falling interest rates, Franklin would issue a CMO and sell the first two (short-term) tranches to investors and keep the residual (long term) tranche for itself.

Exhibit 9   Cash Flows of a Collateralized Mortgage Obligation

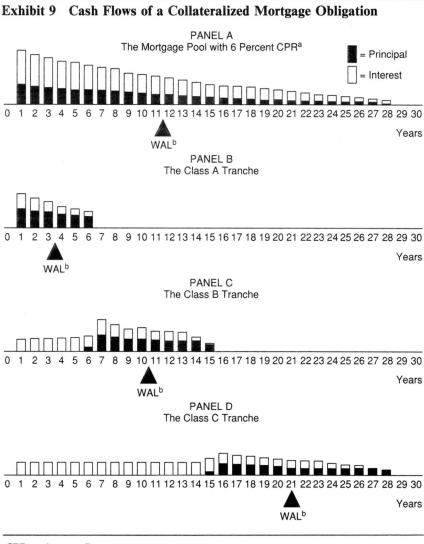

[a]CPR = (assumed) constant prepayment rate

[b]WAL = weighted average life

Source: Don Smith and Mark D'Annolfo, "Collateralized Mortgage Obligations: An Introduction," *Real Estate Review*, Vol. 16, No. 1, Spring 1986, p. 38.

Stripped securities were divided into interest-only strips (IOs) and principal-only strips (POs), which paid holders the cash flows from either the interest or the principal respectively. These had the special characteristic that when interest rates would fall, IOs would decline in value and POs would increase, and vice versa. Sometimes Franklin would purchase POs to hedge its portfolio such as in 1985 and at other times it would purchase IOs such as in 1986 and 1987—depending on the market conditions and the hedging needs in Franklin's portfolio.

John Sun, director of mortgage finance for Kidder Peabody noted, "Fleischer typically leads the street with new products and new structures." One trade in particular that significantly contributed to Franklin's growth was a hedge calculation it made in 1987, based on the new strategy. Franklin paid Merrill Lynch $212 million for an issue of interest-only strips from a mortgage-backed security issue. Typically, a company would buy interest-only strips if it anticipated rising interest rates, because the strips increased in value when interest rates rose. However, Franklin acquired the strips in order to shorten the duration of its assets and internally hedge its returns. Merrill Lynch had been willing to sell the strips while it held onto the underlying principal. When interest rates rose, Merrill booked a trading loss of $377 million on its unhedged investment, while Franklin profited by $10 million.

That particular type of maneuver had helped Franklin become one of the most profitable and fastest-growing of the nation's 3,200 thrifts. It had also helped Franklin weather the damage caused by the U.S. stock market crash on October 19, 1987. Though the company lost money on financial futures, that loss was offset by the rise in its mortgage-backed securities portfolio. Its hedging program even automatically took into account an increase in mortgage prepayments, the result of lower interest payments.

In addition to its mortgage-backed securities business, Franklin was also diversifying into the brokerage business. In late 1986, it completed its purchase of Kansas City-based Stern Brothers, an investment bank specializing in municipal finance. Stern Brothers offered an expanded range of products, including collateralized mortgage obligations. In July 1987, Franklin acquired Underwood, Neuhaus and Company, a Houston, Texas investment banking and securities company. Stern Brothers then became a division of Underwood, Neuhaus. A year later, Franklin acquired another investment bank, L.F. Rothschild Holdings, in June 1988, for $55 million. Rothschild was an investment banking and securities brokerage firm, headquartered in New York. At the time of the acquisition, Rothschild was one of 45 primary dealers of government securities.

Competitor's Strategies

Franklin was one of only approximately 50 thrifts that had insulated itself from interest rate risks as the result of their hedging strategies, setting it apart from traditional thrifts. Other thrifts had achieved various degrees of success by charting different courses. For example, thrifts such as Apple Bank for Savings and Dollar-Dry Dock Savings Bank were trying to become more like commercial banks by offering a wide array of financial products to both consumers and small businesses. Thrifts such as Golden West, Great Western, Dime Savings Bank, and Mercury Savings and Loan, focused on variations of mortgage-banking. Golden West, a no-frills California S&L, had achieved acclaim on Wall Street for its successful strategy of making low-cost adjustable rate mortgages—sticking closely to the traditional business of S&Ls. Still others, such as Anchor Savings Bank, concentrated on building nationwide financial conglomerates by acquiring institutions. In a few cases, S&Ls tried to make themselves attractive takeover candidates, such as Bowery Savings Bank in New York in 1987. See Exhibit 10 for an illustration of the diversity of strategies pursued by S&Ls.

Apple Bank for Savings

Apple's Chairman, Jerome McDougal, was focused on turning his thrift into a full-service bank. Apple provided services such as mortgages, home improvement loans, automobile loans, and financial advice. By 1987, Apple had only half of its asset portfolio in home mortgage loans, the majority of which were located in metropolitan New York City. See Exhibit 11 for financial information on selected thrifts. Since the early 1980s, Apple had become one of the nation's most profitable thrifts, ranked 61st among the top 300 in total assets.

    Part of Apple's recent strength stemmed from problems it encountered in the early 1970s. At that time, the bank was known as Harlem Savings Bank, and held mortgages on many deteriorating buildings across the city. The thrift was faced with rising costs while returns on its assets remained low because of rent controls. When the first oil price shock hit in 1974, many of the buildings' owners abandoned them, leaving Harlem Savings with a portfolio of bad loans. By 1978, Harlem had amortized the bad loans, built its capital to 8 percent of assets, and accumulated plenty of cash. After changing its name to Apple Savings Bank, another acquisition was made. This time it was the Eastern Savings Bank in 1986, which improved Apple's ability to make mortgages and further extended its coverage of the local area. In another effort to become more like its commercial banking counterparts, Apple acquired the commercial lending business of the Long Island Trust Company, the island's largest commercial lender. As a result, Apple had an experienced commercial lending group in a prosperous area.

Great Western Savings and Loan

Great Western, headquartered in Beverly Hills, California, was the third largest thrift in the nation with assets of $29.0 billion in 1987. It was the second largest thrift in California, a state that housed eight of the ten

Exhibit 10 Strategic Emphasis in Asset Deployment for Selected Thrifts in 1987

Thrift	Location	U.S. Ranking on Assets	Mortgage	Non-Mortgage	Credit	Non-Credit	Local	National
Dime Savings Bank	New York	19	X		X		X	
Mercury S&L Association	California	100	X		X		X	
Great Western Savings	California	3	X		X			X
Frankling Savings Association	Kansas	28	X			X		X
American S&L	California	1	X			X		X
Apple Bank for Savings	New York	81		X	X		X	
Dollar Dry Dock Bank	New York	49		X	X			X
Bowery Savings Bank	New York	24		X		X	X	
Anchor Savings Bank	New York	20		X		X		X

Exhibit 11   Assets and Liabilities for Selected Thrifts in 1987

	Franklin Savings (Kansas)	Dime Savings (N.Y.)	Apple Bank (N.Y.)	Anchor Savings (N.Y.)	Mercury S&L (California)	Great Western (California)	American S&L[a] (California)
Cash and money market investments & investment securities	22.1%	10.3%	13.0%	17.1%	11.9%	6.3%	2.6%
Securities (MBS) purchased under agreements to resell	9.5	0.0	0.0	0.0	0.0	0.0	0.8
Loans receivables:							
Mortgage-backed securities (MBS)	54.3	0.0	6.0	18.2	11.9	0.0	53.3
Home mortgage loans	2.6	74.3	53.7	43.6	56.4	73.3	25.2
Commercial real estate loans	0.0	11.3	0.0	10.5	10.8	9.9	7.5
Other loans	0.5	0.0	22.1	0.0	0.0	6.3	0.4
Total loans receivable	57.4	85.5	81.8	72.3	79.1	89.5	86.3
Real estate	0.0	0.9	0.9	0.0	2.8	1.0	2.2
Other assets	11.0	3.2	4.4	10.6	6.2	3.2	8.1
Total assets	**100.0**	**100.0**	**100.0**	**100.0**	**100.0**	**100.0**	**100.0**
Total deposits	24.8	74.0	88.4	85.0	80.0	69.8	50.7
Securities (MBS) sold under repurchase agreements	12.7	0.0	0.0	0.0	0.0	0.0	36.6
Collateralized mortgage obligations	23.4	0.0	0.0	0.0	0.0	0.0	0.3
Borrowed funds[b]	15.0	18.3	2.2	5.5	10.7	5.8	7.5
Bonds payable	20.3	0.0	0.0	0.0	3.3	12.2	0.0
Other liabilities	0.3	1.6	2.3	2.6	3.7	5.8	5.4
Stockholders' equity	3.5	6.1	7.1	6.8	2.4	6.5	-0.5
Total liabilities and stockholders' equity	**100.0**	**100.0**	**100.0**	**100.0**	**100.0**	**100.0**	**100.0**

Source: Company annual reports

[a]Failed in late 1987 and was sold to Robert Bass in 1988.

[b]Consists primarily of FHLBB advances and brokered deposits.

largest thrifts. James Montgomery, Great Western's often-praised chairman, described the thrift as "a real estate-oriented bank." Much of Great Western's success was the result of careful decisions made in the 1970s. Montgomery lent cautiously, avoiding fads, and quietly warning his peers against the twin perils of deregulation and the decade's savings and loans opportunists.

In 1987, almost all of Great Western's loans were real estate based, most of which were mortgages. Montgomery tried to match his mortgage portfolio with liabilities of similar maturity. He also refused to write conventional fixed-rate mortgages, instead pushing Adjustable Rate Mortgages (ARMs). Payments on ARMs were marked up (or down) with underlying interest rates, automatically matching asset and liability maturities (provided that one did not breach the annual and lifetime caps on interest rate movements). By 1987, almost 80 percent of Great Western's portfolio was in ARMs.

Great Western's enviable capital base (a capital to total assets ratio of over 5 percent) made it a logical savior for many ailing thrifts. However, Montgomery was determined "not to mess up the balance sheet." He believed that the current accounting practices that were designed for acquirers of failing thrifts diluted the net worth of the acquiring thrift. Though some thrifts used this method of acquisition to move across state lines, Great Western sought different ways to establish itself around the country. In 1984, Great Western received permission to set up 16 "nonbank" banks in 16 different states. A nonbank bank could make commercial loans or offer checking accounts, but not both. The thrift did not make commercial loans, so it qualified by accepting deposits. In addition, Great Western acquired Aristar in 1984, a consumer loan operation with $1.8 billion in assets. As a result, it gained 272 consumer finance offices in 22 states. In the four years since the Aristar purchase, Great Western's assets had grown by nearly 20 percent, with its real estate loan portfolio alone growing by 25 percent.

Anchor Savings Bank

Anchor Savings, based in Westchester County, New York, had pursued an acquisition strategy that allowed it to swallow more than a dozen failing thrifts. Under the direction of chairman Donald Thomas, Anchor bought thrifts in New York, New Jersey, Georgia, and Florida. Thomas believed that a key part of Anchor's expansion policy was "contiguity." As a result of its acquisition program, Anchor found itself in a number of new businesses that included credit card lending, automobile financing, and a wide variety of mortgage banking activities. It also was the new owner of an equipment leasing company in Connecticut, and an insurance agency in Georgia.

Most of Anchor's acquisitions were made with depositors' cash. Though Anchor had a net worth of $505 million on paper in 1987, it was, almost completely, the result of additions to goodwill. Among other methods, goodwill was created when one thrift took over another that had a large number of low-yielding loans. Because the yield was lower than what the market currently demanded, investors would not pay face value for such loans. The difference between book value and the lower market value would be recorded as goodwill.

Failed Strategies

While some thrifts successfully followed a particular strategy, other thrifts had failed apparently pursuing a similar direction. The thrift industry was littered with quick-fix programs that had turned into disasters. One typical example was Wichita Federal Savings and Loan in Kansas, which needed to cover a $26 million loss it incurred in the mortgage-business in 1981. The thrift plunged into reverse repurchase agreements (reverse repos) in which it bought securities from sellers who agreed to buy them back at a set time and price in the future. The thrift reaped a $26.5 million trading gain from 1981 to 1984. However in 1985, when the thrift's chief executive speculated in financial futures, he lost $17.5 million within two months because of unhedged positions exposed by falling interest rates.

Perhaps the most publicized thrift failure was the case of American Savings and Loan, a California subsidiary of Financial Corporation of America (FCA). American was the nation's largest thrift with assets of $33.8 billion at the end of 1987. In September 1988, FCA declared bankruptcy with $77.2 million in assets and $1.43 billion in liabilities. At that time, the parent company's losses had increased to more than $440 million, and American's net worth had plunged into the red by more than $400 million.

Many in the industry believed that American's problems began in the early 1980s, under FCA's Chairman, Charles Knapp. Knapp quickly became famous for American's aggressive lending and accounting policies. After the thrift sustained a huge loss and a $6.8 billion run on deposits in 1984, Edwin Gray, then Chairman of the Bank Board, forced Knapp out of office. Knapp was replaced by William Popejoy, a seasoned thrift industry executive, but that effort failed as well. By early 1987, American was being dragged down by delinquent loans and foreclosed real estate. Over 70 percent of the thrift's home and commercial loan portfolio was based in California, where 43 percent of it was foreclosed. In Texas, which accounted for 7 percent of the portfolio, 23 percent of the properties were foreclosed. At the end of 1987, American's return on equity was a negative 251 percent. In addition to failed loans, American's $17.9 billion of mortgage-backed securities had been funded by unhedged short-term borrowings. Though that had provided big profits during periods of falling interest rates, by April 1988 rates were starting to rise, and that part of the portfolio was also in trouble.

Questions

1. How do high, volatile interest rates affect thrift institutions? Why would they be more or less vulnerable than any other financial intermediary?
2. Evaluate Franklin's strategy for dealing with the new interest rate environment of the early 1980s. What are the strengths and weaknesses of the strategy? Why didn't all thrifts follow this approach?
3. Recommend an alternative strategy for a thrift institution. Under what conditions would this strategy be superior to Franklin's approach? Could your strategy be applied to turnaround an ailing thrift?
4. Should Fleischer change his strategy now? Why or why not?

CASE 7
Financial Swaps

As with the previous chapter, the core issues in this case can be viewed at both the firm level and at the public policy level. For the firm, the issue raised by this case is how a firm can gain a competitive advantage over its rivals through innovation. For the public policy maker, the issue is what are the causes and consequences of financial innovation.

Financial innovations became increasingly common during the 1980s. Swaps, in their various guises, are just one example of a financial innovation, though a very significant one. Among the various candidates mentioned as a cause of financial innovation are advances in financial knowledge, new technologies, regulatory changes, tax changes, inflation, and the levels and volatility of interest rates and exchange rates.

After we understand the nature of financial innovation, we can focus on whether a financial institution can gain a sustainable competitive advantage over rivals through innovation. We must identify the distinctive edge displayed by the firm and the barriers to additional entry by rivals. If an advantage can be achieved, then we must determine how a financial institution can structure an organization that will be successful in promoting innovation and how that innovation will support its other business activities.

Financial innovation was defined as the change in financial products, processes, or practices of the world's financial institutions. The pace of that change accelerated significantly in the 1980s in the United States and most other industrialized countries. Some of those products, such as interest rate swaps and futures, were designed to help firms reduce their exposure to interest rate risk, which was the sensitivity of net earnings to interest rate movements. Others, such as currency swaps and dual currency bonds, were designed to lessen earnings exposure to fluctuating exchange rates.

Swaps, both interest rate and currency, became one of the most popular of the financial innovations of the decade, quickly gaining acceptance among financial institutions and corporations. In the view of one participant, Cyrus Ardalin, chief of borrowing operations at the World Bank, swaps represented the "single most important financing development that has taken place in recent years." Within a few years, the original swap innovation was transformed to incorporate additions such as caps, floors, and options on interest rate swaps. More recently, the technique was extended to commodity swaps. In 1988, the total dollar volume of swaps outstanding in the world had reached a staggering $1.3 trillion and involved almost 60,000 separate transactions. As recently as the beginning of the decade, the volume of swaps was only a few billion dollars. See Exhibit 1 for the growth in the volume of swaps.

Trends in Financial Markets

The world's financial markets had undergone structural changes which could be grouped into six broad trends: growth, internationalization, securitization, innovation, liberalization, and supervision.

Since the mid-1970s real activity in the financial markets had expanded at a more rapid rate than real output in the major industrial countries. Over that period, the debt-to-income and asset-to-income ratios of the public, corporate, and household sectors rose in most countries. The expansion of financial markets was accompanied by major shifts in the flow of funds among sectors of the industrialized countries. Although the business sector was still a net user of credit, its share of total credit had declined relative to that received by the government sector. Also, major imbalances in the external sector occurred among oil producing countries, developing countries, and industrial countries following the two oil shocks in 1973 and 1979.

The internationalization of financial markets was reflected in the growth of offshore financial markets and greater foreign participation in

This case was prepared by Research Associate Julia Horn under the supervision of Professor Michael G. Rukstad. Copyright © 1990 by the President and Fellows of Harvard College. Harvard Business School Case 9-390-078.

**Exhibit 1   Growth in Swaps Market Currency and Interest Rate
Swaps**

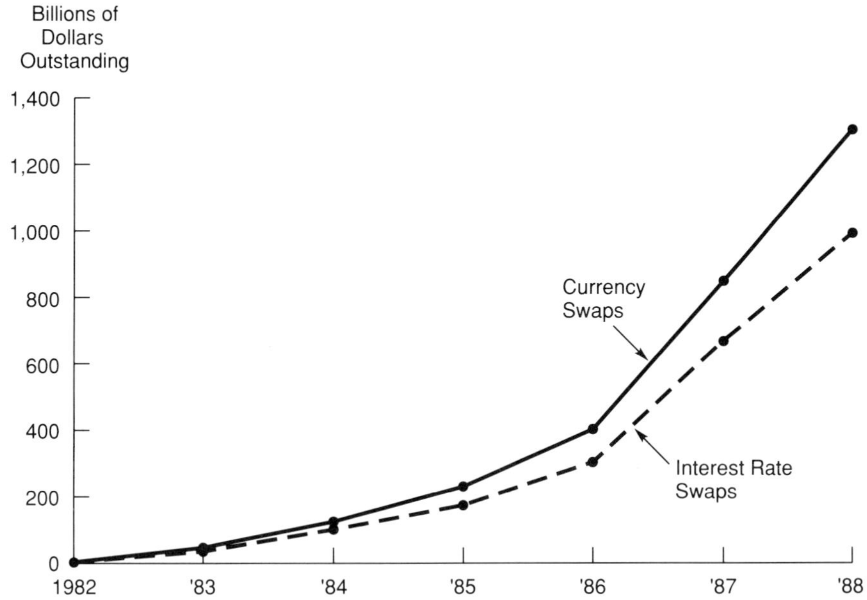

Billions of
Dollars
Outstanding

Source: Economist, May 30, 1987 & ISDA

domestic financial markets. Domestic financial institutions had an increasing proportion of their business in foreign loans and foreign security purchases. Also, the number of foreign financial institutions in the major industrial countries increased sharply and accounted for a considerably greater share of total bank assets and security underwritings.

Securitization occurred simultaneously with the internationalization of financial activity. Securitization involved a greater use of direct debt markets, in which the saver held a direct claim on the borrower, and a shift away from indirect finance, where an intermediary held a nontradable loan asset and issued its own liability to savers. In addition to the shift of credit flows from bank lending to securities markets, a second form of securitization involved the packaging of normally nontradable assets into tradable securities (such as corporate receivables, mortgages, auto loans, and credit card loans). A third form of securitization involved the creation of exchange-traded futures and options contracts. In that case, a certain type of risk, usually one associated with price volatility, was securitized.

Financial innovation was closely related to securitization. There was a significant expansion in the instruments used in international and domestic transactions. Many of those innovations originated either in the domestic U.S. market or in the Eurodollar markets and then spread to other countries. Even though most discussion of financial innovation focused on financial products, many significant innovations also occurred in financial processes and practices. Exhibit 2 gives some examples of representative financial innovations by consumer products, corporate products, financial processes, and financial practices. Analysts had identified numerous factors instigating financial innovations, including the exploitation of tax asymmetries, the reduction of transaction and agency costs, the reduction or reallocation of risk, increased asset liquidity, regulatory or legislative changes, the level and volatility of interest rates, prices, and exchange rates, academic insights, accounting benefits, and technological advances.

A liberalization in the financial markets had been underway since the mid-1970s, most notably in the United States, Japan, Germany, and the United Kingdom. Within the domestic financial markets, liberalization consisted of two related developments: the deregulation of interest rates and brokerage fees, and the expansion of the scope of allowable activities for financial institutions. In international markets, there was a gradual removal of controls on capital inflows and outflows. The removal of exchange controls in the United Kingdom in 1979 along with the lifting of lending restrictions on banks (the "corset"), opened the sterling banking and securities markets to foreign borrowers. In Germany, access to capital markets was liberalized with the removal of a 25 percent withholding tax on interest payments on domestic bonds to nonresidents. Beginning in the early 1980s, Japanese authorities also undertook liberalization of cross-border financial flows by opening up the Euroyen bond market to foreign corporations. Similarly in France, the Eurofranc bond market was reopened during this period.

The supervision of financial markets became more difficult as the risk associated with increasingly complex transactions, such as credit risk, liquidity risk, and interest rate risk, became less transparent. A number of specific actions were taken including the establishment of capital adequacy levels for commercial banks in an effort to strengthen banks' balance sheets and reverse a downward trend in capital relative to assets that had prevailed during the 1970s and early 1980s. Also, regulators were increasingly concerned about the risks associated with the growth in off-balance sheet obligations of all financial institutions in the 1980s.

Currency Swaps

Currency swaps began in the United Kingdom in the late 1970s. They provided a means of financing investment in overseas markets while circumventing the problems of exchange controls in the United Kingdom. Currency swaps evolved from special loans, known as parallel or back-to-back loans, which were popular in the United Kingdom at that time. Parallel loans typically involved two companies, each in a different country and each having a subsidiary in the other's country. Each parent company made an equivalent loan in their national currency to the other's subsidiary. A parallel loan agreement, therefore, entailed two separate loan transactions and two different rates of interest. The drawback of this arrangement was that, if one party failed to make a payment, the other was still obligated to continue payments.

A currency swap was technically different from a parallel loan in that it involved a single agreement. In a currency swap transaction, two counterparties exchanged specific amounts of two different currencies with an agreement to reverse the exchange at a specified time in the future and at a specified exchange rate. Effectively, currency swaps extended the forward foreign exchange markets into longer maturities. One distinguishing feature of a currency swap was that the loan contract did not include an initial exchange of principal but rather the exchange of cash flows, and as such was an off-balance sheet instrument. In addition, credit risk was limited since a performance failure by one counterparty relieved the other counterparty of its obligations. A currency swap could be arranged directly between two counterparties, or as was more often the case, it could be intermediated by some financial institution.[1]

It was generally agreed that the first currency swap was successfully completed in 1976 by a team from Continental Illinois Ltd. (now First Interstate Ltd.) and Goldman Sachs for Bos Kalis Westminster, a Dutch company, and Britain's ICI Finance. The deal involved the Dutch guilder and the pound sterling. That swap was approved by the Bank of England on the basis that the cash flows were identical to those of a parallel loan and thus complied with the spirit of exchange controls at that time. Because that initial deal went unpublicized, currency swaps remained a quiet product. Shortly after, in early 1977, Continental Illinois published a tombstone in *The Wall Street Journal* for a 10-year, $25 million "currency exchange agreement" on behalf of Consolidated Gold Fields, a large gold-mining company. After 1979 when Prime Minister Thatcher came into office, exchange controls were lifted. The recently organized swap groups in most banks started to disband. A few, however, recognized a market for currency exposure management for corporate treasurers and started to sell currency swaps for that purpose.

"It was not until August 1981, however, that currency swaps really came into the international limelight as a market arbitrage technique and became a standard feature of the global capital markets."[2] At that time, the World Bank issued a $290 million bond, arranged by Salomon Brothers, which was swapped into an equivalent amount of Deutsche marks and Swiss francs provided by IBM. The World Bank became a driving force in the development of the currency swap market. Though it could borrow relatively cheaply in the larger dollar markets, the World Bank

[1]For a detailed explanation of currency swaps, see Scott Mason, *Foreign Currency Swaps,* Harvard Business School case 9-286-073.

[2]Denys C. Firth, "Who made the first swap?" *Inside the Swap Market,* (London: IFR Publishing, 1986), p. 21.

Exhibit 2   Selected Financial Innovations

Corporate Products
Debt and Related Securities Innovations

Innovation	Approximate Year of Introduction
Adjustable Rate Notes and Floating Rate Notes	1974
Bull/Bear CDs	1986
Certificate of Accrual on Treasury Securities	1982
Collateralized Mortgage Obligations (CMOs)	1983
Currency Swaps	1979
Dual Currency Bonds	1981
Eurobonds	1963
High-Yield Bonds	1977
Indexed Currency Option Notes	1985
Interest Rate Floors, Caps, and Ceilings	1983
Interest Rate Futures	1975
Interest Rate Swaps	1981
Mortgage-Backed Bonds	1975
Mortgage Pass-Throughs	1969
Negotiable CDs	1962
Options on Treasury Bond Futures	1982
Puttable Municipal Bonds	1980
Stripped Mortgage Backed Securities	1986
Stripped Treasury Bonds	1984
Treasury Bond Futures	1977
Treasury Investment Growth Certificates	1982
Variable Duration Notes	1985
Zero Coupon Bonds	1981

Preferred Stock Innovations

Adjustable Rate Preferred Stock	1982
Auction Rate Preferred Stock	1982
Convertible Adjustable Preferred Stock	1983
Indexed Floating Rate Preferred Stock	1982
Remarketed Preferred Stock	1984
Stated Rate Auction Preferred Stock	1984
Variable Cumulative Preferred Stock	1983

Convertible Debt/Preferred Stock Innovations

Adjustable Rate Convertible Debt	1982
Convertible Exchangeable Preferred Stock	1982
Convertible Reset Debentures	1983
Exchangeable Auction Preferred Stock	1983
Zero Coupon Convertible Debt	1981

Common Stock Innovations

Americus Trust	1983
Master Limited Partnership	1981
Puttable Common Stock	1984

(Continued)

Exhibit 2   (Continued)

Corporate Products
Debt and Related Securities Innovations

Innovation	Approximate Year of Introduction
Consumer Products	
All-saver certificates	1981
Bull/Bear CDs	1986
Debit cards	1980
IRA/Keogh accounts	1981
Money market mutual funds	1981
Money market accounts	1981
Municipal bond funds	1981
NOW accounts	1980
Tuition futures	1986
Variable or adjustable rate mortgages	1974
Processes	
Automated teller machines	1978
Automated clearing houses	1978
Cash management/sweep accounts	1978
Direct public sale of securities	1970
Discount brokerage	1975
Shelf registration	1982
Practices	
Debt-for-debt exchanges	1981
Hedged dividend capture	1985
In-substance defeasance	1986
Leveraged buyouts	1980
Preferred dividend rolls	1979
Project finance/lease	1960

Source: Financial Management, Winter 1988.

sought low interest rate borrowings, mainly in Swiss francs or Deutsche marks, since it sought to make loans in those currencies. Those needs created a natural opportunity to carry out swaps with counterparties who had European currencies or better access to borrowings in Europe, but who needed dollar finance.

Interest Rate Swaps

Interest rate swaps shared many of the features of currency swaps. In an interest rate swap, two parties agreed to exchange their interest payments, but not the underlying principal. One borrower made fixed rate payments and the other made floating rate payments in the same currency, typically dollars. Six-month London InterBank Offer Rate (LIBOR), the rate at which banks loaned funds to one another on the Eurodollar market, was the most commonly used floating rate index against which a fixed rate was priced. Later, other floating rate indices were used including three-month LIBOR, the prime rate, and Treasury yields.

Most interest rate swap transactions took place through an intermediary bank.[3] The intermediary had to be prepared to take on the credit risk of each leg of the transaction—the greatest risk was that the party with the lower credit rating would renege on its fixed rate obligations. The intermediary bank wrote separate contracts with each party and acted as a principal on both sides of the transaction. Intermediaries also performed a payments clearing service and coordinated all rate settings, such as LIBOR.

Interest rate swaps were initially created to take advantage of the fact that the credit worthiness of companies was perceived differently by domestic and foreign lenders and by fixed and floating rate lenders. This allowed borrowers to obtain lower-cost financing and investors to obtain higher-yield assets. For example, in the United States, institutional investors played a larger role in the marketplace and relied heavily on the credit rating system to assess a company's borrowing capabilities. In Europe, on the other hand, investors were less reliant on the credit rating system, which allowed some U.S. companies with widely recognized consumer brand names to have cheaper access to funds than they might have had in the U.S. domestic market. "Swap market participants offered a variety of reasons to account for this relative borrowing cost differential: relatively greater risk aversion in the bond market; over-capacity in the bank loan market, which has reduced the premium for high-risk borrowers; differences in information across markets; banks' superior ability to manage deteriorating credits; or banks' desires to diversify out of their LDC risks."[4] Later, the swap market developed for different motivations than just lower price—participants used swaps to hedge interest rate or currency exposure, to manage asset/liability structures, and to speculate.

Similarly, some lower-rated companies might not have access to the fixed rate debt markets, though they may have had access to floating rate funds. Fixed income investors were more credit sensitive than investors in floating rate instruments. As a result, a greater premium was demanded from lower-rated companies in the fixed rate debt markets, often making fixed rate borrowing prohibitively expensive, if available at all. The lower-rated (and consequently higher-risk) counterparty, typically a BBB-rated industrial company, preferred fixed rate debt in order to reduce its interest rate risk. Its counterparty, typically a AAA-rated commercial bank with cheaper access to both the fixed and floating rate funds, needed floating rate dollars to suit its asset profile, since most of its loans were made at floating rates.

---

[3]Because swaps were forward contingent agreements, they were recorded off-balance sheet for accounting purposes, allowing banks to make intermediate swaps.

[4]Bank for International Settlements, *Recent Innovations In International Banking,* April 1986.

Despite the fact that the commercial bank had an absolute cost advantage in both the fixed and floating rate debt markets, both swap parties in an interest rate swap were able to benefit. For example, a swap agreement might start with a AAA-rated bank that was able to borrow fixed rate funds, for example, at 9.8 percent, but needed floating rate dollars. On the other side of the transaction, the BBB-rated industrial would have to pay 11 percent for the same funds. See Exhibit 3 for a diagram of an interest rate swap transaction. The AAA bank could alternatively borrow floating rate funds at LIBOR[5] plus 0.25 percent, while the lower rated company had to pay LIBOR plus 0.75 percent. Before entering into the swap, both parties issued debt in the rate structures in which they were comparatively best able—the AAA bank borrowed in fixed rate funds, and the BBB industrial borrowed in floating rate funds. Each remained responsible for that debt throughout the life of the swap. The AAA bank then contracted to pay LIBOR to the BBB industrial, in return for 9.9 percent fixed rate payments from the BBB.[6] The AAA bank

Exhibit 3   Interest Rate Swap with Intermediation

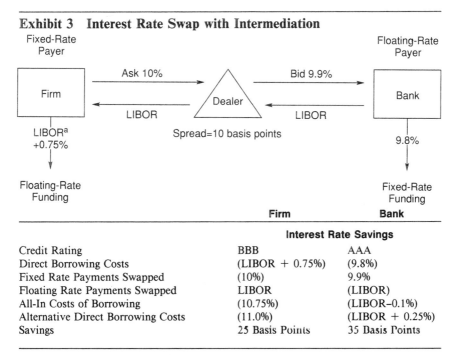

	Firm	**Bank**
Interest Rate Savings		
Credit Rating	BBB	AAA
Direct Borrowing Costs	(LIBOR + 0.75%)	(9.8%)
Fixed Rate Payments Swapped	(10%)	9.9%
Floating Rate Payments Swapped	LIBOR	(LIBOR)
All-In Costs of Borrowing	(10.75%)	(LIBOR−0.1%)
Alternative Direct Borrowing Costs	(11.0%)	(LIBOR + 0.25%)
Savings	25 Basis Points	35 Basis Points

Source: Federal Reserve Bank of Boston.

Note: Payments are swapped at dealer price: 9.9%/10.0% for 6-month LIBOR. Numbers in parentheses are negative interest flows; otherwise positive flows.

[a]Assume LIBOR is 7.25%.

[5]In this example, assume LIBOR is 7.25 percent.

[6]The BBB-rated firm is actually paying 10 percent, however, the intermediary arranging the transaction receives a fee of 0.1 percent (10 basis points), resulting in the net payment of 9.9 percent to the AAA-bank.

return for 9.9 percent fixed rate payments from the BBB.[6] The AAA bank could then use the 9.9 percent income stream to service its 9.8 percent fixed rate funds liability. The BBB industrial used the LIBOR payments from the AAA bank to service its LIBOR plus 0.75 percent floating rate debt, which, when added to its fixed rate payments of 10 percent, resulted in a final cost of funds of 10.75 percent, or significantly less than it would have achieved by entering the fixed-market direction (11 percent).

The interest payments that both parties paid on each other's debt were expressed as a percentage of a mutually determined principal amount (called the "notational amount") and were undertaken for a set period of time. The notional amount of an interest rate swap generally ranged from $10 million to $200 million, with maturity rates ranging from 2 to 12 years. The interest rate swap technique allowed both swap parties to obtain cheaper fixed and floating rate financing than their own individual credit ratings would otherwise allow. "Interest rate swaps enabled a corporation or financial institution to alter the interest rate sensitivity of its balance sheet, to obtain funds that were unavailable through direct borrowing, or simply to obtain a lower cost or different type of financing."[7]

It was generally agreed that the first interest rate swap was arranged in 1981 by Citibank and Continental Illinois. The deal involved a private transaction matched against some privately sourced fixed rate financing and, like many others that followed, it went unpublicized. In June of 1981, Bankers Trust intermediated in a transaction that swapped fixed rate yen payments for floating rate dollar payments between Renault and an unnamed Japanese firm. That deal was the beginning of cross-currency interest rate swaps.

The Evolution of Financial Swaps

During the first stage of swap innovation, intermediary banks typically acted as agents, bringing together two counterparties with matching swap requirements. Frequently, intermediaries also provided letters of credit or other forms of credit enhancement for lower-rated companies. Both commercial and investment banks were active swap intermediaries. In the words of one senior industry executive, "Swaps were one of the few investment banking innovations without regulatory hurdles and in which commercial and investment banks could compete on equal footing right out of the gate." Commercial banks stressed their capacity to provide floating rate funds to fixed rate servicers, while investment banks pointed

---

[6]The BBB-rated firm is actually paying 10 percent, however, the intermediary arranging the transaction receives a fee of 0.1 percent (10 basis points), resulting in the net payment of 9.9 percent to the AAA-bank.

[7]R. C. Merton, "Interest Rate Swaps," Goldman, Sachs and Company, Fall 1985.

to their ability to raise fixed rate funds for their floating rate servicers. At that time, because the swap technology was only understood by a few specialists commanding premium salaries, commercial and investment banks could charge fees as high as $5 million for arranging a swap. In addition to that fee, the intermediary bank typically received 50 to 75 basis points in spread fees on a swap. Swap spreads were independent of the credit quality of the counterparties. The minimum size of the deals in the early years was usually $50 to $100 million or larger. During the first few years of swaps, large commercial banks tended to be the most successful intermediaries in the swap market.

In 1982, the first Eurobond issue with an interest rate swap was done for Banque Indosuez. This opened the floodgates for other firms to access the Eurobond market in order to raise funds at the most favorable rates and then swap them into the currency or interest rate they desired. By the end of the decade 70 percent of all Eurobonds issued were related to swaps. Consequently, the percentage of Eurobonds issued in dollars fell from 57 percent in 1983 to only a third by the end of the decade. Similar large shifts occurred in the amount of fixed bonds and floating rate notes.

The particular financing needs of European AAA-rated banks also aided the development of the interest rate swap market. Those European banks (or banks with European market operations including Citibank, Credit Suisse-First Boston, and Morgan Guaranty) had access to a security distribution network in the European market. Because of the nature of their strong credit rating, the European banks had relatively low-cost access to fixed rate financing in the Eurobond market but desired greater access to floating rate financing at a reduced cost.

During the second stage of swap innovation, which began in the mid-1980s, many intermediaries became less conservative and began to hold one side of a swap in inventory until an offsetting counterparty could be found. That technique, called "warehousing," was aided by the widespread use of sophisticated computers and was considered a "major leap forward" over the technique that involved finding perfect matches. Some intermediaries warehoused swaps for their own account, balancing an entire portfolio of maturities and interest rates. "Warehousing could turn out to be a critical function, enabling [a new issue] to be bought when a yield window opens up even if a swap counterparty is not available at that time."[8]

In the mid-1980s, it became clear that hedging techniques were important until swap counterparties could be found to reduce the bank's exposure to interest rate risk. Intermediaries began to take out a temporary hedge in the bond or futures market until the offsetting swap was found—a technique that involved sophisticated use of duration[9] analysis

[8]"Variations on a Theme of Swaps," *Euromoney,* June 1986.

[9]Duration is the weighted measure of the average life of a security.

for asset and liability structures and other quantitative techniques. Citibank, Salomon Brothers, and Morgan Guaranty, were three of the intermediaries that did well at this stage of the process. Many firms entered the very profitable swap market as dealers during this period. At the same time, the multi-million dollar fees that intermediary banks could once charge disappeared for all but the most complex, "tailor-made" swap deals, and the spread fees were reduced to the range of 12 to 25 basis points. Between 1983 and 1985, the minimum size of swap deals fell from approximately $25 million to as little as $1 million.

Though swaps originated predominantly as international transactions, by 1983 transactions were largely conducted between domestic counterparties primarily in the United States. At that time, regional banks and insurance companies appeared on both sides of the market. U.S. thrift institutions became active as fixed rate payers (i.e. they wanted floating rate funding); U.S. agencies such as the Student Loan Marketing Association (Sallie Mae) usually wanted to pay floating rates. By the mid-1980s, real estate companies, leasing companies, and other financial firms entered the swap market as fixed rate payers as did highly-rated U.S. corporations.

Some of the early innovators acting as intermediaries recognized that swaps were a way of solving particular customer financing problems. However, as intermediaries, commercial and investment banks had different approaches to their customers and to the swap market. Commercial banks tended to view swaps as an extension of their more conventional banking business. For example, when a commercial bank combined a floating rate loan with a swap, it created the equivalent of a fixed rate loan for a customer. "Previously, commercial banks found it difficult to extend fixed rate loans outright because their fixed rate funding costs were sometimes as high as those faced by their customers. In addition, they accepted prepayments on fixed rate funds when rates moved to the disadvantage of the borrower. By unbundling the components (the floating rate loan and the swap) commercial banks could price each more efficiently."[10] Investment banks tended to view swaps as tradable securities, and an outgrowth of their other securities business. See Exhibit 4 for the securities underwriting activity of investment banks. They were also the driving force behind the effort to standardize swap contracts and market practices in order to improve swap market liquidity.

Profiles of Intermediary Firms

The swap strategies of intermediary firms fell into three broad groups. First, there were those firms, such as Goldman Sachs and Credit-Suisse

---

[10]Bank for International Settlements, *Recent Innovations In International Banking,* April 1986.

Exhibit 4   Securities Underwriting Activity of Investment Banks

Top Global Underwriters of Debt and Equity

	1988		1983	
	Rank	Amount (in $ billions)	Rank[a]	Amount (in $ billions)
Firm:				
Credit Suisse/First Boston	1	$51.8	1	$22.1
Merrill Lynch	2	46.9	3	14.1
Goldman, Sachs	3	42.5	4	11.9
Salomon Brothers	4	39.5	2	16.0
Shearson/American Express	5	29.4	5	10.9
Morgan Stanley	6	28.6	6	10.2
Drexel Burnham Lambert	7	21.3	8	7.4
Nomura Securities	8	20.4	—	—
Deutsche Bank	9	12.8	7	7.8
Union Bank of Switzerland	10	12.4	9	4.7

[a]In 1983, Swiss Bank ranked tenth.

Source: Securities Data Co.

Top Eurobond Underwriters

	1988		1983	
	Rank	Amount (in $ billions)	Rank[a]	Amount (in $ billions)
Firm:				
Credit Suisse/First Boston	1	$13.2	1	$9.4
Deutsche Bank	2	11.9	2	8.4
Nomura Securities	3	7.4	9	1.8
Merrill Lynch	4	6.0	8	1.9
Banque Paribas	5	5.9	25	0.7
J.P. Morgan Securities	6	5.7	13	1.4
Industrial Bank of Japan	7	5.6	—	—
Union Bank of Switzerland	8	5.5	7	2.0
Banker Trust	9	5.1	—	—
Daiwa Securities	10	4.2	12	1.4

[a]In 1983, Salomon Brothers ranked third, S.G. Warburg ranked fourth, Morgan Stanley ranked fifth, Goldman Sachs ranked sixth, and Swiss Bank Corp. ranked tenth.

Note: Excludes equity-related issues and private placements.

Source: Securities Data Co.

First Boston, that were involved with swaps predominantly as pure agents of swap transactions. As an agent, the firm brought the two swap counterparties together for a fee and the counterparties contracted without the use of an intermediary. That particular strategy involved little or no credit or interest rate risk. Second, there was the strategy of pursuing only matched intermediary transactions such as that followed by large Japanese banks, which did not involve any trading or interest rate risk. How-

Exhibit 4   (Continued)

Top Underwriters of Corporate Debt (in the United States)

| | 1988 | | 1983 | |
	Rank	Amount (in $ billions)	Rank[a]	Amount (in $ billions)
Firm:				
Goldman Sachs	1	$32.3	4	$ 5.1
Merrill Lynch	2	31.7	5	5.1
Salomon Brothers	3	31.1	1	10.5
First Boston	4	27.6	2	6.6
Morgan Stanley	5	21.1	7	2.7
Shearson/American Express	6	19.3	6	4.8
Drexel Burnham Lambert	7	18.7	3	5.5
Bear, Stearns	8	8.9	13	0.5
Prudential-Bache	9	7.6	—	—
Kidder, Peabody	10	6.0	10	1.1

[a]In 1983, Paine Weber ranked eighth and A.G. Becker Paribus ranked ninth.

Source: IDD Information Services, *The Wall Street Journal*, January 3, 1989.

Top Corporate Equity Underwriters (in the United States)

| | 1988 | | 1983 | |
	Rank	Amount (in $ billions)	Rank[a]	Amount (in $ billions)
Firm:				
Merrill Lynch	1	$7.4	1	$4.9
Shearson/American Express	2	5.6	7	1.9
Prudential-Bache	3	3.3	12	—
Goldman Sachs	4	3.1	2	4.8
Paine Webber	5	2.9	—	—
Wheat, First Securities	6	2.2	—	—
Drexel Burnham Lambert	7	2.0	10	1.5
First Boston	8	1.6	5	2.3
Salomon Brothers	9	1.5	4	3.5
Alex, Brown	10	1.2	—	—

[a]In 1983, Morgan Stanley ranked third, Kidder, Peabody ranked sixth, E.F. Hutton ranked eighth, and Lehman Brothers ranked ninth.

Source: IDD Information Services.

ever, there was still some credit risk because one of the counterparties might be unable to make its payments. Finally, there was a swap trading strategy in which firms took a position and bet on movements in interest rates. That strategy was followed by Citicorp, Morgan Guaranty, Merrill Lynch, and Salomon Brothers.

As the swap market exploded in the 1980s, the growth in swap activity varied significantly among intermediaries. Among the interme-diaries, commercial banks typically had a larger capital base than investment banks, particularly after the regulatory changes following the Third World debt crisis. See Exhibit 5 for comparisons of swap volume for some sample firms. Goldman Sachs was historically a small player in the swap market despite its size as an investment bank. Morgan Guaranty, which had initially pursued an aggressive swap strategy, had not made any significant gains by the end of the decade. Chase Manhattan aggressively sought swap transactions and became one of the leading firms in the industry after a very slow start. Citicorp maintained its dominant role as an innovator since the inception of the swap market.

Goldman Sachs

Goldman Sachs, which was the world's third largest investment bank in 1984, was a relatively late entrant in the swap market. In January, 1984, Arthur Walther became the head of Goldman's swap department, which at the time consisted of one full-time employee. Most swap departments, acting as principals, depended on their firm's capital to fuel their operations by buying swaps outright when counterparties could not be found right away. Walther, on the other hand, favored a different approach. "Walther runs his firm's swap business not on capital, but on pure hustle. His forté is convincing top-drawer clients to pay the company a basis point or two to arrange swaps for them with other firms. One competitor remarked that because Walther had none of the firm's principal capital on the line, he had to 'live by his wits.' "[11]

In the swap market, Walther was known as "a tough negotiator who was willing to scrap for the last basis point." He was also well-respected as a sophisticated technician who had invented a number of swap products that became standards for the industry, such as swaps out of certificates of deposit and private placements. Walther did not want to expose the partners' capital, thus his approach to swapping was that whenever the firm could match swap counterparties directly it would. Occasionally, when it was unable to find a match, it positioned its portfolio to counterbalance the risk. To facilitate the matching of counterparties, Goldman positioned its swap group on the trading floor.

Morgan Guaranty

Morgan Guaranty pursued a more aggressive trading strategy than Goldman Sachs. The firm was one of the early entrants and innovators in the swap market, entering in 1982. By the end of 1988, Morgan was the seventh largest bank in the swap market with $74 billion in swaps outstanding. For Morgan, swaps were primarily a tool used by the firm's corporate finance department. The firm had access to a broad security

---

[11]Joe Kolman, "The sultans of swap," *Institutional Investor,* October 1985.

Exhibit 5   Comparison of Swap Volume

Volume Table of Swaps Outstanding
Mid-1980s
(in $ billions)

Citicorp Bankers Trust Salomon Brothers	27–45
Morgan Guaranty Manufacturers Hanover Chemical Bank Prudential Bache	15–27
First Boston Kleinwort Benson Merrill Lynch First Chicago Chase Manhattan Union Bank of Switzerland Nomura	10–15
Morgan Stanley Drexel Burnham Lambert First Interstate Goldman Sachs	4–10

Volume Table of Swaps Outstanding
Late 1980s
(in $ billions)

Citicorp Merrill Lynch Salomon Brothers Bankers Trust Chase Manhattan First Boston	85–140
Manufacturers Hanover Nomura Shearson Lehman Morgan Stanley Morgan Guaranty Chemical Bank	70–85
Security Pacific First Chicago	40–70
BankAmerica Goldman Sachs Union Bank of Switzerland First Interstate Drexel Burnham Lambert	15–40

Source: *Euromoney*, October 1986, *The New York Times*, July 31, 1989, and *The New England Economic Review*, November/December 1987.

distribution network and was one of the few AAA-rated banks. Unlike others, such as Citibank, the firm was a minimal consumer of swaps for its own funding purposes. Morgan's client base was primarily corporate customers. "Since they have a preference for fixed rate borrowing, Morgan was able to build up inventory on the fixed rate side [of swap deals], amounting sometimes to several hundred million dollars, and to sell it, at leisure, to customers."[12] Most agreed that building up a fixed rate swap inventory was the least risky, since fixed rate payments could always be hedged by buying fixed rate instruments.

At Morgan, Roberto Mendoza was recognized as a leader and an innovator who had pulled the firm away from some of its traditional business outlook. During Mendoza's tenure at Morgan, the swaps team was housed within the department of international financial management, where its purpose was to innovate new products and search out new business. When Mendoza left the firm in 1987, the swaps team was moved into Morgan's treasury department. One swap executive described the atmosphere within the treasury department as, "rather bureaucratic and not conducive to innovation, a crucial function that swap team members needed to perform. Treasury has historically been an area that lacks intellectual curiosity and where swap teams are bound to lose their innovative spirit." However, some believed that firms such as Morgan, which moved their swap operations to Treasury, could better meld swap activities with their other interest rate management activities, rather than aggressively pursuing swap market share.

Chase Manhattan

In 1988, Chase Manhattan was the third largest swap player in the industry with over $85 billion in swaps outstanding, moving up considerably since 1985, when it had just $10 billion in swaps. It took Chase until the end of 1983 to do its first interest rate swap, two years after most competitors. During 1982, Chase was entangled in government bond trades with Drysdale, a government securities firm, which caused Chase to lose $270 million. Shortly thereafter, the firm lost an additional $50 million following the bankruptcy of Penn Square, an Oklahoma bank to which Chase, and a number of other large commercial banks, had lent money.

After a slow beginning, the investment banking group at Chase enthusiastically embraced swaps. Anthony Terraciano, Vice Chairman of Chase, and Robert Lichton, president of Chase's Investment Banking unit, championed this new product and decided that Chase should enter the swap market with full force. Chase significantly expanded their swap personnel from two to almost twenty. The swap department at Chase

---

[12]David Shirreff, "Swaps: Managing the Future," *Euromoney,* October 1984.

then would forward its swap positions to its treasury management to become part of Chase's global funding operations. Chase's philosophy on swaps differed from that of the other commercial banks, as well as from that of other investment banks. "Swaps are heavily integrated with our asset-liability management, as is our fixed rate lending and mortgage business," explained one New York swap executive. "They are a powerful marketing tool backed by our balance sheet."[13]

Citicorp

Citicorp, one of the early innovators in the swap market, was still the largest swap player in 1988, with $138 billion in swaps outstanding. David Pritchard, managing director of Citicorp Investment Banking, Ltd. in London, was often referred to as the "father of swaps." Though Pritchard took credit for getting one of the first currency swaps approved by the Bank of England, he scoffed at the mythology of creativity that surrounded swapping techniques. "Ideas don't tend to come from somebody staring at the ceiling and coming up with a wonderful abstraction," he said. "They almost always come from a customer requirement."[14]

Citicorp was one of the world's largest banks with $270 billion in assets and earning over 80 percent of their income from commercial bank lending. Citicorp was widely recognized for its ability to raise funds for itself and its clients internationally. Becoming a big player in swaps fit with Citicorp's overall strategy of becoming a major corporate finance house in all leading capital markets. "One of Citicorp's advantages is the willingness of its banking units to take on swaps for their own funding purposes."[15] That meant, in many cases, that counterparties could be found at leisure.

In a 1985 reorganization of Citicorp the swap group was incorporated into the capital markets group of their new investment bank, causing some initial disorganization. In one instance, a swap deal was booked with the bank on both sides of the Atlantic simultaneously so that, in effect, Citicorp ended up swapping with itself.

New Directions for the Swap Market in the 1990s

By the late 1980s, the swap market entered a third phase of development, where distribution and the need to disperse new information and technology became increasingly important. Trading sophistication had increased significantly since the early part of the decade. Because swap

---

[13]*Euromoney,* October 1984.
[14]*Institutional Investor,* October 1985.
[15]*Euromoney,* October, 1984.

Exhibit 6   Financial Swaps

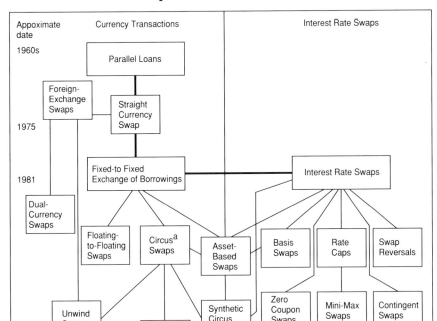

[a]Cross interest-rate currency swaps.

Source: Julian Walmsley, *The New Financial Instruments: An Investor's Guide*, (New York: John Wiley & Sons), 1988.

products had moved along the product lifecycle becoming commodity products, intermediaries' margins were shrinking, even as swap dollar volume grew. As the knowledge base for swaps proliferated, product "half-life" had shrunk to two months compared to two to three years in the earlier part of the decade. In 1989, the bid-ask spread on swaps varied from approximately 7 to 12 basis points.[16]

However, at the same time, the original swap theme had been extended from currency and interest rates to commodities. See Exhibit 6 for variations on the swap theme and Exhibit 7 for an explanation of commodity swaps. Commodity swaps involved the exchange of money and not actual shipments of a commodity, such as oil or a particular metal, and were designed to neutralize the uncertainties of volatile prices for businesses that produced or used commodities. Commodity swaps were being written on a widening range of commodities including oil and

---

[16]Steven Felgran, "Interest Rate Swaps: Use, Risk, and Prices," in New England Economic Review, Federal Reserve Bank of Boston, November/December 1987.

Exhibit 7   How a 'Commodity Swap' Works

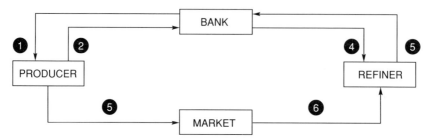

1 The oil producer wants to lock in a set price for its oil. It goes to swap arranger, in this case a bank, which pays the producer that set price over a period of time.

2 Over the same period of time, the producer pays the bank the average market price for the oil.

3 The refiner wants to lock in a price that it will pay for oil, and also goes to the bank to arrange a swap. The refiner pays the bank its predetermined price, again, over a period of time.

4 The bank pays the refiner the average market price for the oil over the same period of time.

5 The oil producer sells oil in the market for the going price.

6 The refiner buys oil in the market for the going price.

The oil producer and the refiner have locked in their desired prices because any gains or losses in the market will be offset by gains or losses on their transactions with the bank.

The bank makes a profit equal to the difference between the producer's desired price and the refiner's desired price.

Source: *The Wall Street Journal*, September 26, 1989.

oil products, as well as gold and base metals, such as copper, zinc, and aluminum. Banks, such as Chase Manhattan, Bankers Trust, and Banque Paribas, were the leaders in commodity swaps, acting as intermediaries. Jack Cogen, vice-president of risk management at Chase Manhattan said, " 'The total value of commodity swaps outstanding now is probably no more than $3 billion.' But, he predicts that the market will grow tenfold over the next few years."[17]

Futures markets were also used to hedge against adverse price moves by farmers, food processors, and others. But futures contracts rarely extended more than a year into the future, while some swap agreements ranged up to twelve years. Futures, however, provided a centralized clear-

---

[17]Stanley Angrist, "Big-Stakes Hedge Starts Branching Out," *The Wall Street Journal,* September 26, 1989.

ing organization, guaranteeing both sides of a trade, whereas the credit for swap participants had to be determined for each swap. Specifications of the commodity futures often did not closely match those for which someone wanted price protection. For example, there was not a futures contract for jet fuel, but swap agreements for it could be arranged.

Questions

1. What conditions account for the timing and the magnitude of the growth in the swap market? Which were most important? Do these conditions apply to all innovations?
2. What are the key success factors in establishing a competitive advantage with a new financial innovation?
3. What might explain the different behavior of Goldman Sachs, Morgan Guaranty, Chase Manhattan, and Citicorp in the swap market?

CASE 8

General Motors and the Dollar

The U.S. dollar appreciated very significantly during the first half of the 1980s. This was, at least partially, a result of the Federal Reserve's policy of high real interest rates in the United States relative to those in other major industrial countries. American exports suffered while foreign imports into the United States reached record levels. The U.S. balance of trade deteriorated more in each successive year. Among the largest industries apparently affected by the appreciation of the dollar was the automotive industry, but many other manufacturers of large durable goods and heavy equipment saw a loss in their competitive position as well.

In this chapter's case, General Motors and the Dollar, we want to analyze how important the appreciating dollar was among the numerous competitive problems facing the U.S. automotive industry in general, and General Motors in particular, during these years. We also want to identify the managerial responses available to companies facing such large changes in exchange rates, including the crucial issue of price setting and the degree to which exchange-rate-induced cost changes are passed through to the customer.

When the dollar exchange rate started depreciating after 1985, we can observe in this case how the Japanese car makers responded to the appreciation of their own currency and contrast this response to that of the American car makers during the previous five years. In fact, the appreciation of the yen after 1985 was much sharper than the appreciation of the dollar earlier in the decade. The objective is to develop an understanding of how exchange rate movements can affect competitive positions and to formulate appropriate responses to those changes.

General Motors (GM) was the largest automaker in the United States in 1989 with a domestic market share of 35 percent. Despite its still dominant position in the U.S. auto industry, the company had lost almost 13 percent of its U.S. market share since 1978. That downward trend at GM was representative of the entire $200 billion U.S. auto industry, as domestic manufacturers over that same period lost a total of 15 percent market share, primarily to Japanese competitors. Though the U.S. economy of the late 1980s was the strongest since the end of World War II, critics charged that GM did not take full advantage of the economic boon while its foreign competitors flourished.

During the period from 1980 to 1985, GM claimed that it had difficulty competing because of rising production costs and the rising value of the dollar, which made U.S. autos more expensive in the world market. Since early 1985, however, the dollar had been falling, particularly against the Japanese yen. Many industry analysts believed that GM and the other U.S. automakers were handed a perfect opportunity to drop prices and to regain their market share positions. Nonetheless, from 1985 to 1988, the Big Three automakers (GM, Ford, and Chrysler), led by GM, raised prices 20 percent faster than Japanese manufacturers.

GM's Competitive Decline in the 1970s

The U.S auto industry had grown rapidly from the 1920s to the 1950s without much foreign competition. Imports, though they had encountered quality and service problems, began to penetrate the U.S. market in the 1950s. Nonetheless, by 1963, they accounted for no more than 5 percent of the market. The largest gain in market share was registered by Japanese producers between 1965 and 1971, when they increased their share by over 6 percent with their inexpensive compact models. In 1973, the auto industry was hit with one of the most significant structural changes in its history—the first oil price shock which quadrupled oil prices. Many potential car buyers postponed purchases because of higher gasoline prices and reduced incomes resulting from the ensuing recession in 1974–1975. Those who did purchase cars were looking for more economical models. In 1974, immediately following the oil shock, small cars captured a record 40 percent of the market. Imports, which focused on the small car buyer, raised their U.S. share to over 18 percent from 15 percent in 1972.

In response, GM led the Big Three, traditionally producers of large "gas-guzzlers," in a program to improve fuel efficiency and downsize their cars. In 1974, domestic cars had an average fuel efficiency of 13.2 miles per

This case was prepared by Research Associate Julia Horn under the supervision of Professor Michael G. Rukstad. Copyright © 1989 by the President and Fellows of Harvard College. Harvard Business School Case 9-389-094.

gallon (mpg) compared to 22.6 mpg for the imported car fleet. New federal fuel efficiency standards were later enacted that provided for a minimum rating of 18 mpg by 1978. While struggling to meet that minimum level and trying to make smaller cars, GM was pushed into the most expensive re-tooling and redesign effort in its history—a $40 billion program that began in 1979 and continued into 1983. "When smaller GM cars did appear, many considered them a disappointment, complaining that they, like other American small cars, were simply big cars made small, while the imported Japanese models were better looking and offered higher quality and value. GM's divisions, scrambling to hang onto their dealers and customers, all demanded their share of the new small cars that the company was devel-oping. The result was too many near clones of each vehicle spread over five divisions."[1] Despite U.S. automakers' slow response to changing market demand for smaller cars, they had curtailed imports' share to 16 percent of the total market in 1978 at the expense of European automakers, leaving the Big Three with a still dominant 84 percent of the U.S. market. See Exhibit 1 for U.S. auto sales by market class.

Consumers began to purchase big cars once again in the late 1970s as gasoline prices became cheap relative to inflation. U.S. automakers found themselves having to reposition their products to satisfy changing market demand. As domestic manufacturers reintroduced larger cars, a second oil price shock in 1979 created long lines at gas stations, moti-

Exhibit 1   U.S. Sales by Market Class Excludes Imports

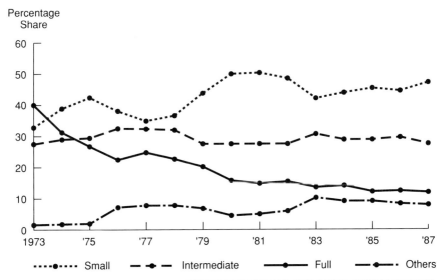

Source: Ward's Automotive Yearbook.

[1]Survey on the Motor Industry, *The Economist*, October 15, 1988.

vating the price-sensitive consumer to seek smaller, more fuel efficient cars.[2] Once again, by 1980, sales of small cars accounted for 51 percent of the market, while sales of large cars shrank to 16 percent from a high of 40 percent of the market in 1973. The combined market share of U.S. auto companies fell 10 percent from 1978 to 1980, while Japanese auto makers enjoyed market share gains of more than 9 percent. See Exhibit 2 for U.S. market share data. In 1980, for the first time, Japan's world car production exceeded that of American car manufacturers. Not only were market shares in flux, but the total number of autos sold in the United States fell from 11 million before the second oil shock to 8 million in the depths of the recession in the early 1980s.

Exchange Rate Fluctuations in the 1980s

The first half of the 1980s marked an unusual period of rapid appreciation of the dollar. Between October 1980 and February 1985, the dollar rose phenomenally on a trade-weighted basis, and to a lesser degree, against the Japanese yen. The dollar rose 63 percent overall against the currencies of U.S. trading partners (a compounded annual growth rate of 12 percent), and 26 percent overall against the yen (a compounded annual growth rate of 5 percent) during that period. See Exhibit 3 for the real and nominal yen-dollar exchange rates.

From 1980 to 1982, the rising dollar could be explained by the improving current account and by the high real interest rates relative to other major countries. The high interest rates and rapidly falling inflation were caused by the unexpectedly tight monetary policy initiated by Chairman Paul Volcker and the Board of Governors of the Federal Reserve in October 1979 and maintained for the next three years. In 1983 and 1984, the primary factor driving up the dollar to record heights was the growing Federal budget deficit. The deficit contributed to America's rapid recovery from the recession relative to the rest of the world. It also attracted foreign savings into the United States in order to finance the deteriorating current account deficit.

However, a reversal occurred in early 1985. From that time until the end of 1988, the dollar fell 38 percent overall against the currencies of U.S. trading partners (a compounded annual decline of 15 percent) and 54 percent against the yen (a compounded annual decline of 23 percent). Even though the budget deficit still remained large, its effects in attracting dollars to the United States were being offset by the huge current account deficit supplying dollars to the world market. Moreover, there was a change in attitudes by the world's financial policymakers, especially by the Reagan

---

[2]It had been estimated that the price elasticity of various classes of automobiles ranged from 1.25 to 2.25. See F. Owen Irvine, "Demand Equations for New Car Models," *Southern Economic Journal*, January 1983.

Exhibit 2 Auto Industry Market Shares in the United States 1976–1988

	United States					Japan						
Year	Total United States[a]	General Motors	Ford	Chrysler	AMC	Total Japan[b]	Toyota	Nissan (Datsun)	Mazda	Honda	Total Europe	Total (units)
1976	85.7%	47.6%	22.6%	13.0%	2.5%	8.1%	3.4%	2.7%	N/A	1.5%	6.2%	10,105.8
1977	83.4%	46.3%	23.4%	12.0%	1.7%	10.6%	4.4%	3.5%	N/A	2.0%	6.0%	11,178.8
1978	83.9%	47.8%	23.5%	11.1%	1.5%	10.9%	3.9%	3.0%	0.7%	2.4%	5.2%	11,310.4
1979	78.7%	46.3%	20.8%	10.1%	1.5%	15.2%	4.8%	4.4%	1.5%	3.3%	6.1%	10,660.4
1980	73.9%	45.9%	17.2%	8.8%	2.0%	19.8%	6.5%	5.8%	1.8%	4.2%	6.3%	8,976.1
1981	73.0%	44.5%	16.6%	9.9%	2.0%	20.6%	6.8%	5.5%	1.9%	4.4%	6.4%	8,533.1
1982	72.8%	44.1%	16.9%	9.9%	1.9%	21.5%	6.7%	5.9%	2.1%	4.6%	5.7%	7,979.3
1983	74.2%	44.2%	17.1%	10.4%	2.5%	20.2%	6.1%	5.7%	1.9%	4.4%	5.6%	9,182.1
1984	75.8%	44.3%	19.1%	10.4%	2.0%	18.9%	5.4%	4.7%	1.6%	4.9%	5.3%	10,390.4
1985	73.7%	42.5%	18.8%	11.3%	1.1%	20.3%	5.6%	5.2%	1.9%	5.0%	6.0%	11,042.1
1986	71.2%	41.0%	18.2%	11.4%	0.6%	21.5%	5.6%	4.8%	1.9%	6.1%	5.5%	11,495.5[c]
1987	67.4%	36.5%	20.2%	10.7%	(d)	24.3%	6.2%	5.2%	2.0%	7.2%	5.2%	10,226.6
1988	69.0%	36.1%	21.6%	11.3%		23.7%[e]	6.5%	4.5%	2.4%	7.3%	4.8%	10,580.8

[a] AMC includes Renault imports and domestic makes after 1980. Chrysler, Ford, and General Motors include captive imports.

[b] Honda total includes domestic production beginning in 1983 and sales of Acura models beginning in 1986. Nissan data includes sales of domestic production beginning in 1985. Toyota data includes sales of domestic built models beginning in 1987. Mazda includes sales of domestic models beginning in 1988. Total also includes Subaru, Isuzu, and Suzuki.

[c] Hyundai of Korea began exporting cars to the United States in 1986. It had a market share of 1.8% in 1986, 3.1% in 1987, and 2.5% in 1988.

[d] AMC was acquired by Chrysler in 1987.

[e] In 1988, of the total cars sold in the United States, Toyota produced 10% of its sales in the United States, Nissan produced 22%, Mazda produced 13%, Honda produced 48%.

Source: Ward's 1987 Automotive Yearbook, Automotive News, various issues.

Exhibit 3   Real and Nominal Exchange Rates, Yen–Dollar

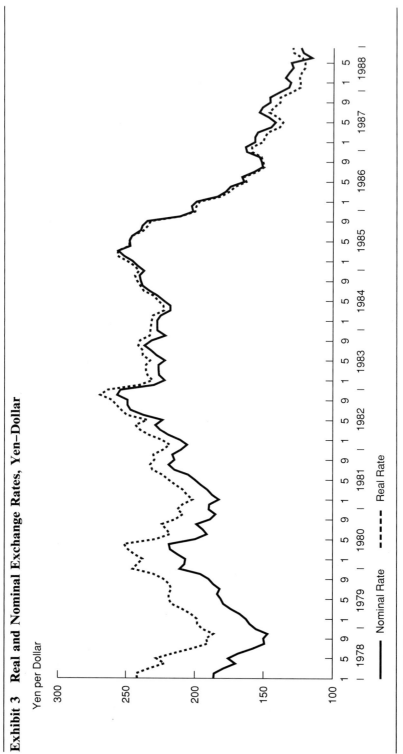

Source: IMF Monthly Statistics

administration, that was demonstrated at a meeting at the Plaza Hotel in New York in September 1985. In the Plaza Accord the central banks of the five leading industrial nations agreed to coordinate monetary and fiscal policies in order to drive down the dollar. Agreement and policies were reaffirmed in February 1987 at a meeting at the Louvre in Paris.

It had been noted by many analysts that during the period from 1980 to 1985 when the dollar was appreciating, the trade deficit in the United States grew from $26 billion to $122 billion. Japan, with its growing exports, managed a trade surplus that grew from $19 billion to $56 billion over the same period. Passenger cars rose from a 7 percent share of the total value of goods imported into the United States in 1980 to an 11 percent share in 1985, while passenger cars and parts accounted for 13 percent of total U.S. exports. Even as the dollar declined between 1985 and 1988, the trade deficit kept growing to a record high of $154 billion by the end of that period. In 1988, GM was still the country's largest exporter, accounting for 3.5 percent of total exports, followed closely by Ford (3.1 percent) and Boeing (2.5 percent).

GM's Market Share and the Rising Dollar: 1980-1985

Despite the period of the rising dollar from 1980 to 1985, American auto producers as a group held market share. However, during that time, GM lost a total of 3.4 percent market share. The decade had an ominous start for GM and the industry. In 1980, GM lost a record $763 million, its first loss since 1921. The company was besieged by foreign imports, and saw its sales of subcompact cars plummet. The decline, however, was offset slightly by the company's highly profitable mid- and full-size product line. Ford and Chrysler did not fare any better. Chrysler, after disastrous losses in 1978 and 1979, received government loan guarantees which gradually returned the company to profitability after four more years of losses. The demand for autos grew briskly after the 1980–1982 recession. In 1983, the industry's growth outlook improved considerably as consumers reveled in lower interest rates, lower inflation, and higher disposable income. However, sales at GM never did recover to their 1978 level, when the company had sold 5.4 million cars, and the industry's sales had peaked at 11.3 million units.

The industry blamed their problems in large part on the rising dollar. "The value of the Japanese yen puts tremendous pressure on U.S. manufacturers," said Roger Smith, CEO of General Motors. "It's helped produce some really stiff competition. For example, in the Saudi Arabian market, we compete head to head with the Japanese. The yen-dollar differential has really been cutting us up."[3] Other American competitors concurred with this analysis of the decline. *The Wall Street Journal* re-

[3]Interview with Roger Smith, *Barron's*, March 12, 1984.

ported that, "Ford pleaded with Washington to help get the dollar down to 180 yen; GM and Chrysler essentially agreed."[4] John V. Deaver, a Ford Motor Company executive, explained the rationale for this lobbying effort, "A weaker dollar should help blunt the continuing competitive pressure from imported cars. A strong dollar got us into this fix and a weak dollar will get us out."[5]

In spite of the rising dollar, the level of Japanese imports remained fairly constant after 1981. One explanation offered by industry analysts was the voluntary export restraint (VER). The VER was signed by the U.S. and Japanese governments in 1981 and limited the number of Japanese auto imports into the United States. The rationale given by the Reagan administration for the VER was that it would give American industry time to adjust to world competition. The export restraints "caused Japanese imports to level off and influenced Asian companies to build assembly plants in the United States. They also led those companies to enrich the mix of vehicles sold here. Unit sales of Japanese cars have crept up slowly since the restraints, but the dollar value of Japanese cars sold in the United States continues to soar."[6]

In the first half of the 1980s, Japanese automakers enhanced their product line in the small car market. Many attributed this upgrading in the image and the options offered in the product line to the VER. Since Japanese producers were limited in the number of units that they could send to the U.S. market, they started offering higher priced, better equipped products for that market. Because of the VER, Japanese auto dealers had more customers than cars available. As a result, the retail price of those cars became the base for extra charges, often as high as $2,000, that included pinstripes, upholstery protection, and paint treatments. The extra charges quickly translated into extra profits for the dealers.

The Quality of GM Cars

Even before the upgrading of their product lines while under the VER, Japanese automakers had developed a reputation for high quality production. The annual editions of *Consumer Reports* indicated that, by 1981, the American consumer rated Japanese import models among the "highest quality" cars available on the market. GM models had fallen in the magazine's quality studies from "slightly above average" in 1972 to "much worse than average" in 1981, a position also shared by Chrysler. Ford models, on the other hand, maintained an "average" reputation over that

[4]Jacob Schlesinger, "GM Officials Get Short-Term Incentives Despite Plan to Emphasize the Long-Term," *The Wall Street Journal*, April 18, 1988.

[5]William J. Hampton, "Detroit's Big Gamble," *Business Week.* January 13, 1986.

[6]Davis Dyer, Malcom S. Salter, and Alan M. Weber, *Changing Alliances.* (Boston: Harvard Business School Press), 1987, p. 1.

decade. During the period from 1982 to 1985, however, GM and the other American producers began to improve their quality ratings. GM's problems per 100 cars dropped from over 350 in 1981 to 250 in 1985, while GM models improved to an "average rating" in *Consumer Reports* studies over that time. Ford cars had the fewest problems of the Big Three from 1981 to 1985, averaging less than 250 per 100 cars. A 1987 *Business Week* poll indicated that 57 percent of those surveyed believed that GM made better cars than overseas manufacturers did. By 1988, a J.D. Power new car quality survey reported that U.S. automakers, led by GM, continued to narrow the quality gap between their cars and those of Japanese manufacturers. GM, for example, had three nameplates among the top ten on the survey's list, outperforming Japan's Honda, Mazda, and Subaru. Mr. Power further predicted that all of GM's nameplates would reach quality parity with such automakers as Honda in the early 1990s.

GM's Declining Cost Competitiveness in the Early 1980s

Because GM's quality had improved significantly in the 1980s, observers turned to other explanations in an attempt to understand the shifts in market share. Most critics charged that GM and other American competitors were not as cost competitive as their Japanese counterparts. For example, one comprehensive study concluded, "U.S. consumers are attracted to Japanese cars for good reasons. Despite massive investments by the Big Three in high technology and wage concessions [in 1981 and 1982] by the United Auto Workers (UAW), Japanese automakers continued to make cars more efficiently than did American automakers."[7] American companies were blamed for not adopting effective management techniques and attitudes, such as Japanese just-in-time inventory systems, long-run market share objectives, and a focus on product innovation. In their defense, U.S. companies maintained that they were addressing their production and inventory problems with substantial investments aimed at increasing labor productivity and product quality. Industry executives preferred to focus attention on labor costs. Roger Smith often cited the $8-per-hour wage differential between American and Japanese workers as a major obstacle for renewed American competitiveness. See Exhibit 4 for hourly compensation data in the auto industry in the United States and Japan. The success of management's efforts at improving productivity can be seen in Exhibit 5.

In an effort to learn production and management techniques from Japan's largest automaker, GM established a 50-50 joint venture with Toyota in 1983 called New United Motor Manufacturing, Inc. (NUMMI).

[7]Dyer, op. cit., p. 151.

Exhibit 4   Hourly Compensation, U.S. & Japan Auto Industry

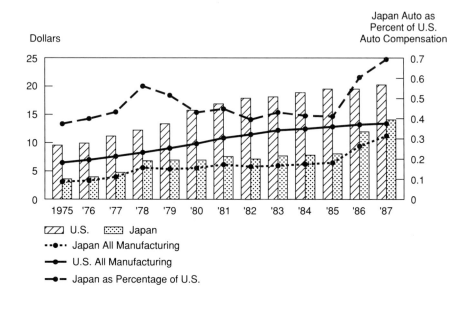

Source: U.S. Bureau of Labor Statistics

Exhibit 5   Unit Labor Costs, Auto Industry

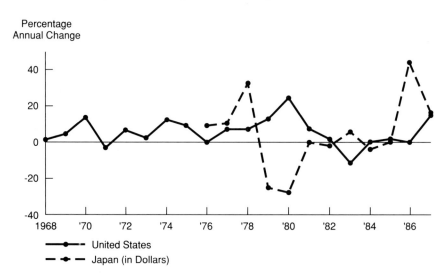

Source: Bureau of Labor Statistics

Under NUMMI, Toyota contributed $150 million and GM contributed $20 million in addition to an assembly plant. In 1984, NUMMI began production of the Chevrolet Nova, a derivative of Toyota's Corolla. Shortly after the announcement, GM's Saturn project was made public. Saturn represented the culmination of GM's newly acquired learning in production techniques and labor relations. The compact Saturn would be the first new GM nameplate since 1918, and the first deliveries were scheduled for 1990.

Despite American progress on cost containment, a U.S. government study indicated that, comparing similar subcompact models of American and Japanese producers, the Japanese cost advantage in 1984 was between $1,500 and $2,500, approximately the same as in 1980.[8] Roger Stempel, president of GM said, "We have too many competitors' cars today that can be priced under us and still make a profit."[9] Despite some plant closings and employee layoffs in the early 1980s, industry analysts waited for GM to outline its plan for bringing costs under control and becoming competitive. "GM must close more plants and cut more costs," said Maryann Keller, an auto industry analyst.[10] "As today's high cost man-ufacturer, GM has given its competition the luxury of pricing their ve-hicles to maximize profits and production."[11] "The one thing that is missing at GM is that no one has stood up as former Ford Chairman Phil Caldwell did and said, 'We have to get $2 billion or $4 billion of cost out of our business.'"[12]

GM's Pricing Policy

Though the Big Three had made some progress on cost reduction, it had not resulted in a pricing advantage for U.S. producers compared to their Japanese counterparts. GM's prices, for example, rose a weighted average of 10.2 percent for all models in the early 1980s—slightly below the weighted average for the U.S. producers and 5 percent slower than the Japanese producers in that same period. The price increases at GM were slower than Chrysler, Ford, Toyota, and Nissan. See Exhibit 6 for auto price increases.

In an attempt to capitalize on the shift to larger cars and the growth

---

[8]U.S. Department of Commerce, *The Automobile Industry, 1983: Report to the Congress from the Secretary of Commerce*, (Washington: Government Printing Office, December 1984).

[9]Joseph Callahan, "Stempel, Reuss See Lower Costs, Better Position in Reorganization," *Automotive Industries*, March 1984.

[10]Michelle Krebs, "Analysts say GM must do more to end its troubles," *Automotive News*, November 10, 1986.

[11]Maryann Keller, "The General's Big Giveway," *Automotive Industries*, September 1987.

[12]Krebs, op. cit.

Exhibit 6   Auto Price Increases

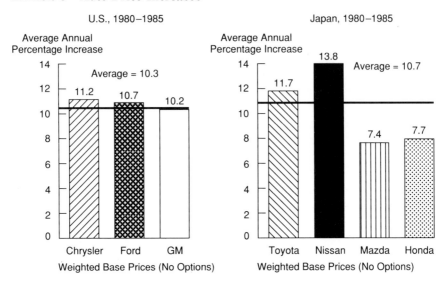

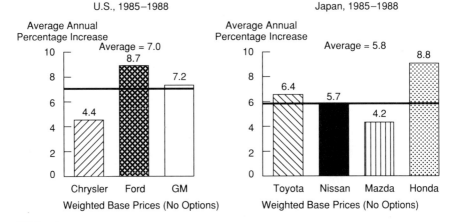

in the industry, GM had experimented with price restraint. In 1983, the company limited its price increases to less than 3 percent; industry analysts observed that a quick recovery in GM's sales following a recession would entice the company to crank up prices, putting an end to a sales rebound. "GM's market share did not respond to massive investment because others were keeping their prices low and offering lots of value," said a management consultant who worked with GM. A company insider admitted, "When the public sees the full-sized GM Chevrolet Caprice costing the same as the subcompact GM Cavalier, it's confusing. It was poor strategic planning."[13]

[13]Corporate Strategies, "General Motors: The next move is to restore each division's identity," *Business Week*, October 4, 1982.

Some estimates determined that the voluntary export restraint may have allowed Japanese producers to increase the price of a typical Japanese car sold in the United States by $600 to $1800 per car—an additional annual increase of 2 percent to 5.5 percent over the first four years of the VER. The reduced competition from the VER also allowed U.S. producers to increase their prices for comparable models by an estimated $150 to $600, which was a compounded annual growth rate of 0.4 percent to 1.5 percent over the same four years.[14]

GM's Performance and the Falling Dollar: 1985–1988

The rapid fall of the dollar, beginning in 1985, brought renewed hope to executives of the Big Three auto companies. After five years of holding ground, however, American automakers lost an additional 5 percent market share from 1985 to 1988. GM's market share suffered the most, falling 6.4 percent. The company's losses were, once again, at the hands of the Japanese producers, who gained an additional 3.4 percent of the market, during a period when the yen was rising and the dollar was falling. Ford's share grew by 2.8 percent, primarily the result of its new Taurus and Sable models, while Chrysler's share remained constant, only because they acquired AMC in 1987. GM's Chairman, Roger Smith, said that his company's goal was to capture 40 percent of the market through 1990. That was higher than the 35 percent that the company got in the first part of 1989, but below the 42 percent goal that GM officials had set in late 1986 and the 45 percent share that GM had averaged over the previous decade. " 'The new goal reflects GM's changing focus towards profitability,' said Leon Krain, GM's treasurer. Smith added that though the company lowered its market share goal, 'it is now in a strong position to provide maximum profitability.' "[15]

There were, however, two structural changes that had occurred in the pattern of trade and production in the auto industry that could affect the future of Smith's market share goals. The first was the introduction of a new player in 1986. Hyundai of Korea successfully launched a line of subcompacts in that year and, within two years, controlled 2.5 percent of the total U.S. market. A second change was the increased U.S. production of Japanese autos sold in the United States. In 1985, only 7 percent of the Japanese cars sold in the United States were produced there (by Honda since 1983 and Nissan since 1985). However, by 1988, four Japanese producers (Honda, Nissan, Mazda, and Toyota) were manufacturing 23 percent of their U.S. sales in the United States. See Exhibit 7 for the distribution of production and sales.

---

[14]Charles Collyns and Steven Dunaway, "The Cost of Trade Restraints: The Case of Japanese Automobile Exports to the United Japanese Automobile Exports to the United States," *International Monetary Fund Staff Papers*, March 1987, pp. 162, 164, 168 and 169.

[15]Doron Levin and Paul Ingrassia, "GM Cuts Market Share Goal but is Poised for Strong Profit, Smith Tells Analysts," *The Wall Street Journal*, April 4, 1987.

**Exhibit 7   Distribution of Auto Sales, Domestic and Overseas,
Average 1985–1988**

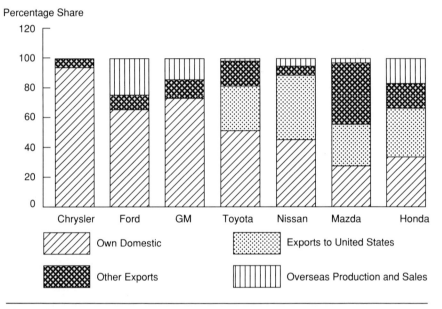

Source: Company Reports.

Though obstacles stood in the way of meeting its market share goals, GM had maintained a strong record of profitability that outshined both its lackluster sales and market share performance. The company's record profits of $4.8 billion in 1988 were 66 percent higher than in 1986—on sales of slightly over $100 billion in each of the last three years. The average after-tax return on sales for all auto producers is shown in Exhibit 8. GM's performance on profits, though strong, was overshadowed by Chrysler's and Ford's phenomenal returns over that period. Beginning in 1986, Ford outearned GM for the first time since 1924, and continued to surpass GM in profitability through 1988. Industry observers attributed the company's performance to improved quality, strong cost-cutting efforts, and an impressive new product line-up, which many agreed was the best in Ford's history. Recent sales and profit performance for the Big Three was reflected in stock prices in 1986 and 1987 when the share prices of Ford and Chrysler increased by 280 percent and 150 percent, respectively, and GM's stock price remained flat. After the stockmarket crash in October 1987, GM and Ford returned to their previous peaks, while Chrysler's stock price remained depressed, reflecting their poor showing in 1988 profits.

The favorable profit results shown by the U.S. automakers were not matched by Japanese producers whose profitability suffered in the mid-1980s. The rising yen boosted Japanese labor costs in dollar terms. Moreover, after years of growing labor productivity in the Japanese auto in-

Exhibit 8   Net Return on Sales

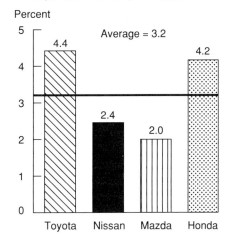

U.S. Auto Companies, 1981–1985

Percent

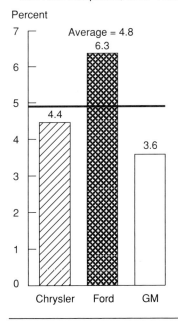

Japanese Auto Companies, 1981–1985

Percent

U.S. Auto Companies, 1986–1988

Percent

Japanese Auto Companies, 1986–1988

Percent

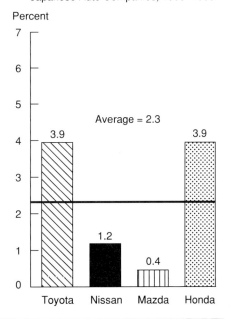

dustry, it had been flat since 1985. Refer to Exhibits 4 and 5 for a labor cost comparison in the U.S. and Japanese auto industry. Despite these rising costs, Japanese producers held their weighted average dollar price increases (Japanese auto production was priced in dollars) in this period to only 5.8 percent compared to American increases of 7 percent. Refer to Exhibit 6. This significantly depressed Japanese auto industry profitability. Their net return on sales was less than half of their pre-1985 level. Refer to Exhibit 8.

Japanese automakers' response to their dwindling profits was five-fold. First, Japanese car manufacturers began to shift their car production to new factories they built in the United States. Second, they started offering more high margin, upscale products in the U.S. market. In 1986, American Honda introduced the Acura and Integra models to the United States. In 1989, after the much-awaited arrival of the Toyota Lexus and the Nissan Infiniti, all of the major Japanese producers had product offerings in the high end, luxury market. Third, Japanese producers squeezed the profit-inflating premiums out of the margins of their American dealers. "In effect, a large portion of the increase in the retail price of Japanese cars was made up for by the elimination of those special dealer charges."[16] Fourth, Japanese producers slashed their production costs. From 1985 to 1988, Japanese auto companies mounted an austerity program described by industry observers as, "squeezing water out of a dry rag."[17] Fifth, they placed more emphasis on meeting their own domestic demand, particularly with high margin products, since they had experienced difficulties with earning profits overseas. In the Japanese domestic market, "growth in demand was at the highly profitable upper end of the market where Japanese manufacturers were starting to compete intensely. Nissan, which was in the process of renewing its model range from the top down, said its gains in market share and profits in 1988 were due almost entirely to sales of bigger cars."[18]

The only encouraging indicator for Japanese auto executives was the 3.4 percent market share gain in the U.S. auto market from 1985 to 1988, since Japanese auto profitability had taken a beating in the mid-1980s. During that time, big cost reduction programs were launched, internal procedures were streamlined, and automakers worked with their suppliers to increase productivity. But by 1988, Toyota's pre-tax profits, for example, jumped 31 percent. *The Economist* concluded: "This demonstrates another Japanese trait: the nerve to suffer short-term financial setbacks rather than risk losing market share."[19]

Criticism of Big Three Auto Pricing

By 1987, critics charged that GM and the other American automakers were not taking advantage of competitive opportunities. *The Wall Street Journal* queried in the subtitle of their lead story on U.S. automakers'

---

[16]Maryann Keller, "Japanese Cars Are Cheaper Than You Think," *Automotive Industries*, April 1988.

[17]Guy de Jonquieres, "Vehicle demand accelerates," *Financial Times*, December 7, 1988.

[18]de Jonquieres, op. cit.

[19]Motor Industry Survey, "Hard drive from the East," *The Economist*, October 15, 1988, p. 7.

improved chances, "Will They Blow It Again?" The news story noted that, "over the years, they have proved adept at blowing opportunities. True to form, they used the past year's surge in prices of Japanese and German cars to raise their own prices aggressively instead of holding the line to widen their price edge. 'This would have been a perfect opportunity to recapture market share,' fumed Wayne Angell, a governor of the Federal Reserve Board, 'These companies lack the vision of a world marketplace.' "[20] The management of the Big Three were starting to recognize that the problem might reside at their own doorstep. In 1987, for the first time since Arthur Andersen and Company's biennial survey of auto executives began in 1979, the auto industry's "own management practices" was cited first among the industry's problems.[21]

The price increases were confusing because not everyone was comparing comparably equipped automobiles. Most critics preferred to examine the base prices of automobiles, whereas management often preferred to talk about "options packages." For example, GM's Chevrolet Cavalier model, was base priced at $8,120 in 1988, a 12 percent base price increase over 1987. That "base" price contained $638 worth of now-standard equipment, including a glove box lock, color-coordinated seat belts, and an AM-FM stereo, all of which was optional equipment in 1987. In fact, the customer could not buy the 1987-equivalent standard model without those options in 1988. GM tried to further entice Cavalier buyers with an extra package of options, which included air conditioning, tinted glass, and sport mirrors, for an additional $1,477, minus a "discount" of $675. That discounted options package, which was unavailable previously, drove the price of the car up to $8,922, or 23 percent above the base price in 1987. Critics charged that some options, such as an upgraded transmission and color-coordinated seat belts, were purchased by fewer than 10 percent of car buyers in 1987.

In 1988, GM was compelled to spend $4.3 billion on rebates and incentives compared to $2.7 billion in 1987. Originally used only to reduce huge vehicle inventories, rebates and other sales programs had become a regular part of everyday car marketing by the end of the 1980s, especially for the Big Three. Typically, one company led the Big Three in offering a particular incentive package, such as special financing rates, and the other two companies followed suit. Most foreign car manufacturers offered rebates of their own, though not necessarily following the lead of the Big Three. As the dollar began its fall in 1985, foreign automakers increasingly began to offer cash back and financing incentives to make up for slow sales. By 1987, virtually every Japanese automaker offered incentives on a regular basis, often matching the promotions from domestic manufacturers. Prior to the late 1980s, Japanese producers had

---

[20]Paul Ingrassia, "U.S. Auto Makers Get Chance to Regain Sales From Foreign Rivals," *The Wall Street Journal*, April 16, 1987.

[21]Ibid.

offered incentives to dealers who could then choose whether or not to pass those savings on to customers. Since that time, however, most Japanese automakers aimed their incentives directly at the consumer.

"Incentives are eating up cost savings," said David Healy, and auto analyst at Drexel Burnham Lambert. By Healy's calculations, "GM was spending $1,000, or 10 percent of the average car price, on incentives for every vehicle sold in North America during the fourth quarter of 1988."[22] "That figure compared with $700 per car (7.4 percent of the average car price) in the first quarter of 1988 and the previous record of $400 per car (4.4 percent of the average car price) in third quarter 1987."[23]

In response to a front-page *Wall Street Journal* article in early 1988 asking, "Fateful Choice: Did U.S. Car Makers Err by Raising Prices When the Yen Rose?," Robert Stempel, president of General Motors responded with the following letter to the editor:

Contrary to your April 18 page one story, "Fateful Choice," domestic car manufacturers have been responsibly pricing their products. To report otherwise is a disservice to the American consumer.

An in-depth assessment of General Motors' pricing would reveal that, in terms of the way customers buy cars, they are paying slightly more than 6 percent over the price they paid three years ago; this is below the overall increase in the general U.S. economy. Today's marketplace has become very complex, so a thorough assessment of new-car prices has to consider much more than traditional "base-car" prices. It is also necessary to evaluate the major sales incentives that have become so prevalent in the marketplace.

For example, substantial discounts are available on many GM car lines when options are purchased in a pre-specified "package," which is designed to include the items most people would order separately. On a 1988 Chevrolet Cavalier, a package of popular options costing the customer $1,477 when purchased separately is discounted by $675 when ordered as a complete package. In addition, the competitive marketplace has frequently required the use of cash rebates or low-interest-rate financing on many car lines. While these sales incentives may vary during the course of the year, the same 1988 Chevrolet Cavalier already mentioned with the $675 option-package discount also pays a cash rebate of $400 currently.

Continuing with the Cavalier example, the current customer would pay $8,597 today compared with $8,908 three years ago—a reduction of $311, or 3.5 percent. For GM's passenger cars as a whole, the combination of lower-than-inflation base-car price adjustments and the introduction of option-package discounts and retail sales incentives has held overall 1988 model prices to about 6 percent more than for 1985 models—an average increase of slightly more than 2 percent over this three-year period.

[22]Doron Levin, "G.M. Net Rises 67.5% in Quarter," *The New York Times*, February 15, 1989.

[23]Schlesinger, op. cit.

Looking at price developments for the industry as a whole shows a similar picture. The U.S. Bureau of Labor Statistics Price Index for new domestic passenger cars, which also reflects incentives, shows a cumulative increase of only 3.9 percent from the summer of 1985 through March of 1988, the most recent data available. The same index has decreased 5.6 percent since last October, the month of model year 1988 introduction.

This particular index provides a measurement of the wholesale price of a select sample of specifically contented passenger cars. As such, the fleet mix and option content availability are held constant, so it more closely approximates a "pure" price series than does the GM fleet average figure cited above.

On the basis of both GM and BLS statistics, the implication that domestic cars are not responsibly priced ignores the facts and misleads the consumer. Clearly, domestically produced automobiles offer the American consumer better value today."[24]

Despite Stempel's response to the article, *The Wall Street Journal* launched another offensive in their lead article on May 23, 1989. "The cheaper dollar created a window of opportunity for many U.S. industries to recover ground lost to cheap imports. But Detroit seized the opportunity to boost short-term profits by raising prices, instead of seeking long-term gains in market share. Now the Big Three's window of opportunity seems to be slamming shut [the dollar rose from 120 yen to 140 yen]."[25] Meanwhile, critics charged that though U.S. automakers, aided by the cheaper dollar and the VER, were able to close the gap on quality and productivity in the mid 1980s, Japanese automakers were gaining on the Big Three once again. In the first four months of 1989, Japanese car companies increased their sales in the U.S. by 6 percent, while U.S. producers car sales dropped 10 percent. Thomas Wagner, general manager of Ford Motor's Ford Division, said of Japan's auto companies, "I believe they are gaining strength. It's going to get down and dirty in the next three years."[26] Industry analyst Christopher Cedergren of J.D. Power expected Japan's share of the U.S. market to grow to 27 percent by 1992. Toyota, for example, had not raised prices in over six months on its cars and was providing sales incentives to dealers who turned them into cash rebates. In preparation, U.S. automakers were spending billions of dollars on rebates and financing packages—the types of programs that observers expected to dig into domestic profits.

[24]"GM Cars Aren't Overpriced," *The Wall Street Journal*, June 6, 1988.

[25]Joseph B. White, "After a Brief Pause, Japanese Auto Makers Gain on Detroit Again," *The Wall Street Journal*, May 23, 1989.

[26]Ibid.

Questions

1. What were the causes of GM's declining market share? Were the primary factors the same over the past decade or have some factors become more or less important?

2. What was the contribution of the rising dollar to GM's problems between 1980 and 1985?

3. Did GM price its cars "responsibly" between 1985 and 1988, as GM President Robert Stempel claims?

4. Did GM miss a competitive opportunity as Federal Reserve Governor Wayne Angell maintains?

CASE 9

Colgate-Palmolive in Mexico

The problems of hyperinflation and devaluation are always interrelated in practice and both are phenomena greatly influenced by monetary policy. At the broadest level of analysis, the data in the Colgate-Palmolive in Mexico case allows one to reconstruct the conditions that led to the cycle of hyperinflation and devaluation in Mexico starting with the oil shocks of the 1970s. In the 1980s there were typically dozens of countries that were experiencing hyperinflation at any one time, therefore the situation described in this chapter's case is not a unique managerial problem. Typically these situations involved Third-World countries attempting to maintain rapid economic growth as well as a managed exchange rate system that did not allow completely unrestricted capital flows and foreign exchange transactions.

Managers in such an environment must decide whether hyperinflation will require a change in their business strategies, and whether the exchange rate adjustments will affect their competitive position against any actual and potential rivals. Much of the richness of this analysis results from examining the implications of hyperinflation and exchange rate changes for various functional policies, such as the options for the marketing, financial, production, purchasing, R&D, and the data processing department.

Finally, there is the issue of how one should evaluate the performance and integrate the operations of a corporate subsidiary competing under conditions of hyperinflation and devaluation. Traditional measures of performance such as dollar remittances to the corporate home office are distorted by inflation and exchange rate changes. At the same time devaluations result in changes in competitive advantage for products produced in that country. These are opportunities that the corporation may want to seize by reevaluating their corporate strategies.

Colgate-Palmolive's worldwide market presence was built on the strength of its household and personal care products. Long known for its Colgate brand toothpaste and Palmolive brand soap, the company was a major global force in the packaged goods field and had an international reputation for excellence. Chairman and chief executive officer, Reuben Mark, believed that strengthening its current activities as well as selectively introducing new products would be the vanguard of Colgate's continued growth in world markets.

Colgate's products were sold in over 100 countries around the world. Colgate had manufacturing or distribution facilities in 54 countries. See Exhibit 1 for an organizational chart. Its major overseas manufacturing facilities were located in Australia, Brazil, Canada, Colombia, France, Germany, Italy, Mexico, and the United Kingdom. The company's operations were organized into seven subsidiaries: The United States, Mexico, France, Europe, Latin America, Asia-Pacific, and Africa and the Middle East. Excluding the parent operation in the United States, only two divisions, Mexico and France, were free-standing subsidiaries, both of which were among the largest subsidiaries in terms of sales and profits. Colgate's Mexican operating results were not aggregated with those of the Latin American division, and France's operating results were not included with those of Colgate's European division. The president of the Mexican operation, Michael Tangney, reported directly to Senior Executive Vice President Roderick Turner in New York, rather than to the president of the Latin American division. Tangney was also an international vice president. All general managers of the subsidiaries were expected to recommend and then implement decisions regarding strategy and operating policy.

During the two oil price shocks in the 1970s, Colgate's Mexican subsidiary had responded remarkably well. Its new product launches, particularly those in powdered cleansers and hand dishwashing detergents, during those years kept it healthy through the early 1980s. However, the economic changes that the country had undergone since the beginning of the Mexican debt crisis in August 1982 made Colgate-Mexico a special concern among Colgate's subsidiaries because of Mexico's relative inexperience in operating under hyperinflationary conditions. At the beginning of 1987, Mexico's annual inflation rate for the 1987 calendar year was forecasted to increase to 120 percent , and gross domestic product, a measure of the economy's growth, was expected to slow to 1 percent. See *The Mexican Economy: Selected Data Exhibits for 1967–1987*, reproduced as Exhibits 6–18 at the end of this case for data on the economic policies and performance of the Mexican economy. In the year preceding the U.S. stock market crash on October 19, 1987, Mexico's

The case was prepared by Research Associate Julia Horn under the supervision of Professor Michael G. Rukstad. Copyright © 1989 by the President and Fellows of Harvard College. Harvard Business Case 9-389-105.

Exhibit 1   Colgate-Palmolive in Mexico

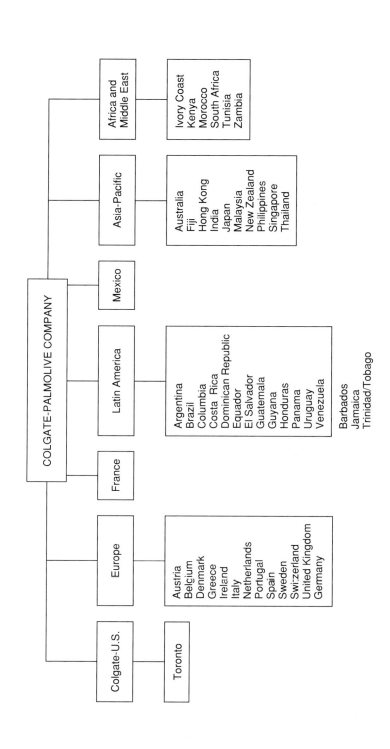

stock market was the fastest growing in the world. However, the decline of the U.S. stock market on that day precipitated declines around the world and Mexico was no exception. Just five weeks after its all-time high on October 5, 1987, the Mexican stock market lost 75 percent of its value.

On November 16–20, 1987, in the midst of continued fear of economic decline in Mexico, management from both Colgate Corporate and Colgate-Mexico, including Turner and Tangney, conducted the annual budget meeting in Mexico City. See Exhibits 2 and 3 for Colgate-Mexico's financial performance.

Economic and Political Background of the Mexican Economy

Beginning in the 1940s and continuing through the 1960s, Mexico's economic policy was based largely on protectionism and import substitution. When President Luis Echeverria took office in 1970, he addressed the unresolved matter of excessive dependency on foreign capital by announcing an aggressive trade policy to limit imports in order to boost

Exhibit 2   Colgate-Mexico—Balance Sheet (Thousands)

	1985	1986	1987
Cash and marketable securities	$ 8,336	$ 8,087	$ 950
Accounts receivable	12,774	14,728	23,006
Inventories	21,574	24,178	24,927
Total Prepaid Expenses	*(2,464)*	*82*	*4,130*
Total Current Assets	*40,220*	*47,075*	*53,013*
Total Intercompany Balances	*(512)*	*13*	*4,403*
Property, plant and equipment:			
Land and buildings	1,940	1,940	1,940
Machinery and equipment	42,562	45,921	49,701
Total property, plant and equipment	44,502	47,861	51,641
Depreciation and amortization	19,535	22,531	25,182
Total Property, Plant and Equipment (Net)	*24,967*	*25,330*	*26,459*
Miscellaneous investments	4	1	1
Total Assets	*$64,679*	*$72,419*	*$83,876*
Short-term debt	0	637	11,120
Long-term debt payable in one year	811	70	5
Accounts payable	9,248	14,576	12,094
Miscellaneous accruals	8,348	5,973	4,090
Total Current Liabilities	*18,407*	*21,256*	*27,309*
Long-term debt	1,247	18	0
Deferred liabilities	1,863	1,298	1,242
Common stock	26,533	8,409	8,409
Retained earnings	16,629	41,438	46,916
Total Stockholders' Equity	*43,162*	*49,847*	*55,325*
Total Liabilities and Stockholders' Equity	*$64,679*	*$72,419*	*$83,876*

Exhibit 3 Colgate-Mexico—Income Statement (Thousands)

	1985	1986	1987
Sales	**$217,205**	**$193,409**	**$229,474**
Cost of sales	151,298	136,902	156,386
Gross profit	65,907	56,507	71,088
Media	9,583	5,817	6,468
Promotion	1,050	980	2,312
Total Advertising	**9,633**	**6,797**	**8,780**
Total marketing and selling	4,287	3,614	4,151
Total freight and warehousing	13,095	11,075	11,285
General and administrative	20,546	13,952	26,342
Total Operating Expenses	**47,561**	**35,438**	**50,558**
Net profit before taxes	18,346	21,069	20,530
Total provision for taxes	11,331	9,908	11,553
Net Profit After Taxes	**7,015**	**11,161**	**8,977**

foreign exchange earnings. In addition, he passed a new and restrictive law on foreign investment. Nonetheless, slowing exports resulting from the slowdown in world growth and a fivefold increase in interest payments tripled the deficit on the external current account from 1970 to 1976. Unfettered Mexican growth spurred on by stimulative government policies caused inflation, which had been largely nonexistent since 1950, to climb. In August 1976, only a few months before the end of Echeverria's term, the Bank of Mexico devalued the peso by 64.8 percent, the first devaluation since 1954.

In 1976, President Lopez-Portillo took office just after the peso had lost over half of its value and $3 billion of capital had fled the country. At the beginning of his term, estimates of the huge number of new oil finds were first made public. In the five years of oil price increases that followed, Mexico borrowed an additional $60 billion abroad against future oil revenues. "However, by 1981, during which one-third of the money was borrowed, the borrowing was not to finance investment; it was designed to prop up the country against the effects of a softening oil price, high interest rates abroad, and a world recession. Inflation was on the rise, anticipating the inevitable devaluation of the peso, and capital left the country."[1]

The first devaluation of the peso by 45 percent occurred in February 1982. By early August, following wage and price increases, a new flight of capital began. On August 5, the government restricted interest payments and vital imports to the current exchange rate of 49 pesos to the dollar, while an open market was in effect for all other transactions. The result was a second devaluation of the peso by 50 percent on that day.

[1]*Economist*, September 5, 1987.

On August 13, the Mexican government announced that it could no longer service its foreign debt. Following the announcement, the Federal Reserve Board and the International Monetary Fund encouraged public and private bankers to help, resulting in an aid package that totaled $11 billion, including a 90-day postponement of principal repayments.

Following the onset of the debt crisis and the nationalization of the banks in September 1982, President Miguel de la Madrid took office in December 1982. He was committed to a new, broad economic policy that would open Mexico's economy to world markets, roll back the extent of state ownership of resources, and take strides toward fiscal stability. After the rescheduling of all of Mexico's $80 billion in debt repayments over 20 years in 1982, real GDP in 1983 contracted by 5 percent from the previous year, the worst decline in postwar years. In 1984 real GDP grew by 3.5 percent as the worldwide recession in 1981 and 1982, particularly in the U.S., came to an end and demand for Mexican exports increased by 8.4 percent. However, by 1985, the flight of capital and the strain of servicing the $100 billion debt put renewed pressure on public finances. In addition, Mexican oil, which sold for $26.70 a barrel in February 1986, had collapsed to $8.60 by July 1986. The lower oil price reduced government revenues by more than 30 percent and forced new changes in the management of the Mexican economy.

Mr. de la Madrid's new trade policy, part of his broader economic policy of opening the Mexican economy to the outside world, was based on exposing Mexican businesses to competitive pressure from abroad and encouraging the growth of nonoil exports. In 1986, Mexico ratified membership in the General Agreement on Tariffs and Trade (GATT), which began to open up trading channels and to reduce protectionism. And by 1986, only 38 percent of the value of Mexico's exports were from oil and mining, down from 78 percent in 1982. Some state-owned industries, primarily the energy industry, continued to be outside GATT rules and the country still enjoyed some of the concessions of GATT that protected developing countries. However, Mexico was reducing both the level of its tariffs and the number of tariff rates. By the end of 1987, when the country's new duty law (written to abide by GATT rules) would come into effect, the higher official prices for imported goods, used to calculate tariff levels, would be abolished.

Colgate's Corporate Strategy

Colgate-Palmolive's corporate goals focused on increasing global profitability and enhancing shareholder value. By 1991, the company hoped to reach and maintain a 15 percent return on capital. It had averaged 10.5 percent since 1984, when Mark first established the 15 percent goal. In the company's 1985 annual report, Mark stressed that Colgate was also taking strides to achieve global low-cost producer status. New product introductions and product revitalizations were also numerous and important to the overall growth and profitability of the company. In 1985 alone, Colgate worldwide launched or revitalized 277 products.

In that same year, Colgate-Palmolive began a strategic restructuring to increase profitability. The restructuring primarily involved selling off a food company, Riviana, and the Etonic and Bike athletic lines. Colgate was then able to concentrate on three core businesses: Household and Personal Care, Health Care, and Specialty Marketing, made up of smaller businesses that occupied distinct market niches. The largest business, household and personal care, comprised 74 percent of total company sales and 56 percent of operating profit in 1986. The health care business accounted for 20 percent of sales and 26 percent of operating profit, and the specialty marketing business accounted for 6 percent of sales and 18 percent of operating profit in 1986.

Colgate's Mexican Strategy

The main goal of Colgate-Mexico's strategic plan, common for all of Colgate's subsidiaries, was to improve market shares with high-quality products while working to gradually improve dollar profits and remittances. As Assistant Controller Morgan O'Brien summarized, "Our primary financial charge is to achieve our budgeted profits while simultaneously building consumer franchises and brand equity." Profitable volume growth and protection of shareholder equity were basic, ongoing goals. "In 1986," Tangney explained, "we even reduced tonnage growth because that growth was not predicted to be profitable." All of Colgate-Mexico's functional goals related to its broader strategy of being a cost-competitive producer of high-quality household and personal care products for the Mexican domestic market, while continuing to be a good corporate citizen. Management described the market boundaries of Colgate-Mexico as a company devoted to, "caring for consumers, their possessions and their environment by cleaning, treating, protecting, and enhancing their personal appearance as well as the surfaces around them."

Key Operating Policies in a Hyperinflationary Environment

Products

Colgate-Mexico produced 40 different products in 16 product categories. In comparison, there were 43 products in 13 categories in the United States. The subsidiary had dominant market shares of 70 percent to 90 percent in some products such as fine fabric detergents, fabric softeners, and dental creams. Beginning in the 1960s, the Mexican government exerted price controls on certain essential consumer goods as a means of protecting the consumer's purchasing power. Included in the Mexican government's "basket" of price-controlled goods were soaps, laundry detergents, and dental creams. In 1986, 86 percent of Mexican households already used laundry detergents and 83 percent used dental creams, whereas 35 percent used liquid cleaners and 21 percent used scouring powders.

Colgate-Mexico's product line targeted a wide range of the 82 million consumers in Mexico. Though most of its products were targeted toward the basic needs of all consumers, some products such as fine fabric detergents and fabric softeners, were aimed at high- and middle-income groups. Vice President of Marketing and Sales, Ken May, noted that certain products, such as bar soaps and some detergents, were largely recession-proof. However, all buyers were sensitive to price rises, and often stopped buying products that were considered luxury items, such as the floor cleaners, when their prices increased in comparison with necessity items. In fact, in tough economic times buyers often switched from more expensive shampoos and liquid floor cleaners to less expensive bar soaps and powdered detergents that could be used inexpensively to clean their hair and wash floors in addition to their intended purpose.

Marketing

One of the primary responsibilities of May and the rest of the Marketing Department was staying at least even with inflation. "In the past two years," said May, "prices for all products have had to increase in response to faster increases in our cost structure as a result of growing inflation." Margins were forecasted to be between 30 percent and 45 percent in 1987. In price-controlled categories, the government gave Colgate and other companies a complicated formula based on documented cost increases so as to recover these cost increases when they accumulated to a 10 percent change. During 1987, however, the government began to slow down the price increase authorization procedure, and to grant only a fraction of the price increases needed to offset the cost increase.

Colgate-Mexico began implementing a stricter policy in 1987 on price-controlled products that would disallow shipping to clients until they accepted the approved selling price increases. Specifically, on those controlled products with the lowest margins, soaps and detergents, Colgate-Mexico's policy was to immediately adopt the price increases and to cut the orders of those customers who did not intend to accept the immediate price change. Notably, government-run accounts which could account for as much as 30 percent of Colgate's volume, would refuse to accept a new purchase price until private sector retail accounts had already raised prices to the public. In noncontrolled product categories, Colgate's general policy was to allow a one-week grace period for customers to accept selling price increases. May estimated that the pretax income effect of Colgate's stricter selling price increase implementation policy was a partial help to offsetting the delays in approved price increases.

For those products that were not price-controlled, there was free-market pricing. Selling price increases were typically announced to customers one week before they became effective. The percentage by which individual product prices rose varied from month to month. The company's product costing was based on replacement cost estimates and projections. This method was initiated in 1985 (the company had been on LIFO accounting since 1982) and was based on what the company expected it would have to pay to restock its inventory. Restocking costs were based on costs directly related to supplier price increases. Therefore, the marketing department had to keep close contact with the purchasing department which had the task of monitoring the prices for some 2,000 items of raw and packaging materials on a daily basis. These costs had to be projected into the next month while also projecting the inflation rate's impact on those costs. Colgate-Mexico's latest price increases before the November budget meeting were on October 25, in response to the local inflation rate of 8.3 percent for the month of October. The nominal interest rate for October was 11.6 percent for 30-day loans.

The management of customer credit was another key function of the marketing department. May's goal was to reduce accounts receivable from over 30 to under 25 days by offering new, stricter credit and trading terms. Furthermore, May believed that a significant opportunity laid in accelerating the steps involved in recuperating invoice and collection documents more rapidly from clients, especially the government. If this were accomplished, May believed it could save the company as much as $5 million on a pretax income basis which would partially offset the decline in profits resulting from price controls. May emphasized the point that incremental sales can often come with a significant fall in margin. "Profitability can disappear quickly if we must purchase incremental or replacement raw and packing materials with borrowed money only to sell to customers who will delay paying us by as much as 30 days beyond our stated terms."

Credit terms within Mexico had historically been set by product category. Price-controlled categories were generally 21 days, non-controlled household products between 30 and 45 days, and personal care products, with higher margins and slower in-store rotation, 45 to 60 days. Government accounts generally demanded 10 to 15 days more credit than the private sector. With an average "days outstanding" of about 30 days Colgate-Mexico was already the strictest among its competitors in selling terms and in the discipline of their application. Given the wide range of Colgate-Mexico's categories, with almost 50 percent of sales in personal care categories, the company stood in very good financial shape relative to its competitors. Procter & Gamble's receivable period was estimated at 25 days because 90 percent of its business was in price-controlled categories. Local competitor La Corona averaged about 45 days because of their reliance on government distribution channels and on their long-term policy of relying on promotions to the exclusion of all media advertising. Gillette and Cheseborough-Pond's, personal care product companies, had standard credit terms of 60 days.

Colgate-Mexico hoped to generate $18 million (or 7 percent) of incremental sales by the end of 1988 on a wave of new product introductions that would return at least a 20 percent contribution (margin less advertising and promotion), while maintaining the company's profitability into the 1990s. The new products ranged from what May termed "fast payback engines" such as a fresh breath gel toothpaste, to those that were part of a portfolio expansion, such as a new line of colognes. In 1987, it was estimated that new products would increase tonnage by 13,000 tons (4.7 percent) and add $10.4 million (4.5 percent) to total sales. By the end of 1988 new products could add 34,000 tons (13.3 percent) and $45.3 million (16 percent) to total sales. The Marketing Department had set minimum standards for new product launches, including: Net yearly sales of greater than $1.0 million, a contribution margin greater than $300,000 or 30 percent by the third year, and a five-month payback period. For new personal care products, the criteria included: Net yearly sales of greater than $650,000, and a payback period of eight months. Flanker or side brands, such as Ajax Pine Cleaner, a flanker brand of Ajax, had to comprise at least 10 percent of main brand sales, and offer a higher operating profit than the main brand and an eight-month payback period to be considered for introduction.

Competitors

Colgate-Mexico's largest competitor across all product categories was Procter & Gamble (P&G), which sold in 4 of Colgate's 16 product categories. See Exhibits 4 and 5 for competitor information. P&G in Mexico had not followed Colgate-Mexico's strategy in the 1970s of launching new products in non-price-controlled categories. Consequently, P&G's strength was in the price-controlled categories of soap and detergents. P&G's Mexican subsidiary was established in 1948. It operated two plants in Mexico City, one of which it acquired when it bought Richardson-Vicks in 1986. The Mexican subsidiary employed an estimated 3,600 people, including Richardson-Vicks. In 1986, P&G in Mexico had roughly the same amount of revenues as Colgate and was believed to have reported a minor pretax loss (excluding Richardson-Vicks) due to the price controls on soaps and detergents. P&G was the market leader in both toilet soaps and detergents with 45 percent and 49 percent market shares, respectively. Colgate was the leader in more than half of the product categories in which it competed. May believed that the reason for Colgate-Mexico's financial and marketing successes in so many product areas was that, "Many important new product launches were made in the 1970s in the non-price-controlled categories, where P&G was less aggressive in expanding its product lines."

Unilever, a potential new competitor, was essentially not active in Colgate's product categories in Mexico. However, the company was active

Exhibit 4 Consolidated Financial Data of Colgate-Palmolive, P&G, and Unilever (in $ millions)

	1987	1986	1985	1984	1983
Colgate-Palmolive					
Sales	5,647	4,985	4,524	4,985	4,855
Net income	54[a]	177	109	72	198
ROE	6.2%	18.8%	15.7%	11.7%	14.9%
ROC	12.7%	11.2%	10.2%	10.0%	11.8%
Total Assets	***3,288***	***2,846***	***2,814***	***2,568***	***2,664***
Proctor and Gamble					
Sales	17,000	15,439	13,552	12,946	12,452
Net income	327	709	635	890	866
ROE	7.5%	12.6%	12.3%	18.4%	38.8%
ROC	7.5%	8.5%	9.2%	14.1%	
Total Assets	***13,715***	***13,055***	***9,683***	***8,898***	***8,135***
Unilever					
Sales	29,790	25,368	24,205	18,670	19,410
Net income	1,361	982	748	583	559
ROE	24.8%	17.5%	16.9%	13.6%	12.3%
ROC	12.2%	10.2%	9.2%	8.6%	8.8%
Total Assets	***17,998***	***20,413***	***13,521***	***11,236***	***11,206***

Source: Company annual reports

[a]Colgate-Palmolive undertook a major restructuring in 1987. The charge of that restructuring was $150 after taxes.

in dental creams, fabric softeners, shampoos, and body cleaners in the U.S. and other countries, and was estimated to be the world's largest producer of detergents outside of the United States. Unilever had a strong Mexican presence in foods and artificial flavors through its acquisition of five local companies, each with its own plant. The company had also acquired Cheseborough-Ponds in 1986, a U.S.-based manufacturer of personal care products and toiletries including lotions, with a plant in Mexico. Cheseborough-Ponds of Mexico had 1986 estimated sales of $36 million and pretax profits of $8 million. There was a possibility that Unilever could become a direct competitor in Mexico in the next year or two. Because detergents, one of Unilever's leading product categories, were price-controlled in Mexico, Colgate's management believed that they could maintain their current market share in that category without significant concern for the presence of a new detergent entry from Unilever.

In four of Colgate-Mexico's markets it faced a third competitor, La Corona, a local household products company that produced soaps and detergents. La Corona had one plant in Mexico, employed an estimated 2,600 people, and had 1986 sales of about $200 million and pretax profits

Exhibit 5   Household and Personal Care Products' Competitive Position in Mexico

	Five-Year Average Growth in tons (1982–1986)[b]	Percent of Colgate-Mexico's Sales in 1987	Competitors and Market Share[a]				
			Colgate-Mexico	Proctor & Gamble	La Corona	Del Centro	Total
Price-controlled Products:		67	14/48[c]				
Detergents	(3)	25	3/22	4/49	3/27		10/98
Hand dishwashing products	6	9	1/57	1/42	1/1		3/100
Laundry bar products	(9)	1	3/3	1/1	2/55		6/59
Toilet soap	(0)	12	6/32	3/45	3/13		12/90
Dental creams	9	20	1/90	1/8			2/98
Nonprice-controlled Products:		33	14/54[c]				
Powder cleansers	(4)	2	2/80				2/83
Liquid all-purpose cleaners	7	4	2/18	1/12			3/30
Fabric softeners	27	8	1/90	1/1			2/98
Fine fabric liquid detergents	6	4	1/90				1/98
Shampoos	17	9	3/22	1/1		3/18	7/41
Male hair preparations	(1)	1	2/23				2/23
Toothbrushes	na	1	2/13				2/13
Baby line	4	3	1/40				1/40
All other	na	1					

[a]Number of brands/share of market

[b]Total growth in tons is over the four-year period from 1982–1986

[c]An average weighted by the number of shares

of $20 million. Unilever had a licensing agreement with La Corona to market two of Unilever's soaps locally (Lux and Rexona) and some industry sources had speculated in the past that Unilever would eventually buy La Corona. La Corona was also an active competitor in margarines and cooking oils, two significant and traditional categories for Unilever.

Distribution and Sales

Colgate-Mexico distributed its products through three different channels in Mexico. The first channel was the food wholesaler, who sold to both the small supermarket chains and "mom and pop" stores that were not government clients. These chains made up over half of Colgate-Mexico's business. The food wholesalers typically paid Colgate quickly and on time. The second channel was national supermarket chains, made up primarily of five major clients. The third channel was composed of the government clients, the largest of which was CONASUPO, which accounted for 12 percent of total sales. CONASUPO owned 25 percent of Mexico's supermarkets in addition to controlling the movement of agricultural commodities in Mexico. Government clients typically extended credit terms the furthest. A smaller channel was the drug wholesaler, who distributed the product to drugstores around the country and accounted for approximately 10 percent of sales.

Colgate had its own distribution and salesforce of 120 people. An estimated 100 to 150 trucks carried the products out of the single factory in Mexico City each day. The salesforce's performance was evaluated by account, territory, and zone. Key accounts, made up of such customers as CONASUPO, represented 60 percent to 70 percent of the business. Salespeople typically visited those key accounts once or twice per week. Nelson Garcia-Mella, director of trade marketing, explained, "The main traditional direct expenses of each retail account are: salespeople, freight, promotional allowances, the shelf staff who arrange the products on the shelf, and the push staff who demonstrate the products to customers in the store. More importantly, however, is the 'accounts receivable cost,' or the financial cost of waiting for these accounts to pay us. The financing of account receivables is a key factor in measuring if a given sale or order is profitable or not."

Purchasing and Production

The primary function of Purchasing Director Michael Vander May and his staff of 25 was obtaining some 2,000 individual chemicals and packaging materials necessary for Colgate's products. In 1986, Colgate-Mexico purchased $150 million of material inputs. Of that total, approximately $125 million was purchased locally, with the remainder imported. Fifty-five percent of the inputs purchased were raw materials, 35 percent were packaging materials, and 10 percent were essential oils.

The department's packaging goals included the reduction of costs to increase competitiveness. The subsidiary had been negotiating for the purchase of a local bottle producer, Demi, which had 1986 sales of about $1 million, some of which were to Colgate. If purchased, Demi could produce almost 35 percent of Colgate's total bottle purchases. Colgate-Mexico's in-house packaging group had also developed lighter-weight, less expensive plastic bottles for liquid cleaners and fabric softeners which were expected to reduce packaging costs.

The remaining 10 percent of inputs that the company purchased were essential oils such as perfumes, flavors and their components, most of which were imported. In 1986, Colgate-Mexico spent over $20 million on essential oils, from mostly international suppliers.

Vander May worked closely with the finance department on price negotiations with suppliers in order to monitor the effect on margins and the need for new selling prices for Colgate products. Vander May and the Purchasing Department met weekly to discuss ways to reduce costs. "The first step in negotiations with suppliers is simply indicating that you want to do business with them," said Vander May. Long-term contracts with all suppliers were typically three months, unless imported materials were involved, in which case contracts were generally one month because of the possibility of exchange rate fluctuations. "All contracts are open to negotiation, and suppliers usually will not guarantee a price," Vander May added. Colgate often bundled credit terms with prices in the total package they offered to suppliers. The largest supplier, Pemex, the state-owned petroleum company, often demanded payment in 24 hours on certain products.

Negotiations and purchasing contracts, regardless of whether materials were imported or purchased domestically, were based on the less volatile controlled exchange rate, which was set by the government, rather than the free-market exchange rate, which fluctuated daily. Many of the company's imported raw materials waited on the U.S. side of the border for the import documentation needed to purchase controlled rate dollars. The free-market rate was used to purchase dollars for dividend remittances. The controlled rate was used to buy raw materials and to pay monthly royalties. The government estimated that 80 percent of all transactions in Mexico occurred at the controlled rate.

Vander May explained the purchasing options available to Colgate-Mexico. "Though there is alternative sourcing, we are not as flexible as we would like to be. For many of the necessary materials, there are only a few suppliers. In the case of detergents, the government owns many of the companies that supply the chemicals we use such as sodium sulfate, meaning that we have only one supplier. This makes negotiations somewhat difficult." However, Vander May explained that Colgate-Mexico did have leverage. In addition to the option of using imported raw materials (which were not necessarily cheaper), Colgate-U.S.'s international purchasing department could help find the best alternative sourcing by combining its worldwide purchasing and competitively bidding on sources. Prior to Mexico's accession to GATT in 1986, import permits were required and were especially difficult to obtain when sourcing inputs for which there were local substitutes. By 1987, permits were easier to obtain and were not needed in most cases. The country was reducing import duties, and opening the border to make Mexican raw materials more competitive.

Sixty-percent of Colgate-Mexico's total product costs were input costs. The company's direct labor costs were just 3.5 percent of total product cost. Mexico's minimum wage of approximately $.44 per hour was among the lowest in the world, compared to $3.35 per hour for the minimum wage in the United States. The company was one of the largest employers in Mexico, employing 2,130 people directly and between 5,000 and 6,000 people in total throughout the country. David Stinson, vice president of manufacturing, further explained Colgate-Mexico's manufacturing operations, "Because capital expenditures for equipment are almost nonexistent, we have to get more out of the equipment we have." In 1986, the company imported $3 to $4 million of equipment for its only plant located in Mexico City, "The government understands that we have to import equipment. Some sophisticated equipment is just not available here," Stinson said.

Colgate's Mexico City plant had been built in 1948 and was thus relatively antiquated. Unlike modern plants, it utilized much equipment that had been fully depreciated. Specifically, it employed batch production as opposed to the modern continuous flow production seen in many U.S. plants. As a result, for example, it took 180 minutes to switch production from one type of dental cream to another. In total, the company produced approximately 1,100 tons of its products per day. In 1986, over 200 tons were produced per worker at Colgate's Mexican plant. Management believed that installing significant additional capacity or vertically integrating at the current site in Mexico was improbable because of government restrictions on expansion.

Finance and Control

Colgate-Mexico's main thrust was to develop strong brands by strengthening market share, by gradually growing profits, and increasing both remittances and Colgate-Palmolive shareholder value.

The Mexican operation was a wholly-owned subsidiary of the U.S. parent. O'Brien explained the rationale for the subsidiary's financial objectives: "Maximizing market share in the long run allows us to slowly improve profits and remittances. Our growth in dollar remittances helps fulfill the parent company's need for an adequate return on investment, and provides a measure of protection against future devaluation."

Remittances were sent in the form of dividends and royalties, both of which were tax deductible in Mexico. Royalties were subject to a 21 percent withholding tax while dividends suffered a 55 percent withholding tax. Both of these were subject to a 46 percent U.S. tax for the parent, yet the foreign taxes paid were available for credit.

In terms of reducing exposure and optimizing cash remitted, royalties were preferred over dividends due to the lower withholding tax. Colgate-Mexico's royalty payments to Colgate-Palmolive were authorized by the Mexican government under a "transfer of technology" agreement in which Colgate-U.S. provided the know-how and technology to its subsidiary, in exchange for royalties calculated as a percent of sales. In 1986 the company sought to change its technology agreement and increase the royalty percent above the 2 percent of sales which had been in force for many years. In a two-month period Colgate's legal and research departments had gathered a substantial amount of documentation from all over the company that showed the appropriateness of a move towards the 5 percent to 7.5 percent rate paid by its other subsidiaries worldwide. This documentation was presented to the Mexican Transfer of Technology Department. After a few months of review and negotiation, the company achieved a new contract which increased royalties to either 3 percent or 5 percent, depending upon the product.

The new contract also permitted the subsidiary to remit royalties on a monthly rather than a quarterly basis. The government did not allow Colgate-Mexico or any other Mexican subsidiary to renegotiate its royalty contract every year. The government typically granted a contract for a 10-year period, and often requested that the company provide a service to the Mexican economy in return. Examples of such services included improving the company's technology and improving the company's balance of payments. Colgate further offered to start a voluntary program to help Mexican Ph.D. candidates with scholarships. Colgate also became an active supporter of the Mexican Rural Development Foundation with, among others, a specific long-term project to develop Mexican essential oils to substitute imports used by Colgate.

In reporting financial information, O'Brien noted that the requirements for companies operating in Mexico were probably among the most complicated of any in the world. The Mexican subsidiary had to comply with several different reporting requirements: U.S. GAAP, Mexican tax, and the corporate management requirements. In 1984, under an IRS allowance, Colgate-U.S. began reporting Colgate-Mexico as a tax branch rather than as a subsidiary for U.S. tax purposes. Foreign activity undertaken as a branch was regarded as part of the parent's own operation and branch earnings were fully taxed in the year they were earned, whether they were remitted to the parent in that year or not. The real benefit to Colgate-U.S. was that as a tax branch, foreign exchange translation losses could be written off immediately against U.S. taxes owed for all foreign operations owned by the company. The result, while not reducing Mexican taxes, was a U.S. tax savings of millions of dollars after restatement of all tax years from inception in 1926.

In addition to the broader reporting requirements, Colgate-Mexico had to comply with the Financial Accounting Standards Board (FASB) rule No. 52. FASB-52 established uniform standards for translating a subsidiary's foreign currency-denominated financial statements into dollars for consolidation with U.S.-based multinationals. According to FASB-52, all foreign currency revenue and expense items on the subsidiary's income statements had to be translated at the exchange rate in effect on the date those items were recognized, while foreign exchange losses on monetary assets and liabilities were recognized as exchange rates changed. FASB-52 rules allowed companies to uniformly translate the local currency, used by the subsidiary on a daily basis (pesos at Colgate-Mexico), to the functional currency which was the currency of the primary economic environment in which the parent operated (dollars at Colgate-U.S.).

In non-hyperinflationary countries, translation gains and losses bypassed the parent's income statement and were accumulated in a separate equity account on the parent's balance sheet, typically called "cumulative translation adjustment." In the case of a hyperinflationary country, defined as one that had cumulative inflation of 100 percent or more over a three-year period, FASB-52 required that translation losses go directly to profit and loss. The balance sheet of a foreign entity was translated at the rate used to remit dividends. Thus, the profits of a subsidiary in a hyperinflationary country were generally converted at the dividend rate as of the balance sheet date.

Colgate-Mexico's borrowing requirements were generally denominated in local currency. As was the case with many other subsidiaries of multinationals, Colgate-Mexico was expected to borrow money to finance working capital. In June 1987, however, instead of borrowing pesos, the company entered into a dollar-denominated, six-month loan for $4 million. Athole Stewart, director of finance, explained this special case. "There was a window period where dollar-based borrowing looked better because dollar interest rates were much cheaper." This loan was cheaper than local borrowings even when the cost of a controlled-rate hedge contract purchased to protect against the eventuality of a devaluation was included.

Colgate typically borrowed from the local banks which offered better interest rates than the debt markets. The average long-term debt in Mexico was six months, and the typical loan was 30 days at that time.

The November Budget Meeting

When Tangney and the other members of management met to review the budget from November 16-20, 1987, they began with a framework of their expectations for the Mexican economic and political situation for the remainder of the year and into early 1988. Their initial expectations were that, though the economy continued in a depressed state, consumer demand had not fallen off in Colgate's principal product categories to date. They expected moderate (3 percent) growth in consumer demand into 1988. At the beginning of the year, Colgate-Mexico had estimated an inflation rate of 80 percent for 1987, but had updated that estimate to 120 percent for the year as a result of continuing increases in monthly inflation right up to the meeting in November. The company also expected rising interest rates in the months ahead, due to a lack of liquidity in the market and as a government move to compensate for expected inflation and to prevent the likely outflow of capital that a devaluation could produce.

Following the stock market crash on October 19, 1987, the Mexican government had proposed a recovery plan under which they would participate with brokers to purchase and hold large volumes of stock to increase investor confidence. However, just days before Colgate-Mexico's budget meeting, the Mexican government announced that it would not institute any recovery plan, and that the year-to-date inflation rate of 109 percent for 1987 had already surpassed the highest annual level in Mexican history. Those announcements, together with two days of sharp stock market declines on November 16 and 17, created a rush by investors to buy dollars which were perceived as a safer haven for liquidity. On November 18, 1987, after spending between $1 and $3 billion to buy pesos in the market (7 percent to 20 percent of reserves), the Bank of Mexico announced its decision to withdraw support for the free-market pesos, resulting in a 32.8 percent devaluation in the free-market rate. The controlled rate declined only slightly. See Exhibit 9 on the two exchange rates.

Estimates of 1987 inflation, set at 120 percent before the budget meeting, were raised to 160 percent at the conclusion of the meeting. The peso's daily devaluation rate had been governed mainly by the gap between Mexican and U.S. inflation rates. At the end of October, Colgate-Mexico had concluded that year-to-date devaluation had in fact not been sufficient to balance the inflation differential between Mexico and the United States, Mexico's principal trading partner. However, the company had not anticipated either the precise timing or the magnitude of the November devaluation.

In 1987, because the free and controlled exchange rates had been quoted at essentially the same rate, Colgate had transacted its business at essentially one exchange rate. However, because the free rate devaluation of 32.8 percent was larger than the controlled rate devaluation of 1.0 percent, the widening of the differential between the free and control exchange rates posed many opportunities and problems for the company. At the end of the meeting on November 20, 1987, Tangney and the rest of management had to quickly assess the actions that Colgate-Mexico must take given the events of the previous few days.

Exhibit 6   Mexican Real Economic Growth, 1967–1987

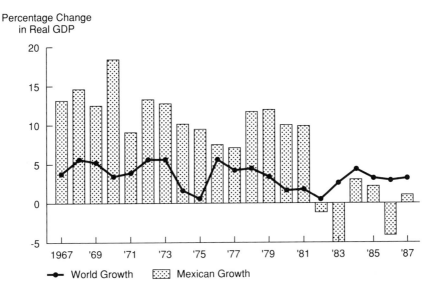

Source: IMF, World Bank

Exhibit 7   Mexican Inflation, 1967–1987

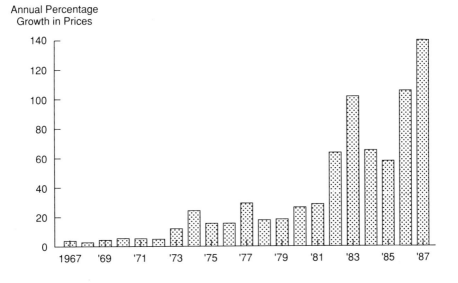

Source: Banco de Mexico, World Bank

Exhibit 8   Mexican Current Account, 1967–1987 (Excluding Interest Payments)

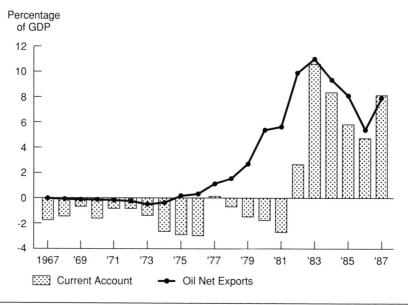

Source: Banco de Mexico, World Bank

Exhibit 9   Mexican Foreign Debt, 1967–1987

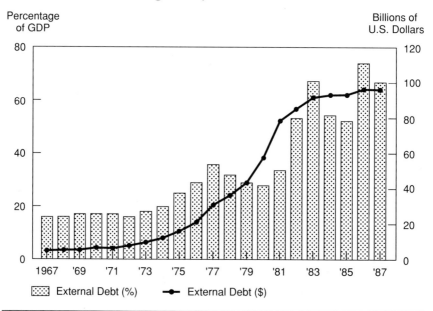

Source: Banco de Mexico, World Bank

Exhibit 10   Capital Flight from Mexico, 1970–1987

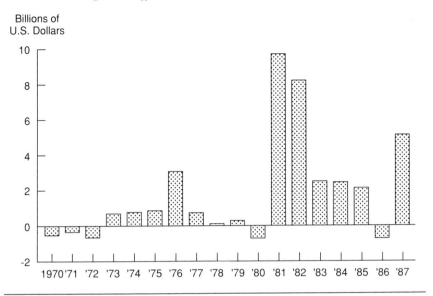

Source: Dornbusch (1988), World Bank

Exhibit 11   International Reserves, 1967–1987, Mexican Central Bank

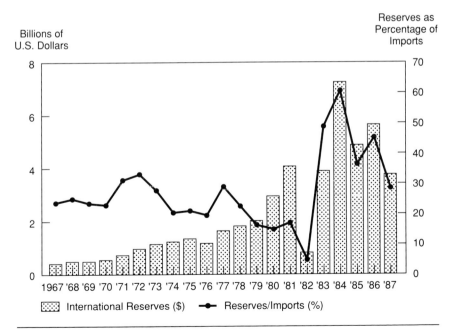

Source: World Bank

Exhibit 12   Mexican Real Exchange Rate, 1970–1987

Real Exchange
Rate Index:
1980-1982 =100

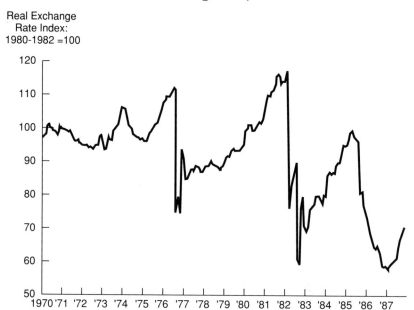

Source: *World Financial Markets*, Morgan Guaranty.

Exhibit 13   Controlled vs. Free Exchange Rate

Pesos per
Dollar
(Thousands)

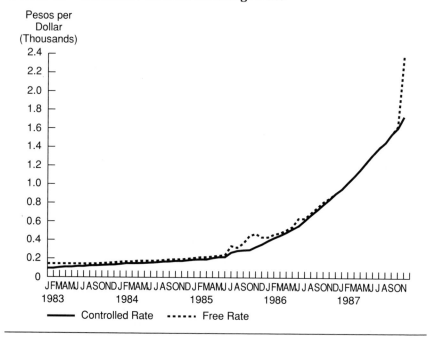

Source: Colgate-Palmolive, Mexico.

Exhibit 14   Mexican Money Supply Growth, 1967–1987

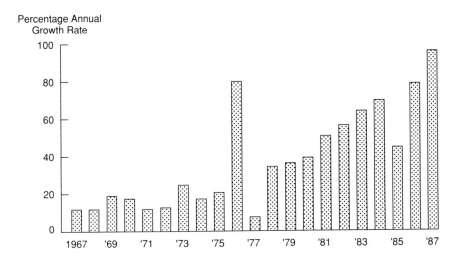

Source: World Bank

Exhibit 15   Mexican Fiscal Deficit, 1967–1987

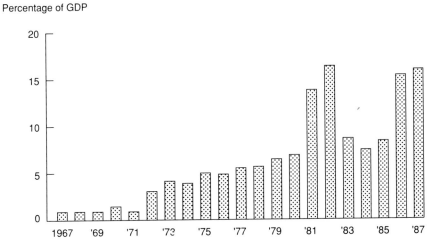

Source: Banco de Mexico

Exhibit 16   Real Interest Rates, 1 Month Deposits (% p.a.)

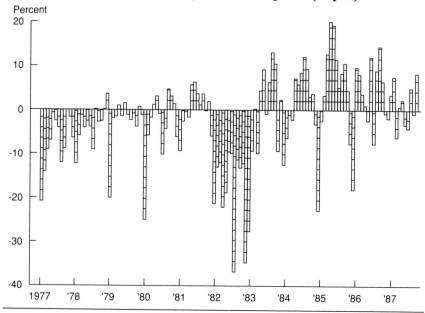

Source: Data Resources Inc.

Exhibit 17   Real Oil Prices, 1970–88 (1972 = 100).

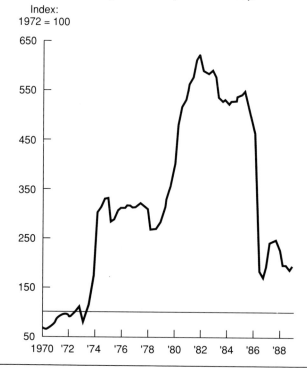

ªNominal prices deflated by export prices of manufacturers.

Exhibit 18   The Real Manufacturing Wage (1980–82 = 100)

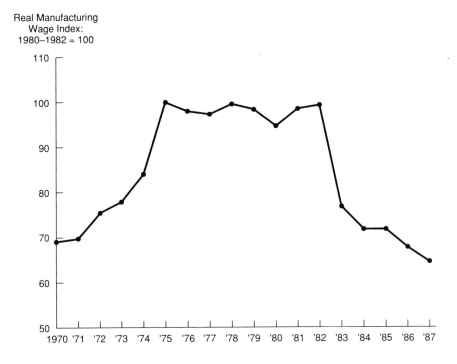

Source: Indicadores Economicos, Banco de Mexico.

Questions

1. What are the most important problems in the Mexican economy that concern Colgate-Mexico?

2. What is unique about managing in a hyperinflationary environment?

3. Describe Colgate-Mexico's strategy. How does this strategy help its performance in Mexico's hyperinflationary environment?

4. How well-positioned is Colgate-Mexico to deal with its competitors in Mexico?

5. What would your immediate response to the November 1987 devaluation of the peso? What long-term changes, if any, would you recommend to President Mike Tangney to improve Colgate-Mexico's future performance? Do you have any recommendations for Reuben Mark, Colgate's CEO?

PART III

Corporate Management of Fiscal Policy Changes

Fiscal policy encompasses a government's policies regarding its expenditures, taxes, and the financing of any fiscal deficits or surpluses. These variables affect all businesses indirectly by affecting the level of aggregate demand in the economy. However, we will be most interested in the direct effects of fiscal policy on a business, such as when the government's expenditures are the sales of the business or when the change in tax policy directly affects the taxes paid by the business.

Among the major industrial countries in the 1980s, the United States has been particularly active in changing tax policy. The Economic Recovery Tax Act (ERTA) of 1981 was the largest tax cut ever passed. Among the many provisions for reducing the taxes of the business sector was the Accelerated Cost Recovery System (ACRS). The following year Congress removed some of the tax benefits granted in the 1981 act when they passed the Tax Equalization and Fiscal Responsibility Act (TEFRA) of 1982. Relatively smaller tax bills followed in the ensuing years, but the next major overhaul of the tax system came in 1986 with the passage of the Tax Reform Act (TRA). Other countries too have engaged in massive changes in their tax policies. Countries with value-added taxes have made changes in their tax structures, which effectively reduced their reliance on direct income taxes and increased their reliance on indirect sales taxes. The United Kingdom, for example, tried this in the early 1980s, and Japan tried in the mid-1980s.

Fiscal expenditures have also been changed on a large scale during the past decade. In all industrial countries, expenditures for social welfare programs have been rising steadily for the past two decades. In recent years, governments have found the ability to cut military expenditures, or at least to significantly slow their growth. Demand for infrastructure spending has increased in most countries, though it has not always been satisfied. In the mid-1980s, for example, Japan boosted its infrastructure spending, not only to satisfy its growing needs at home, but also to stem criticisms abroad of its continued trade surpluses.

These dramatic changes in tax and expenditure policies provide opportunities for a change in competitive position among rivals in an industry. The cases in Part III illustrate how fiscal policy decisions can affect a business and how a business might respond. The Chapter 10 case, Ryder System, examines a company that explicitly coordinated its strategy to take advantage of tax policy changes. In Chapter 11, we analyze whether Honeywell's investment decisions were helped by the tax incentives of the early 1980s. The last tax policy case, Schlumberger and Fairchild Semiconductor, which is presented in Chapter 12, focuses on a narrower issue—the tax considerations in the acquisition of Fairchild. The remaining three cases explore different aspects of expenditure policy. In Chapter 13, The Privatization of British Airways is classified as an "expenditure" case since privatization can substitute for government expenditure, and it will have consequences for a firm's competitiveness. In Chapter 14 and 15, we have parallel cases in which a firm is trying to cope with large changes in a particular government expenditure—cuts in defense expenditures for Martin Marietta and increases in social welfare expenditures for Saab-Scania.

CASE 10
Ryder System

Ryder System is an example of a company that explicitly incorporated tax considerations into the design of its corporate strategy. In our analysis of the case, we must identify the components of Ryder's strategy and assess its fit with the firm's environment. At that point, we are in a position to evaluate whether it made sense for this company to take advantage of the government's tax incentives.

A more complicated issue is whether a strategy based on a transient government policy can be the source of long-term competitive advantage. In this case, the tax benefits afforded by the Economic Recovery Tax Act of 1981 were largely abandoned in the Tax Reform Act of 1986. The unresolved question is whether Ryder can transform any tax benefits it might have received during this period into a more sustainable competitive edge.

The cases in this chapter and the following chapter raise some important questions about the efficacy of tax policy. Policy makers in the nation's capitol change tax policies because, ostensibly, they want managers to respond to the new incentive in order to promote some social or economic objective. If we can better understand the conditions under which managers will respond, we can better understand what makes tax policy most effective as an economic tool. The degree of responsiveness may vary from industry to industry, and even within the same industry. In fact, it is this differential responsiveness to the same tax incentive within the same industry that can lead to a change in competitive positioning. Consequently, this is an issue that cannot be ignored by managers or policy makers.

Ryder System in the early 1980s embarked on an aggressive acquisition strategy concentrating on the truck leasing business. The company had grown from a nascent regional competitor in the southeastern states in the 1930s to the largest in the U.S. truck leasing business in the 1980s. In 1986 Ryder ranked twelfth in the Fortune Service 500. From 1983 to 1986 alone, Ryder spent nearly $1.1 billion acquiring 65 companies. Management claimed that this acquisition drive was financed in part by the increased cash flow from tax incentives allowed by the Economic Recovery Tax Act (ERTA) of 1981. However, the Tax Reform Act (TRA) of 1986 reduced the generous depreciation benefits and eliminated the investment tax credit at the same time it lowered the maximum corporate tax rate. Ryder's CEO Anthony Burns was forced to reevaluate his acquisition strategy and the company's growth-oriented philosophy.

Company History

Ryder System was formed in 1933 when founder James A. Ryder started a local cartage business in Miami, Florida called the Ryder Trucking Company. In 1938, Mr. Ryder provided his first truck leasing customer, a beer distributor, with five trucks and a servicing agreement. In 1955, Ryder System with $50 million in revenues, was incorporated with Mr. Ryder serving as President and Chairman of the Board. In the same year, the entire capital stock of Great Southern Trucking Company, the largest motor freight carrier in the Southeast, was acquired for $1.0 million.

Ryder continued to expand throughout the 1950s and 1960s, with 42 acquisitions. Of those acquisitions, approximately one-third were trucking companies, one-third were truck leasing companies, and one-third were truck rental companies. Trucking companies purchased their trucks and hauled freight with their own company logo on the truck, whereas truck leasing firms leased their trucks to shippers, who in turn hauled freight under the shipping company's logo. Leasing was a long-term rental agreement in order to obtain the use of capital equipment, whereas renting referred to a short-term contract, usually by the day or the week.

In early 1970, Ryder diversified outside the transportation business for the first time by acquiring Southern Underwriters Inc., thus starting the Company's Insurance Division. Nearly two years later, Ryder acquired Truckstops of America, a chain that provided restaurants, hotels, maintenance, and retail shops for truck drivers on long hauls. Mr. Ryder diversified the company further in the early 1970s, when he bought a truck driving school, a credit-card operation, Toro Petroleum Corpora-

This case was prepared by Professor Michael G. Rukstad with the assistance of Research Associate Julia Horn. Copyright © 1989 by the President and Fellows of Harvard College. Harvard Business School Case 9-389-095.

Exhibit 1   Consolidated Income Statements (in $ million)

	1986	1985	1984	1983	1982	1981	1980	1979	1978	1977
Revenue and Net Sales	3,768.3	2,905.3	2,485.9	2,383.6	2,075.9	1,946.5	1,694.1	1,454.7	1,124.1	914.5
Operating Expense	2,404.9	2,105.2	1,875.7	1,588.8	1,369.7	1,258.2	1,091.0	965.9	742.4	612.7
Cost of Sales	485.6	123.4	17.5	281.5	301.6	305.0	261.6	179.9	129.8	103.6
Depreciation, net of gains	425.5	325.2	289.6	264.8	217.8	201.7	177.9	142.5	112.8	91.3
Interest Expense	192.0	156.7	115.0	93.8	81.6	76.6	83.6	63.1	44.0	33.8
Miscellaneous income	(17.1)	(7.4)	(6.2)	(10.7)	(19.2)	(9.7)	(4.5)	(2.2)	(4.7)	(2.5)
	3,490.9	2,703.2	2,291.5	2,218.2	1,951.4	1,831.7	1,609.6	1,351.4	1,029.0	841.4
Earnings from continuing operations before income taxes	277.5	202.1	194.3	165.4	124.5	114.7	84.6	105.6	99.8	75.6
Provision for income taxes	116.5	76.8	76.8	64.3	41.9	40.7	28.4	43.2	44.5	34.9
Earnings from continuing operations	160.9	125.3	117.6	101.1	82.6	74.0	56.2	62.4	55.3	40.7
Discontinued operations, net of taxes	–	–	18.4	–	–	–	–	–	–	–
Net Earnings	160.9	125.3	135.9	101.1	82.6	74.0	56.2	62.4	55.3	40.7

Exhibit 2   Consolidated Balance Sheets (in $ millions)

	1986	1985	1984	1983	1982	1981	1980	1979	1978	1977
Assets										
Current Assets:										
Cash and marketable securities	84.3	74.9	55.2	40.2	32.1	134.9	28.1	35.2	27.8	24.7
Receivables	498.0	440.3	278.6	235.6	216.1	188.6	175.1	174.6	115.3	90.1
Inventories	317.2	185.8	70.9	77.5	71.1	48.4	58.5	39.6	27.6	19.6
Tires in service	120.6	101.3	92.2	65.9	57.6	47.6	49.1	49.9	36.7	34.5
Prepaid expenses	70.2	59.7	46.7	32.4	25.6	22.0	20.2	18.2	14.4	11.6
Total current assets	1,090.4	862.0	543.5	451.7	402.4	441.5	331.1	317.5	221.8	180.4
Revenue earning equipment, net	2,421.9	1,964.6	1,790.0	1,341.4	1,172.7	964.8	1,006.3	930.3	709.5	551.6
Operating property and equipment, net	462.7	395.6	259.5	313.6	299.9	285.3	262.5	229.7	172.0	144.3
Investments and other assets	298.5	195.8	139.5	84.5	73.3	35.5	15.1	29.9	10.7	12.5
Intangible assets and deferred charges	510.4	322.6	77.5	65.5	36.8	32.4	31.2	29.8	27.3	26.7
	4,783.9	3,740.6	2,810.0	2,256.6	1,985.0	1,759.5	1,646.2	1,537.2	1,141.2	915.5

Exhibit 2 (Continued)

Liabilities and Shareholders' Equity

Current liabilities										
Current portion of long-term debt	190.8	93.9	43.9	35.5	3.5	2.5	6.4	6.6	2.4	11.2
Accounts payable	342.2	316.0	252.8	231.8	231.7	180.7	185.1	183.5	134.1	120.2
Accrued expenses	396.6	294.5	232.5	175.9	129.3	115.8	105.8	95.8	78.8	63.9
Equipment obligations	—	—	—	24.5	18.8	59.2	22.8	22.8	20.6	14.4
Total current liabilities	929.6	704.3	529.2	443.2	383.3	358.2	322.6	308.8	236.0	209.7
Long-term debt	1,888.8	1,539.3	1,092.2	828.5	765.0	656.8	739.0	714.3	501.9	390.1
Limited recourse debt	77.1	—	—	—	—	—	—	—	—	—
Other non-current liabilities	154.0	110.4	74.2	62.3	53.9	49.4	46.8	41.1	36.1	30.8
Deferred income taxes	463.3	366.7	298.6	242.2	206.9	191.5	170.4	144.0	78.5	57.7
Deferred investment tax credits	31.9	46.6	49.5	33.6	18.1	13.3	15.8	21.8	32.3	21.3
Total Shareholder' Equity	1,239.2	973.3	766.4	646.9	557.9	490.2	351.6	307.1	256.5	205.9
	4,783.9	3,740.6	2,810.0	2,256.6	1,985.0	1,759.5	1,646.2	1,537.2	1,141.2	915.5

Exhibit 3   Statement of Changes in Financial Position

	1986	1985	1984	1983	1982	1981
Cash Provided from Operations:						
Continuing operations:						
Net earnings from continuing operations	160.9	125.3	117.6	98.9	82.6	74.1
Depreciation, net of gains	425.5	325.2	289.6	258.2	217.8	201.7
Deferred income taxes and tax credits	89.0	67.6	80.8	54.2	24.0	20.0
Property and equipment sold	170.4	232.2	166.4	132.1	158.0	135.4
Other noncash items, net	49.9	40.0	18.6	11.2	2.8	4.4
Discontinued operations	—	—	20.1	9.6	—	—
Cash provided from operations	895.8	790.2	693.1	564.2	485.2	435.6
(Increase) decrease in working capital	(37.1)	(68.2)	5.8	11.3	13.8	(71.3)
Cash provided from operations and working capital	858.6	722.0	699.0	575.5	471.4	506.9
Financing Activities:						
Debt:						
Incurred	629.3	625.9	376.5	122.3	160.3	26.2
Repaid	(407.9)	(292.6)	(100.6)	(82.0)	(114.5)	(74.1)
Preferred shares issued	—	98.3	—	—	—	—
Common shares issued	142.0	13.3	12.5	13.3	13.6	84.8
Total financing activities	363.4	444.9	288.4	53.5	59.4	36.9

Exhibit 3 (Continued)

Investment Activities:

Purchases of property and revenue earning equipment	(896.7)	(788.4)	(972.0)	(563.0)	(544.1)	(305.4)
Acquisitions:						
Working capital	(53.4)	(105.5)	(5.1)	(5.7)	–	–
Goodwill	(238.4)	(208.8)	(16.0)	(28.0)	(6.2)	(2.8)
Operating property, net	(304.1)	(136.2)	(26.5)	(47.8)	(66.8)	(12.9)
Debt assumed	256.4	159.9	20.0	38.0	25.4	2.3
Total acquisitions	(339.5)	(290.6)	(27.6)	(43.5)	(47.6)	(13.4)
Net assets of businesses sold	70.9	–	52.1	–	–	–
Other, net	(9.7)	(39.7)	0.2	9.6	(1.4)	(0.4)
	1,175.0	(1,118.8)	(947.3)	(597.0)	(640.7)	(332.6)

Dividends Paid to Shareholders:

Common	(32.4)	(28.5)	(25.0)	(24.0)	(22.5)	(20.3)
Preferred	(5.3)	–	–	–	–	–
	(37.6)	(28.5)	(25.0)	(24.0)	(22.5)	(20.3)
Increase in Cash and Marketable Securities	9.4	19.7	15.0	8.1	(132.4)	190.9

tion, Pancon Oil Properties (crude oil), and a check cashing company. By the end of 1974, hurt by rising fuel costs and a weak economy, Ryder System lost over $20 million on revenues of $565 million and had a debt-to-equity ratio of seven, putting the company on the edge of bankruptcy. Under pressure from lenders, Ryder hired Leslie O. Barnes from Allegheny Airlines in mid-1975 as chief executive. Under Barnes' direction, the new management sold off Truckstops of America, the two oil companies, the truck-driving school, and the credit-card operations. Mr. Ryder left the Company in 1978 to start a competitor, Jartran, which eventually went bankrupt. Exhibits 1–3 show Ryder's financial performance.

The Trucking Industry in the 1970s

The trucking industry could be segmented into for-hire carriers and private carriers, as shown in Exhibit 4. For-hire carriers transported the goods of customers for a fee, whereas private carriers transported their own goods, often as the in-house shipping department of a manufacturer or retailer.

Both branches of the industry could be further segmented into owner-operators and nonowner-operators. Owner-operators purchased their trucks and then hauled freight either for hire or for themselves. The nonowner-operators leased their trucks from large companies such as Ryder, Gelco, Leaseway, and Lilly or from the numerous small truck-leasing companies scattered throughout the country. Leasing operations

Exhibit 4   Trucking Industry of the 1970s

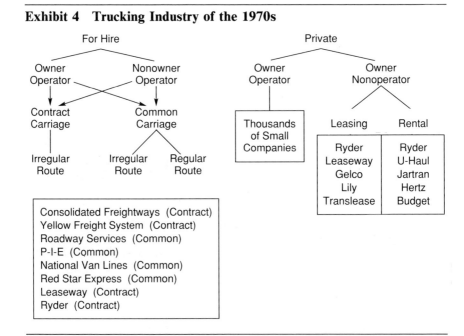

arranged a long-term rental agreement for the truck, fuel, and maintenance (but not the driver). A special case of the private nonowner-operator was the consumer or commercial truck renter, who typically rented by the day or by the week. The largest firms in the truck rental business were Ryder, U-Haul, Hertz/Penske, and Budget.

Within the for-hire carrier segment, there was a complicated division of service segments in the 1970s, regulated by the Interstate Commerce Commission (ICC). Carriers of agricultural commodities were exempt from ICC regulation. Those carriers that were subject to ICC regulation had to be licensed as either a common carrier or a contract carrier. Under the regulations before 1980, they could not operate as both. A common carrier, such as National Van Lines, Roadway Services, and Red Star Express, offered to haul the freight of any person or company. Regulations required entrants in this field to prove that currently licensed carriers were not providing the service that they could offer. Certificates were very specific regarding the types of freight that an operator could carry. On the other hand, contract carriers such as Consolidated Freightways, Yellow Freight System, and to a much smaller degree, Ryder, provided semi-private service for up to eight customers under long-term agreements.

The regulatory restrictions extended to operating licenses, which specified whether common and contract carriers could operate a regular route or an irregular route. Regular route carriers provided service between specific points over fixed routes. Irregular route carriers served general areas. For example, a regular route carrier, such as Red Star Express, might provide service between terminals in Los Angeles and Chicago, whereas an irregular route carrier, such as Consolidated Freightways or Roadway Services, might deliver anywhere in the area of California and Arizona. Common carriers could follow either regular or irregular routes. Contract carriers were granted irregular route authority, because at the time that authority was granted, the ICC did not know which specific shippers the contract carrier would be serving, and therefore, which exact route would be followed.

The trucking industry as a whole competed against other industries to haul shippers' inventories. The railroad industry provided the toughest competition, and a few trucking companies, such as Consolidated Freightways, set up links with railroad companies in effort to gain geographic expansion while increasing business. Competition also came from the airline industry, though for larger shipments of goods, trucking was typically a lower cost alternative.

In the mid-1970s, the trucking industry, like most other industries, felt the pain of both the economic recession and the oil shortage. In 1974, a temporary 6 percent fuel surcharge levied on truck operators was made permanent. The rising fuel costs were particularly painful because they were combined with reduced revenues leading to lower margins. Despite the damage to trucking companies from the recession, the ICC worsened the situation by cutting from 6 percent to 2 percent the general rate increase that it allowed truckers to charge their customers. In 1976, with the U.S. economic recovery, the industry climbed out of the depressed level it reached during the previous year. By the late 1970s, rising traffic and some ICC-allowed rate increases brought higher revenues and profits for all companies in the industry. The slump was over by 1978, as major shippers began to restock their inventories of goods again. In addition, because truckers had been faced with escalating fuel costs for several years, they had gone to great lengths to conserve through the use of fuel-saving engines and radial tires.

A Changing Environment

The second oil price shock in 1979 pushed inflation into double-digit rates. In response to the renewed bout of inflation, Federal Reserve Chairman Paul Volcker tightened monetary policy by allowing short-term interest rates to rise in order to control monetary growth. By 1980, corporations felt the general squeeze on the economy and saw revenues and earnings fall. The revenues of the trucking industry were closely tied to the growth in GNP. See Exhibit 5 for GNP growth versus trucking industry revenues. Consequently, the trucking industry experienced a significant slowdown in growth.

In June 1980, the Motor Carrier Act was passed, which deregulated the trucking industry and led to major structural changes. One of the most significant changes was the increased competition on both price and service in the common and contract trucking business. Much of the increased competition came from the thousands of entrants into the trucking business. From 1980 to 1985, the number of motor carriers, freight forwarders, and freight brokers skyrocketed from 17,300 to 33,500, despite the many business failures along the way. Most entrants were non-union carriers. Deregulation provided new incentives for companies to enter the private carriage business, particularly in intercorporate hauling. The increased competition also came from eliminating the prohibition against a single carrier operating as both a common and a contract carrier. Following deregulation, the largest carriers such as Consolidated Freightways, Yellow Freight System, Pacific-Intermountain-Express (P-I-E), Roadway Services, and Ryder expanded to both businesses.

Deregulation did not directly affect the truck leasing business. However, as a result of the freewheeling rate competition among truckers, trucking companies were demanding new services, ranging from truck maintenance to financial services, which would help them control costs. New suppliers brought lower prices for many highway transportation services, such as maintenance, route planning, and fleet management, while also focusing shippers' attention on the quality of those services. Truck leasing companies argued that they could provide trucking services at a lower cost than owner-operators because of efficiencies in purchasing, maintenance, and administration.

Exhibit 5   GNP and Final Sales vs. Trucking Revenues

Ryder Systems, Inc.

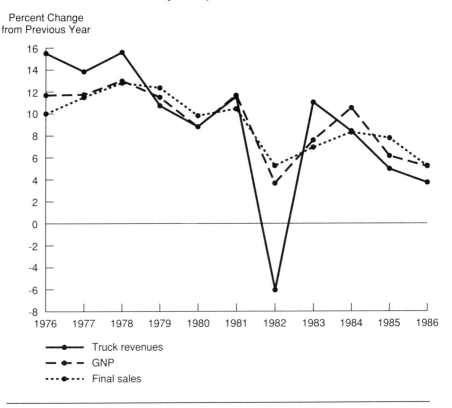

In addition to deregulation, tax cuts in the following year provided a stimulus to trucking and other industries. Throughout 1981, after Reagan's election to the Presidency, his proposed tax cut was making front-page news. By August, Congress passed the Economic Recovery Tax Act (ERTA), which embodied major changes in the personal income tax rates, depreciation schedules, and definitions of taxable income. Two of the most important provisions for participants in the trucking industry were the accelerated depreciation benefits and accompanying investment tax credit.

Prior to ERTA, depreciation was an annual expense that varied with the "useful life" or durability of the assets. However, after ERTA, the concept of the useful life of an asset was replaced with a new definition, the Accelerated Cost Recovery System (ACRS). Under ACRS, newly acquired assets were grouped into four depreciation classes based on capital recovery periods of 3, 5, 10, and 15 years. For example, the trucking industries' primary assets, heavy duty trucks, fell into the 5-year class. Under ERTA, heavy duty trucks had shorter depreciation periods, helping trucking companies to recapture asset costs more quickly. Under the previous depreciation law, heavy duty trucks already received very favorable treatment if companies elected to depreciate those assets in the minimum allowable time. Consequently, the increase in tax benefits for heavy trucks under ACRS was not as great as for most other assets.

The investment tax credit (ITC) was also changed by ERTA. Under prior law, an ITC of 6.6 percent of the asset purchase price was allowed on all assets with a useful life of 5 years. Under the ACRS provisions of ERTA, however, the ITC was based on the class of recovery period. For heavy duty trucks, and all other assets in the five year class, the ITC was raised from 6.6 percent to 10 percent, providing even greater benefits. See Exhibit 6 for a comparison of the present value of tax benefits for heavy duty trucks.

The expanded benefits of ACRS and the revised ITC were not available to many companies engaged in heavy capital spending programs or in a tax loss position, such as steel, mining, and forest products companies. The benefits of depreciation deductions and ITCs were available only to the owner of the asset with sufficient taxable income to offset any deductions and credits. However, after ERTA, those companies unable to use tax benefits were more inclined to obtain a portion of the benefits indirectly by leasing equipment from companies that had sufficient taxable income to use the benefits. For example, a company such as Ryder could lease equipment to another company and use the ITCs. The use of the tax benefits by Ryder was reflected in reduced rental charges or cash payments by the lessee, a point emphasized in Ryder's marketing efforts.

Ryder's Response to the Changes

In 1980, Ryder's net earnings dropped 11 percent from the 1979 level, following industry trends. As interest rates soared higher, so did Ryder's interest payments on its floating-rate debt, forcing a temporary surge in

Exhibit 6   Comparison of the Present Value of Representative Tax Benefits for Heavy-Duty Trucks (for $100 investment)

		Before 1981 Pre-ACRS	1981–1986 ACRS	Percentage Increase under ACRS
10 percent Discount Rate	ITC	$ 6.60	$10.00	
	Depreciation	32.57	34.94	
	Total tax benefits	$39.17	$44.94	15.0%
15 percent Discount Rate	ITC	$ 6.60	$10.00	
	Depreciation	29.20	31.00	
	Total tax benefits	$35.80	$41.00	14.5%
20 percent Discount Rate	ITC	$ 6.60	$10.00	
	Depreciation	26.36	27.68	
	Total tax benefits	$32.96	$37.68	14.0%

Source: Calculated by author; based on Deloitte, Haskins, & Sells, *Accelerated Cost Recovery System*, 1981, p. 11.

their interest costs. Interest expense in 1980 was $83.6 million, nearly double the level of only two years earlier. In the high interest rate environment of the early 1980s, Ryder would have difficulty paying the finance charges of an additional $100 million to $200 million for truck replacements and new purchases. As the recession deepened, instead of going on the defensive, Ryder went on the offensive. For example, when business began to fall off in one-way consumer truck rentals, Ryder did not hesitate to attack its competitors. They cut truck rental prices from $40 to $19.95 per day. "When we cut the price by 50 percent," said then-President M. Anthony Burns, "utilization more than quadrupled, and we brought more profit dollars to the bottom line."[1]

In 1981, Ryder offered 2.4 million shares of common stock, which was more attractive than the long-term fixed-rate debt that carried interest rates in excess of 17 percent. Ryder used one-half of the $80 million proceeds to reduce their floating rate debt to 10 percent of total debt outstanding, which also reduced their debt-equity ratio to 135 percent. The remainder was used to fund acquisitions.

Despite the economic recession that began in 1981, Ryder's first priority was continued growth through acquisition and consolidation. The changes in the tax laws under ERTA facilitated Ryder's acquisitions. Ryder's annual purchases of new trucks (capital expenditures for the Vehicle Leasing and Services Division) represented $270.4 million or 89 percent of total capital expenditures in 1981. Under ERTA, Ryder was entitled to huge ITCs and accelerated depreciation. CEO Barnes and President Burns were "searching for an acquisition outside the trucking business that would sop up excess tax credits that Ryder's truck purchases would throw off."[2]

Under the previous tax laws, Ryder banked $5.6 million in unused credits in 1980, a figure that more than doubled in 1981 to $13.4 million. Under ERTA, deferred taxes rose from $170.4 million in 1980 to $191.5 million in 1981. See Exhibit 7 for Ryder's income tax information for 1980–1986. The new tax laws gave companies greater flexibility in deciding how to use their excess credits. Truck lessors could split credits with lessees if both parties agreed. Ryder and some of the other big trucking lessors would be able to shield more of their own income with the tax credits. At the same time, they could use the new law to persuade more corporate clients to lease, rather than buy, new trucks.

Given the nature of their primary business—vehicle leasing and services—Ryder's acquisitions to use up excess tax credits could take them outside the truck leasing industry and change their overall business mix. Ryder was searching for an acquisition candidate that, "when combined with Ryder's small non-trucking operations would provide one-quarter

---

[1]"How to Beat the Recession—Any Recession," *Forbes*, December 20, 1982.

[2]"Ryder System: A tax break fuels a drive into acquisitions," *Business Week*, September 28, 1981.

Exhibit 7　Income Information (in $ millions)

	1986	1985	1984	1983	1982	1981	1980
Current tax expense (benefit)							
Federal	15.5	3.1	(4.6)	7.7	13.1	15.1	6.6
State and foreign	12.0	6.1	0.6	1.9	4.7	5.5	(0.8)
Total	27.5	9.2	(4.0)	9.6	17.8	20.6	5.8
Deferred tax expense							
Federal	93.4	58.3	48.7	32.1	15.3	19.5	22.2
State and foreign	10.1	12.0	14.7	6.9	3.9	3.3	6.3
Total	103.5	70.2	63.4	39.0	19.2	22.8	28.5
Deferred investment tax credits							
Generated during year	13.5	28.9	40.3	29.4	17.4	11.1	6.4
Amortized during year	(27.9)	(31.7)	(22.9)	(13.7)	(12.6)	(13.8)	(12.4)
Total	(14.5)	(2.7)	17.4	15.6	4.8	(2.8)	(6.0)
Provision for income taxes, continuing operations	116.5	76.8	76.8	64.3	41.9	40.7	28.4
Discontinued operations, including gain on disposal	–	–	7.7	–	–	–	–
Total income tax expense	116.5	76.8	84.5	64.3	41.9	40.7	28.4

Exhibit 7 (Continued)

Deferred tax expense for continuing operations							
Tax depreciation over book depreciation	103.6	101.8	97.5	37.3	(12.2)	(10.1)	6.3
Book gains over (under) tax gains on disposition of assets, principally vehicles	(21.8)	(12.7)	4.0	3.2	15.2	10.0	14.0
Net change in unrealized tax credits	53.6	(10.5)	(26.8)	(2.7)	14.0	13.4	5.6
Deferred state and foreign income taxes, net of federal income tax	8.1	8.4	9.3	3.0	2.7	2.4	3.7
Expenses for book purposes in excess of amounts currently deductible for tax purposes	(32.4)	11.4	(16.8)	5.9	2.7	(2.1)	2.6
Other items, net	(7.7)	(5.2)	(3.8)	(7.6)	(3.2)	(2.5)	(3.7)
Total	103.5	70.3	63.4	39.1	19.2	22.8	28.5
Statutory rate (%)	46.0	46.0	46.0	46.0	46.0	46.0	46.0
Amortization of investment tax credits (%)	(10.1)	(15.7)	(11.8)	(8.3)	(10.1)	(12.0)	(14.7)
Basis reduction resulting from investment tax credits (%)	2.3	3.3	1.9	0.7	(1.0)	(0.0)	(1.8)
State income taxes, net of federal income tax benefit (%)	3.2	3.8	3.5	3.2	3.2	3.5	3.3
Miscellaneous items, net (%)	0.6	0.6	(0.1)	(1.3)	(4.5)	(1.6)	0.7

to one-half of total profits. 'We can't use all of our tax advantages,' said Burns. 'This is part of the strategy for seeking an acquisition.' "[3]

Ryder recognized that there were still many opportunities for rapid expansion within the trucking industry, though they also looked outside the industry for a company that would absorb ITCs. Deregulation and ERTA were the catalysts for Ryder's aggressive acquisition strategy in the 1980s. Between 1981 and 1983, Ryder acquired 20 companies, and, between 1983 and 1986, an additional 65 companies. The majority of the acquisitions were trucking, and truck-leasing companies.

In searching for an acquisition candidate, Ryder was looking for a company without debt, with positive cash flow, and with high tax payments. Burns argued that, "With regard to acquisitions to offset tax credits, we can afford to be patient because our core businesses performed remarkably well during the recession years of 1981–1982."[4] Barnes' overall corporate goals for Ryder were 15 percent annual growth in revenues and earnings, 17 percent return on equity, and a position among the top 200 companies in profit growth. Through most of the 1980s, Ryder had exceeded those goals. Between 1982 and 1985, Ryder's average revenues and earnings grew at record rates of 19 percent and 17 percent, respectively.

Companies such as Leaseway and Gelco had opted for strategies quite different from that pursued by Ryder. Though Ryder's competitors also reaped the benefits of the ITC and accumulated depreciation from ERTA, nowhere did it play as central a role in strategic planning as it did at Ryder. The largest of Ryder's competitors at that time, broad-based Leaseway Transportation, continued its strategy of internally funding growth, making just three carriage and three auto carrier acquisitions in the period from 1981 to 1983. In 1985, Leaseway described their strategic objective: "To provide transportation services—any strategic redeployment of assets will be consistent with this objective. We are not in the financial services business."[5] Gelco, which also competed with Ryder in the vehicle leasing business, followed a strategy similar to that of Leaseway. It made six acquisitions following ERTA, all of which were in its principle business. See Exhibit 8 for data on Ryder's largest competitors.

Expansion Outside the Trucking Industry

In 1981, Ryder had four main divisions: Vehicle Leasing and Services, Distribution Systems, Truckstops of America, and Automotive Carriers. The Vehicle Leasing and Services division was, and continued to be, the

---

[3]Ibid.

[4]*The Wall Street Transcript*, April 21, 1986.

[5]Leaseway, *Anual Report*, 1985.

Exhibit 8 Comparative Financial Data

	Ryder	Gelco	Leaseway
Revenues (CAGR)[a]	19.2%	3.6%	6.2%
Total Assets (CAGR)	22.1%	4.4%	3.8%
Revenue Earning Equipment (CAGR)	20.2%	−0.3%	−6.3%
Capital Expenditures (CAGR)	24.1%	−7.7%	−4.9%
Debt to Total Capital (Average 1981–1986)	60.2%	88.0%	48.3%
Return on Equity (Average 1981–1986)	14.9%	5.3%	14.3%
Return on Assets (Average 1981–1986)	4.3%	0.5%	5.0%
Number of Acquisitions, 1981–1986	85	6	15
Dollar Value of Acquisitions ($ millions), 1981–1986	1,400	50	127

[a]CAGR is computed annual growth rate for 1981–1986.

mainstay of their business, accounting for 65 percent of total sales and 84 percent of operating profit in 1981. It included full-service truck leasing, commercial and consumer truck rental, and routine truck maintenance. The Distribution Systems division accounted for 3 percent of total revenues and 3 percent of operating profit and included contract and common carriage. Truckstops of America contributed 31 percent to revenues and 6 percent to operating profit, and Automotive Carriers accounted for 12 percent of revenues and 6 percent of operating profit. The remainder was Insurance Management Services.

In late 1981, Ryder began buying stock (a total of 9.5 percent) in the fourth largest international insurance broker, Frank B. Hall. Hall's services income would have absorbed the rising tax credits Ryder expected to generate on its equipment purchases. Management described this stock purchase leading to the anticipated acquisition as predominantly tax motivated. Hall, concluding that a hostile takeover attempt was being launched, avoided the acquisition by buying one of Ryder's competitors, Jartran, which went bankrupt the following year.

In the summer of 1982, Barnes made a succesful attempt in his diversification-through-acquisition strategy by entering into a joint venture with Forstmann-Leff Associates, a New York investment management firm, to manage pension fund assets. These assets would be used to buy well-run, growing companies for the benefit of the participating pension funds. Barnes commented on the new venture, "It fits well into our goal of finding companies that are not capital-intensive, not energy-intensive, and do pay a high cash tax rate. We will be able to use a lot of tax benefits against the earnings we receive."[6] In October 1983, Ryder bought its partner's interest in the joint venture, renamed the operation "Corporate Management Associates," and made it a wholly-owned subsidiary of Ryder System.

[6]*Forbes*, December 20, 1982, p. 55.

In March 1982, Ryder entered the $12 billion worldwide aviation service market by acquiring the Aviation Sales Company, a small replacement parts distributor in Miami, and its subsidiary, General Hydraulics Corporation, a parts repair and overhaul facility. Though Ryder didn't specifically target the aviation business, Barnes' previous experience at Allegheny Airlines made him particularly interested in it. Barnes believed that the repositioning of airline companies as a result of deregulation would force them to be more efficient. Therefore, Ryder could capitalize on providing third party services. Later Ryder broadened the scope of its airline services activities by entering the aircraft leasing business. It acquired 16 used Boeing 727 and 737 aircraft for $104 million, which made Ryder's fleet of aircraft larger than that of many airlines.

Management then turned its attention to providing more value-added services in a segment of the aviation industry where they could service the same customers. The engine overhaul business looked particularly promising because of significant barriers to entry, including economies of scale. In 1985, Ryder acquired Aviall for $150 million. Aviall, a leader in the engine overhaul business, was Ryder's first acquisition of a public company. Because Aviall had a high debt ratio from its previous leveraged buyout, Ryder refinanced the company, bringing its average interest cost down from 16 percent to 10 percent. Shortly after, Ryder entered the new aircraft parts business by acquiring Van Dusen Air. Though margins on replacement parts were larger than the 20 percent margin on new parts, the replacement supplier typically provided them only in emergencies, and not on a steady basis.

Despite these significant diversifications outside of the trucking industry, Ryder continued to expand its base business through acquisitions. During 1983, under new CEO, M. Anthony Burns, Ryder acquired Interstate Contract Carrier Corporation, which accounted for 42 percent of the Distribution System's revenue in that year. Ryder achieved a record gain in earnings in 1984, driven in part by the capital gains on the sale of Truckstops of America for $85 million. In 1985, Ryder entered the student transportation market by acquiring Rustman Bus Company, building a fleet of 3800 buses in the two years after that acquisition, making them the largest school bus company in the country.

Ryder's acquisitions during the early 1980s, made a new divisonal structure necessary. By 1986, the restructured Ryder had three main divisions: Vehicle Leasing and Services, Automotive Carriers, and Aviation Services, with Insurance Management Services still comprising a small remainder. Distribution Systems and Truckstops of America were replaced by Aviation Services, which after 3 years of 170 percent average growth in revenues became a new division in 1985.

In 1986, the Vehicle Leasing division's revenues were $2.4 billion, accounting for 64 percent of Ryder's revenue. Operating profit was $340 million, or 71 percent of the total, and the division had $3.4 billion in assets. Sixty-one percent of Ryder's highway transportation-related revenue was from vehicle leasing and rental, and the remainder was from automotive carriage, contract carriage, buses, and freight transportation services (including common carriage). Ryder's competitors included Leaseway Transportation, Gelco, U-Haul, Hertz/Penske, Consolidated Freightways, Roadway Services, P-I-E, Carolina Freight, and Yellow Freight System. Though these firms competed with at least one segment of the Division, none competed with all of the division's operations.

The Automotive Carrier Division provided transportation of new cars, trucks, components, and parts to domestic auto assembly plants, and produced auto transports for its own use and for sale to other autocarriers. In 1986, the division transported 5 million new cars and trucks, making Ryder the largest automotive carrier in the U.S., with revenues of $619 million, operating profit of $55 million, and $290 million in assets. Ryder carriers transported 31 percent of the cars and trucks produced and sold in North America, up from 23 percent in 1981. Ryder's largest competitor, Leaseway Transportation, delivered 3 million vehicles in 1986 or approximately 18 percent of all the cars and trucks produced and sold in North America. Automotive carriers was Leaseway's largest business.

Aviation Services contributed 18 percent of revenue in 1986, with revenues of $663 million, an increase of 265 percent over 1985. The division leased 30 jet aircraft to commercial operators, such as Trans World Airlines, Pan American World Airways, DHL Airways, and The Flying Tiger Line, and leased $99 million of aircraft parts and engines. Ryder's competitors included United Airlines and General Electric in the engine repair business.

The Insurance Division had revenues of $88 million and operating profit of $6 million in 1986, comprising 2.3 percent and 1.2 percent of total revenues and operating profit, respectively. With regard to the future of the division, Burns said, "Insurance management systems will be roughly 5 percent of company earnings. It will probably be less of a percent of the assets and less of the revenue."[7] He also stated two reasons for being in the insurance management industry: "First, it is advantageous to have a strong, sound relationship with major insurance companies to provide insurance and liability coverage for the 134,000 vehicles and 30 aircraft that Ryder has out on lease. Second, it provides an opportunity for good service income. We can shelter most of our cash tax payments."[8]

Ryder in 1986 and Beyond

In 1986, Congress passed the Tax Reform Act, creating some of the most sweeping changes ever in the tax structure of the United States. Tax reform included a number of changes for businesses. Among the most

[7]"Interview with M. Anthony Burns," *The Wall Street Transcript*, April 21, 1986, p. 81.
[8]Ibid.

important were the repeal of the ITC, the lengthening of the time period over which investments in assets could be depreciated, and the lowering of the statutory corporate tax rate from 46 percent to 34 percent. See Exhibit 6. In addition, Congress cut individual tax rates with the provision that the total revenue raised through the tax system remain unchanged.

Though the trucking industry lost its ITCs under tax reform, it did, unlike many other industries, retain the shorter periods permitted for asset depreciation. Because of those favorable depreciation periods, major national and regional trucking companies, many of whom had supported tax reform, were still spending considerable amounts to re-equip their fleets after 1986. In addition, the industry's earnings had shown steady improvement in the mid-1980s, as the recovery in consumer durables increased demand for transportation services. However, because freight volume was not increasing, industry participants were competing for a slice of nearly the same-sized pie.

In light of these changes in tax policy, CEO Burns re-examined his corporate strategy at the end of 1986. He wondered whether Ryder should continue with its acquisition-driven growth strategy and whether Ryder should reconsider the businesses in which it would compete.

Questions

1. Evaluate Ryder's corporate strategy from 1981 to 1985.
2. What was the contribution of the Economic Recovery Tax Act of 1981 to the success of Ryder's corporate strategy? To what extent should managers change strategy in response to changes in tax policy?
3. What will be the effect of the Tax Reform Act of 1986 on the success of Ryder's strategy?
4. What should Ryder CEO Anthony Burns do in 1986?

CASE 11

Honeywell's Investment Decisions

Perhaps the two most frequently cited rationales for a new tax proposal are that it will create jobs and that it will stimulate investment. Most of us have an intuitive understanding of how this process works, and, with the help of economists, we have formalized a model of how a rational firm ought to behave when confronted with a change in taxes. The consensus model says that investment will be determined by expectations of changes in future sales and the cost of capital. Taxes are one of the many variables, including the real interest rate for borrowing funds and the percentage depreciation rate, which affect the cost of capital. If the tax change lowers the cost of capital, the desired capital stock will rise and firms will invest in order to reach the desired level.

And yet, in reality, there are many steps between the legislator's pen and the cancelled check for a new investment project. In the Chapter 11 case, Investment Decisions at Honeywell, we will attempt some detective work. The case sketches the actual steps in the investment decision making process for Honeywell Corporation in the early 1980s. The payoff in this case comes from tracing the flow of decisions through the five stages of strategy formulation, divisional plans, aggregation of plans, appropriations, and expenditures. Try to identify where the Economic Recovery Tax Act (ERTA) of 1981 could reasonably have influenced the investment decision in any way. Consider not just the quantity of funds to be invested, but also other characteristics such as the timing, location, quality of the project, and so forth.

The process described in this case is not atypical of the investment decision making process at many large corporations. Some companies are more "responsive" to a given tax incentive and others are less so. To the extent that this case study is truly representative, and depending on your evaluation of the effectiveness of ERTA in increasing investment at Honeywell, one might want to reevaluate their stand on the use of tax policy to stimulate investment.

255

During the 1980s, tax policy had been the central focus of the U.S. economic agenda. In 1980, Ronald Reagan was elected President on the promise of the largest tax cut in U.S. history. The Economic Recovery Tax Act (ERTA) of 1981 embodied that promise by slashing individual tax rates 25 percent over 3 years and greatly accelerating business depreciation schedules. The Joint Committee on Taxation estimated that ERTA would save individuals almost $700 billion and save businesses over $200 billion in taxes during the period 1981 to 1986. But in 1982 and 1984, Congress whittled away at ERTA tax savings in an attempt to reduce the burgeoning fiscal deficit. The final blow to ERTA came in 1986, when Congress passed a landmark tax reform package. It drastically cut depreciation write-offs to a pre-1981 level and eliminated the investment tax credit in return for a reduction in the corporate tax rate from 46 percent to 34 percent.

A major component of all tax policy debates was the anticipated effect of tax changes on business investment. The tax system had been used by the federal government to stimulate investment ever since accelerated depreciation and the investment tax credit were first introduced in 1954 and 1962 respectively. Indeed, one former presidental advisor called the income tax code "an industrial policy in disguise, and a capricious one at that."[1] Estimates of the impact of the 1981 tax reductions on U.S. investment vary, but one estimate, for example, attributes an increase in net corporate investment of approximately 20 percent or $17 billion in 1982.[2] Honeywell, like other U.S. industrial giants, serves as a representative corporate example of how tax policy may or may not affect investment decisions.

History

The Honeywell Corporation started in Minneapolis in 1885 with the production of residential heating controls. Initially known as the Thermo-Electric Regulator Company, Honeywell adopted its current name when it merged in 1927 with Honeywell Heating Specialty Company. Each company held patents before the merger that blocked the other company's continued growth. By 1934, the rapidly-growing firm had opened international subsidiaries in Canada and Europe.

In the same year, Honeywell diversified into the industrial controls

This case was prepared by Professor Michael G. Rukstad, with the assistance of Research Associates Julia Horn and Brad Kirchhofer. Copyright © 1989 by the President and Fellows of Harvard College. Harvard Business School Case 9-389-128.

[1]Walter W. Heller, "A Guarded Yes for Tax Reform," *Wall Street Journal,* January 22, 1986.

[2]Martin Feldstein and Joosung Jun, "The Effects of Tax Rules on Nonresidential Fixed Investment," in Martin Feldstein, ed., *The Effects of Taxation on Capital Accumulation,* (Chicago: University of Chicago Press, 1987), p. 117.

business by purchasing Brown Instrument Company of Philadelphia, which was the precursor of Honeywell's industrial controls segment. During World War II, Honeywell's experience in the mass production of precision instruments put the company in a unique position to supply the war effort. Among Honeywell's contributions was the development of a top-secret autopilot system, which launched the company's still-successful aerospace and defense business.

Because electronics were so important to Honeywell's instrument and control products, the Transistor Division was formed in 1954 to expand electronic circuit research and production. In 1957, Honeywell bought Datamatic Corporation to establish the Datamatic Computer Division. General Electric and Honeywell merged their computer businesses in 1970 to form Honeywell Information Systems, the second largest computer company in the country at the time. Honeywell's initial share of 81.5 percent later became complete ownership.

By 1985, Honeywell's centennial year, it had $6.6 billion dollars in revenue and employed 94,000 people throughout the world. Technology's importance to Honeywell was exemplified by the 7 percent of revenue spent on research and development in 1984, compared to an average of 4.2 percent for the top 200 electronic firms in the United States, and an average of 2.5 percent for the 819 firms in *Business Week's* all-industry composite listing. Honeywell ranked 15th in the United States in absolute level of R&D spending in 1984. The company received over a quarter of its revenue from outside the United States and ranked 55th in the United States in absolute level of foreign revenue in 1984. The top 200 U.S. firms in terms of foreign revenue derived an average of 32 percent of their total revenue from foreign sources.

Business Segments

Before 1986, Honeywell divided its activities into the four major product segments shown below with their respective 1985 share of sales and profits:

Segment	Percent of Total Sales	Percent of Total Profits
Aerospace and Defense	29%	21%
Control Products	15	20
Control Systems	26	24
Information Systems	30	35

Aerospace and Defense

This segment included the design, development and production of guidance systems and controls for military and commercial aircraft, space vehicles, missiles, naval vessels, and military vehicles. Many large, well-known firms participated in the Aerospace and Defense (A&D) markets, including Martin Marietta, Raytheon, Allied-Signal, TRW, Sperry, Litton, Texas Instruments, Singer, GenCorp and Gould (ranked by 1985 A&D revenue from largest to smallest). Though these firms competed with at least one division of Honeywell's A&D, none competed with all of A&D's operations.

The outlook for the Aerospace and Defense segment was particularly promising because of the rapid growth of the defense industry in the mid-1980s. Segment sales had grown almost 14 percent annually from 1980 to 1985 and were expected to continue growing quickly, although not at the rate of the early 1980s.

Control Products

The Control Products segment included microelectronic and electro-mechanical components and products for residential, commercial, and industrial application. Most of these products were sold to wholesalers, distributors, and OEMs, rather than to end users. Sales had grown erratically in the early 1980s and had fallen again in 1985. The segment's products included residential environmental controls, precision switches, and semiconductors (for both internal use and external sale). In early 1985, Honeywell sold its Synertek unit, a merchant producer of integrated circuits for consumer products, to AT&T.

Residential environmental controls were very effective in helping homeowners to reduce energy consumption; as a result, sales of these controls exploded after the oil shocks of the 1970's, growing 15 percent annually from 1974 to 1980. Slower sales growth in the Control Products segment was expected in the mid-1980s as the residential market, in addition to the consumer product and industrial markets, experienced moderate growth. Competitors in the Control Products segment included a few larger firms, such as Matsushita and Johnson Controls, and many smaller control firms (with parent company in parentheses): Advanced Micro Devices, Allen Bradley (Rockwell), AMP Banner, Barber Coleman, Cherry Electric, Cutler-Hammer (Eaton), ELDEC, Keytronic, Master Specialties (Eaton), Omron, Photo Switch, Robert Shaw, Square D, Uni-Max, and White Rogers (Emerson Electric).

Control Systems

This segment grew 9.6 percent annually in 1981 and 1982, declined slightly in 1983, and grew 5.8 percent annually in 1984 and 1985. The Control Systems segment included sophisticated commercial-building and industrial systems which were designed for data acquisition monitoring, control, and management of customer processes and equipment.

Most segment sales were made directly to the builders and manufacturers who used the products, and as such were very dependent on capital spending by these customers.

In the commercial building market, the Control Systems segment provided energy-management systems, fire and security systems, computer and communication systems, and building services. Communication systems were built around private branch exchanges (PBXs) produced by Honeywell's joint venture with L.M. Ericsson of Sweden. Commercial building competitors included Johnson Controls, MCC Powers, Lardis & Gyr, and Staefa.

Industrial products included computerized plant management systems, process control systems, and test management systems. For example, Honeywell's TDC 3000 process management system integrated process control in the chemical process industries with production scheduling, inventory control, maintenance, and administration. This system gave the plant manager a single monitoring and control point for the entire plant. Foxboro, Fisher Controls, Yokogawa, Bailey, Allen Bradley, and Siemens were Honeywell's major competitors in the industrial control market.

Information Systems

Honeywell's largest product segment, Information Systems (IS), included products and services related to electronic data processing systems for business, government, and scientific applications. With nearly $2 billion in revenue in 1985, Honeywell ranked about eighth in the world in information systems revenues. Since Honeywell was strongest in mainframe computers, its major competitors included IBM, Burroughs, Fujitsu/Amdahl, Control Data, Sperry, NCR and Hitachi as ranked by 1984 worldwide shipments of mainframes.

The IS segment experienced several difficulties in the early 1980s. Segment operating profit dropped precipitously between 1980 and 1982. James Renier took over the IS segment in late 1982. He acted swiftly, slashing costs and reducing the IS work force of 27,000 by 3,500 people through layoffs, retirements, and transfers. In addition, cooperative agreements were entered into with other manufacturers, such as CDC and Sperry in peripherals and Japan's NEC in large-scale mainframes. NEC had licensed Honeywell's mainframe technology for years; now that NEC had developed its own strongly competitive mainframe line, a reverse relationship would find Honeywell obtaining its large computers from NEC. Results were immediate and dramatic: IS operating profit was 250 percent greater in 1985 than in 1982, on a sales increase of only 16 percent in the same period.

Renier did not stop at cutting costs and reorganizing; he fully revamped Honeywell's IS marketing strategy. No longer would Honeywell compete across the board with IBM (25 times Honeywell's size). Honeywell would instead attempt to complement IBM systems already installed. Honeywell viewed IBM as "the environment" rather than as competition.[3]

Corporate Strategy

Honeywell Corporation's general goals in early 1986 were to exploit the growth potential in the automation and control businesses, to capitalize on the firm's technological strengths, and to manage assets carefully. The first two goals involved the market for integrated systems where Honeywell hoped to combine its strengths in computers, controls, communications, and software into unique new products. The third goal indicated a desire to avoid another reduction in group operating profits such as the drop in Information Systems in 1982. Specific financial objectives included a return on equity of 18 percent, a 14 percent return on investment, a debt-to-total-capital ratio of 30 percent or less, and steadily increasing dividends. See Exhibits 1 and 2 for Honeywell financial information.

Honeywell saw its major product focus in the 1980s as systems which integrated the firm's computer, communications, and control hardware into a cooperative whole. A massive software development effort was crucial to the ability to integrate these various hardware components. The two biggest potential markets were manufacturing automation and commercial buildings.

Manufacturing Automation

Honeywell envisioned combining computers, communications, and controls in integrated systems to automate every aspect of manufacturing operations. This concept in its various forms was popularly referred to as "the factory of the future." The $10 billion market for such systems in 1985 was expected to be $20 billion by 1990 and $35 billion by 1995. Honeywell expected to have sales on the order of $4 billion in this market by 1990. The company faced formidable competition from DEC (the computer leader on the factory floor), IBM, Allen-Bradley (a Rockwell International subsidiary), and General Electric.

Integrated manufacturing systems would include process control; manufacturing planning, control, and communication; programmable controllers; and sensors. Honeywell segmented the market into process industries (refining, chemicals, pulp and paper), hybrid industries (food, pharmaceuticals), and discrete manufacturing industries (automobiles,

---

[3]June Altman, "Bunch Eyes Niches," *MISWeek*, May 29, 1985, p. 1.

Exhibit 1 Balance Sheet (in $ millions)

	1976	1977	1978	1979	1980	1981	1982	1983	1984	1985
Assets										
Current Assets	1,046	1,233	1,431	1,780	2,069	2,152	2,434	2,498	2,562	2,671
Investments and Advances	243	262	314	368	468	615	409	408	400	393
Property, Plant, and Equipment										
Equipment for lease to others	1,123	1,042	1,043	1,038	1,010	1,005	810	690	605	557
Less accumulated depreciation	614	548	557	569	556	546	440	377	310	287
	508	494	488	469	454	459	370	312	294	277
Other PP&E	548	622	720	860	1,103	1,395	1,636	1,762	1,953	2,312
Less accumulated depreciation	263	295	322	365	427	518	614	707	815	1,002
	285	327	398	495	676	877	1,022	1,055	1,137	1,310
Total PP&E	794	822	887	964	1,130	1,337	1,392	1,367	1,432	1,580
Other Assets	110	112	194	228	225	228	236	390	366	390
Total Assets	2,204	2,429	2,826	3,340	3,893	4,331	4,471	4,664	4,760	5,034
Liabilities and Stockholders' Equity										
Current Liabilities	511	643	820	937	1,114	1,199	1,266	1,338	1,387	1,549
Long-Term Debt	262	240	300	440	470	606	676	695	666	642
Deferred income taxes	140	155	180	240	293	283	307	253	192	197
Other Liabilities	163	182	139	81	142	145	78	64	134	79
Stockholders' Equity	1,128	1,209	1,387	1,642	1,874	2,098	2,143	2,314	2,381	2,567
Total Liabilities and Stockholders' Equity	2,204	2,429	2,826	3,340	3,893	4,331	4,471	4,664	4,760	5,034

Source: Company Annual Reports.

Exhibit 2 Consolidated Income Statement (in $ millions)

	1976	1977	1978	1979	1980	1981	1982	1983	1984	1985
Revenue										
Sales	$1,973	$2,313	$2,846	$3,505	$4,119	$4,472	$4,594	$4,779	$5,185	$5,754
Computer rental and service income	522	598	702	705	806	879	897	888	889	871
Total Revenue	$2,495	$2,911	$3,548	$4,210	$4,925	$5,351	$5,491	$5,667	$6,074	$6,625
Costs and Expenses:										
Cost of Sales	1,637	1,870	2,239	2,226	2,712	2,917	3,054	3,241	3,495	3,914
Cost of computer rental and service revenue	—	—	—	433	464	505	488	483	485	452
Research and development	126	152	187	235	295	369	397	414	422	452
Selling, general and administrative	561	636	794	902	1,016	1,146	1,207	1,149	1,217	1,353
Other income	(28)	(7)	(17)	(24)	(37)	(1)	(91)	—	—	—
Earnings Before Interest and Taxes	$199	$260	$345	$438	$475	$415	$436	$380	$455	$454
Interest:										
Interest expense	25	—	—	65	91	123	118	92	88	104
Interest income	—	(24)	(22)	(43)	(51)	(72)	(66)	(70)	(64)	(44)
	25	(24)	(22)	22	40	51	52	22	24	60
Income before taxes	$174	$284	$367	$416	$435	$364	$384	$358	$431	$394
Income Taxes	70	101	141	176	159	107	111	107	96	115
Other net income	8	11	20	21	13	3	—	(20)	(96)	6
Net Income	$112	$194	$246	$261	$289	$260	$273	$231	$239	$282

Source: Company Annual Reports.

aerospace, appliances), and expected to be strong in all three. Honeywell considered itself well-positioned to exploit this market because of its strength in industrial control and the fact that one-third of its 10,000 computer customers were manufacturing companies.

Commercial Buildings

Modern commercial buildings incorporated many sophisticated electronic systems in their structures; Honeywell planned to integrate and augment these systems in ways which would reduce costs and enhance service to building owners and tenants alike. In 1986, this market was estimated at $2.2 billion and was projected to be $6.6 billion by 1995. Competition included a United Technologies-AT&T joint venture formed in December 1984 to attack the building automation market, as well as other communications companies planning to enter this market.

The components of an integrated building system included energy/environmental controls, fire and security systems, PBX systems for voice and data transmission, computer services (time-sharing and office automation) for tenants, and preventive-maintenance/building-operation services. All of these products and services were available from Honeywell individually; the integrated systems approach tied them all together under one efficient organization in a building. The same computers could control heating and cooling, warn of security breaches, switch telephone calls, advise of the need for maintenance, and provide information processing to tenants. Combining and coordinating these services would eliminate redundant hardware while expanding the service available to tenants (and Honeywell's revenue opportunities). The target market for these systems included office buildings, hotels, hospitals, university campuses, shopping centers, and any other large building or complex of buildings.

Capital Expenditures
Total Capital Expenditures

Honeywell's total capital expenditures grew an average of 16 percent annually for the five years from 1976 to 1981, fell 9 percent annually for the three years from 1981 to 1984, and then rebounded 10 percent in 1985. However, the pattern of total capital expenditures was misleading since it included "equipment for lease to others" (ELTO). Unlike the capital decisions made by Honeywell managers, the level of ELTO expenditures was determined during the course of the year by customer decisions. For customers desiring to lease computer equipment, Honeywell would manufacture the equipment and accept payment in the form of lease payments. The manufacturing cost of such equipment was considered a capital expenditure, while its depreciation was a "cost of computer-rental revenue."[4] (Refer to Exhibit 2). Capital expenditures net of leased equipment grew nearly 33 percent annually for the six years from 1976 to 1982, declined somewhat in 1983 and 1984, and in 1985 increased to 16 percent over the 1983 level. Exhibits 3-5 show capital expenditures for the four businesses by segment and asset type.

Depreciation and Tax Trends.

The pattern of tax depreciation write-offs was determined by the historical pattern of capital expenditures and the current and past tax laws. For example, the 1981 current tax depreciation write-offs was the sum of current ACRS depreciation for assets placed in service during 1981, and

Exhibit 3   Capital Expenditures by Segment

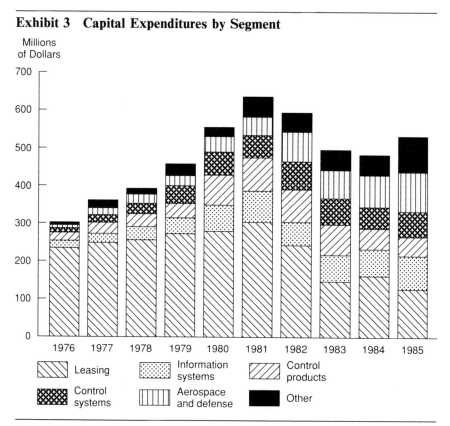

Source: Annual Reports.

[4]In the early 1980s, Honeywell made a conscious decision to shift the financing of these leases to third-party leasing companies, because Honeywell did not want to be "a financial institution." By raising the borrowing rate implicit in its lease plans slightly above market rates, Honeywell encouraged customers to arrange lease financing through firms such as General Electric Credit Corporation (GECC) and Security Pacific Leasing. The decline in the level of capital expenditures for ELTO after 1981 reflects this effort by Honeywell.

Exhibit 4   Capital Expenditures by Segment (without ELTO)

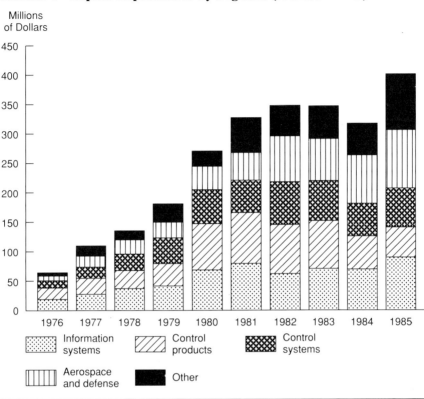

Source: Annual Reports.

the current portion of ADR depreciation for assets placed in service between 1971 and 1980 (but still not fully depreciated).[5] Therefore the full effect of a particular change in the depreciation tax law would not be felt for many years. Nonetheless, one could summarize the relative effects of all applicable tax laws on the firms particular portfolio of assets by examining the effective depreciation rate, which was defined as the total of current depreciation expenses divided by the total cost basis of all assets. The effective depreciation rate for Honeywell for the years 1976 to 1985 is shown in Exhibit 6. From the relatively low rate of 12.3 percent in 1981 (which implies an average depreciable life of 8.1 years ($=1/12.3$ percent)), it has risen to a high of 14.6 percent in 1985 (an average depreciable life of 6.8 years).

[5]ACRS is Accelerated Cost Recovery System, which is the title of the depreciation plan in the Economic Recovery Tax Act of 1981. It was retroactive to the beginning of that year. ADR is Accelerated Depreciation Range, which is applicable to assets placed in service during the years indicated. Bulletin F gave the recommended depreciation schedules for assets placed in service between 1962 and 1970.

Exhibit 5   Capital Expenditures by Type

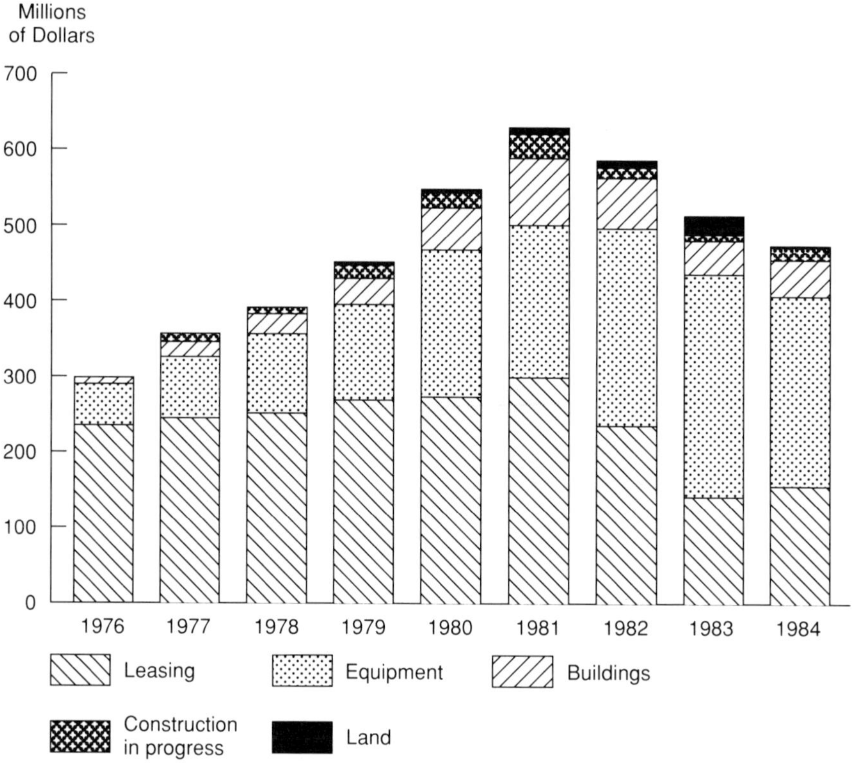

Millions
of Dollars

Source: Annual Reports.

Exhibit 6   Capital Asset Analysis (in millions)

Year	Average Capital Asset Cost	Current Tax Depreciation	Depreciation Rate
1976	$1,174	$158	13.5%
1977	1,184	143	12.2
1978	1,214	164	13.6
1979	1,322	190	14.4
1980	1,449	200	13.8
1981	1,599	196	12.3
1982	1,773	219	12.4
1983	1,947	272	14.0
1984	2,100	300	14.3
1985	2,230	325	14.6

Source: Casewriter Estimates.

In order to better understand the origins of the total depreciation charges, one could disaggregate the depreciation for any particular year into ACRS, ADR and pre-ADR. This detail is shown for the years 1981 to 1983 in Exhibit 7. In 1981 only a quarter of the total depreciation came from ACRS, but by 1983 ACRS accounted for approximately three-quarters of the total depreciation write-offs. If one reconstructed the depreciation write-offs, assuming Honeywell invested in the same assets but that ADR was in effect after 1980 rather than ACRS, one would have had the pattern of depreciation charges shown in Exhibit 8. The simplified corporate tax forms presented in Exhibit 9 show the relative importance of depreciation write-offs in determining the corporation's tax payment.

Honeywell's tax department was representative of the tax departments of most large U.S. corporations. By 1986, as tax issues grew in complexity and pervasiveness, twelve tax professionals centralized at

Exhibit 7   Contribution to Total Tax Depreciation from ACRS and ADR (1981–1983)

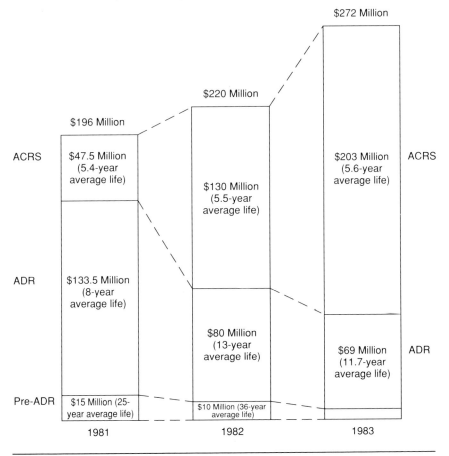

Source: Casewriter Estimates.

Exhibit 8   Total Tax Depreciation from 1981–1983 if ACRS were not enacted and ADR remained

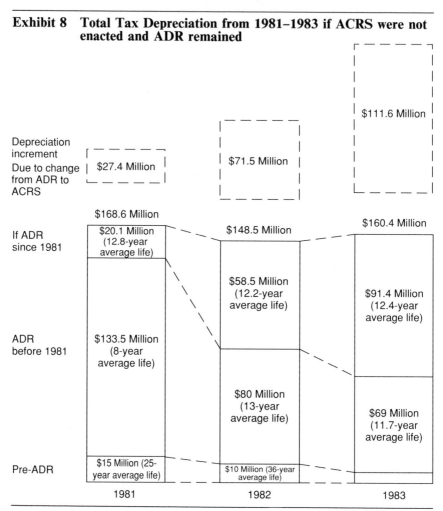

Source: Casewriter Estimates.

Honeywell Plaza were needed to deal with federal and international tax issues. The department's role in the investment decision process in 1986 was still that of an educator. The department promulgated knowledge about tax policy throughout the firm, but did not participate directly in the capital acquisition decision process. In making acquisition decisions, the tax department maintained close involvement because of the complex ways in which taxes could affect such transactions. Some managers felt that tax effects could be the deciding criterion in some acquisitions.

Honeywell's Planning and Capital Budgeting Process

The observed trends in capital expenditures, and hence in depreciation and taxes, were the outcome of a complex planning and capital budgeting

Exhibit 9   Simplified Tax Reports ($ Millions)

	1980	1981	1982
Gross Receipts	3,251	4,285	4,071
− Cost of Goods Sold	− 1,800	− 2,140	− 2,390
Gross Profits	1,451	1,723	1,681
+ Other Income	+ 223	+ 234	+ 326
Total Income	1,674	1,957	2,007
− Salaries, Rents, Taxes, Interest, & other Expenses	− 1,275	− 1,506	− 1,562
− Depreciation	− 200	− 196	− 220
Total Income Before Operating Loss	199	255	255
− Operating Loss	− 10	− 13	− 9.6
Taxable Income	189	242	215.4
− Total Tax Before Credits	− 108.5	− 142.6	− 112.1
After-Tax Income Before Credits	80.5	99.4	103.3
+ Foreign Tax Credits	+ 34.5	+ 38	+ 12.3
+ Investment Tax Credits	+ 27.6	+ 30	+ 32.0
+ R & D Tax Credits	0	0	+ 6.3
+ Other credits and Adjustments	− 3.1	+ 5	− 6.6
After-Tax Income	139.5	172.4	147.3
Effective Tax Rate (=Total Tax/Taxable Income)	26.2%	28.8%	31.6%

Source: Casewriter Estimates.

process. The corporation had established formal guidelines, however, most managers developed more informal decision making processes for allocating capital. In order to understand the key planning and capital budgeting decisions, the process can be decomposed, for purposes of simplification, into the following stages.

Formulate Strategy

The process began with the formulation of the corporate strategy. The chairman and senior executives defined the businesses in which Honeywell would participate and the performance objectives of the corporation. The business definition, ROI and ROE goals, and target capital structure were "policy constraints" under which Honeywell's capital was allocated. These policy constraints changed very little from 1976 to 1985. See Exhibit 10 for Honeywell's financial goals and actual performance over that period.

Exhibit 10   Honeywell Performance Measures (Actual and Goals)

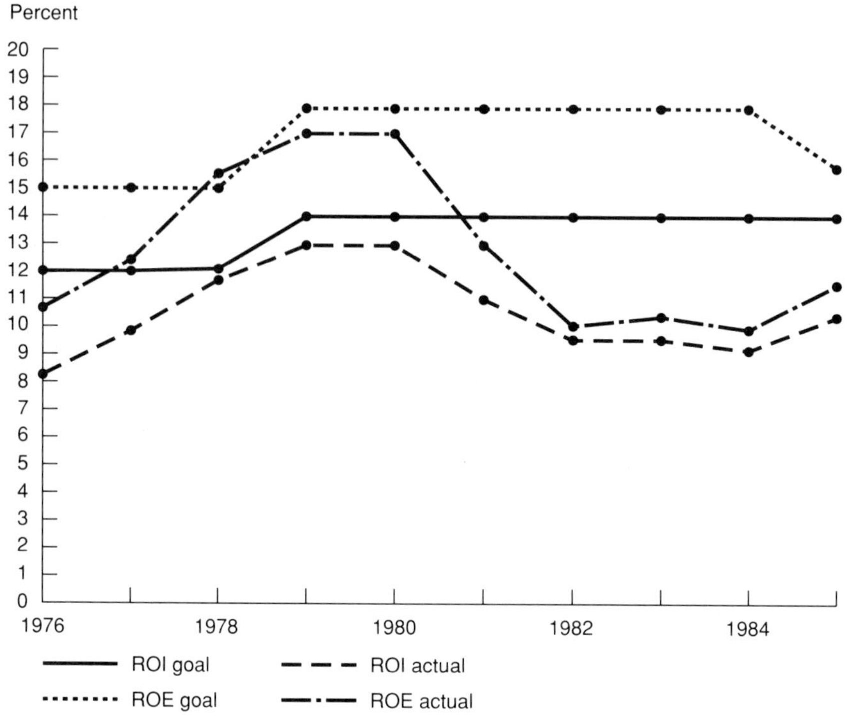

Percent

Source: Annual Reports.

Year-End Divisional Plan

The second stage began with the "Year-End Planning Process." Division managers proposed the capital expenditures which they deemed necessary to meet the performance goals received from headquarters. Each operating unit submitted a one year operational plan and a forecast for the following four years by November 1 (two months before the start of the fiscal year). The operational plan for the next twelve months included financial forecasts, budgets, and plans on a monthly basis, along with detailed descriptions of division objectives and strategies.

The operational plan specified that the division manager's bonus would be based on four performance measures: division return on investment (ROI), operating profit/sales, sales/assets, and revenue growth rate. The standards for evaluating these measures were unique to each division. In 1979, ROI was made the primary performance measure of division managers in order to make Honeywell's internal measurement system consistent with the way the corporation measured itself externally. At the same time, the ROI calculation was changed to allow accelerated depreciation (through deferred taxes) to reduce the "investment" portion of the ratio. Then in 1981, the "return" portion of the ROI measure was changed to include all tax credits accrued to the division.

Aggregation of Year-End Divisional Plans

In the third stage, all of the division capital expenditure proposals were aggregated at the corporate level. During December preceding the fiscal year, the year-end divisional plans were reviewed by a corporate management committee selected by the chairman. This committee examined the total requested level of expenditure and received advice from the Planning Department on the quality of data, the prospects for certain businesses, and the track records of division managers in forecasting sales and meeting plans. With this information, the committee revised the plans (if necessary) to accommodate the aggregate level of capital expenditure which they believed would maximize corporate ROI. If cuts from the level proposed by the division managers were necessary, they generally occurred across the board. Cash remaining after capital expenditures was used for dividends, acquisitions, and retained earnings. After review, the plan was presented by the committee to the board of directors along with recommendations for corporate objectives for the next year.

The approved year-end plan was returned to the divisions in January (the beginning of the fiscal year) for implementation. By the end of February, the corporate financial planning department had incorporated the approved plan into the consolidated corporate financial plan, which encompassed all investment and financing activities for the coming year.

Appropriations Process

The fourth stage was the appropriations process, which commenced as the planning process drew to an end (in the beginning of the corporate fiscal year). After a capital project was identified in the year-end plan, the next step was to complete the appropriation request form. See Exhibit 11 for a sample form. An investment analysis was required if the total investment was $10,000 or more and an economic return or cost reduction could be identified. In theory, divisions used a standard set of tools for evaluating their capital expenditure proposals, including discounting the cash flows at a corporate hurdle rate equal to the corporate ROI goal. However, Honeywell's extremely decentralized structure allowed for a great deal of diversity in the use of these tools. Some senior managers felt that the divisions could manipulate the assumptions to make projects satisfy corporate criteria. On the other hand, most managers felt that the division ROI goal provided the discipline to prevent abuse of this flexible project evaluation system. In addition, if the request required the approval of the Honeywell Board, a discounted cash flow or ROI analysis had to be offered in support.

Final approval of an appropriation request was authorized according to the type of request and/or the dollar amount of the total investment. Most projects were approved by the Division General Manager, and for smaller projects, by the Engineering or Production Manager. All projects over $1.0 million had to be approved by the chairman, CEO, or vice

Exhibit 11   Honeywell Appropriation Request Form

Honeywell
APPROPRIATION REQUEST

1. ORGANIZATION	2. APPROPRIATION NUMBER

3. DEPARTMENT	NUMBER	4. REQUEST NUMBER

5. LOCATION OR PLANT	NUMBER	6. DATE SUBMITTED

7. TITLE OF REQUEST	8. SUPPLEMENT TO APPROPRIATION NO.

9. Classification: Complete and attach support form as indicated below classifications

☐ Machinery ☐ Telecommunications ☐ Land and Buildings ☐ Building or Leasehold Improvements ☐ Unusual Expenses
☐ Test Equip. ☐ Office Automation
☐ Tooling ☐ Computer Products
☐ Turn &Fix   FORM A   FORM B   FORM C   ☐ ACQUISITION/ DIVESTITURES

10. REASON (CHECK ONE)
☐ Replacement   ☐ Contact
☐ Expansion   ☐ Work Conditions
☐ Savings

11. FINANCING   ☐ OPERATING LEASE
☐ Purchase   ☐ In House Make   ☐ CAPITAL LEASE

12.
☐ General Purpose   ☐ Special Purpose

13. FINANCIAL ANALYSIS OF INVESTMENT
Internal Rate of Return _____

14. SUMMARY OF ITEMS TO BE ACQUIRED OR WORK TO BE DONE   TOTAL COST OR COMMITMENT

QTY. or YEARS	DESCRIPTION	UNIT COST / ANNUAL RENT	EXPENSE	CAPITAL	ACCOUNT NUMBER

15. THIS CAPITAL REQUEST (Check One)

☐ Is included in this year's capital plan as line no. _____ .

☐ Was not planned but will be charged to this year's capital plan.

☐ Was not planned and this year's capital plan will be overrun by $ _____ .

Sub Total	
Transportation	
Site Preparation	
Sales Tax	
Less Trade-In	
TOTAL AMOUNT OF REQUEST	$ $ $

16. APPROPRIATION IS NECESSARY FOR FOLLOWING REASONS:

☐ We have verified that no suitable surplus equipment of this size is available

17. PROJECT COMMITMENT:

If this request is only a portion of a project/program outline additional investment required.
Project title _____

Previous appropriations	$ _____
This request	$ _____
Estimated future requests	$ _____
Current Total estimated commitment	$ _____
Original Total estimated commitment	$ _____
Previously approved commitment	$ _____

18. REQUESTED AND CERTIFIED BY:

REQUESTOR (PLEASE PRINT)	PHONE	DATE
CONTROLLER CERTIFICATION		DATE

19. APPROVALS (As Required)

NAME	DATE
NAME	DATE
NAME	DATE
DIVISION VICE PRES.	DATE
GROUP VICE PRES.	DATE
CORP. VICE PRES.	DATE
SR. VICE PRES.	DATE
EXECUTIVE VICE PRES.	DATE
CHIEF FINANCIAL OFFICER	DATE
PRESIDENT	DATE
CHAIRMAN AND CHIEF EXEC. OFFICER/VICE CHAIRMAN	DATE

Be sure to Attach Appropriate Support Form   Before filling out this form see Instruction on Back of Set.
81-2901-008 REV. 2-83

Exhibit 12 Total Appropriations 1976–1985 (Plan vs. Actual)

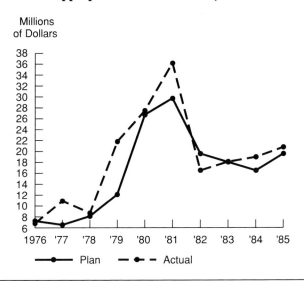

Source: Compiled by Casewriter.

Exhibit 13 Percent Change Planned vs. Actual: 1976–1985

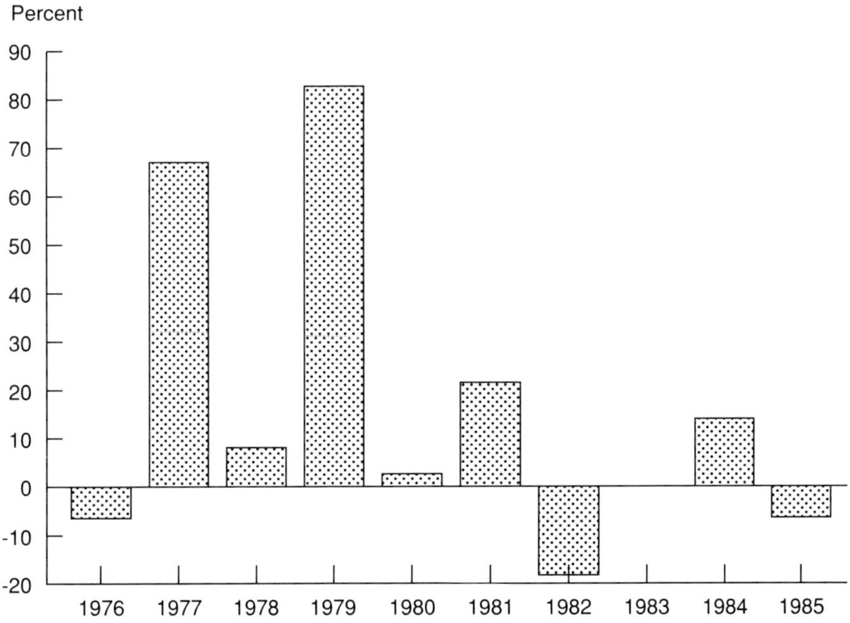

Percent

Source: Compiled by Casewriter.

Exhibit 14   Number of Projects per Month

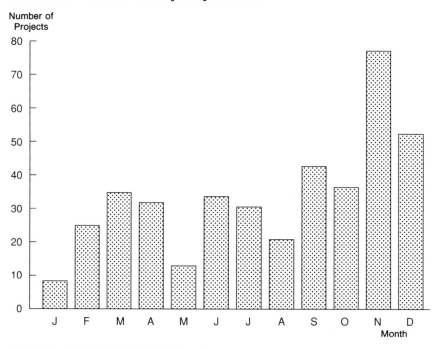

Source: Compiled by Casewriter.

chairman, as did all purchases, construction, or sales of land and buildings, and all acquisition and divestiture proposals. In practice, typically less than one percent (in number and value) of the formal appropriation requests were rejected in any year. Only 35 percent of the year's total planned capital appropriations could be appropriated in the first six months of the year.

Capital Expenditure

After the planning and appropriation stages, the final stage was the actual expenditure of the capital. Some capital expenditures were made in the same fiscal year in which they were appropriated, but often the capital expenditures were made in subsequent fiscal years, depending on purchasing and construction lags. The division controller managed this process but had no discretion regarding the timing of expenditures.

Honeywell Residential Division Capital Expenditures in 1981

The capital budgeting process could be best illustrated by recounting the events leading to the appropriations in the residential division in fiscal year 1981, which extended from January 1 to December 31, 1981. The

Exhibit 15   Total Dollar Amount per Month

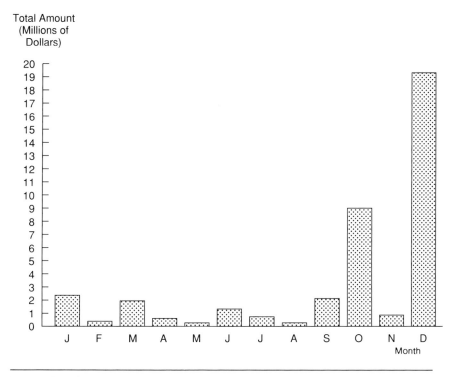

Source: Compiled by Casewriter.

residential division, part of the Control Products segment, was the largest and oldest division in Honeywell and had been a good contributor to overall profits. The division manufactured home heating control units, fire protection equipment, and other control products for the home. The following timeline presents an overview of the process for 1981.

Stages of the Budget Process ($ millions)	1981	1982	1983 and Beyond
(1) Year-End Divisional Plan Request for 1981 (received November 1, 1980)	$30.0		
(2) Approved Divisional Plan for 1981 (received December, 1980)	$30.0		
(3) Appropriation Requests Approved			
1st Quarter 1981	$ 4.7		
2nd Quarter 1981	$ 2.2		
3rd Quarter 1981	$ 3.1		
4th Quarter 1981	$29.2		
Total (Including Supplements)	$39.2		
(Total (New Appropriations only)	$36.6)		
(4) Capital Expenditures of the 1981 Appropriations	$ 1.6	$11.8	$25.8

Exhibit 16   Number of Projects per Range

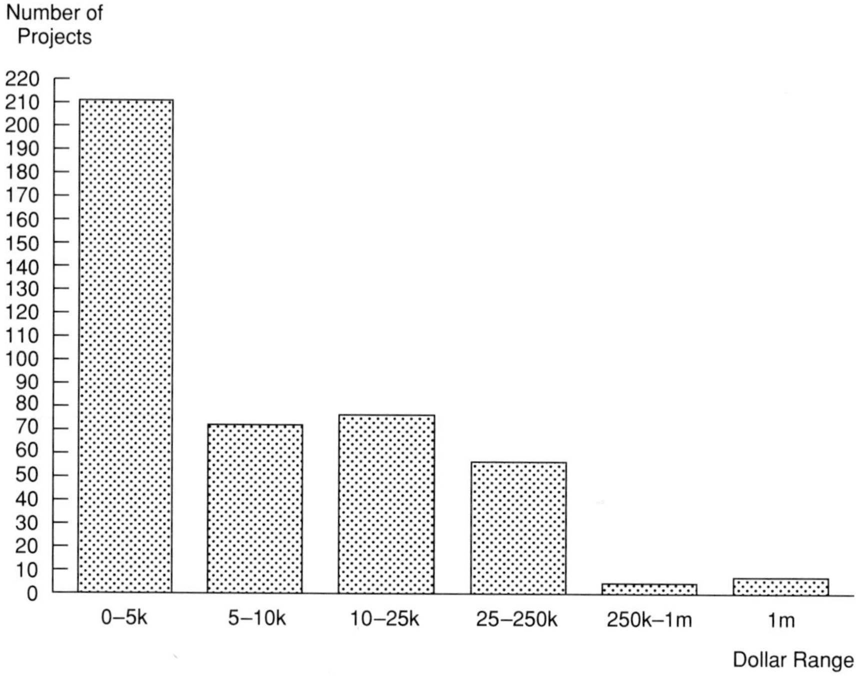

Number of
Projects

Source: Compiled by Casewriter.

In mid-October of 1980, while the Residential Division was preparing its plans for the upcoming fiscal year 1981, the capital appropriations committee held a meeting at corporate headquarters in Honeywell
Plaza. At the meeting, it was agreed that corporate performance goals
would continue to be 18 percent ROE, 14 percent ROI, a debt-to-total-
capital ratio of 30 percent or less, and steady growth in dividends. The
committee reviewed both the 1980 Honeywell sales and the sales forecast
for 1981. In 1980, Honeywell sales increased 4.5 percent from the first
to the second quarter followed by a slight decline in the 3rd quarter.
Fourth quarter sales were expected to show an increase of approximately
20 percent, similar to their average growth in that quarter in the previous
two years.

By November 1980, the Residential Division had completed their
year-end plans for presentation to management. Sales of the division were
expected to increase steadily in each quarter of 1981, except for a slight
downturn expected in the 3rd quarter. Residential division sales were
similar to company sales forecasts.

As December drew to a close, the appropriations committee, after
reviewing divisional proposals, set a constraint of $30 million for capital
expenditures in 1981 for the Residential Division. This was an increase
of $3.2 million over the 1980 level and was based upon sales forecasts

Exhibit 17   Total Dollar Amount per Range

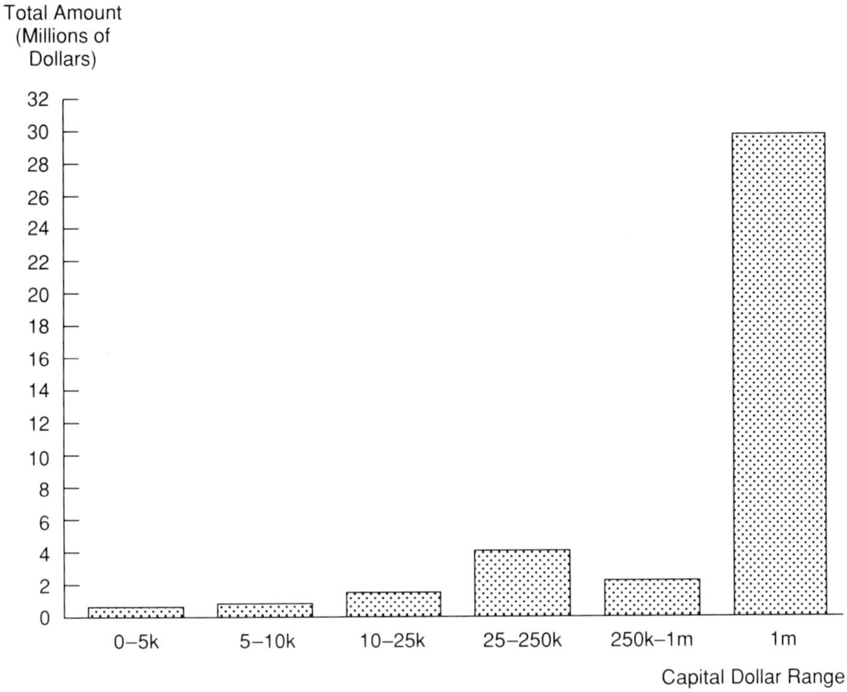

Total Amount
(Millions of
  Dollars)

Source: Compiled by Casewriter.

and financial schedules submitted by the division. Exhibits 12 and 13 plot the planned and the actual capital expenditures for Honeywell's Residential Division and the percentage change from plan. During the 1976 to 1985 period, Honeywell's Residential Division spent $159 million in capital expenditures with $111 million of that total in the last five years.

Residential sales in the first two quarters of 1981 were 19 percent and 10 percent below the level achieved in the fourth quarter of 1980, though they were 7 percent and 10 percent above their comparable quarters in 1980. Compared to plan, however, actual sales for the first two quarters were 11 percent and 14 percent below forecasted sales. This pattern of depressed sales continued into the second half of the year. Despite the unexpectedly low sales for 1981 and the likelihood of a similar performance for 1982, the actual capital appropriations in fiscal 1981 were $36.6, an overrun of $6.6 million *above* plan. Exhibits 14 and 15 summarize the monthly distribution of the number and dollars of capital expenditures during 1981. Most of the 469 projects accepted in 1981 were approved in the fourth quarter of the year. This pattern was typical for the company as a whole and similar to previous years' appropriations.

Exhibit 18   Appropriations

Classification	Planning Index[a]		Month Index[b]	
Computer	0.9		10.1	
Equipment	0.4		8.7	
Furniture	0.8		7.8	
Land	−1.0		10.0	
Machinery	0.7		4.4	
Tooling	0.9		5.7	
Unusual	−0.1		5.9	
Buildings	−0.7	(0.9 without the $18.1 million project)	11.5	(9.2 without the $18.1 million project)
Reason				
Work Conditions	0.7		8.9	
Replacement	0.9		9.4	
Expansion	0.8		5.3	
Savings	−0.8	(−0.2 without the $18.1 million project)	11.5	(9.4 without the $18.1 million project)
Financial Analysis				
Yes	−0.4		10.6	
No	0.0		6.5	
Not Available	0.7		7.0	

[a]The planning index is a weighted average of the number of projects in each category. An index of 1 indicates that all projects were planned. An index of −1 indicates that all projects were unplanned. Substitutions of one project for another were not included in the index.

[b]The month index is a weighted average of the dollar value of projects that occurred in each month. For example, an index of 1 indicates that all projects occurred in January, whereas an index of 12 indicates that all projects occurred in December.

Source: Casewriters Estimates.

    The seven largest projects (those over $1 million) accounted for the largest dollar amounts (84 percent of total spending) in 1981. Small projects (those under $5,000) accounted for 234 of the 469 projects but they amounted to less than $500,000 million in total (less than 1 percent of total spending). See Exhibits 16 and 17 for the distribution of projects by size of capital expenditure. Financial analysis was available in only 46 of the 469 projects, but this accounted for 75 percent of the total dollar value of appropriations. The difference between the planned and actual year-end capital expenditure totals resulted from unanticipated projects that were not in the Residential Division's operational plan. There were 21 unplanned projects totaling $18.4 million which were approved during the last quarter of 1981. The certainty and the timing of investment projects varied depending on the type, reason, and level of analysis of the investment. Exhibit 18 shows the diversity among investment projects.

    The largest of the unplanned projects in 1981, occurring in the fourth quarter, was the $18.1 million office consolidation plan, which accounted for half of the year's capital appropriations. In fact, this one project accounted for over 11 percent of the total capital expenditures for the Residential Division in the 10 years from 1976 to 1985. In 1981 the Residential Division offices were housed in five separate locations in Minneapolis (Corporate Headquarters Downtown, Parkdale, Golden Valley, Shady Oak, and Eden Prairie). The project would consolidate the group by mid-1983 under one roof (360,000 square feet) at the Golden Valley site. On June 18, 1981, the first formal appropriation request for $12,600 for an architectural study of the consolidation plan was submitted. The project had not been included in the 1981 plan but it had been discussed in general terms for years. The reason most often given for the timing of this project was the expiration of long-term leases of approximately 260,000 square feet of office space in 1983 and 1984. The justification for building a new office complex was that it would yield a cost savings. The cost savings would come from the avoidance of lease costs, the elimination of duplicate services (cafeterias, maintenance, etc.), the reduction in personnel, and the elimination of travel time and mileage between facilities. The return on investment was expected to be 15 percent, which exactly equaled the corporate hurdle rate.

On December 10, 1981, the appropriation request on the $18.1 capital expenditure for the Residential Division office consolidation project was submitted. The $18.1 million project would generate approximately $223,000 in investment tax credits and $820,000 of annual increases in depreciation write-offs. On December 18, Chairman Edson Spencer approved the request. The approval resulted in a $6.6 million year-end overrun for the Residential Division in 1981.

Questions

1. Did Reagan's 1981 tax cut affect Honeywell's investment decisions? If yes, by how much and through which channels or stages of the decision process?
2. Should Honeywell be more responsive to tax incentives? How could one change Honeywell's investment decision-making process so that it could be more responsive.
3. What impact do you expect that the 1986 Tax Reform Act would have on Honeywell's investment?

CASE 12

Schlumberger and Fairchild Semiconductor

Our final example of the influence of tax policy on business decisions is Schlumberger's sale of its Fairchild Semiconductor business. Initially the sale was arranged with Fujitsu Corporation of Japan, but after that deal collapsed following some government rumblings, the final sale was negotiated with American-based National Semiconductor. In this case we see the impact of taxes on a particular divestment/acquisition transaction. Schlumberger was quite concerned with the tax consequences of the structure of this deal. We will discuss whether this concern was well founded or not.

In addition to the tax issues, the case allows one to evaluate Schlumberger's strategy and its fit with Fairchild, when Fairchild was still one of its operating subsidiaries. Also, there is a question as to whether Schlumberger could have managed the sale of Fairchild better than it did, once it decided that a sale was in order. Or perhaps the criticism is not with Schlumberger, but rather with the meddling of the government. These are topics that will arise during the class discussion.

Beyond the specific issues of this transaction, this case also illustrates the impact of the tax code on the wave of mergers and acquisitions during the 1980s. We first encountered this issue in the Chapter 4 case, RJR/Nabisco and Leveraged Buyouts. The case raises the issue of whether the tax code was an effective means for the government to intervene in such decisions by the private sector and whether it was having some unintended consequences.

Schlumberger, Ltd., headquartered in both New York and Paris, was the world's largest company in the oilfield service industry in the 1980s. Schlumberger, recognized on Wall Street as one of the world's best-managed multinational corporations, had been under the guiding genius of Chairman and CEO Jean Riboud since 1965. Riboud, a native of France and a loyalist to French Socialist ideology, oversaw the company's greatest successes. Included among those was Schlumberger's outstanding earnings record in the early 1980s, a period during which profits of most oil and oilfield service companies fell sharply.

Riboud also led Schlumberger's expansion into businesses outside of its traditional operations. He recognized that although the oilfield service industry was very profitable he also wanted to be able to exploit economies of scope with new businesses. The company's first step in that direction was the acquisition of a French industrial group, Compagnie de Compteurs, in 1970 for $79 million. The acquired company's major activities were in metering and measurement instruments. After returning these new businesses to profitability, Riboud spent $425 million in 1979 to acquire Fairchild Camera and Instrument Corporation, a major U.S. manufacturer of semiconductors. In 1981, Schlumberger acquired Manufacturing Data Systems (MDSI), a provider of numerical-controlled software systems, for $190 million. The following year, the company acquired Applicon, a computer-aided design (CAD) manufacturer, for $220 million.

By 1985, Schlumberger was organized into five businesses: wireline services, drilling and production services, Fairchild Semiconductor, computer-aided systems, and measurement and control devices. See Exhibit 1 for the corporate organization chart. The first two businesses, which comprised the Oilfield Services group, accounted for two-thirds of corporate revenues. Wireline operations provided measurement services to help locate and evaluate underground oil and gas reserves. Schlumberger controlled almost 70 percent of the world wireline market. The next largest competitor was Dresser Industries with 10 percent of that market. In fact, one Schlumberger subsidiary of the drilling and production services business was, by itself, the world's largest oil-drilling company. The computer-aided systems group, including Applicon, MDSI and others, specialized in automated test equipment for semiconductor and other electronic applications. The smallest of the five businesses, Measurement and Control, produced water, electric, and gas meters, defense control systems and electronic transaction equipment. This business group was the world's largest manufacturer of electric meters, and ranked second in the production of water meters.

Schlumberger, N.V. was incorporated in the Netherlands Antilles,

This case was prepared by Research Associate Julia Horn under the supervision of Professors Michael G. Rukstad and Mark A. Wolfson. Copyright © 1989 by the President and Fellows of Harvard College. Harvard Business School Case 9-389-133.

Exhibit 1 Schlumberger Ltd.: Corporate Organization Chart

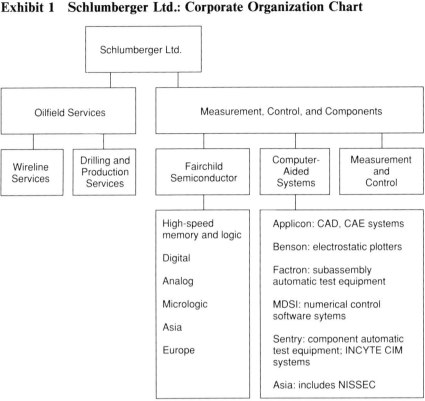

giving it significant tax advantages over companies incorporated in other locations. In addition to an income tax rate of just 3 percent, one of those advantages was the tax treatment of dividend payments. Although any company that conducted business in the United States paid a corporate tax at a rate of 46 percent (prior to the Tax Reform Act of 1986, which dropped corporate rates in two steps to 34 percent by 1988) regardless of its place of incorporation, companies incorporated in the United States faced an additional withholding tax on dividends, interest, and royalties paid to foreigners at a rate of up to 30 percent. The 30 percent withholding tax rate could be reduced by tax treaties between the United States and foreign countries. For companies such as Schlumberger that were incorporated in the Netherlands Antilles, dividend repatriations to parent companies were taxed at a rate of only 5 percent, and interest and royalty payments attracted no withholding tax at all. Overall, Schlumberger operated in 92 tax jurisdictions with statutory rates of up to 50 percent. Allen Klein, Schlumberger's vice president and director of taxes said, "Many American companies have lower effective tax rates than Schlumberger, because they may take advantage of tax breaks not available to foreign companies."[1] However, a member of the U.S. Congressional Joint Committee on Taxation asserted, "The tax advantages available to companies that are incorporated in the Antilles can be matched or surpassed by only a fraction of American companies."[2]

Along with the tax benefits it enjoyed, Schlumberger had always maintained a highly liquid portfolio of assets.[3] The company's current assets typically accounted for over 60 percent of total assets. In addition, because of its incorporation in the Netherlands Antilles, it had been able to generate substantial amounts of net interest income, largely free of tax. Schlumberger's profit position continued to be favorable. In each year from 1981 to 1984, Schlumberger's reported net income exceeded $1 billion. During that period, the Oilfield Services group had accounted for approximately 60 percent of total revenues and over 90 percent of total profits. In 1985 and 1986 profits of the Oilfield Services group tumbled along with oil prices to virtually zero. This coincided with the period of relatively small cumulative profits for the Measurement and Control group, which had earned on average over $100 million in each of the preceding five years. See Exhibit 2.

Schlumberger's Acquisition of Fairchild in 1979

With the acquisition of Fairchild in 1979, Riboud defined Schlumberger's boundaries to the shareholders in the Annual Report as follows:

We are in the right businesses; luck or not, we are. I cannot imagine for the eighties fields of activity with greater growth than the ones we are in: the technical services for the exploration and production of hydrocarbons, the technical products tied to the distribution of electrical power, and the advanced products of the semiconductor industry.

In particular, the Fairchild acquisition fit with Riboud's long-term vision for his company.

I felt strongly that twenty years down the road we had to have semiconductor capability." He said that because Germany had not invested in semiconductors it had become a captive of Japanese and American computer technology. Schlumberger's basic business, he went on, is information, not oil, and what the Wireline division does is provide information to oil companies to help them make accurate decisions. The next generation of wire-

---

[1]Ken Auletta, "Profiles: A Certain Poetry," *The New Yorker*, June 6, 1983, p.59.
[2]Ibid.

[3]Of Schlumberger's $6.7 billion in assets in 1987, $2.8 billion were identified as a corporate assets. The company's other identifiable assets were distributed around the world as follows: $1.3 billion in the United States, $400 million in other Western Hemisphere countries, $800 million in France, $800 million in other European countries, and $700 million in other Eastern Hemisphere countries.

Exhibit 2 Schlumberger Limited Financial Data (in $ millions)

Year Ended December 31,	1987	1986	1985	1984	1983	1982	1981	1980	1979ᵃ	1978	1977	1976
Revenue:												
Oilfield Services	$2,306	$ 2,652	$ 3,966	$ 3,616	$3,414	$4,054	$3,788	$2,814	$2,037	$1,636	$1,310	$1,005
Measurement, Control and Components	2,096	1,916	1,619	1,630	1,577	1,971	1,995	2,070	1,513	983	850	805
Interest and other income	325	370	434	390	279	259	195	253	91	65	46	30
	$4,727	$ 4,938	$ 6,019	$ 5,636	$5,270	$6,284	$5,978	$5,137	$3,641	$2,684	$2,206	$1,840
Percent increase (decrease) over prior year	(4%)	(18%)	7%	7%	(9%)	5%	16%	41%	36%	22%	20%	16%
Cost of goods sold and services	$3,273	$ 3,506	$ 3,650	$ 3,659	$3,388	$3,479	$3,244	$2,813	$2,061	$1,499	$1,231	$1,071
Operating income:												
Oilfield Services	$ 147	$ 8	$ 1,039	$ 1,170	$1,187	$1,656	$1,702	$1,184	$ 809	$ 648	$ 540	$ 383
Measurement, Control and Components	107	74	69	147	143	34	131	230	189	122	93	77
Eliminations	(2)	(1,614)ᵇ	1	10	13	(18)	(25)	(14)	(14)	(6)	(1)	—
	$ 252	$(1,532)ᵇ	$ 1,109	$ 1,327	$1,343	$1,672	$1,808	$1,400	$ 984	$ 764	$ 632	$ 450
Percent increase (decrease) over prior year	NA	NA	(16%)	(1%)	(25%)	(8%)	29%	42%	29%	21%	37%	27%

(Continued)

Exhibit 2 (Continued)

Year Ended December 31,	1987	1986	1985	1984	1983	1982	1981	1980	1979[a]	1978	1977	1976
Interest expense	$ 166	$ 410	$ 209	$ 146	$ 110	$ 117	$ 108	$ 102	$ 52	$ 18	$ 16	$ 15
Taxes on income	116	106	324	401	363	451	580	522	355	295	248	168
Net income	353[c]	(2,108)[d]	351[e]	1,182	1,084	1,348	1,266	994	658	502	401	293
Percent increase (decrease) over prior year	NA	NA	(17%)	2%	(19%)	6%	27%	51%	31%	25%	37%	34%
Net income as percent of revenue	11%	NA	16%	21%	22%	21%	21%	19%	18%	19%	18%	16%
Return on average stockholders' equity	13%	NA	14%	19%	21%	28%	34%	36%	31%	29%	28%	25%
Fixed asset additions	$ 276	$ 447	$ 650	$ 559	$ 394	$1,094	$1,063	$ 748	$ 503	$ 393	$ 212	$ 187
Total assets	6,741	8,012	11,282	10,913	8,353	7,846	6,525	5,242	4,350	2,955	2,385	1,995
Long-term debt	125	504	1,014	966	455	462	278	238	490	85	17	72
Stockholders' equity	3,836	4,123	6,877	6,992	5,819	5,226	4,235	3,218	2,400	1,900	1,550	1,280

[a] Results of Fairchild were consolidated beginning July 1, 1979.

[b] Includes nonrecurring charges relating to operating income of $1.6 billion.

[c] Includes nonrecurring credit relating to continuing operations of $222 million.

[d] Includes nonrecurring charges relating to continuing operations of $1.7 billion including pretax interest expense of $228 million.

[e] Includes unusual charges relating to discontinued operations of Fairchild Semiconductor with an after-tax effect of $486 million.

line and meter equipment, he said, will be more dependent on tiny micropro-
cessors and semiconductors, and he predicted that in five years Fairchild
would be "among the top five semiconductor companies in the world, including the Japanese."[4]

Schlumberger acquired Fairchild after it outbid Gould, the initial
suitor. In the first three months of 1979, Fairchild's market value was
$180 million, with the shares selling at an average price of $32.75. On
April 26, Gould Inc., one of the nation's largest producers of electrical
parts and auto batteries, announced that it would purchase Fairchild for
$300 million in cash and securities, a share price equivalent to $54.
Fairchild's market value on the announcement rose $45 million to $287
million. After initial reluctance on the side of Fairchild, Gould increased
the offer to $315 million or $57 per share. On May 20, Schlumberger
entered the bidding with a $363 million cash offer at $66 per share.
Despite a subsequent Gould offer of $70 per share in cash and securities,
Schlumberger acquired the company at its $66 per share cash offer. At
the close of the transaction on July 1, Schlumberger had paid $425 million
in cash and expenses for all of Fairchild's shares in a taxable transaction
that included approximately $253 million in goodwill.[5]

Wall Street critics and even some Schlumberger employees feared
that Schlumberger overpaid for Fairchild. "Fairchild was flat on its back
when Schlumberger acquired it," said Richard E. Belcher, general manager of Fairchild's hybrid products division. "It was saved in the nick of
time."[6] In 1975, Fairchild was the second leading supplier of integrated
circuits behind Texas Instruments but ahead of National Semiconductor,
Intel, and Motorola. Fairchild, along with Texas Instruments, was the
first to develop integrated circuit (IC) technology. It built the IC market
in the 1960s by taking circuit design away from its customers and per-
suading them to design systems instead. In the early 1970s, Fairchild was
the third largest producer of semiconductors. However, by the end of the
decade, when the next generation of semiconductor chips was being developed, Fairchild was no longer a viable player.[7] Nonetheless, Fairchild
retained ownership of numerous patents and licenses on ICs and other
chip designs, which would be valuable for many years into the future.
From 1974 to 1978, Fairchild's sales had grown at a compounded annual
rate of 8.5 percent , but net income declined 2 percent per year over the
same period. Fairchild had not sustained any losses, but its return on
sales declined from 7 percent in 1974 to 4.6 percent in 1978 after re-
bounding from a low of 2.4 percent in 1977. See Exhibit 3. In a period

---

[4]Ken Auletta, "Profiles: A Certain Poetry," *The New Yorker*, June 6, 1983, p.89.

[5]Goodwill is not amortizable for tax purposes in the United States, but it must be amortized
in computing income reported to shareholders.

[6]Is the worst over for Fairchild Camera?" *Business Week*, December 14, 1983, p.78.

[7]Richard N. Foster, *Innovation: The Attackers' Advantage*, (New York: Summit Books,
1984).

Exhibit 3   Fairchild Camera and Instrument Corporation Summary of Operations (in $ thousands)

	Years ended December 31st				
	1978	1977	1976	1975	1974
Net Sales	$533,832	$460,108	$443,221	$291,542	$384,933
Royalties and other income	6,608	10,340	7,157	8,188	10,619
Total Sales and Income	550,440	470,448	450,378	299,730	395,552
Percent increase (decrease) over prior year	17%	5%	50%	(24%)	—
Cost of Sales	373,144	342,576	327,381	208,712	264,194
Provision for discontinued product line	5,932	—	—	—	—
Administrative and selling expenses	123,484	102,392	94,427	69,732	75,882
Interest expense	7,284	7,182	5,504	4,154	3,868
Income before income taxes	40,596	18,298	23,066	17,132	51,608
Net Income	$ 24,764	$ 11,162	$ 12,456	$ 13,073	$ 27,032
Percent increase (decrease) over prior year	121%	(10%)	(5%)	(52%)	—
Net income as percent of revenue	4.5%	2.4%	2.8%	4.4%	6.8%
Return on average stockholders' equity	12.0%	6.0%	7.0%	7.9%	17.6%
Total Assets	339,660	288,734	314,596	265,592	256,468
Capital expenditures	31,991	22,047	36,076	20,693	41,342
Long-term debt	73,703	72,358	68,088	46,825	49,592
Stockholders' equity	205,916	184,865	177,609	166,329	153,875

when total capital spending for all other U.S. semiconductor companies had increased by 80 percent, Fairchild's capital expenditures had fallen to half its 1974 level.[8]

Fairchild and the Semiconductor Industry, 1979-1986

After Schlumberger acquired Fairchild, its performance did not improve over the next eight years. Despite Fairchild's small contribution to Schlumberger's overall earnings, some critics charged that Fairchild's dismal profitability brought Schlumberger's stock price down from a high of $87 per share in November 1980 to $34 per share in August 1982.[9] By 1982, Fairchild's market share in semiconductors was only half of its 1977 level despite climbing revenues. Fairchild's performance plummeted even though Schlumberger injected over $1 billion in capital additions and research and development expenditures in the first five years following the acquisition. Despite the fact that Fairchild had been grappling with losses, analysts identified Fairchild's strengths as application-specific integrated circuits (ASICs), particularly gate arrays, standard logic products such as emitter-coupled logic (ECL) devices, and memory products such as programmable read-only memories (PROMs). See Exhibit 4. In 1986, Fairchild was the fourth largest U.S. gate array producer and was particularly known for its success in ECL, a bipolar process technology that offered significant speed advantages for system performance. Fairchild produced its products in eight U.S. plants located in California (four plants), Maine (three plants), South Carolina, and Washington. The company also had two smaller manufacturing facilities in West Germany and Japan.

After strong growth in the early part of the decade, the U.S. semiconductor industry had its worst year on record in 1985. See Exhibit 5. From 1981 to 1985, Japanese semiconductor companies had posted significant market share gains in the U.S. market, while U.S. companies lost market share in both Japan and at home. Three dumping suits, legal actions charging that Japanese producers were selling chips in the United States and third markets below production cost, were initiated by U.S. semiconductor firms and the U.S. Department of Commerce during 1985. In addition, the U.S. Semiconductor Industry Association (SIA) filed a Section 301 unfair trade case against Japan. Japanese companies denied all charges, arguing that their market was open and that they had lower production costs than U.S. producers. Japanese producers further claimed that they had difficulty selling their products through independent U.S. distributors, where nearly one-quarter of chips were sold, because many

---

[8]Daniel I. Okimoto, et. al., eds., *Competitive Edge: The Semiconductor Industry in the U.S. and Japan*, (Stanford, California: Stanford University Press, 1984), p.166.

[9]Ken Auletta, "Profiles: A Certain Poetry," *The New Yorker*, June 6, 1983, p.88.

Exhibit 4   Semiconductor Product Tree (approximate percentages of consumption in the mid-1980s in parentheses)

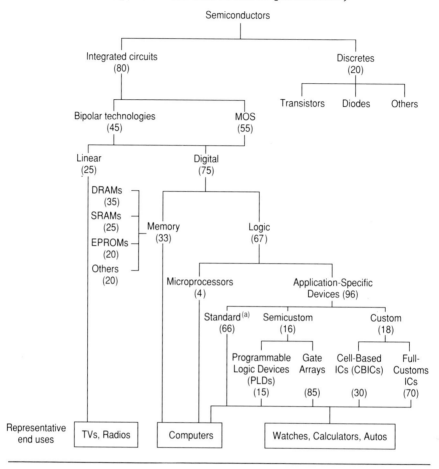

[a] Includes ECL devices among other products.

of those distributors did not want to risk losing business from U.S. chip makers.

All major semiconductor firms in the United States fared poorly in 1985, but Fairchild fared among the worst. Schlumberger was forced to writeoff $511 million because of the continued Fairchild losses, including the writeoff of what remained of the $253 million of Fairchild goodwill on Schlumberger's books. "Although Riboud had acknowledged that he may have paid too much for Fairchild, he predicted in 1979 at the time of the acquisition that Fairchild's problems would take no more than five years to resolve"—a horizon he subsequently extended to seven years.[10]

[10]Ken Auletta, "Profiles: A Certain Poetry," *The New Yorker*, June 13, 1983, p.89.

Exhibit 5   Growth in U.S. Semiconductor Consumption vs. U.S. GNP Growth (year-to-year percentage change)

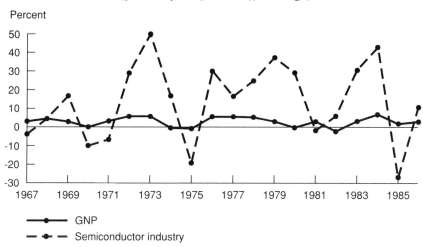

Source: Dataquest, March 1987.

Of the top twenty semiconductor manufacturers in 1986, only Advanced Micro Devices lost a higher proportion of its market share during the period from 1984 to 1986. Fairchild's sales declined by 23.3 percent over the same period, while sales of the top twenty firms grew by 4.5 percent (5.4 percent excluding Fairchild).

In 1986, trade disputes between U.S. and Japanese semiconductor manufacturers came to a head over continued alleged dumping of computer chips and the lack of access to Japanese markets for foreign producers. On July 31, 1986, after months of negotiations, the United States and Japan reached an historic agreement, the U.S.-Japan Semiconductor Trade Arrangement, which was to eliminate Japanese dumping in the United States and third markets and to double foreign market share in Japan in the next five years. The agreement led to the suspension of the 301 and dumping suits.

After seven years of sizeable investments in Fairchild with no corresponding returns, Schlumberger wondered how it could rid itself of the Fairchild operation. In August 1986, the decision was made that Fairchild could not be fixed by Schlumberger and that it no longer fit with Schlumberger's corporate strategy. Therefore, Schlumberger decided to sell Fairchild.

Negotiations with Fujitsu Leading to a Joint Venture Proposal

In August 1986, Schlumberger began preliminary discussions with Fujitsu Ltd. of Japan regarding the purchase of Fairchild. Fujitsu, a producer of semiconductors, computers, and telecommunications devices, was Japan's largest computer builder, second largest manufacturer of telecommunications equipment, and the country's fourth largest semiconductor manufacturer. In semiconductors, the company's strengths were in ASICs, particularly gate arrays and cell-based integrated circuits (CBICs), and in standard logic products, such as ECLs. Fujitsu was the world's largest supplier of ASICs and bipolar digital memory products in 1986 and the seventh largest semiconductor supplier overall. See Exhibit 6. Fujitsu's sales had grown at a compounded annual rate of 21 percent from 1982 to 1986. Over that same time period, the company's profits grew 41 percent per year from 1982 to 1985, but fell 57 percent in 1986 due, in part, to the rapid appreciation of the yen against the dollar. See Exhibit 7.

Fujitsu produced its products in eighteen plants around the world. Thirteen of those plants were located in Japan, the largest of which was an 84,000 square meter plant in Iwate that fabricated and assembled MOS memory products. In the U.S., Fujitsu had one disk drive plant located in Hillsboro, Oregon. The company also had fabrication and assembly operations in England, Ireland, and Malaysia.

After a month of discussions, a preliminary deal was announced in September 1986. That preliminary agreement was structured as a joint venture that would hold certain U.S. assets of Fairchild as well as the company's overseas manufacturing facilities. Schlumberger would retain an 18 percent interest in the joint venture, with Fujitsu holding the remaining 82 percent. Fujitsu would contribute approximately $225 million in cash and would provide both operating cash for the venture and certain Fujitsu facilities in the United States and Europe. Fujitsu would be in charge of managing the venture's operations and would secure a seat on the Schlumberger board.

The preliminary joint venture agreement, however, proved to be much more complex when the tax consequences were examined more carefully. Fujitsu and Schlumberger had different agendas. Fujitsu insisted that it receive the licensing agreements of Fairchild. Schlumberger management was adamant that they retain the $600 million net operating loss (NOL) tax carryforward in the United States which they "earned" as a result of Fairchild's losses while part of Schlumberger. For tax purposes Schlumberger was entitled to use those losses to offset future profits earned by Schlumberger's U.S. operation for up to 15 years, since Schlumberger and Fairchild filed consolidated tax returns in the United States. Under the U.S. tax laws, the only way in which that tax loss carryforward could survive the Fairchild-Fujitsu deal was if the transaction was structured as a "bona fide" purchase by Fujitsu of the stock or assets of Fairchild.

The preliminary agreement had called for both Fairchild and Fujitsu to contribute certain assets to the "old" Fairchild entity. However, at the time of the initial discussions, the companies did not realize that the transfer of these assets would cause the entire agreement to be recharacterized as a Section 351 transaction under the tax code. Under Section

Exhibit 6 World Semiconductor Market Share Ranking

1984 Rank	1985 Rank	1986 Rank	Company	1984 Sales	1985 Sales	1986 Sales	Percent Change 1985–1986
3	1	1	MEC	2,251	1,984	2,638	33.0%
4	4	2	Hitachi	2,052	1,671	2,305	37.9%
5	5	3	Toshiba	1,561	1,468	2,261	54.0%
2	2	4	Motorola	2,320	1,830	2,025	10.7%
1	3	5	Texas Instruments	2,480	1,742	1,820	4.5%
6	6	6	Philips-Signetics	1,325	1,068	1,356	27.0%
9	7	7	Fujitsu	1,190	1,020	1,310	28.4%
12	10	8	Matsushita	928	906	1,233	36.1%
10	11	9	Mitsubishi	964	642	1,177	83.3%
8	8	10	Intel	1,201	1,020	991	−2.8%
7	9	11	National Semiconductor[a]	1,263	925	990	7.0%
11	12	12	Advanced Micro Devices[b]	936	615	629	2.3%
15	14	13	Sanyo	455	457	585	28.0%
13	13	14	Fairchild	665	492	510	3.7%
29	22	15	Sony	177	252	475	88.5%
16	15	16	Siemens	450	420	457	8.8%
20	16	17	Sharp	354	329	456	38.6%
22	17	18	Thomson-Mostek[c]	301	324	436	34.6%
19	19	19	Oki	362	307	427	39.1%
24	23	20	Rohm	252	249	379	52.2%
			Top 20 Total	21,487	17,721	22,460	30.7%

[a] National acquired Fairchild in 1987.

[b] Advanced Micro Devices merged with Monolithic Memories in 1987.

[c] Mostek and Thomson revenues are aggregated in 1986 but not in 1984 or 1985.

Source: Dataquest, January 1987.

Exhibit 7   Fujitsu Summary of Operations (in ¥ millions)

	Years ended March 31st				
	1988	1987	1986	1985	1984
Net Sales	2,046	1,789	1,691	1,562	1,209
Percent Increase (decrease) over prior year	14%	6%	8%	29%	27%
Costs of goods sold	1,339	1,232	1,140	959	749
Setting general and administrative expenses	588	494	466	408	325
Operating Income	119	62	84	194	134
Percent increase (decrease) over prior year	92%	(26%)	57%	45%	38%
Net income	42	21	38	89	66
Percent increase (decrease) over prior year	100%	(45%)	(57%)	35%	38%
Net income as percent of revenue	2.0%	1.2%	2.2%	5.7%	5.5%
Return on average stockholders' equity	5.1%	3.1%	6.0%	14.6%	15.2%
Total Assets	2,316	1,998	1,871	1,720	1,277
Long-term debt	302	338	356	252	205
Stockholders' equity	827	680	636	609	434

351, which was a common way of forming a new corporation, each party contributed assets to a "new" corporation and received, tax-free, stock in exchange for the assets they contributed. However, because this was technically an "exchange" and not a "bona fide" purchase, Schlumberger would lose their tax carryforward benefits. In addition, because the "old" entity was no longer preserved, Fujitsu would lose the licensing benefits.

Analysts observed that Schlumberger was probably showing negative profits for U.S. tax purposes during the early 1980s as its capital writeoffs accelerated under the Accelerated Cost Recovery System (ACRS)[11] and its booming oil business demanded increased capital expenditures. Fairchild's sizeable net operating losses (NOLs) could not be used at that time by Schlumberger and had to be carried forward. However, Schlumberger's "negative taxable profits" position was expected to be reversed in the mid- to late-1980s. Analysts reasoned that Schlumberger could use the tax benefits more quickly than a purchaser since under the provisions of the tax code, a purchaser could only offset the NOLs with the profits of Fairchild, and not the profits of its other operations. These rules, known as "separate return limitation year" (SRLY) rules, prevented trafficking in NOLs whereby companies could be purchased solely for the benefit of their NOLs.

A Brief Overview of Tax Laws for Mergers and Acquisitions

A corporate acquisition or divestiture could be structured as either a taxable or a tax-free transaction. The transaction might be accomplished by the sale or exchange of either assets or stock.

In the following examples, we will consider in more detail the different types of transactions for mergers and acquisitions. We will compare them along three dimensions: (1) the tax consequences of the transaction on the buyer and seller, (2) the tax basis of the assets of the target company, and (3) the ownership of the surviving tax attributes, if any, of the target company. The tax basis of assets was the value used to determine the amount of depreciation over the life of the asset and any gain or loss on the subsequent sale of the asset. Tax attributes included NOL carryforwards and investment tax credit (ITC) carryforwards, among others. The tax code (Section 382) imposed limits on the use of a target company's tax attributes by any acquiring corporation.

Consider first the taxable transactions in which cash or debt was used to acquire either the assets or stock of another corporation. In the first case, which is illustrated in Exhibit 8A, all the net assets of the target company were acquired, followed by a complete liquidation of the proceeds to the shareholders. If the acquiring company (say, Fujitsu) bought

---

[11]ACRS was the accelerated depreciation system introduced by the Economic Recovery Tax Act passed in August 1981. The system provided for very rapid depreciation over depreciable lives that were much shorter than the economic lives of the depreciable assets.

Exhibit 8A   Taxable Acquisition: Liquidating Sale of Net Assets

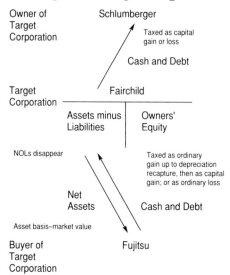

all the assets and liabilities of the target company (Fairchild), it would have effectively acquired the business functions of the target company (Fairchild) even if the original shareholders (Schlumberger) in the target company were unchanged. In this case, Schlumberger would own the corporate shell of the old Fairchild, which would be dissolved upon the liquidation of Fairchild. Prior to the Tax Reform Act of 1986, capital gains on the sale of assets at the corporate level could be avoided by electing liquidation treatment under Section 337 of the Tax Code. But in the case of Fairchild, the sale would have given rise to losses, not gains, so liquidation treatment would not have been desirable. Moreover, a liquidation would result in the disappearance of Fairchild's NOLs and investment tax credits (ITCs). In the absence of liquidation, the gains or losses on the assets would be taxable to Fairchild. The tax basis of the assets in the hands of the new owner (Fujitsu) would be revalued to fair market value.

In the second case of a taxable transaction, illustrated in Exhibit 8C, Fujitsu would acquire all of the stock of Fairchild. This would be a nontaxable event for Fairchild, but Schlumberger would be taxed on any capital gain or loss on its investment in Fairchild. Once again, the NOLs would disappear since the ownership shift in the Fairchild stock was very large. The tax basis of the assets would be carried over to Fujitsu's books unchanged from Fairchild's books.

Tax-free acquisitions (see Exhibits 8B and 8D) were accomplished by exchanging Fujitsu's stock for either the assets or the stock of Fairchild. In either case, the transaction would not be taxable for Schlumberger, Fairchild, or Fujitsu. The NOLs of Fairchild would be available to Fu-

Exhibit 8B   Tax-Free Acquisition: Liquidating Sale of Net Assets

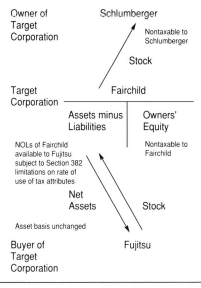

Exhibit 8C   Taxable Acquisition: Sale of Stock

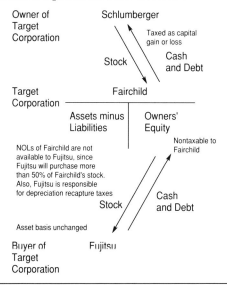

jitsu, but they would be subject to Section 382 limitations on the rate at which they could be used to shelter Fujitsu's income from taxes.

Under certain conditions, the tax code allowed purchasers to elect, for tax purposes under Section 338, to treat the purchase of stock as a purchase of assets followed by a complete liquidation of the company. See Exhibit 8E. The rationale for this provision was that these two avenues provided the same end result and a stock purchase was easier to

Exhibit 8D   Tax-Free Acquisition: Sale of Stock

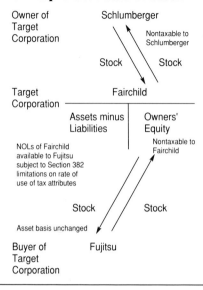

Exhibit 8E   338 Election: Sale of Stock as Sale of Assets

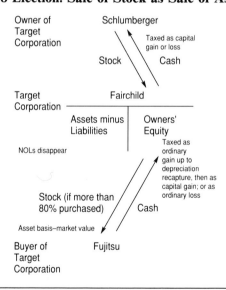

implement. The tax treatment of a 338 election was equivalent to the tax treatment of a liquidating sale of net assets shown in Exhibit 8A. In the special case where a target company was wholly-owned by another company and they filed a consolidated tax return, as was the case of Fairchild and Schlumberger, the purchaser could elect a 338(h)(10) transaction. See Exhibit 8F. This was equivalent to a general 338 election except that the NOLs would be available to Schlumberger.

Exhibit 8F   338(h)(10) Election: Sale of Stock as Sale of Assets

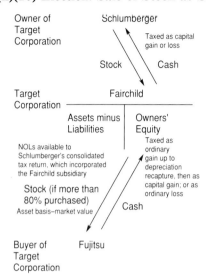

Schlumberger's Options regarding Fairchild in 1986

The key decision for Schlumberger was how to structure the deal so that they could retain as much of the residual value of Fairchild as possible. At this point Schlumberger's four options were defined by the tax and legal rules governing mergers and acquisitions and by the needs of the potential buyer. The set of options were:

1. Sell Fairchild's assets in either a taxable or tax-free transaction (*Exhibits 8A and 8B*).
2. Sell Fairchild's stock in either a taxable or tax-free transaction (*Exhibits 8C and 8D*).
3. Sell Fairchild's stock with a 338 election (*Exhibit 8E*).
4. Sell Fairchild's stock with a 338(h)(10) election (*Exhibit 8F*).

The first option, selling Fairchild's assets, was treated for tax purposes as a disposition of the individual assets of the business.[12] Fujitsu would form a new company with the Fairchild assets (or integrate them into their existing operations), and Schlumberger would retain the corporate

---

[12]Sales of accounts receivable and inventory at a gain or loss would produce ordinary income or losses. Sales of depreciable business property at a gain produce ordinary income on the recapture of past depreciation and capital gains on the excess. Losses on the sale of such assets produce ordinary tax deductions under Section 1231. Gains or losses on the sale of nondepreciable assets yield capital gains and losses. Any losses would be available to Schlumberger to offset future income. Recapture of previously claimed ITCs would also be required for assets held an insufficient length of time under this type of transaction for Schlumberger.

shell of the "old" Fairchild. Fujitsu would not be entitled to any of Fairchild's licensing and cross-licensing agreements, tax attributes, or any other assets attributable to the "old" Fairchild legal entity. In a non-liquidating transaction, Schlumberger would be entitled to keep Fairchild's NOLs that they had earned during the years in which Fairchild was unprofitable (because Schlumberger filed a consolidated tax return with Fairchild). Once Fairchild was liquidated, the NOLs of Fairchild disappeared for both Schlumberger and Fujitsu.

Schlumberger's second option was to sell Fairchild's stock. The NOLs would still be available to any purchaser subject to the 382 limitation, which limited the rate at which NOL carryforwards could offset taxable income of the purchaser. Assets would remain valued at Fairchild's book value, not the lower market value. The purchasing company would lose the opportunity to write off the overvalued assets immediately. However, this loss was somewhat offset by the fact that the purchaser could depreciate assets from a larger basis. If this "built-in loss potential" was greater than 25 percent of non-cash assets, then it too was subject to the 382 limitation.

Schlumberger's third option was to sell Fairchild's stock with a 338 election. Under this type of transaction, Fairchild's NOLs would disappear and would not be available to Schlumberger. In addition, the purchaser would again be responsible for any recapture taxes, which would be levied on any accelerated tax benefits received to date.

Finally, Schlumberger could sell Fairchild's stock with a 338(h)(10) election, which was treated identically to the first option for tax purposes. This option involved a "bona fide" purchase of at least 80 percent of Fairchild's stock followed by an election to treat the stock sale as an asset sale for tax purposes only. Fairchild's assets would be stepped down to market value (rather than book value) on Fujitsu's books for U.S. tax purposes. This option also had the advantage of facilitating the transfer of certain intangibles, such as licensing agreements, relative to the individual sales of assets.

After months of research and additional discussions, Schlumberger and Fujitsu finally came up with a joint venture agreement that would preserve both Schlumberger's carryforwards and Fujitsu's licensing rights. Under the final joint venture plan, structured as a 338(h)(10) transaction, Fujitsu would not contribute any of its assets. Instead, Fujitsu's assets would be purchased by or leased to the "old" Fairchild at a fair value. Following the restructuring of "old" Fairchild (which entailed removing unwanted assets and liabilities, and selling off all non-U.S. Schlumberger stock or assets), Fujitsu would purchase 82 percent of "old" Fairchild stock. Following that purchase, each party would contribute cash and notes proportionate to their respective interests to purchase the Fujitsu assets. All transactions would be at fair market values. This final agreement would then qualify as a "bona fide" purchase, and both parties' agendas would be satisfied.

The Fairchild-Fujitsu Deal Collapses

The date of March 16, 1987 was set aside for Schlumberger and Fujitsu to meet in California to work out the final details of the agreement. On that very morning, as the Schlumberger management team was preparing to fly west, Fujitsu abruptly announced that they were withdrawing from the deal. Most industry analysts speculated that the reasons for Fujitsu's termination of the agreement were political in nature.

The proposed purchase had been hounded from the start by protests from other semiconductor manufacturers and from Reagan Administration officials. Many semiconductor company executives expressed fears that if the deal was finalized, it would give a Japanese company access to advanced technology and leave American companies dependent upon Japanese chips suppliers, who also competed with them in computers. U.S. semiconductor companies were also incensed because they saw it as, "rewarding Japan's electronics giants for past unfair trade practices that had undermined the U.S. semiconductor industry."[13] They cited as evidence the decision in 1986 by the International Trade Commission that found Japanese companies guilty of dumping chips in the United States, and estimated that such dumping had caused them to lose over $1 billion in revenues in 1986. Others feared that the deal would be the first in a wave of acquisitions by which Japanese chip makers could someday gain control of all U.S. semiconductor technology. Overall, most executives in the industry revealed their excitement when the deal was finally terminated. "At last, the United States is waking up and realizing that we've been had by the Japanese, and we're no longer willing to be their patsy,"[14] said Wilfred Corrigan, LSI Logic President and the former President of Fairchild during its 1979 acquisition by Schlumberger. Corrigan believed that, had the deal gone through, every Japanese semiconductor maker would have rushed to the United States with their large bankrolls and American companies would have become big marketing and distribution companies for Japanese products.

The U.S. government also had reservations about the proposed Fairchild-Fujitsu deal. On March 11, 1987, even before Fujitsu terminated the agreement, Commerce Secretary Malcolm Baldridge and Defense Secretary Casper Weinberger asked the Reagan Administration to consider blocking the deal. Baldridge was concerned about trade issues and the threat that Japanese chip manufacturers could make strong inroads into the U.S. semiconductor industry through such acquisitions. He also questioned whether or not Japan had been fulfilling its part of the 1986 Trade Arrangement regarding dumping practices. Weinberger, on the other hand, was concerned about the deal's defense implications. Fairchild was

---

[13]John W. Wilson and Steven J. Dryden, "What the Fairchild fiasco signals for trade policy," *Business Week*, p. 28.
[14]Ibid.

a major vendor of ECL process technology used in highly classified high-speed weapons and military equipment. In 1986, Fairchild received revenues of close to $150 million for such defense work. It was estimated that one-third of that work was proprietary and could not be duplicated by other companies. The Defense Department was worried not only about "protecting the sensitive ECL technology as it was applied to military chips, but also about maintaining the American production base for such chips."[15]

Though Fujitsu had backed out of the Fairchild purchase agreement in the wake of political pressure, it still planned to carry out its plans with Fairchild to cooperate in semiconductor manufacturing through a series of joint ventures. Those joint venture agreements covered future technology development, joint manufacturing in both the United States and Japan, and exchange of manufacturing rights for new and existing products. "Plan One didn't work, so we're moving on to alternative plans for cooperation," said Ken Katashiba, vice president for corporate ventures and the spokesman for Fujitsu's U.S. semiconductor operations.[16]

Schlumberger Sells Fairchild to National Semiconductor

Meanwhile, Schlumberger was still eager to sell Fairchild. The company had prepared a sizeable brochure and sent it to fifteen potential buyers, in which it stressed that it wanted to maintain its NOL carryforward benefit in any transaction that would occur. The sales brochure thus made it perfectly clear that any purchase of Fairchild would be a purchase of assets or a purchase of stock with an election (338(h)(10)) to treat such a purchase as an asset purchase for U.S. tax purposes. Two serious offers were received. The first was from National Semiconductor, the eleventh largest semiconductor manufacturer in the world, and the other was from the Fairchild management group, led by President Donald Brooks. Both parties were interested in purchasing most, but not all, of Fairchild's worldwide operations. In addition, Schlumberger was unwilling to sell Fairchild's automatic test equipment subsidiary, which had been incorporated as a tax-free subsidiary of Fairchild in early 1986. Many in the industry thought that it was rather ironic that National Semiconductor's Chairman, Charlie Sporck, who had aided the Semiconductor Industry Association in its lobbying efforts against the Fairchild sale to Fujitsu, was interested in acquiring Fairchild.

After months of ironing out the details of both offers, which differed on the amounts of debt, cash, and stock that were offered as well as the transfer taxes and foreign taxes that were involved, the offer from Na-

---

[15]"Government reviewing Fujitsu-Fairchild deal," *San Jose Mercury News*, November 1, 1986, p. 3.

[16]Brenton Schlender, "Fujitsu, Fairchild Semiconductor Plan Ventures Even Though Merger Is Ended," *The Wall Street Journal*, March 18, 1987, p. 3.

tional Semiconductor was accepted. The final $122 million offer was paid for in National stock and warrants for the U.S. shares of Fairchild with a 338(h)(10) election, preserving the $600 million carryforward benefit for Schlumberger. National also assumed $50 to $100 million in Fairchild debt. The acquisition gave National ten more plants, half of which were in the United States, and made the company the third largest semiconductor manufacturer in the United States, and the sixth largest in the world. National, however, did not gain control of Fairchild's plants in Japan, West Germany, and South San Jose, California. National's purchase price amounted to just 20 percent of Fairchild's annual sales. Schlumberger suffered a $220 million loss, which it wrote off in 1987.

Questions

1. What are the sources of value of Fairchild in 1986? Why might Fujitsu have valued Fairchild so much more than National Semiconductor did?
2. How well did Schlumberger manage the Fairchild deal with Fujitsu? What option would have been best for Schlumberger? for Fujitsu? Was Schlumberger too concerned about the tax consequences of the sale of Fairchild?
3. What should be U.S. government policy regarding the acquisition of high-technology U.S. companies by foreign companies?

CASE 13

The Privatization of British Airways

Privatization is an issue that is not obviously, nor exclusively, a topic of fiscal policy. The relationship becomes clearer if one views privatization as a means of reducing a government's future fiscal expenditures and obtaining current revenues from the sale of that asset. Conversely, the nationalization of a formerly private company almost always involves the commitment of government resources to purchase the equity of the former shareholders, and perhaps later, additional capital injections to keep a typically less efficient company operating.

With the ownership resulting from nationalization, there is not only a commitment of resources (the fiscal policy issue) but also the control of management decisions (a regulatory/competitive policy issue). Much of the debate over privatization centers on this latter issue. It is often argued that a private company will be more efficient than a public company, because the private company does not have to contend with political considerations interfering with the efficient allocation of resources.

The Chapter 13 case, The Privatization of British Airways, evaluates the effects of this privatization on the competitiveness of the British Airways. The evaluation will have two components: whether the competitive position of British Airways has indeed improved, and the identification of the channels by which privatization was responsible for the improvement. The second component will be the more difficult and the most important.

British Airways (BA) flew more international passengers than any other carrier in 1989 and was Europe's largest airline. The company's profits had grown at a compounded annual rate of 28 percent during the previous two years. Revenues reached an historic high of $7.5 billion (£4.7 billion) in that year as BA carried 25 million passengers, virtually one in two of the entire British population. BA was also the recipient of numerous awards, including "Airline of the Year."

BA had not always been profitable nor had it always been perceived as a provider of top quality service. Before the company was privatized in February 1987 under the administration of Prime Minister Margaret Thatcher, it had been declared technically bankrupt and its service was commonly referred to as "*Bloody Awful.*" In gearing up for the privatization, BA's Chairman Lord John King and Chief Executive Sir Colin Marshall had taken radical steps toward transforming the airline's image, level of service, and financial results. With that transformation firmly in place in 1989, Lord King and Sir Colin were eager to continue BA's global expansion through strategic alliances and by gaining additional airport gate space and access to new routes. With the unification of the European market in 1992, BA was concerned about what kind of reshaping would take place in the world airline industry.

The History of BA

BA was created in 1972 by the merger of British Overseas Airways Corporation and British European Airways. British Overseas had been formed in 1939 when BA and Imperial Airways merged to form a public corporation. British European Airways was formed in 1946, originally as the European division of British Overseas. "Both British Overseas and British European were manifestly inefficient and overstaffed during the 1960s, in British Overseas' case essentially because it had been deliberately protected from external competition by the government."[1] Because of employee disputes, excess employees, the oil price shock, and logistical problems, the merger was not fully completed until 1977.

Following the merger, BA, sought to increase operating efficiency while expanding operations so that it could fully utilize its large staff. In 1979, Britain's newly elected Prime Minister, Margaret Thatcher, announced her intentions to sell shares in BA to the public, making BA one of her government's first proposed candidates for privatization. At the same time, BA's Board of Directors announced plans for a substantial long-term expansion of the airline, aimed at doubling its passengers by

This case was prepared by Research Associate Julia Horn under the supervision of Professor Michael G. Rukstad. Copyright © 1990 by the President and Fellows of Harvard College. Harvard Business School Case N9-390-079.

[1] Peter J. Curwen, *Public Enterprise* (New York: St. Martin's Press, 1986).

1986 but keeping its staff at existing levels. That plan also called for the replacement of a large portion of its aging fleet that would no longer comply with international noise regulations due to take effect in 1986. In 1979, BA placed orders worth £270 million for Boeing 737s, 757s, and 747s, not only for replacement purposes but to provide for the growth in volume it anticipated. The company also cut prices to attract more customers at the same time that the worldwide recession and a second oil price shock began in 1979. The full force of the recession hit BA during the vital summer months, when it traditionally expected to earn the operating surpluses it needed to carry it through the winter; traffic volumes fell almost 10 percent. Fuel costs grew from 1979 to 1980 to account for 30 percent of total operating costs at BA while every one cent rise in the price of a gallon of jet fuel translated into an additional cost of £5 million for BA.

In fiscal years 1980 and 1981, BA lost a total of £240 million before taxes. At the same time, BA's debt had nearly doubled to £780 million. See Exhibit 1 for financial information on British Airways. In late 1981, Lord King, a veteran industrialist from the ball bearings and power engineering industries and a Conservative Party loyalist, was installed by Mrs. Thatcher as the new chairman of BA. He was the company's fourth chairman in ten years, and with his appointment the Conservative Party declared that it was aiming to privatize the company as early as 1982. Lord King's initiative was to repair BA's financial condition in preparation for its return to the private sector.

The Restructuring in 1981 and 1982

Despite the government's hopes to privatize BA the following year, they could not risk a stock offering while the company was sustaining losses. The government believed that BA would need £250 million in pretax profits before privatization could take place. In addition to its mounting debt burden and confusion among executives about its strategic objectives, BA continued to finish last among the six largest European airlines in both the number of passengers per employee and operating revenue per employee. One BA manager described the company's operating philosophy up to that time with the following phrase: "If we needed a pint of milk, we went out and bought the cow."

In the fall of 1981 just months after taking office, Lord King brought in a new team of senior managers and instituted a major restructuring plan, called BA's "survival plan." He drastically cut the number of profitable routes the airline served, the number of stations where flight operations were based, and began cuts that would gradually reduce the workforce from 52,000 to 43,000 employees. BA had to make nearly £300 million in severance payments through a redundancy plan for those employees, forcing the company to turn to the government to guarantee additional bank lending. Keith Wilkins, director of planning at BA, recalled additional cutbacks the company had to make to ensure survival

Exhibit 1   British Airways Financial Data (in £ millions)

For the years ended March 31	1989	1988	1987	1986	1985	1984	1983	1982	1981	1980	1979	1978	1977
Revenues	4,257	3,756	3,263	3,149	2,943	2,514	2,497	2,241	2,060	1,920	1,640	1,355	1,248
Operating expenses	3,921	3,520	3,090	2,951	2,651	2,246	2,312	2,230	2,153	1,891	1,549	1,301	1,154
Operating surplus (loss)	336	236	173	198	292	268	185	11	(93)	29	91	54	94
Other income and charges	18	12	19	36	12	26	19	(2)	24	26	19	11	3
Interest payable	(86)	(20)	(30)	(39)	(113)	(109)	(130)	(120)	(68)	(38)	(30)	(23)	(19)
Profit before taxes	268	228	162	195	191	185	74	(111)	(137)	17	80	42	78
Income taxes	93	77	14	2	5	2	10	5	4	9	13	21	41
Profit before extraordinary items	175	151	148	193	186	183	64	(116)	(141)	8	67	21	37
Extraordinary items	—	—	4	(12)	(12)	33	26	(429)[a]	—	—	—	—	—
Net profit	175	151	152	181	174	216	90	(544)	(141)	8	67	21	37
Other Financial Data:													
Total assets	3,494	3,106	2,082	1,913	1,961	1,794	1,673	1,632	1,683	1,473	1,252	1,161	978
Long-term debt	896	851	270	340	591	899	1,074	1,074	739	493	385	297	237
Capital expenditures	698	499	245	282	120	253	180	153	271	291	225	207	163

[a]Extraordinary items consisted of provisions to write down the unamortized cost of the aircraft fleet (£208) and provisions for severence costs (£220).

Source: Company documents.

in the 1980s, "Besides having to reschedule major investments in new aircraft, we were forced to sell four Boeing 747s to TWA, eight Lockheed TriStars to the Royal Air Force, and two highly coveted launch positions for the Boeing 757 to Air Europe, a new competitor on some European routes. The two Boeing 757s later became the stars of Air Europe's fleet. We literally paid employee wages from the cash those asset sales generated." BA also sold its helicopter business and its hotel interests for a total of £150 million. At the same time, "the government was, in accordance with its belief of opening up markets to competition, taking away BA's exclusive routes and giving them to British Caledonian, the U.K.'s second largest airline, thereby becoming the first European government to stop outright protection of a state flag-carrier."[2] Despite BA's problems, it was not the only airline in financial trouble at the time. Most major airlines were experiencing a crunch in profitability during the worldwide recession of the early 1980s. See Exhibit 2 for airline profitability.

By March 1982, nearly three years after Mrs. Thatcher named the company as one of her government's first candidates for privatization, BA was legally bankrupt. Operating costs, particularly fuel, flight oper-

Exhibit 2   Airline Industry Operating Profits

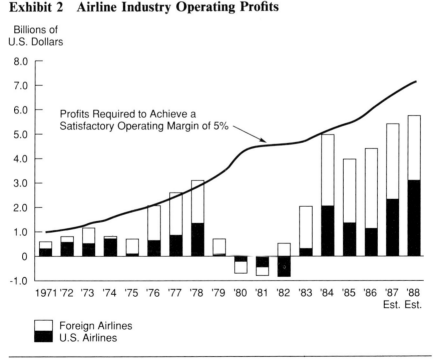

Billions of U.S. Dollars

Foreign Airlines
U.S. Airlines

Source: Boeing

[2]Ibid.

ations, and maintenance were rising to unmanageable levels. See Exhibits 3 and 4 for the airline industry's and BA's operating costs. The company's measure of passengers carried and the distance over which they were carried, passenger revenue miles (one paying passenger flown one mile), was depressed by the airline's reputation for poor service. By the end of the year, losses and write-offs reached a staggering £545 million. Mrs. Thatcher's government believed that privatization was not feasible until

Exhibit 3   Airline Operating Cost Distribution 1987

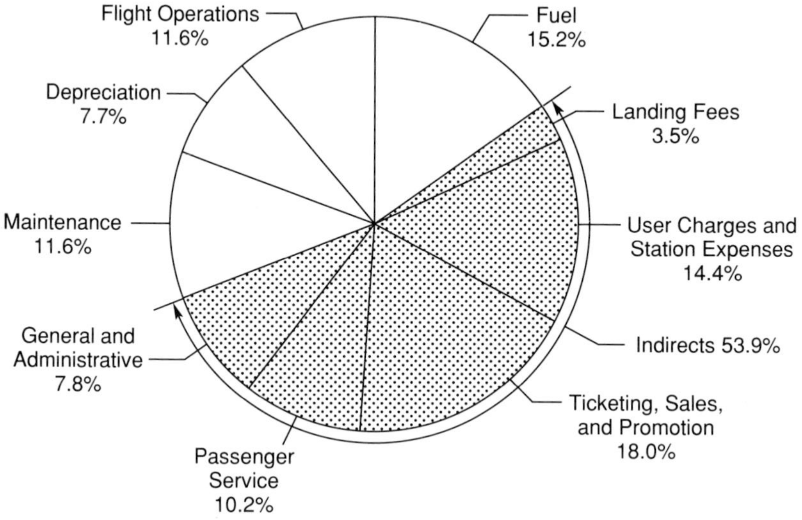

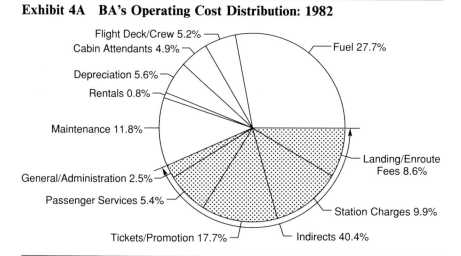

Flight Operations 11.6%
Fuel 15.2%
Depreciation 7.7%
Landing Fees 3.5%
Maintenance 11.6%
User Charges and Station Expenses 14.4%
General and Administrative 7.8%
Indirects 53.9%
Ticketing, Sales, and Promotion 18.0%
Passenger Service 10.2%

Source: Boeing

Exhibit 4A   BA's Operating Cost Distribution: 1982

Flight Deck/Crew 5.2%
Cabin Attendants 4.9%
Fuel 27.7%
Depreciation 5.6%
Rentals 0.8%
Maintenance 11.8%
Landing/Enroute Fees 8.6%
General/Administration 2.5%
Passenger Services 5.4%
Station Charges 9.9%
Tickets/Promotion 17.7%
Indirects 40.4%

Source: Company Documents

Exhibit 4B   BA's Operating Cost Distribution: 1987

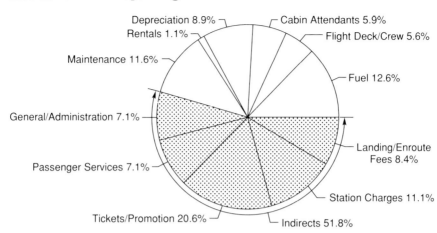

Source: Company Document

the company was pulled out of insolvency. Lord King made the first of many appeals to the Thatcher government to write off the company's debt, which had grown to £1 billion. Up to 1982, the U.K. government had infused only £180 million of equity capital into BA.[3] However, the government did not write off the debt and refused to guarantee any additional bank borrowing by the company.

The Road to Recovery

In 1983, Lord King again tightened the company's belt, reducing the number of employees (including 2,000 managers) even further from 43,000 to 36,000 and its fleet from 250 to 144 aircraft. The company's routes were regrouped into three separate operating divisions, and individual profit centers were established. Later in the year, the three divisions were reorganized into three separate businesses (cargo, charter, and tour) in eight marketing centers around the world. Meanwhile, the company hired a new advertising agency, Saatchi and Saatchi PLC, who came up with a slick new ad campaign for the carrier based on the slogan, "The World's Favorite Airline." The company, however, was in need of even greater image-burnishing and cost reduction, so Lord King and the board brought in Colin Marshall (later Sir Colin) as the new chief executive. Sir Colin was a seasoned marketing professional, having held posts at Avis Inc. and Sears Holdings, a large British retail concern unrelated to the American retailer.

When Sir Colin joined BA, the airline was still beleaguered by a

[3]Ibid.

reputation for poor customer service and employee morale was low. Sir Colin believed that if BA were to compete successfully in a service-driven industry, it needed to project an image of good service to its customers. With that in mind, Sir Colin began looking at BA's flights inside Great Britain where as many as 60 percent of BA's customers traveled. Many of the airline's international customers were also its domestic customers, and Sir Colin believed that the poor reputation of BA's domestic flights was undermining the company's international business. By promoting BA domestically as the "Super Shuttle" through a new ad campaign, he was able to build customer allegiance to BA within its home market. He also initiated a number of other marketing measures on a global scale to signal a change in direction to customers—planes were repainted, workers' uniforms were redesigned, and the company was given a new insignia and motto, "To Fly, to Serve." On the Concorde aircraft, Sir Colin refurbished interiors, raised prices, and introduced advertising that emphasized the time saved by and the prestige associated with flying the supersonic jet. The Concorde, once considered a costly mistake, immediately boosted the company's profits.

At the same time, many BA employees believed that their jobs were in danger if the privatization proceeded and that those who were not fired would be subject to pay cuts. Sir Colin introduced measures to boost employee morale including a profit-sharing plan and employee motivational programs. The profit-sharing plan was the first ever offered by a public U.K. company and was not negotiable as part of the BA employees' union contract. The motivational programs began with, "Putting People First," a two-day training program that every BA employee worldwide was required to attend. The program, which ran continuously for two years, involved a clear statement of corporate objectives, morale boosting, team activities, and roleplaying to pinpoint customer needs and help employees understand the customer. Successive programs included "A Day in the Life," where employees learned about the day-to-day operations of other jobs in the company, "To Be the Best," which educated workers about BA's competitive environment and the growing need for quality service at BA, and "Managing People First," a five day course which gave managers specific feedback from subordinates and peers on behaviors and style. At the end of both of those courses, Sir Colin or another member of senior management made closing remarks and held informal discussions with the employees in attendance.

Despite improved profits at the end of the 1983 fiscal year, BA was still faced with close to £1 billion in debt. Lord King reiterated his requests that the government write off at least part of that debt. The government proposed a £700 million bridge loan for BA under which it would write off a large portion of the debt and recoup that money from the proceeds of the eventual privatization. Many people, including Sir Adam Thomson, chairman of rival British Caledonian, felt that if BA were privatized and its debt written off, it would have the largest international route network in the world under one ownership. BA already had an 83 percent market share of all U.K. scheduled domestic and international flights. Others expressed the fear that, "a privatized BA would still be regarded by the government as the U.K. flag carrier and would as a consequence receive preferential treatment in the future allocation of routes, both domestic and international.[4]

Boosted by the economic recovery in the United States and a strong dollar, both of which increased air travel, BA began to recoup profits by the end of the summer of 1984 and its passenger volume increased 11.4 percent. In addition, productivity as measured by the industry yardstick, available ton kilometers (ATK) per employee,[5] rose nearly 11 percent from 1983 to 1984. "This augured well for privatization, but a dispute rumbled on between BA, who wanted the government to convert a large chunk of outstanding debt into equity, and the Transport Department, who wanted BA to contribute more [to the privatization] itself even though a capital injection would be recouped through a higher sale price."[6] Later in 1984, BA's debt fell to £900 million, and the airline ceased to be insolvent for the first time in nearly three years.

Despite steadily increasing profits at BA, the privatization continued to be delayed into 1986. This time, the problem was an antitrust lawsuit that had begun in 1982 with the bankruptcy and later dissolvement of Laker Airlines. Laker, a low-cost airline, charged that BA, Pan Am, and TWA had forced the airline out of business by conspiring to eliminate it. Travelers who were hurt by Laker's collapse also brought a class action suit against the group of airlines, claiming that they had to pay higher fares for transatlantic flights because of Laker's bankruptcy. Though losing the Laker antitrust case would not have cost the company a large sum, "it would have strengthened Laker's hand in pressing for punitive damages in the civil courts, and would thereby cast a heavy shadow over the proposed privatization of BA."[7] The Laker case succeeded in slowing down the privatization and was not settled until 1986 when the three defendant airlines, though they maintained their innocence, paid a total of $30 million in air travel coupons.

The Privatization

Following the Laker settlement, and with three years of solid profit performance, Sir John Moore, the Secretary of State for Transport, announced in the fall of 1986 that the privatization would take place in early 1987. In February of 1987, 720 million common shares, or 100 percent of the company, were offered to the public. Though the govern-

---

[4]Ibid.

[5]Available ton kilometers is the measure of salable aircraft capacity.

[6]Curwen, op. cit.

[7]Ibid.

ment would sell all of its BA stock, it would still retain one special "golden share" to prevent the airline from falling into foreign hands. The government decided on a cautious approach (a 125 pence per share compared to 130 pence per share) to the floatation of shares primarily as an "eleventh-hour" attempt to stimulate interest in the issue among U.K. investors, who had remained less than enthusiastic. The share offering price put a value on BA of £900 million. U.K. institutions received 36 percent of the shares while another 36 percent went to private applicants. Seventeen percent of the shares were sold overseas through public offerings in the United States and Canada and through private placements in Japan and Switzerland. The remaining eleven percent of the shares went to BA employees and pensioners. Nearly 97 percent of eligible BA staff applied for shares in the company. Because of the demand for the shares, most applications from the general public were heavily scaled down in the process of allocation. Only those applying for 200 shares or less received their allocation in full. Those applying for up to 1,500 shares received only 200, while those applying for over 100,000 received none. By the time the sale was completed, over one million private investors had received a small allocation of BA shares.

    BA's stock issuance was successful as judged by the stock market. After the first day of trading, the price had appreciated by 63 percent. That premium together with the fact that the offer was 21 times oversubscribed, left the government open to criticism that the issue was underpriced. The government, on the other hand, could hardly believe its luck. "Airline stocks are volatile, and BA has had a bumpy earnings record. As it is, the company is predicting that profits will fall to £145 million from £195 million in the year ending March 31, 1987. It was the riskiest of the privatizations and could easily have been the first real flop."[8] Trading in BA shares began on the London, New York, and Toronto Stock Exchanges on February 11, 1987. The total cost of the privatization was £28 million, or less than 5 percent of the total proceeds, slightly below the average for the ten largest U.K. privatizations since 1981. The cost was comprised of £8 million for advertising and marketing, £8.5 million for underwriters' commissions, £6 million for bankers' fees, and £5.5 million for overseas sales.

The Private Life of BA

British Caledonian

In December 1987, less than one year after joining the private sector, BA acquired a major British airline, British Caledonian Airways (BCal), for £250 million. BA called the acquisition a move toward the expansion of

---

[8]William Kay, "With a Little Help, BA Deal Flies," *Barron's,* February 16, 1987.

its network. Despite several years of losses at BCal, BA gained valuable landing slots at London's Gatwick Airport as well as additional routes. BA was given the opportunity for expansion across the BCal network, including flights to the Middle East and Africa, between Gatwick and Los Angeles, Houston, and Atlanta and lucrative flights to East Asia. The merger raised BA's share from 83 percent to 95 percent of all British international flights. To comply with U.K. monopolies and mergers regulations, BA had to release several of BCal's domestic and European routes as well as some slots at Gatwick airport. "Lord King argued that the takeover would protect Britain's national interest from U.S. 'megacarriers.' "[9] When another European carrier, Scandinavian Airlines System (SAS) offered to rescue BCal, BA and its supporters fumed. "Viking pillage!" cried Norman Tebbitt, the former chairman of the ruling Conservative Party.[10] After the acquisition, BA had the largest share of available gates at both Heathrow and Gatwick airports, the two busiest intersections in global aviation, where BA had 45 percent and 33 percent of the gatespace respectively. Almost immediately, BA slashed costs at BCal, in part by cutting half of its workforce of 7,000.

BA's competitors, however, were bitter toward the British government for allowing the merger, claiming that the government was overly kind to the company. "The problem is that they [BA] have assumed that they can carry into the private sector the public privileges they used to enjoy. They've pushed it a bit too far,"[11] said Michael Bishop, Chairman of Airlines of Britain Holdings, PLC, a competitor. Still others commented that, "the airline relies on the regulatory and political advantages conferred by its former status as a state-owned carrier, rarely missing a chance to throw its hefty weight around."[12]

Sir Colin commented that, contrary to what some critics believed, "the acquisition did not remove a one of BA's British competitors from the world airline market, because BCal primarily served domestic routes. Rather, it gave BA access to parts of the world which the airline had been excluded from during its period under government ownership."

The BCal acquisition was just one of many new liberties BA was allowed when it became a private company. BA had endured a number of bureaucratic hardships while it was in the public sector. For example, in the early 1980s BA needed new replacement engines for some of its aircraft. The company had to wait six months before government approval was granted, even though the request was well within the government's guidelines. Sir Colin identified the source of the hardships: "When we were in the public sector, we were competing against the Department

[9]John Marcom, Jr., "BA Throws Its Weight Around, *The Wall Street Journal*, August 8, 1988.
[10]Ibid.
[11]*The Wall Street Journal*, August 8, 1988.
[12]Ibid.

of Health, Education, and Welfare as well as number of other social service and transportation programs for government spending, and we were rather low on the list."

In the two fiscal years that followed the privatization, BA continued to reap record pretax profits, despite having to absorb the losses produced by BCal (in 1988 alone, BCal produced pretax losses of £32 million). By most financial measures, BA's performance had continued to improve after it joined the private sector. In fiscal year 1990, BA's revenues were expected to reach £4.7 billion, a 10 percent increase over the prior year, and operating profit was expected to top £370 million, making BA one of the world's most profitable airlines. Productivity at BA grew at a compounded annual rate of nearly 5 percent from 1987 to 1989. See Exhibit 5 for average airline productivity data. By the mid-1990s, BA planned to invest £8 billion in a massive re-equipment program, which would bring down the average age of its fleet from 9.8 to 8.0 years, well below the industry average of 12.0 years.[13]

The World Airline Industry

In the 1990s, the world airline industry was undergoing some of the most dramatic changes in its history. Already, a handful of American "megacarriers" threatened to dominate the industry. In addition, the 12-nation European Community, partly forced by America's lead in dereg-

---

Exhibit 5   Productivity: U.S. vs. Non-U.S. Airlines

ATMs per Employee[a]

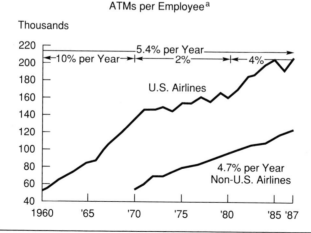

Source: Boeing

[a]ATMs = available ton miles.

---

[13]The average age of jet airplanes at retirement was 22 years.

ulation and partly because of its own commitment to abolish internal trade barriers in 1992, was moving toward a liberalized market in air travel. Elsewhere in the world, the concept of deregulation was also gaining considerable emphasis. Many, including BA, hoped that liberalization would occur and put an end to the bilateral agreements in some countries that governed which airlines could serve particular routes and countries. In some cases, only one carrier from each country was allowed to serve a particular city.

BA was especially concerned with liberalization because nowhere in Europe was the airline competition greater than in Great Britain. Ninety foreign airlines flew scheduled services in and out of Britain. However, certain markets, such as Luxembourg and Amsterdam had already begun to break down the barriers to competition even before 1992. Though the timing of the complete deregulation in Europe was uncertain, most analysts did not expect the process to be as rapid or as wrenching as it had been in the United States in 1978. It was, however, expected to reduce the number of carriers, particularly government-owned carriers, and offer the big, efficient airlines a chance to establish several hubs throughout Europe.

For the 1990s, analysts predicted a 5.4 percent average annual expansion in scheduled international air traffic. See Exhibit 6 for world air travel. That growth rate would ensure that the 1988 figure of 1.1 billion scheduled service passengers would double by the end of the decade, putting further pressure on the world's air traffic control systems. Most of that growth was expected to occur in Trans-Pacific routes and routes between Europe and the Orient. At the same time, the world's airlines were expected to spend "close to $516 billion by the beginning of the

Exhibit 6   World Air Travel Forecast

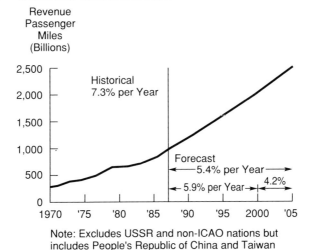

Note: Excludes USSR and non-ICAO nations but includes People's Republic of China and Taiwan

Source: Boeing

next century on new jet airliners, of which $295 billion would cover new aircraft to meet the anticipated traffic growth, another $125 billion to cope with the replacement of existing aging jets, and some $96 billion to cover the outstanding order backlogs."[14]

While aircraft orders and world air traffic were expected to grow, so were fuel costs. See Exhibit 7. In 1989 fuel costs rose more than 30 percent over the previous year to 70 cents per gallon, catching airline management off guard. Most airlines were forced to increase fares as rising fuel costs began to erode their profitability. At BA, for example, for every 1 percent rise in fuel costs, profits fell $4.9 million.

Competitors

BA competed against a number of carriers, ranging from smaller domestic airlines to larger international carriers, many of which were government owned. On every major BA international route, there was at least one foreign competitor. BA segmented those competitors by the markets they served. For example, in the North Atlantic, it competed against American, Delta, and Northwest. In Europe, SAS, Swissair, and KLM were its biggest competitors, while Singapore Airlines, JAL, and Cathay Pacific were strong players in the Far East. See Exhibits 8–10 for the world's ten largest airlines and operating data on selected airlines. Among BA's largest competitors, American, SAS, and Singapore Airlines were pursuing different

---

Exhibit 7   Fuel and Oil Prices: Current Terms

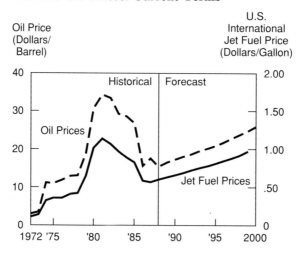

Source: Boeing

---

[14]Michael Donne, "International Travel in the 1990s," as cited in *The World's Favourite Airline, A Special Review*, 1989.

Exhibit 8   The World's Ten Largest Airlines

(Billions of revenue passenger miles 1988)[a]

1. Aeroflot	136.6
2. United	69.1
3. American	64.7
4. Delta	51.7
5. Continentai	40.7
6. Northwest	40.6
7. British Airways	35.5
8. TWA	34.8
9. JAL (Japan Airlines)	30.1
10. Pan Am	29.6

[a]A revenue passenger mile is equal to one paying passenger flown one mile.

Source: *Airline Business Magazine*, cited in *The New York Times*, May 7, 1989.

Exhibit 9   Airline Productivity Growth: ATM/Employee, 1979–1988[a]

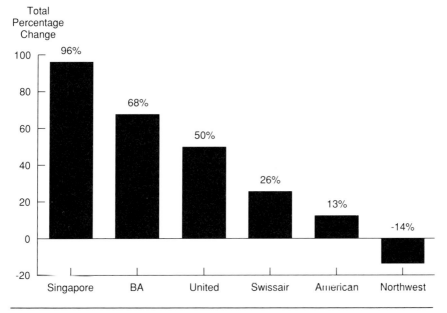

[a]ATMs = available ton miles.

Source: Company Documents

strategies for growth. While American had not built any significant alliances with other world airlines, SAS was dependent on these alliances
in the 1990s. Similarly, Singapore Airlines established two key alliances
in its effort to better exploit opportunities in markets where it could not
compete previously.

Exhibit 10   Comparative Traffic Volume for Selected Airlines

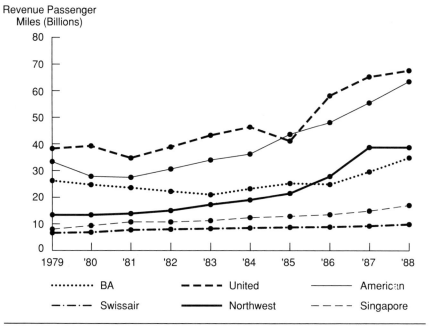

Source: Company Documents

American Airlines.   American Airlines was the second largest airline in
the free world and had the biggest share of U.S. passenger traffic in 1988
with sales of $8.8 billion. While some of its domestic competitors had
tried either to build an empire through acquisitions to become a complete
travel-services company, American had deliberately built from within.
American spent up to $3 billion a year for three years in the mid-1980s,
constructing new hubs, buying new planes, and developing computer
reservation and yield-management systems. The company's SABRE computer reservation system was the world's largest. By 1988, American's
profits surged to $477 million, more than doubling from 1987 levels.

   In its effort to take on global carriers in a bid for a larger share of
foreign markets, American was rapidly gaining strength in Europe, where
it had been exploiting niches that other carriers had overlooked. For
example, American had 119 flights per week to 13 secondary cities, such
as Manchester (England), Stockholm, and Lyons (France) as well as to
bigger cities such as Brussels, Paris, and London. As part of that expansion
in 1989, American announced one of the biggest airline orders in history—
the purchase of up to 150 McDonnell Douglas MD-11s for a total of $7
billion.

Scandinavian Airlines System (SAS).   Based in Stockholm, Sweden, SAS
had revenues of $4.4 billion in 1988. Beginning in the 1980s, in an effort
to avoid being shut out as a large player in the Europe of the 1990s, SAS

began to spin a web of overseas routes by forging strategic relationships with other airlines. By the sheer number of alliances it sought and the money it had invested in those alliances, SAS had been the boldest of dealmakers. SAS's goal was to pick up more passengers from other carriers, preferably business travelers. SAS would lure them with such conveniences as coordinated international flight schedules with the minimum number of stops and connections, simplified ticketing and check-in procedures, and shared facilities in hubs and terminals on almost every continent.

The first of SAS's alliances was with Thai Airways, in which SAS agreed to coordinate flights and services between Bangkok, Stockholm, and Copenhagen while sharing a hub with the airline in Bangkok. SAS also gained gatespace at London's Heathrow airport through its 25 percent stake in Airlines of Britain PLC whose largest single carrier was British Midland Airways, BA's major domestic competitor. One of SAS's most visible U.S. alliances was its 9.9 percent share of Texas Air, which gave it links with Continental Airlines at its Newark hub. In late 1989, just one year after the alliance with Continental, SAS had registered a 28 percent increase in passenger traffic between Scandinavia and the U.S. SAS had also signed agreements with All Nippon Airways, Japan's second largest carrier, Swissair, and Finnair, providing even more links to routes and hubs across Europe.

Singapore Airlines.   Singapore Airlines (SIA) was known throughout the world as an airline with excellent inflight service and one of the most efficient aircraft fleets in the world that operated non-stop long hauls. In addition, the airline had the youngest fleet in commercial aviation with an average age of just 4.5 years. SIA had established important alliances with other carriers throughout the world as SAS had, but for very different reasons. The country of Singapore, located at the crossroads of the world's principal trade routes, maintained a strict adherence to an "open skies" policy where air traffic routes were exchanged liberally with other countries with reciprocal rights for SIA. The country planned to further liberalize air service agreements in the 1990s to ensure its position as one of the largest and fastest growing air centers.

SIA, however, had not always benefited from the country's reciprocity with other carriers, and unlike many of its competitors it had not received any government subsidies. As a result, in 1988, the airline established a $360 million stock swap and a 10-year marketing agreement with Delta Airlines. Under the agreement, SIA gained greater access to Delta's U.S. network through passenger transfers made possible by timetable coordination and would achieve cost savings through shared facilities at common destinations. Among the reasons for the Delta alliance was SIA's continued frustration with restrictions on its U.S. operations. Michael Tan, deputy managing director for SIA explained, "We are not allowed to operate more than a daily frequency through Tokyo to the United States because of an out-moded, one-sided restriction. We can only fly to the United States via the Pacific and not the Atlantic."[15] On the other hand, any number of U.S. carriers could fly to Singapore from any direction and from any U.S. point. SIA had negotiated a similar stock swap and marketing agreement with Swissair. That agreement gave SIA indirect access to markets in Africa, the Middle East, and South America, which were previously economically unjustifiable. In addition to those alliances, SIA was stepping up its investment in aircraft in its effort to create a global network. In early 1990, the company placed an $8.6 billion order for 50 planes (Boeing 747-400s and McDonnell Douglas MD-11s) to be delivered between 1994 and 1999.

BA's Strategy For Growth

Sir Colin planned to keep BA in the global aviation race through mergers and joint marketing ventures. In addition to the acquisition of BCal, BA had instituted a joint marketing program with United Airlines in 1988. The program integrated their route networks and flight schedules. The venture was widely regarded as a prototype of global alliances of the future. The two airlines also coordinated their ticketing, schedules, and baggage handling. The move effectively opened a gateway for BA to the 150 American cities served by United. BA would use United's terminals in Chicago, Washington, and Seattle; United would use BA's terminal at Kennedy Airport in New York. United, which did not fly to Europe, hoped to feed BA passengers into its domestic market, while BA hoped to gain extra Europe-bound fares. John Zeeman, a United executive vice president believed that, "each partner should initially gain 200 to 300 passengers per day."[16] Sir Colin hoped to line up similar partnerships in other countries. In addition, in early 1990, BA bought a 20 percent share of Sabena World Airlines, a new subsidiary of the Belgian national carrier. That deal gave BA a share of an important new hub in Brussels.

BA was also busy modernizing is fleet and taking strides to further upgrade its service reputation. BA had embarked on the largest re-equipment program in its history, which was estimated to cost £5 billion by 1990. The airline had ordered 19 Boeing 747-400 jets, the first of which was delivered in 1989. That order, plus an option to purchase 12 additional 747-400s, totaled almost $4 billion. In the fall of 1989, BA announced that it planned to acquire at least 31 new Boeing aircraft or an addition of almost one-fifth to modernize its short- and medium-range fleet. Those orders were expected to total over £1 billion. At the same time, BA had invested $43 million to upgrade its business class service,

---

[15]"Open Skies Policy Pays Off," *Financial Times,* February 5, 1990.

[16]Mark Maremont, "British Airways Is Out To Create Its Own United Kingdom," *Business Week*, December 27, 1987.

and by 1989, it had recorded a 20 percent gain in intercontinental business class traffic and a 9 percent rise in Europe. A similar $41 million effort to spruce up first class service was completed in early 1990.

The Bid For UAL

In the fall of 1989, as part of its world growth strategy, BA offered to buy a $750 million stake in a management buyout of UAL, the parent of United Airlines. In return for its cash, which represented the largest piece of equity in the buyout, BA would receive preferred shares equal to 15 percent of UAL's voting stock. Said John Pincavage, a partner at Transportation Group, an investment banking firm that specialized in airline-related finance, "If you said you wanted to build the most powerful airline combination in the world, on paper this has to be the one."[17] However, after the buyout group, which included UAL's management and pilot's union, failed to obtain financing for the $6.79 billion transaction, BA formally ended its involvement with the project in October of 1989.

Despite the setback to its overall expansion goals caused by the collapse of the UAL buyout, BA continued to forge ahead on a large scale to supplement its position as the world's largest international carrier. Sir

Exhibit 11 Comparative Load Factors for Selected Airlines

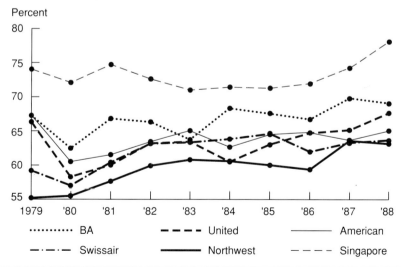

Source: Company Documents

[17]Christopher Power, "From Bloody Awful to Bloody Awesome," *Business Week*, October 9, 1989.

Colin explained BA's outlook for the coming decade. "We decided it is not possible for one airline by itself to be a truly global airline," Sir Colin explained. "So we have set out in search of other associations to give us and our customers the equivalent of a global airline."[18]

[18]Lohr, p. 1.

Questions

1. Evaluate British Airways strategy. What were the key factors in the turn-around of BA?
2. What effect did privatization have on BA's performance? Would BA's performance have been better if the privatization had occurred earlier?
3. What are the lessons of the BA experience for managers of other privatized firms?

CASE 14
Martin Marietta

For a company that is exclusively a defense contractor, government defense expenditures are that company's sales. It is obvious that such a company must carefully monitor and respond to changes in defense expenditures. However, it is not obvious what the optimal strategy should be in such an environment. Cuts in defense expenditures are only one example of a change in a government's fiscal policy that would directly affect private sector firms—firms delivering services for health care, education, or municipal services could also benefit from the experience of the defense contractors.

In this chapter we examine an apparently successful defense contractor, Martin Marietta, in order to distill some principles that may guide managers when one of their large customers (or perhaps their sole customer) is the government. The case describes a multi-year four-stage strategy that was introduced before the crumbling of the Berlin Wall, before the Gulf War, and before the dissolution of the Soviet Union. We must decide what in that strategy is still valid, and what must change to fit the new realities. The menu of options is broad, if one were to survey strategies being pursued by the other large defense contractors. There seems to be no consensus in the industry in this early stage on how best to respond to the apparent future decline in U.S. defense expenditures.

In 1989, Martin Marietta was the sixth largest defense contractor in the United States. The company, based in Bethesda, Maryland, built its success in the 1980s after warding off a hostile takeover attempt in 1982 and subsequently restructuring its operations. At the same time, the company had embarked on the first phase of a four part strategy that would carry them into the 1990s. After the restructuring and renewed strategic direction, Martin Marietta had emerged as a company that targeted its investment toward growth areas in the defense field and submitted fiercely competitive bids. Senior managers at Martin Marietta also believed that the company kept a tight rein on costs.

Martin Marietta's sales in 1989 had reached almost $6 billion while its contract backlog had grown to $13.4 billion. Almost three-fourths of the company's revenues in that year were defense related. Because of expectations about future constraints on the growth of U.S. defense spending, primarily as a result of the dramatic and unexpected easing of East-West tensions in 1989, Martin Marietta management was reevaluating the future of some of its defense and space programs.

The Defense Contract Industry

The defense industry included over 100,000 companies ranging from prime contractors (companies that delivered the final product) to subcontractors and suppliers that engaged in every facet of defense work. In 1989 the industry was dominated by approximately 100 prime contractors whose revenues accounted for two-thirds of total defense spending. Defense contractors developed, manufactured, and supplied equipment ranging from missiles and aircraft to engines and radar devices primarily for the U.S. Department of Defense (DoD). The DoD, the largest and most complex organization in the United States, encompassed the Army, Air Force, and Navy, and shaped the country's defense strategy. In 1989 more than 90 percent of all defense industry sales went to the U.S. government, primarily the DoD, which executed more than 15 million contracts per year (more than 60,000 per day). The individual regulations that applied to the DoD's procurement of defense products numbered over 1,200 in 1989. Defense companies also contracted with organizations outside the DoD particularly the National Aeronautics and Space Administration (NASA), which presided over all of the country's space exploration. The dollar outlays for those contracts outside of the DoD were not included in the total defense spending figures.

The defense procurement process was composed of two stages: research and development (R&D) and production. "R&D included plan-

This case was prepared by Research Associate Julia Horn under the supervision of Professor Michael G. Rukstad. Copyright © 1990 by the President and Fellows of Harvard College. Harvard Business School Case 9-390-080.

ning, testing and evaluation. That stage began with the DoD identifying a national security threat or defense mission, and encompassed Congress's appropriation of the necessary funds, designs, and proposals by interested contractors, and selection of the contractor."[1] In 1990 government defense contracts were one of two basic types: cost-plus-fee or fixed-price. Under cost-plus-fee agreements, the contract allowed for a range of reimbursement plans for those additional costs incurred by the defense contracting company that the Pentagon deemed allowable. Under fixed-price contracts, work was performed and paid for at a fixed amount without adjustment for actual costs experienced in connection with the contract. Therefore, all risk of loss due to increased costs was borne by the contractor. Since 1987, the number of fixed-price contracts had grown to more than one-third of all defense contracts.

As part of the contractor selection process, the DoD prepared and issued a request for proposal (RFP) to any and all interested contractors, though in some cases, only certain qualified companies were invited to bid for a system. The RFP spelled out performance requirements, timetables for development and delivery, contractor qualifications, deadlines for submission, and information on the type of contract that would be issued. Throughout the selection process, price was an overriding factor; product and quantity were determined, not by the management of the firm, but by governmental authority. For example, in 1990, Martin Marietta's Air Defense and Anti-Tank System (ADATS) program was undergoing two years of testing before the government would make a decision on whether or not to go ahead with initial low-level production. Once the appointed selection committee narrowed the field of qualified contractors, "at least two contractors would be kept in the running to the end so that the government could squeeze out the best possible price before it made its final judgment."[2]

For most large programs, the contractor(s) that was awarded the R&D portion of a contract ended up producing the system during the second phase of the defense procurement process. In some cases, however, the government selected another contractor(s), through its selection process, that could "blueprint" the R&D work on the system and produce it at a lower cost or in a shorter time frame. Some companies, such as Raytheon, did not compete for a contract in the R&D phase. Instead, they waited for the government to announce a new bidding process for the production of a system and then tried to make the lowest bid.

Since the 1950s, the major products of the defense industry had been referred to as weapons systems, such as aircraft, missiles, ships, and tanks. "A weapon system includes not only the major piece of equipment

[1]Ronald Fox with James L. Field, *The Defense Management Challenge: Weapons Acquisition*, (Boston: Harvard Business School Press, 1988), p. 22.

[2]William Gregory, *The Defense Procurement Mess*, (Lexington, MA.: D.C. Heath and Company, 1989), p. 68.

itself but the subsystems, logistical support, software, construction, and training needed to operate and support it. Subsystems can include power plants, armaments, equipment for guidance and navigation, communications, and spare parts."[3] Those subsystems and other related items accounted for an average of 25 percent of total defense expenditures.

Following the end of the Vietnam War in 1972, defense spending by the U.S. government fell an average of 2.2 percent per year in real terms until the late 1970s, when it rose slightly at the end of President Carter's administration. See Exhibit 1 for actual and projected defense spending figures. When President Reagan was elected in 1980, he made it clear that a strong national defense would be at the core of his foreign policy. "With public support behind him, Reagan proposed a huge budget increase in March 1981, adding over $30 billion above inflation to the Carter administration's defense budgets for 1981–1982."[4] During Reagan's tenure from 1980 to 1988, increasing percentages of the defense budget were allocated toward major weapons systems. See Exhibit 2 for defense purchases. In 1986, nearly 100 major systems (those requiring more than $200 million in R&D or $1 billion in production) were at various stages of development and production, including jet fighters, bombers, aircraft, tanks, and missiles. The total cost of the 100 major systems was estimated to exceed $750 billion, or more than the gross

---

Exhibit 1A   Defense Budget Authority and Outlays in Billions of Constant Dollars

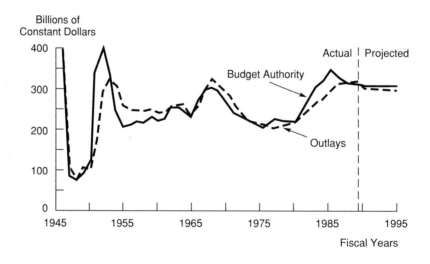

---

[3]Fox, p. 9.

[4]Richard A. Stubbing with Richard A. Mendel, *The Defense Game* (New York: Harper and Row Publishers, 1986), p. 29.

Exhibit 1B   Defense Budget Authority and Outlays in Billions of Current Dollars

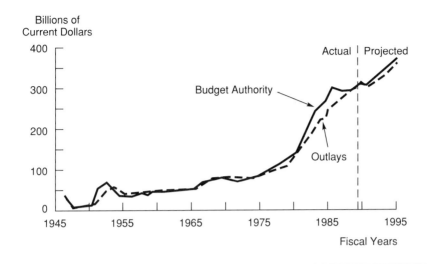

Exhibit 1C   Outlays as Share of GNP, National Defense

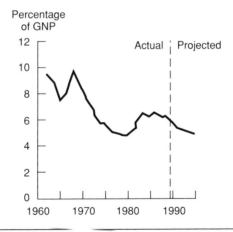

Source: Congressional Budget Office

national product of most countries of the world.[5] From 1980 to 1988 alone, the Pentagon doled out more than $2 trillion to defense contractors, giving producers of everything from munitions to spy satellites all the work they could handle.

In 1989, the $303 billion defense budget accounted for approxi-

[5]Fox, p. 9.

Exhibit 2 National Defense Purchases of Goods and Services (in billions of dollars)

	1989	1988	1987	1986	1985	1984	1983	1982	1981	1980
National Defense Purchases	302.8	298.0	295.3	277.5	259.1	234.3	200.5	179.5	153.7	131.2
Durable Goods	81.9	83.9	89.8	83.5	76.4	66.0	59.1	49.4	40.0	33.5
Military Equipment	72.0	72.9	77.3	71.1	64.5	55.7	49.3	39.9	31.0	26.5
Aircraft	26.5	29.3	33.4	32.9	26.6	21.8	20.6	16.6	12.7	10.9
Missiles	13.7	12.4	13.0	11.5	9.6	8.5	7.4	5.7	4.6	3.7
Ships	9.8	8.4	8.5	8.5	8.4	7.7	6.9	5.9	4.9	4.2
Vehicles	3.6	4.2	4.8	4.7	4.8	5.1	4.2	2.9	1.9	1.8
Electronic equipment	6.2	6.0	5.8	5.1	4.9	4.1	3.6	3.2	2.7	2.2
Other	12.2	12.5	11.8	8.4	10.1	8.5	6.8	5.6	4.2	3.7
Other durable goods	9.9	11.0	12.5	12.4	11.9	10.3	9.8	9.5	9.0	7.0
Nondurable Goods	11.1	10.9	10.5	11.1	11.9	12.1	12.4	13.3	12.5	10.7
Petroleum products	4.6	4.4	4.2	4.3	6.5	6.6	7.6	9.2	8.9	7.6
Ammunition	3.8	3.9	3.8	4.3	3.0	3.1	2.7	2.3	1.8	1.6
Other nondurable goods	2.7	2.6	2.5	2.5	2.4	2.3	2.1	1.9	1.7	1.6
Services	203.3	196.1	187.8	176.4	164.8	151.3	124.4	112.9	98.0	83.8
Compensation of employees	119.8	113.2	108.9	104.0	100.9	94.8	73.1	68.4	61.2	53.1
Military	79.3	76.0	73.2	70.2	67.4	63.5	43.6	40.9	35.9	30.5
Civilian	40.5	37.2	35.7	33.8	33.5	31.3	29.5	27.5	25.2	22.6
Other services	83.5	82.9	78.9	72.4	63.9	56.5	51.3	44.5	36.8	0.7
Contractual R&D	30.8	30.7	28.5	28.6	25.8	22.6	16.5	13.8	12.0	10.0
Installation support[a]	23.9	23.8	22.3	18.6	16.6	15.0	1.1	1.1	0.9	0.7
Weapons support[a]	9.0	8.9	9.0	7.8	7.5	6.7	5.9	4.6	3.6	2.9
Personnel support[a]	12.1	11.8	11.3	10.4	7.2	5.5	21.7	19.1	15.5	12.8
Transportation of material	3.9	3.7	4.0	3.4	3.2	3.4	3.6	3.2	2.9	2.6
Travel of persons	3.9	4.0	3.8	3.5	3.3	2.9	2.6	2.6	2.1	1.6
Other[a]	-0.1	0.0	0.0	0.2	0.2	0.3	0.0	0.0	0.0	0.0

(Continued)

Exhibit 2 (Continued)

	1989	1988	1987	1986	1985	1984	1983	1982	1981	1980
Structures	6.6	7.0	7.2	6.6	6.1	4.9	4.6	3.9	3.2	3.2
Military facilities	4.1	4.7	4.9	4.1	3.5	3.0	2.8	2.3	1.9	2.1
Other	2.4	2.4	2.4	2.4	2.6	1.9	1.8	1.5	1.3	1.0
National Defense Purchases	256.2	261.5	264.9	251.4	237.2	218.5	207.3	196.3	183.7	176.1
Durable Goods	81.8	84.6	87.9	78.1	72.1	61.2	56.4	50.3	45.2	42.4
Military Equipment	69.0	70.8	72.5	64.0	59.1	50.7	46.9	40.7	35.2	34.0
Aircraft	26.5	29.0	30.7	28.0	22.8	18.1	18.7	17.1	15.5	15.0
Missiles	14.7	13.5	12.8	10.9	9.0	8.0	7.0	5.5	4.8	4.6
Ships	7.9	7.1	7.3	7.4	7.6	7.0	6.7	5.9	5.2	4.9
Vehicles	3.8	4.5	5.1	5.0	5.3	5.5	4.5	3.2	2.6	2.9
Electronic equipment	5.6	5.6	5.5	4.8	4.7	3.9	3.4	3.1	2.7	2.3
Other	10.5	11.2	11.0	8.0	9.7	8.1	6.7	5.7	4.5	4.3
Other durable goods	12.8	13.8	15.4	14.2	13.0	10.5	9.5	9.5	9.7	8.2
Nondurable Goods	14.0	14.3	14.7	15.4	13.4	13.4	13.5	14.0	12.8	12.1
Petroleum products	7.8	7.9	8.4	8.5	8.2	8.2	8.6	9.6	8.5	8.5
Ammunition	3.9	4.1	4.0	4.6	2.9	3.0	2.6	2.3	2.1	1.8
Other nondurable goods	2.3	2.2	2.3	2.3	2.3	2.2	2.3	2.1	2.1	1.8

(Continued)

Exhibit 2   (Continued)

	1989	1988	1987	1986	1985	1984	1983	1982	1981	1980
Services	155.5	156.9	156.4	152.3	146.2	139.2	132.7	127.4	122.2	118.1
Compensation of employees	89.7	89.1	89.3	88.8	88.3	86.8	85.2	83.4	81.4	79.2
Military	59.6	60.0	60.2	59.9	59.4	58.5	57.2	56.3	54.9	53.5
Civilian	30.1	29.1	29.0	28.9	28.9	28.3	28.0	27.1	26.7	25.8
Other services	65.9	67.8	67.2	63.4	57.9	52.4	47.5	44.0	40.8	38.9
Contractual R&D	24.7	25.5	24.7	25.3	23.2	20.8	18.6	16.5	15.4	14.3
Installation support[a]	17.6	18.2	17.9	15.5	14.5	13.4	13.0	13.0	13.0	13.0
Weapons support[a]	7.4	7.6	7.9	6.9	6.6	6.2	5.9	5.9	4.8	4.5
Personnel support[a]	8.7	8.9	8.8	8.5	6.5	5.2	3.7	3.6	2.8	2.5
Transportation of material	4.0	3.9	4.2	3.7	3.7	3.6	3.6	3.7	2.8	2.8
Travel of persons	3.6	3.8	3.7	3.4	3.2	2.9	2.5	2.5	2.0	1.8
Other[a]	-0.1	0.0	0.0	0.2	0.2	0.3	0.2	0.0	0.0	0.0
Structures	4.9	5.7	5.9	5.6	5.6	4.7	4.6	4.6	3.5	3.5
Military facilities	3.1	3.7	3.9	3.4	3.2	2.9	2.8	2.8	1.9	2.4
Other	1.8	2.0	2.0	2.2	2.4	1.8	1.8	1.8	1.5	1.1

[a]These categories were reorganized after 1983.

Source: U.S. Department of Commerce, Survey of Current Business.

mately 30 percent of the federal budget, and 6 percent of GNP, and employed 10 percent of the country's labor force. The defense budget also played an important role in local economies by distributing bases, contracts, and jobs across the country. However, as President George Bush took office in that year, Mikhail Gorbachev's policies of Glasnost (political openness) and Perestroika (economic reform) in the Soviet Union, the tearing down of the Berlin Wall in October, and the emerging democratic elections and easing tensions in Eastern Europe resulted in prospects for a drastically lower defense budget in the coming decade.

The Effect of Cost Overruns

In an effort to deal with increased costs incurred on contract work, defense contractors were allowed to defer taxes on unfinished projects. By the end of 1985, the ten largest contractors had deferred $7 billion worth of taxes. For example, deferred taxes during the period from 1985 to 1988 accounted for an average of 17.3 percent of total assets at Martin Marietta, 16.3 percent at Lockheed, and 15.8 percent at McDonnell Douglas. Congress, in need of revenue and infuriated with the extent of the corporate tax liabilities, changed the industry's "completed contract" accounting rules in the Tax Reform Act of 1986 to eliminate most tax deferrals. As a result, by the end of 1991, $7 billion of the defense industry's unpaid taxes would come due. For some companies, the burden would be staggering. From 1990 to 1992, Lockheed would owe the government $1.2 billion, while General Dynamics would have to pay an estimated $750 million. In addition, contractors could no longer defer taxes on new projects in the pipeline.

The defense industry in the United States had suffered from a poor public image because of reports of fraudulent cost claims on cost-plus-fee contracts and wrenching schedule delays. Reported occurrences rose significantly in the early and mid-1980s when defense spending began to rise. Most Americans were outraged at reports that the Defense Department spent $400 for hammers or $3,000 for coffeemakers. However, it was often an overlooked fact that government regulations required that overhead costs be distributed equally among a contractor's products and that products conform to specific customized specifications, thus artificially inflating the costs of many smaller items. Nonetheless, some cost overruns were genuine. "Schedules had been extended by about 33 percent in approximately one-third of the programs. In addition, more than nine in ten programs exceeded initial cost estimates, and the average increase in cost for the majority of programs was more than 50 percent, excluding the effects of quantity changes and inflation."[6] Poor estimates

[6]Jacques S. Gansler, "Program Instability: Causes, Costs, and Cures," paper prepared for the Defense Acquisition Study, Center for Strategic and International Studies, Georgetown University, March 1, 1986, cited in Fox, *The Defense Management Challenge*, p. 33.

of both development and production costs as well as scheduling delays typically accounted for cost overruns.

In 1986, many of the government's allegations of fraud made newspaper headlines. In that year the procurement activities of two firms in particular, Lockheed and General Dynamics, came under attack. Both suffered little more than a slap on the wrist and were able to maintain sales and earnings growth for the year. Lockheed was accused of not reporting to the Air Force that it inflated labor costs by $500 million on the production of fifty aircraft.

General Dynamics, historically one of the largest defense contractors, was not a stranger to allegations of fraud and cost overruns. The company was first barred from bidding as a second source integrator to IBM for a Navy submarine in late 1985. A second suspension in the late 1980s lasted more than two months and barred the company from receiving any government contracts. That suspension came after company officials were indicted for alleged cost switching on General Dynamics' early work on an Army tank program. Pentagon officials explained that the suspensions were not intended to function as punishment for erring contractors but rather to assure the government that wrongs would not be repeated. Amid the condemnations from Washington, General Dynamics achieved its third consecutive year of record profits. "General Dynamics' surging profits, contrasted with its dismal public image, demonstrate how difficult it is for Washington to translate its outrage toward big contractors into actions that have any economic consequences."[7]

In 1987 partly as a response, the Pentagon had made numerous procurement policy changes, including a greater use of fixed-price contracts. By 1989, fixed-price contracts made up 35 percent of the dollar value of all new DoD contract work, and that percentage was growing as new allegations of fraud were made public. The Pentagon also began insisting that contractors contribute as much as 50 percent to the development costs of some weapons systems. Many contractors loaded up on debt to fund those development costs only to be faced with President Bush's budget cuts. For example, Tenneco had a debt to capitalization ratio of 64 percent, and McDonnell Douglas and Grumman both had debt ratios of 45 percent. Eventually, the development money for particular projects was to be repaid to the companies that won the contract to produce the weapon systems. But in 1988, when Northrop spent more than it had estimated on the Stealth bomber project, the Pentagon refused to pay its cost overrun. That forced Northrop to take $300 million in write-downs.

[7]John Koten and Tim Carrington, "For General Dynamics, Scandal Over Billing Hasn't Hurt Business," *The Wall Street Journal*, April 29, 1986.

Competitors

The top defense contractors were among the largest corporations in the United States. The defense business was highly competitive on the basis of both price and technical capability, involved rapidly advancing technologies, and was subject to many uncertainties, the greatest of which was the government's defense outlay. Some of the contractors, such as Boeing, specialized in designing aircraft, while others, such as General Electric, were multi-defense-industry companies, producing jet engines, electronic and communications equipment, and missiles. See Exhibit 3 for defense contractors' representative product specializations.

The structure of the defense industry had changed from the 1970s to the 1980s. For example, General Electric, consistently one of the ten largest contractors in the 1980s, was not a big player in the 1970s. Like others, it had dedicated more resources to defense activities as defense spending under President Reagan skyrocketed. In addition, some companies, including Rockwell International, manufacturer of the B-1 bomber, and Northrop, which made the B-2 Stealth bomber, faced very significant cutbacks of their largest contracts and were forced off the top ten list.

With the forecast of leaner Pentagon defense spending in the future, defense contractors were aggressively trimming their costs while trying

Exhibit 3 Categorizations and Size (in $ billions) of the Largest Defense Companies in 1988[a]

	Aircraft or Astronautics	Missiles/ Space System	Ships	Tank/ Automotive	Electronics
McDonnell Douglas	5,925	2,146			
General Dynamics	3,417	2,485	1,548	1,001	
General Electric	6,481[b]	5,343			
Tenneco			1,671		
Raytheon					4,994
Martin Marietta	2,467	2,055[c]			
General Motors (Hughes Electronics)	11,243[b]				
Lockheed	3,446	5,407			818
United Technologies	2,300[d]	1,657			
Boeing	3,668				1,457
Grumman	2,643	514			
Rockwell	1,611	2,360			1,663
Northrop	4,232				938

[a]Categorized by those businesses that account for the largest dollar volume of the company's defense-related sales.

[b]Includes sales to both government and commercial customers.

[c]Category also contains the company's military electronics sales.

[d]Aircraft engines.

Source: Company documents.

to improve productivity. See Exhibit 4 for financial data on selected firms and Exhibit 5 for the ten largest defense contractors. Their general "belt-tightening" signaled that the companies believed that the procurement reforms that began in 1987 would have a lasting effect through President Bush's tenure and that cost competitiveness was more crucial than ever. For example, "after seeing its profit margins on aircraft engines cut nearly in half, the Pratt & Whitney unit of United Technologies reduced its staff by 10 percent. Meanwhile, Boeing slashed overhead costs 25 percent, and General Dynamics was hoping to cut 40 percent off its [overhead] costs."[8] General Dynamics also planned to cut its $400 million R&D budget by as much as 25 percent in 1990 while Grumman had reduced its workforce by 15 percent since 1987 and had moved many of its operations to plants in Florida and Texas, where corporate tax rates were lower. If Grumman's F-14 fighter aircraft program were cancelled in the early 1990s, the company would have to layoff 3,000 more Grumman employees and as many as 20,000 subcontractor employees. Hughes Aircraft had also made workforce cuts, trimming its payroll by 8 percent or 6,000 jobs in 1989. At the same time, Lockheed sold off two shipyards and its Dialog Information Services business for a total of $500 million.

In the 1990s, defense contractors had different strategies for growth. Some companies, such as Rockwell and Tenneco, were diversifying outside the defense business through a series of related commercial acquisitions. This was similar to the strategies of McDonnell Douglas and Boeing, which exploited synergies between their military and commercial businesses. Others such as Lockheed and General Motors' Hughes Aircraft hoped to diversify but looked for new businesses that continued to serve government markets in some form, such as information systems, field-training, and simulation. Other companies, such as Ford Aerospace and Litton Industries were looking overseas for defense business. For example, Ford positioned itself to help the European space agency replace billions of dollars worth of ground stations. Unlike many of its competitors, General Dynamics was not planning to diversify. The company believed it could survive cuts in defense spending because it was the only U.S. maker of tanks, the dominant maker of submarines, a key supplier of cruise missiles, and its F-16 fighter was the staple of the domestic and many foreign air forces.

The most common strategy among defense companies, however, was to enter the field of defense electronics, such as Raytheon, Honeywell, and Grumman had done. In 1989, military electronics accounted for 78 percent of Raytheon's total earnings, and the company was the largest defense electronics firm in the United States. Raytheon had also taken strides in the 1970s to diversify beyond the defense business, and by 1988, 39 percent of its sales came from non-defense businesses such as

---

[8]Eileen White, "Defense Industry Slims Down to Survive," *The Wall Street Journal*, September 30, 1987.

Exhibit 4   Financial Performance of the Thirteen Leading Defense Contractors in 1988 (all $ figures in millions)

| | Yearly Sales | Percent Change | Net Income | Percent Change | Return on | | Capital Spending | Debt to Capitalization | Deferred Taxes/Total Assets |
					Equity	Assets			
McDonnell Douglas	15,069	10.2%	347	11.9%	10.9%	2.9%	651	45.0%	15.8%
General Dyamics	9,551	1.5%	379	(13.2%)	19.7%	8.7%	496	33.6%	7.7%
General Electric	50,089	4.0%	3,386	16.2%	19.4%	3.1%	3,681	44.9%	3.0%
Tenneco	13,234	10.8%	822	477.0%	26.0%	4.7%	688	63.9%	7.6%
Raytheon	8,192	7.0%	490	10.1%	23.1%	10.3%	421	1.9%	4.5%
Martin Marietta[a]	5,728	10.9%	359	55.4%	29.9%	10.8%	362	28.7%	14.3%
General Motors[a]	11,243	8.0%	257	17.4%	9.5%	6.0%	469	11.3%	0.1%
Lockheed	10,590	(6.5%)	624	43.1%	25.2%	9.4%	380	21.9%	16.3%
United Technologies	18,001	4.8%	659	11.3%	14.6%	5.4%	875	25.4%	3.0%
Boeing	16,962	10.5%	614	27.9%	11.4%	4.9%	629	4.4%	1.6%
Grumman	3,649	9.7%	87	141.7%	11.1%	3.4%	118	49.4%	5.5%
Rockwell	11,946	(1.5%)	812	27.9%	21.9%	8.8%	555	16.8%	14.6%
Northrop	5,797	(4.2%)	(31)[b]	(133.0%)	(3.1%)	(9.8%)	254	36.5%	14.8%

[a]Data is for Hughes Electronics division only.

[b]Net income was before cumulative effect on prior years of change in accounting for income taxes. Net income was 104 after that extraordinary item was figured in.

Source: Company Documents.

Exhibit 5 Top Ten Defense Contractors

Rank			Awards	
FY1988	FY1981[a]	Company	FY1988	FY1981
1	1	McDonnell Douglas	8.0	4.4
2	3	General Dynamics	6.5	3.4
3	4	General Electric	5.7	3.0
4	—	Tenneco	5.1	—
5	8	Raytheon	4.1	1.8
6	12	Martin Marietta	3.7	1.3
7	7	General Motors[b]	3.6	2.6
8	6	Lockheed	3.5	2.7
9	2	United Technologies	3.5	3.8
10	5	Boeing	3.0	2.7
—	9	Grumman	—	1.7
Total of Top Ten Contractors			46.7	27.4
Percent of All Awards Accounted for by Top Ten			34.1%	28.0%
Total of Top 100 Contractors			90.1	64.7
Percent of All Awards Accounted for by Top 100			65.8%	67.0%

[a]In FY1981, Chrysler was ranked tenth with $1.4 billion.
[b]Hughes Aircraft division only.
Source: Aerospace Facts and Figures, 1988–1989, Department of Defense.

Exhibit 6 U.S. Military Electronics Procurement and R&D, Testing, and Equipment (in constant fiscal year 1990 $ billions)

	1989	1990	1991
Program			
Aircraft	12.9	12.2	12.0
Missiles	7.5	7.2	7.1
Space	6.1	6.4	6.4
Ships	4.7	4.2	4.3
Ordnance and Weapons	1.2	1.2	1.2
Vehicles	0.8	0.8	0.8
Electronics and Communications	9.9	8.8	8.7
All Others	7.1	6.6	5.9
Total	50.2	47.4	46.4

Source: Electronic News, October 9, 1989.

Beech Aircraft and Amana home appliances. Raytheon and many other observers believed that the field of defense electronics would be less affected by the declining defense budget in the 1990s than the traditional defense businesses of aircraft assembly and shipbuilding. However, in fiscal year 1990, federal funds allocated to the DoD for electronics programs were forecasted to drop by five percent from fiscal year 1989 to $47 billion. See Exhibit 6 for military electronics funding. Sixty-five percent of the total funding would be allocated for procurement with the remaining 35 percent allocated to R&D, testing, and equipment. Overall, U.S. defense electronics, used in everything from missile systems to antisubmarine warfare to advanced tactical fighters, would account for one-quarter of the total U.S. electronics market. Possible commercial applications from defense electronics included artificial intelligence, high definition television, factory automation and control, and semiconductor manufacturing technology.

McDonnell Douglas In 1988, McDonnell Douglas was the largest defense contractor with a total of $8.0 billion in DoD contracts. Eighty-eight percent of the company's total dollar awards were for combat aircraft. McDonnell Douglas competed closely with several other large military aircraft contractors including Lockheed, Boeing, and Grumman. Unlike Grumman, however, McDonnell Douglas manufactured a number of different fighter and transport aircraft models including the F-15, the FA-18, the AV-8B, the CF-18, and the C-17, and did not rely on any single program for the majority of its profits. Historically, slightly more than one-half of the company's sales were to the U.S. government (including combat aircraft, space systems and missiles); commercial jet production accounted for one-third of sales; and information systems (primarily government-related) comprised the remainder. However, in 1989, McDonnell Douglas sold off most of its information systems division after several years of weak profit performance.

Despite losses from cost overruns in 1989, McDonnell Douglas's goal was to continue to be the largest defense contractor by capturing a leadership position in the award of development and production contracts for the DoD's largest projects. In an effort to achieve that goal, the company completed a large restructuring in early 1990 to reduce costs and layers of management. Though McDonnell Douglas realized that its military transport aircraft business was the fastest growing and most likely to have the strongest impact on company sales through 1993, it was also investing heavily in its commercial aircraft business to balance the commercial side of the business with the military side. The company hoped to build a strong commercial presence in the large, long-range jetliner market as well as in the smaller, short- to medium-range aircraft market.

Rockwell In 1986 Rockwell was the fourth largest defense contractor in the United States, but by 1988, the company had fallen to twelfth place. The main reason for the company's fall was the termination by the government of the production of the B-1 bomber aircraft. In 1986, that particular combat airplane pumped $4 billion into the company, and accounted for nearly one-third of the company's total revenues. As a result of the program's termination, Rockwell's B-1 revenues shriveled to a $1 billion per year maintenance contract. "The challenge for Rockwell is to hold on to what it's got in aerospace and also show that there are opportunities for the company after the B-1 bomber," said Wolfgang Demisch, aerospace analyst at First Boston.[9]

Following the cancellation of the B-1 program, Rockwell's goal was to grow through strategic diversification outside of the aerospace business. For example, the company planned to increase the scope of its defense electronics business group, and make strategic acquisitions outside of the defense business by establishing joint ventures. In 1986, the company spent $500 million to buy back 8 percent of its common stock, which it then used for additional acquisitions. Later in that year, Rockwell acquired Allen-Bradley, an automation-equipment maker for $1.7 billion. In addition, to strengthen its non-aerospace operations, Rockwell acquired more than ten smaller companies, including truck parts and newspaper printing press manufacturers. By the end of 1988, sales from non-B-1 business increased by more than $1.6 billion and the company's DoD contracts totaled 31 percent of sales compared to 45 percent in 1987.

Grumman   Grumman, the country's premier supplier of naval aircraft, was still reeling from a number of setbacks it incurred in the late 1980s. In 1989, Grumman fell victim to defense budget cuts that resulted in the gradual phasing out of production of the company's F-14 Tomcat fighter aircraft (that starred in the movie "Top Gun") and remaining A-6 bomber production by Congress in 1991. In that one stroke, Grumman lost one-third of its $3.6 billion in annual revenues and was slated for elimination as a major aircraft manufacturer. "Once the Navy moves on to the next generation of fighters," Grumman Chairman John O'Brien conceded, "I see us having a difficult time staying in the carrier fighter business."[10]

To outlive defense budget cuts, Grumman hoped to move into other businesses such as military electronics, data systems, and commercial aviation parts without forsaking the company's aerospace heritage. However, the company was plagued with more than $800 million in debt and shrinking earnings, much of which was a legacy from failed diversification efforts in the 1970s that led the company into buses, solar energy, and refrigerators. Some observers expressed concern over Grumman's plans. "They can't think about growth," said William Deatherage, an analyst at Dean Witter Reynolds. "They have to worry about survival."[11] In looking toward the future, Grumman was spending less than 1 percent of its annual revenues on R&D, compared with an industry average of 3 percent to 4 percent. "I don't see the need to spend any more than that," said Grumman Chairman John O'Brien. "Why should I be wasting

[9]Timothy D. Schellhardt, "Beall, Tapped to Become Rockwell Chief After Anderson, Faces End of B-1 Order," *The Wall Street Journal*, October 8, 1987.

[10]Andy Pasztor, "Grumman F-14s Fate and Firm's Course Face Day of Decision," *The Wall Street Journal*, July 27, 1989.

[11]Eric Weiner, "Grumman Girds for Arms Cuts," *The New York Times*, December 12, 1989.

company money on R&D? I saw these [defense budget] cuts coming all along."[12]

Lockheed   Lockheed, once one of the nation's defense leaders, was the eighth largest defense contractor in 1988 with contracts totaling $3.5 billion. In 1987 three of the company's multi-billion dollar programs were significantly slowed down or canceled. Lockheed was also hurt by the increasing use of a cost cutting reform called "second-sourcing," which began in the mid-1980s. Second-sourcing, in effect, threw open to competition all production contracts on hardware that had typically been developed and produced by a single firm. Second-sourcing was considered a two-edged sword because, though it presented opportunities for growth, it also challenged a company's existing position. For example, in 1987, one of Lockheed's longest running monopolies, the P-3 Orion submarine hunting aircraft was auctioned off to other bidders.

In 1988, Lockheed's sales slipped 6 percent to $10.6 billion. Close to 43 percent of those sales were derived from defense electronics, and software products and services. In early 1989, Lockheed announced a new two-part strategy to help it reach its goal of focused diversification in both domestic and international markets. First, the company planned to maintain and enhance its defense and NASA business by seeking out new business in non-traditional areas where its skills were transferable. These included submarine warfare technology, and the management and technical service business. Second, Lockheed planned to build its non-defense portfolio by applying its data management and systems skills to the needs of other government markets and through its information systems division. The company was vying to become the systems integrator in a $1.5 billion Air Force program linking all DoD office computers. In addition to its diversification efforts, Lockheed was competing against Northrop for the Air Force's Advanced Tactical Fighter. Some analysts believed that winning that competition to build $35 billion of fighter aircraft throughout the 1990s could help insulate Lockheed from many defense cuts. However, they were also aware that Congress could vote to reduce drastically funding for the project.

Martin Marietta

Though most defense contractors were diversifying and cutting costs to shield themselves from a declining budget, the approach of the sixth largest defense contractor, Martin Marietta, had won the praise of Wall Street. Many analysts believed that even if defense spending levels plummeted, the company would still be less vulnerable than its competitors

---

[12]Ibid.

because its defense business was spread over a number of specialized markets. The company had successfully cut costs and diversified in an effort to remain competitive in the 1990s.

Business Segments

Martin Marietta had focused on aerospace defense products since the company's formation in the 1960s. Its business mix and structure however, had changed considerably during the period from the 1970s to the 1980s. In the 1970s, Martin Marietta's sales, though dominated by the aerospace segment, were also concentrated in a number of basic industry segments. One-fourth of sales were aluminum products while one-third was cement, aggregates, and chemical products. Throughout the 1970s the company enjoyed strong sales and earnings growth that extended into the 1980s. See Exhibits 7 and 8 for data on Martin Marietta's financial performance.

In 1988, Martin Marietta had four main business segments: Astronautics, Electronics and Missiles, Information Systems, and Materials. The company had undergone a major reorganization of its segment reporting operations in early 1987, moving from a geographical basis to a product group basis for the organization of its divisions. Over 90 percent of the sales of the company's three largest groups were made to the U.S. government, either as a prime contractor or as a subcontractor, principally to the DoD and NASA. The Astronautics and the Electronics and Missiles divisions had historically been and continued to be the largest of the company's businesses since a company-wide restructuring in 1982, contributing 14 percent and 34 percent to total operating profit in 1988 respectively.

The Astronautics division, located in Denver, Colorado, designed, developed, tested, and manufactured systems for space and defense. It was comprised of four companies: Space Launch Systems, the prime integration, systems, and launch contractor for the company's Titan series of space launch vehicles; Martin Marietta Commercial Titan, formed in 1987 to launch satellites for commercial customers; Space Systems, which produced planetary spacecraft and instruments for NASA and the military; and Strategic Systems, a U.S. Air Force contractor for the development of the Peacekeeper (MX) missile system. See Exhibit 9 for a list of Martin Marietta's largest defense contracts.

The Electronics and Missiles division, located in Orlando, Florida, was engaged in the design, development, and production of missiles and electronic systems. The group's responsibilities included the development of the Pershing missile system for the U.S. Army, the production of electro-optic navigational and targeting equipment for military aircraft, and the manufacture of shipboard missile storage units and fan reverser assemblies for jet engines.

Martin Marietta's Information Systems division, located in Bethesda, had accounted for approximately 17 percent of total revenues in

Exhibit 7   Martin Marietta Financial Data (in $ millions)

	1989	1988	1987	1986	1985	1984	1983	1982	1981	1980
Operating Results										
Net Sales	5,796	5,728	5,165	4,753	4,410	3,920	3,228	3,527	3,294	2,613
Cost of Sales, other costs, and expenses	5,331	5,331	4,758	4,422	4,116	3,634	2,999	3,453	3,073	2,383
Earnings from operations	465	397	407	331	294	286	230	74	222	230
Other income and expenses, net	8	117	(3)	18	160	55	135	87	72	55
	473	514	404	349	454	341	365	160	293	285
Interest expense on debt	43	39	24	21	36	32	64	68	10	7
Earnings before taxes	430	475	380	327	418	309	301	92	283	279
Taxes	122	155	149	125	169	133	139	0	83	90
Earnings from Continuing Operations	308	320	231	202	249	176	162	92	200	188
Losses from discontinued aluminum business	—	—	—	—	—	(368)	(20)	—	—	—
Utilization of tax capital loss carryforward	—	39	—	—	—	—	—	—	—	—
Net Earnings (Losses)	308	359	231	202	249	(192)	141	92	200	188
Total Assets	3,516	3,319	2,794	2,471	2,258	2,224	2,380	2,838	2,546	2,069
Capital Expenditures	282	362	277	282	316	206	159	225	391	353
Long-term Debt	478	484	295	241	233	349	549	1,235	359	163
Long-term Debt to Capital (as a percent)	26.0%	28.7%	24.5%	22.2%	24.8%	33.7%	39.4%	73.9%	23.0%	12.9%
Return on Equity (as percent)	22.7%	29.9%	25.4%	24.0%	34.8%	(32.4%)	15.4%	21.0%	16.7%	17.1%
Deferred taxes	515	473	541	466	367	267	446	495	330	304
Deferred taxes as percent of Capital	38.0%	28.1%	44.9%	42.9%	39.0%	27.4%	31.9%	29.6%	21.2%	24.0%
Deferred taxes as percent of Assets	14.7%	14.3%	19.4%	18.9%	16.3%	12.0%	18.7%	17.4%	13.0%	14.7%

Source: Company documents.

Exhibit 8   Martin Marietta Sales by Industry Segment (in $ millions)

	1989	1988	1987	1986	1985	1984ᵃ	1983	1982	1981ᵃ	1980
Astronautics	2,754	2,467	2,044	1,831	1,790	2,077	1,655	1,554	1,923	1,234
Electronics and Missiles	2,117	2,055	2,021	1,887	1,698	1,018	910	755	—	—
Information Systems	748	998	939	889	756	539	279	245	—	—
Materials and Other	423	462	415	375	358	428	499	598	1,369	1,382
Total segment salesᵇ	6,042	5,982	5,419	4,981	4,601	4,062	3,343	3,152	3,292	2,616

Operating Profit by Industry Segment (in $ millions)

	1989	1988	1987	1986	1985	1984ᵃ	1983	1982	1981ᵃ	1980
Astronautics	197	82	120	120	134	178	135	105	137	90
Electronics and Missiles	194	195	201	182	147	78	79	69	—	—
Information Systems	21	214ᶜ	51	2	2	19	16	12	—	—
Materials and Other	86	77	82	76	164	86	91	25	142	188
Total segment operating profitᵇ	498	568	455	380	447	361	321	211	279	278

ᵃThe company's segment reporting was changed in both 1984 and 1981. In 1981 Astronautics, Electronics, and Missiles were all included in the Astronautics segment.

The Company's aluminum operations were sold in 1982.

ᵇMay not equal total company sales and operating profit due to intersegment sales.

ᶜInflated by capital gain on sale of U.K. data systems company.

Source: Company documents.

Exhibit 9   Martin Marietta's Largest Defense Contracts

Year	Project	Customer	Contract Value (in $ millions)
1989	Sixty external tanks for the Space Shuttle	NASA	1,800
1989	Titan IV launch vehicles	U.S. Air Force	1,600
1989	Shoulder-fired anti-tank weapon system	U.S. Army	3,000[a]
1988	Strategic Defense Initiative's National Test Bed	DoD	508
1987	Air defense and anti-tank system	U.S. Army	4,000[a]
1986	Titan IV launch vehicles	U.S. Air Force	2,100
1985	Titan IV launch vehicles	U.S. Air Force	2,300
1984	Magellan Spacecraft	NASA	216
1983	Modernization of air traffic control system	U.S. Department of Transportation	984
1982	Pershing Missile System	U.S. Army	1,730
1980	LANTIRN Navigation System	U.S. Air Force	3,000
1979	Peacekeeper (MX) missile	U.S. Air Force	2,600

[a]Potential value over the life of the contract.

Source: Martin Marietta.

the late 1980s. Companies within the division designed, built, and integrated advanced information systems in electronics, communications, and data processing. Its largest customers included the Federal Aviation Administration, for which it was the principal contractor for upgrading the air traffic control network, the U.S. Army, and the U.S. Air Force. The division also provided information systems integration and custom software solutions for both commercial customers and the U.S. government.

Through the company's smallest division, Materials, it was the second largest producer of crushed stone in the United States, supplied refractory materials for basic steelmaking, and produced aluminum and titanium components primarily for the aircraft industry. The company also managed and operated three of the Department of Energy's uranium enrichment facilities.

Corporate Strategy

In 1982, Martin Marietta underwent a dramatic restructuring brought about by a hostile takeover attempt. Early in that year, Bendix Corporation, led by Bill Agee, attempted an unfriendly takeover of Martin Marietta. On the advice of a Wall Street dealmaker, Martin Marietta borrowed more than $1 billion to finance a retaliatory acquisition of Bendix. The company's defense, later termed the "Pac Man" defense because it countered Bendix's hostile bid with a takeover bid of its own, was successful. When the dust had settled, Martin Marietta owned more than half of Bendix's stock.

The end of the battle with Bendix in 1982 marked the beginning of a new corporate strategy at Martin Marietta. The company had to face the enormous hurdle of paying back the $1 billion it borrowed to finance the Bendix deal. Its debt to capital ratio had climbed from 23 percent in 1981 to 74 percent by the end of 1982. In absolute terms, long-term debt rose 243 percent over that same period. Norman Augustine, chairman and chief executive officer of Martin Marietta reflected, "We knew we had to fix the balance sheet immediately. In the defense industry, companies begin to worry when debt to total capital ratios reach 30 percent." To reduce that debt, the company sold its extraneous cement, chemical, and aluminum divisions and began to focus directly on its aerospace business. "Bendix forced Martin Marietta to focus on what kind of company it wanted to be years before that was popular," said Peter Aseritis, a vice president at First Boston.[13] By 1987, the company's debt to capital ratio had been reduced to 28 percent.

In 1985 Martin Marietta embarked on the second phase of its corporate strategy which was to bid for and win twenty-four new contracts. That phase was tied to the fact that Martin Marietta's senior management believed that defense spending in the United States would not continue to grow in the late 1980s, primarily because of the growing burden of the U.S. budget deficit. Instead, the company forecasted that the defense budget would flatten in 1987 and decline 1 percent per year (in real terms) through 1994. "With that in mind," Augustine explained, "We decided to invest heavily in defense-related R&D between 1985 and 1987 in an effort to bring in a lot of contracts. That way we would have enough ongoing contracts in-house for seed material downstream during the years of cutbacks." In addition, Martin Marietta was careful in choosing contracts that at least half of the company's business be spread out over ten or more contracts. The company surveyed the Reagan administration's defense buildup and targeted twenty-four government contracts it considered crucial; the list was called "Must Wins," and included ADATS and Titan IV launch contracts and other systems with "recurring add-ons." Martin Marietta announced their R&D investment strategy to Wall Street analysts in the fall of 1985. The company's stock reacted by losing $750 million of its market value.

Martin Marietta's strategy, however, proved to be more successful than the analysts had anticipated. In 1986 the government began to demand more fixed-price contracts from defense companies which were typically easier to win than cost-plus-fee contracts because, as Augustine explained, "Winning became simply a matter of the amount of risk that management was willing to take—not technical capability, innovation,

---

[13]Laurie Hays, "Martin Marietta Scores Successes in Defense Industry," *The Wall Street Journal*, February 18, 1988.

etc." As Augustine explained, "We were able to win 50 percent of the contracts we targeted while maintaining a relatively prudent pricing policy by very selectively choosing target contracts." By garnering 50 percent of the contracts it targeted, the company far surpassed the industry average of 28 percent. In dollar value terms Martin Marietta was even more successful, winning 65 percent of the total dollar value of the contracts they targeted, again surpassing the industry average of 65 percent.

In 1986 the government abandoned most commercial satellite launching after the Challenger Shuttle disaster. Therefore, commercial launch opportunities existed for companies such as Martin Marietta. In 1987, the company began to market its Titan launch vehicles to companies that wanted to launch their own satellites that would have gone into space on the shuttle. By the end of 1988, the company had committed to twenty-three launch reservations valued at approximately $110 million each. However, a number of other U.S. companies, such as McDonnell Douglas, and government subsidized foreign companies from countries such as France and China had entered the commercial launch business leading to an overabundance of launch vehicles. Caleb Hurtt, president and chief operating officer of Martin Marietta added, "That excess supply drove prices down. Therefore, we no longer have an inventory of Titans, and we will build more only on the basis of a firm order."

Martin Marietta was careful in its assessments of the probabilities of individual projects and whether or not to bid on them. The company believed that accurate forecasting was a critical factor in managing the company's strategic direction. "Senior managers are heavily involved in managing our planning and forecasting system. From early August to early January of each year, those managers do not have any operating responsibilities, and are solely responsible for planning," said Augustine. Among the issues the company considered when assessing various projects were, the probability that the government would want a particular system, the probability that Martin Marietta could submit the winning bid for that system, the development cost to the company, and the system's payoff. If the contract was fixed-price (which it generally considered to be the easiest contracts to win but the most difficult to profit from), the company needed to surmise whether the DoD or other customer's decision would be based on cost estimates or technical capability. Some companies, such as Boeing and Norden, had been forced to take large write-offs because of losses incurred on fixed-rate contracts. Augustine maintained that "conservative bidding" in terms of cost projections was the best overall long-term strategy for Martin Marietta to pursue.

In addition to forecasting the risks of a project under consideration, Martin Marietta also had to assess and manage the risks of a project once development and production were underway. Hurtt explained, "Our first task is to ensure quality and what we call 'Mission Success;' after that we focus on cost and schedule controls. Mission Success means that we can address the customer's mission rather than try to create a need for a component or technology we have already built." Hurtt pointed to the low altitude navigation and targeting night-vision testing system (LANTIRN) project as an example of how the company managed the business risk of a project. In the development phase of the LANTIRN project, the customer (the U.S. Air Force) had encountered a number of cost overruns, forcing the government to demand that the production phase of the contract, which Martin Marietta was working on, be on a fixed-price basis. At the time, Senator Barry Goldwater, chairman of the Senate Armed Services Committee, told Martin Marietta that the LAN-TIRN was a necessity, that the company would be given $3.2 billion, and that it "must step up and take the contract." (Under the worst scenario, the company stood to lose $600 million on the project.) In an effort to ameliorate the risk, Martin Marietta built a new factory incorporating the latest technology. Hurtt added, "That new factory gave us a way to reduce the project's risk. Now we are making money on LANTIRN and we have not missed one production delivery date."

At the end of 1987, Martin Marietta's contract backlog reached a record $10.8 billion compared to $3 billion in 1983. Among the largest contracts the company was awarded from 1985 to 1987 were a contract to build an air defense and anti-tank system for the Army ($4 billion over the course of five years), a contract to develop a National Test Bed (computer simulation facility) for the Strategic Defense Initiative ("Star Wars" Project), and a contract to design the Magellan spacecraft, which will travel to Venus.

In the third phase of Martin Marietta's strategy, which began in 1988, the company planned to "follow on" its backlog. Augustine explained the plan as follows: "During this phase, which we expect to last until 1994, we will not pursue large new contracts, but will look for add-ons to existing contracts, such as additional orders for our Titan IV series of launch vehicles and our LANTIRN navigational system." Augustine hoped that the backlog would grow through modifications and updates of existing systems with new technology. Hurtt added that, "Our projects are not just one-shot affairs, they have recurring add-ons. Therefore, once we get in the barn, we get to stay there." In addition, the company would continue to act as a subcontractor for some projects. In 1990 one-half of its sales were from subcontracting projects, the same as the industry average.

During its fourth strategic phase, Martin Marietta hoped to take advantage of what it predicted would be a 1 percent real growth rate in the defense budget beginning in the mid-1990s. At that time, the company wanted to be equipped with the best technology possible. To lay the groundwork for the fourth phase, the company had established the Advanced Development and Technology Organization (ADTO). ADTO pursued advanced technology developments across the broad spectrum of the company's interests but focused primarily on new developments in defense electronics, missiles, astronautics, and information systems.

Martin Marietta and the Defense Industry in the 1990s

Most observers agreed that Martin Marietta's diversified, cost cutting strategy had brought nothing less than success by the end of the 1980s. At that time, 50 percent of the company's business was in ten or more contracts. George Shapiro, aerospace analyst at Salomon Brothers noted, "Martin Marietta is well-positioned because of its product line (in specialized markets). The company has established a strong position in tactical missiles, night vision equipment (LANTIRN), and expendable launching vehicles (Titan IV). These new markets are likely to continue to grow in the new military environment of stricter procurement policies and a decreased military budget."[14] Such praise was echoed by other Wall Street analysts who had hailed Martin Marietta's strategy. "Martin Marietta will be less vulnerable to cutbacks than other defense contractors," noted Wolfgang Demisch, aerospace analyst for First Boston, "because its defense business is spread over so many areas, and a lot of its contracts carry the highest priority with the government."[15]

Despite its strong record of success in the defense business, Martin Marietta and the country's other defense contractors faced a number of uncertainties in the 1990s. Most analysts believed that the largest factor that would affect the level of defense spending in the United States was the success of Soviet Union leader Gorbachev's economic and political reform programs. As part of the reforms, the United States and the Soviet Union had agreed to a number of arms reductions. Following Gorbachev's reforms in the Soviet Union, tensions eased dramatically in Eastern Europe in early 1990, again signaling that President Bush and the Pentagon might further decrease defense spending.

In 1990, the U.S. government was considering defense budget cuts that could average between 5 percent and 10 percent per year through the mid-1990s. "But the impact of those cuts on the defense industry," according to Jack Modzelewski, a former Rockwell executive and now a Paine Webber vice president, "will be far greater than 5 percent to 10 percent. It's harder for the government to make cuts in personnel or operations than in R&D or procurement plans. So the big cuts have to come out of the industry's bread and butter. These companies haven't even begun to feel the pain."[16] Some defense insiders spoke publicly about the grim prospect that Northrop or Grumman or some other particularly vulnerable contractor could go bankrupt or be forced into the arms of a rival in a merger. Defense contractors faced the likelihood that almost

---

[14]Kurt Eichenwald, "Arms Contractors Found Attractive," *The New York Times*, June 23, 1988.

[15]Ibid.

[16]Howard Gleckman, "It's Bombs Away for Defense Stocks," *Business Week*, December 4, 1989.

every major weapons project would be reduced in size or stretched out, with some programs facing the possibility of being canceled. "Keeping programs alive on a smaller scale or at a reduced rate of production carries a financial penalty for the companies involved as they fail to reach the levels of manufacturing efficiency they had planned when making their original bids."[17]

Norman Augustine and other senior managers at Martin Marietta were contemplating what course they should follow if the defense budget declined steeply by the mid-1990s. Realizing that their present strategy of defense product diversification might need to be extended, they were considering ways to develop new technologies. Augustine was careful to keep in mind, however, that the industry's record of diversification outside of the defense business had not met with much success.

---

[17]Richard Stevenson, "Behind the Military Stock Selloff," *The New York Times*, November 21, 1989.

Questions

1. What are the key factors for success in the defense contract industry?
2. How well positioned is Martin Marietta to compete in the 1990s?
3. What strategic options are available to Martin Marietta in 1990? Are these same options available to other competitors in the defense contract industry?
4. Should the company change its strategy now in light of the prospects for sharply reduced defense expenditures?

CASE 15
Saab-Scania: The Car Division

In the last chapter we examined a government expenditure (defense spending) that directly affected revenues on the income statement of a firm. In this chapter we will view the role of another government expenditure (social welfare spending) that also affects the income statement, but through costs, not revenues. The hypothesis is that social welfare spending has grown so large in Sweden that it is placing a burden on Swedish manufacturers, which makes it difficult for them to compete in the international marketplace.

As with many of the other chapters in this book, we will try to identify the means by which a government policy affects business—in this case, how social welfare spending imposes its burden on manufacturers. As we will see, the burden of the social welfare state will be transmitted through both direct and indirect channels, but we need to assess how significant this burden is for Saab. We will also find that the burden depends, in part, on the market conditions in that country. The most interesting managerial question is whether a firm can devise a strategy which will allow it to compete successfully in the world economy despite some country-based disadvantages in the location where they produce. Also, we would like to identify characteristics of industries which will be more vulnerable to such competitive burdens.

Entitlements spending is rising in all major industrial countries (but at significantly different rates) and workers have increased demands for health care, child care, and other social benefits. This makes the issues raised by this case relevant not only in Sweden, but in most advanced industrial countries whose industries are competing against rivals domiciled in countries whose social welfare benefits (and burdens) are less generous.

The Saab Car Division, headquartered in Nyköping, Sweden, had been increasingly successful in the international car market during the 1980s. In 1988, the company produced nearly 130,000 cars of which 80 percent were sold outside of Sweden, primarily in the United States and Western Europe. Though auto sales in its home market had slowed slightly, the division had maintained eleven years of increasing profitability. Saab had also made significant inroads in the European car market and was beginning to penetrate the market in Japan.

Saab had developed an international reputation as a manufacturer of technically superior cars. The company manufactured virtually all of its cars in Sweden, a country with a unique labor environment. The policies of the Social Democratic government of Sweden, in conjunction with the Swedish labor unions, had produced the highest social welfare benefits of any country in the world. As a result, Saab and other Swedish employers were required by the government to pay an average of 56 percent of employees' salaries in benefits compared to the 11.4 percent required in the United States. Despite its social welfare cost burden, Saab had evolved into a top international competitor by the end of the 1980s.

Background of Saab-Scania

Saab-Scania was the result of a merger that took place in 1969 between Saab (*S*venska *A*eroplan *A*ktie*b*olaget), manufacturers of aircraft since 1937 and passenger cars since 1949, and Scania Vabis, Sweden's oldest truck manufacturer, dating back to 1891. The merger was heavily promoted by Stockholm Enskilda Bank, Sweden's largest private bank, and by its chairman, Marcus Wallenberg, often referred to as the John D. Rockefeller of Sweden. Wallenberg was elected Chairman of the new Saab-Scania company, a position which he held until his retirement in 1980.

By 1988, Saab-Scania had three divisions (Scania, Saab Cars, Saab Aircraft) and two subsidiary units (Combitech and Enertech). Scania, the largest division, manufactured heavy trucks and buses, and industrial and marine engines. As the third largest truck manufacturer in Europe, Scania produced 7 percent of the total world output of heavy trucks and 15 percent of the world exports of heavy trucks. Scania trucks were sold through 1,200 dealers in nearly 100 countries, primarily in the Nordic countries, Europe, and South America. In 1987, Scania trucks accounted for 50 percent of the heavy truck market in Sweden and 14 percent in Europe. Of the 30,000 trucks and buses it produced in 1987, more than 90 percent were exported, placing Scania third among the world's truck

This case was prepared by Research Associate Julia Horn under the supervision of Professor Michael G. Rukstad. Copyright © 1989 by the President and Fellows of Harvard College. Harvard Business School Case 9-389-103.

exporters. Scania's truck production strategy focused on the production of heavy trucks that, because of technical superiority, could be sold at higher prices than those of their rivals. Truck sales represented 65 percent of the Scania division's total sales of $2.95 billion in 1987. See Exhibits 1 and 2 for Saab-Scania and Saab Car Division financial statements.

The Saab Car Division sold over 127,000 cars throughout the world in 1987 and accounted for 38.6 percent of Saab-Scania's sales, making it the second largest division. Beginning in 1969 when the merger of Saab and Scania took place, the company marketed its cars along with Scania trucks, until it was decided to form a separate car division in 1972. By 1987, the United States had become Saab's biggest single market with sales of 45,102 cars. Saab's unit market share among U.S. imports had also grown at a compounded annual rate of 18.7 percent from 1980 to 1987. See Exhibit 3 for a geographic breakdown of Saab's car sales.

The Saab Aircraft division had grown from its early days as a pure military producer to a manufacturer of both combat and passenger aircraft. Its military production was primarily oriented to meet the Swedish Armed Forces' demand for combat aircraft and to export aircraft to other countries with the approval of the Swedish government. Commercial production, which included the popular 340 Turboprop, was focused on the market for regional (commuter) aircraft. In 1987, Saab's worldwide market share of the commercial turboprop market was 30 percent and Saab planes were used by seven different airlines in the United States alone. The aircraft division's total sales in 1987 were $717 million.

Combitech and Enertech divisions were the company's smallest units. Combitech products included missiles, target materials and simulators for weapons training, and control systems and instruments for aircraft, missiles and submarines. Total sales in 1987 were $224 million. The Enertech division, which manufactured heating products, was sold in late 1988.

The Early Years of Auto Production

The evolution of Saab's small cars began in 1945 when Saab, then an aircraft maker, began to build three prototypes of the Saab model 92. (See Exhibit 4.) Early sales were primarily in Sweden and in neighboring Scandinavian markets where pent up demand for cars after the war generated waiting lists for new cars lasting well into the 1950s. In 1950, after the initial series of cars were built based on those prototypes, Saab entered its first European car rally and won. Saab later entered a number of other rallies with the Saab 93 and 96, successors to the 92 model. The rally triumphs were the cars' own best advertising and began to open up new markets for Saab. Later, in the early 1960s, Saab's legendary race car driver, Erik Carlsson, won numerous rallies including two victories at Monte Carlo. Saab's rallying successes, which lasted well into the 1970s with the introduction of the 99 model, were responsible for launching

Exhibit 1   Saab-Scania Consolidated Income Statements (in $ millions)

	1987	1986	1985	1984	1983	1982
Operating Revenue:						
Sales	$6,530.4	$4,947.0	$3,702.3	$3,138.5	$2,708.3	$2,981.8
Costs and Expenses:						
Manufacturing, selling, and administrative	5,861.7	4,385.4	3,295.2	2,737.2	2,345.3	2,621.9
Depreciation	217.2	168.8	115.5	102.2	92.7	93.4
Total costs and expenses	$6,078.9	$4,554.2	$3,410.7	$2,839.4	$2,438.0	$2,715.3
Operating Income	451.5	392.8	291.6	299.1	270.3	266.5
Interest Income	192.7	127.7	117.4	107.1	83.6	87.5
Interest Expense	(127.8)	(102.8)	(100.1)	(112.2)	(108.3)	(135.8)
Operating non-operating income	38.9	44.1	8.2	7.6	13.7	0.3
Income Before Income Taxes and Extraordinary Items	$ 555.3	$ 461.8	$ 317.1	$ 301.6	$ 259.3	$ 218.5
Extraordinary income and expenses	5.5	5.3	1.8	3.9	0.8	(0.3)
Minority interest in subsidiaries	(6.9)	(5.2)	(0.6)	(0.8)	(0.6)	(0.7)
Appropriations	(212.0)	(169.1)	(179.2)	(174.7)	(177.1)	(111.5)
Income Before Income Taxes	$ 341.9	$ 292.8	$ 139.1	$ 130.0	$ 82.4	$ 106.0
Income Taxes	(117.7)	(109.6)	(68.3)	(50.9)	(37.0)	(33.4)
Net Income	$ 224.2	$ 183.2	$ 70.8	$ 79.1	$ 45.4	$ 72.6

(Continued)

Exhibit 1 (Continued)

The Saab Car Division's sales and net income were as follows:

	1987	1986	1985	1984	1983	1982
Sales	$2,520.8	$1,985.9	$1,338.7	$1,218.6	$1,081.1	$1,003.0
Net Income	91.3	132.2	106.2	113.1	107.0	
Net Income as % of Sales	3.6%	6.7%	7.9%	9.3%	9.9%	
(a) Swedish kronor were converted to U.S. dollars at						
the following exchange rates:						
average for the year	6.34	7.12	8.60	8.27	7.67	6.28
year-end	5.84	6.82	7.61	8.99	7.99	7.29

Source: Company Annual Reports.

Exhibit 2   Saab-Scania Consolidated Balance Sheet

	1987	1986	1985	1984	1983	1982
Assets						
Current Assets:						
Cash and marketable securities	$1,014.9	$ 749.7	$ 562.4	$ 407.6	$ 430.2	$ 336.6
Accounts receivable	994.3	724.9	635.4	483.7	491.6	449.6
Prepaid expenses and accrued income	117.6	76.4	77.6	31.5	27.7	19.8
Inventory	1,617.5	1,285.5	1,023.6	822.2	743.3	768.5
	$3,744.3	$2,836.5	$2,299.0	$1,745.0	$1,692.8	$1,574.5
Blocked investment reserves	10.3	35.0	35.4	4.5	4.0	2.6
Bond obligations from Denmark	13.0	14.8	16.7	16.9	22.3	27.9
Fixed assets:						
Long-term receivables	$ 150.7	$ 67.7	$ 40.7	$ 46.1	$ 51.0	$ 75.3
Shares, bonds, and other securities	459.5	241.9	36.0	24.3	21.5	21.0
Property, plant, and equipment	1,947.4	1,417.3	1,080.2	759.2	681.1	605.3
Total Assets	$6,325.2	$4,613.2	$3,508.0	$2,596.0	$2,472.7	$2,306.6
Liabilities and Stockholders' Equity						
Current liabilities:						
Bank loans	$ 253.1	$ 189.0	$ 195.3	$ 143.5	$ 238.5	$ 322.7
Accounts payable	643.2	440.8	381.3	309.3	186.3	133.1
Accrued expenses and prepaid income	672.1	434.9	377.0	221.5	189.5	212.9
Other current liabilities	255.1	215.0	165.5	134.1	131.3	122.2
Advance payments from customers	479.5	392.8	279.5	231.2	232.1	186.1
	$2,303.0	$1,672.5	$1,398.6	$1,039.6	$ 977.7	$ 977.0

(Continued)

Exhibit 2   (Continued)

	1987	1986	1985	1984	1983	1982
Bond loans from Denmark	12.8	14.7	16.4	16.7	21.9	27.4
Long-term liabilities:						
Long-term loans	$ 651.2	$ 432.1	$ 222.7	$ 192.8	$ 218.5	$ 235.0
Provisions for pensions	367.5	287.5	234.3	179.2	177.6	177.3
Provision for vehicle damage	20.7	14.7	10.6	7.6	7.5	7.6
Minority interest in subsidiaries	55.3	42.1	4.9	4.0	3.7	4.0
Untaxed investment reserve	1,768.5	1,318.5	1,054.0	721.8	632.2	507.8
Stockholders' equity:						
Common stock	$ 290.6	$ 177.7	$ 159.3	$ 134.8	$ 151.7	$ 138.6
Preferred stock	1.0	0.9	0.8	0.7	0.8	0.8
Statutory reserves	256.7	240.6	155.0	125.7	139.4	101.5
Unappropriated earnings	350.3	220.4	166.9	97.2	94.1	64.9
Net income	247.6	191.5	84.5	75.9	47.5	64.7
Total Liabilities and Stockholders' Equity	**$6,325.2**	**$4,613.2**	**$3,508.0**	**$2,596.0**	**$2,472.7**	**$2,306.6**

Source: Company Annual Reports.

Exhibit 3   Geographic Breakdown of Saab Car Sales

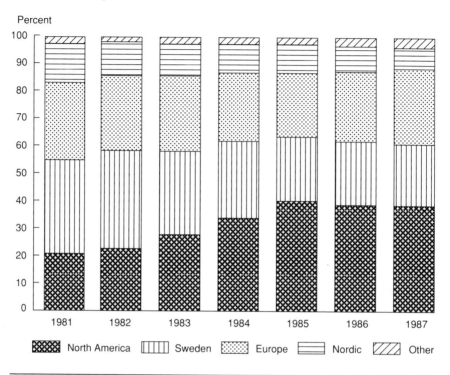

Source: Company Documents

the car division into export markets. People flocked to the rallies in hopes that they could meet Saab officials and be allowed to set up small dealerships to sell Saab cars in their home country. As a result of the interest of those enthusiasts, small numbers of Saabs were being sold everywhere from South America to Asia to Africa. It was also during the earlier rally days that Saab Motors USA, an export arm in the United States, was established in 1956.

As Saab continued riding on the coattails of its rally victories in the mid-1970s, management realized that the division was fighting against mass-produced cars from other countries with lower labor costs. It needed to find a new product to help cover those and other growing costs while enriching the product line. Saab's general manager at the time, Sten Wennlo, provided the inspiration for a new breed of Saab car. The result of his efforts was unveiled at the 1977 Frankfurt Motor Show, when the production model of the Saab 99 Turbo was introduced to the public. The turbo car prototype had been ready for test driving one year earlier than anticipated and just three months after Wennlo told the development team to deliver him such a car. After test driving the turbo car, Wennlo was convinced that the turbo was the answer to Saab's cost problems.

Though the turbo-charger had been used by German car maker BMW for its rally cars and by Porsche in its expensive model 911, Bengt Ödmann, Vice President of Sales and Marketing, observed that the turbo had not been a commercial success in the market that served the ordinary motorist. Both Ödmann and Wennlo agreed that Saab's version of the "family turbo" involved a more civilized approach to gaining the extra power from a turbocharged engine. The Saab-pioneered turbo concept allowed the company to charge a premium price for their turbo cars. The Saab turbo also proved to be a large commercial success in export markets. As Ödmann explained, "The turbo is our anchor when it comes to profitability. The turbo buyer is less sensitive about prices. However, we're not out to save the world. We're out to reach the one person in 20,000 to 30,000 who wants what the turbo delivers." In 1987, 33 percent of all Saab cars sold were turbo models.

By the early 1970s, Saab had evolved into a small, specialty auto producer. Its rally successes, coupled with the popular support of a group of Saab enthusiasts turned dealers, had made the Saab car division an international exporter without any real planning in that direction. Wennlo remarked that Saab had sold twice as many cars in Kenya as in West Germany in the 1960s. It was the need to eliminate extraneous export markets with small "garage-type" dealers (borne from the rally days) that led the company to establish the Saab Car Division in 1972. At that time, Saab began the task of categorizing its markets geographically and the division focused on those markets that were close to home (Europe, Nordic countries, United States). The division's top management all agreed, however, that they needed to build both volume and profitability.

Indeed, both Saab and Volvo, the other large Swedish automaker, were so apprehensive regarding the future of the auto industry, that a merger of the two auto companies was briefly considered in 1977 to increase Sweden's world car presence. At that time, Saab cars, though they had competed well at home, were not doing well in the world market. However, Saab ultimately rejected the merger proposal because closer study of the proposal by both the passenger car and truck units led to the idea being abandoned for various strategic reasons. Moreover, Saab believed that home market competition was healthy and would lead to a more finely honed organization for competition in export markets.

A New Strategic Decision in 1979

By 1979, Saab management wondered if the car division would survive into the 1980s. Edur Karlsson, sales and marketing planning manager, recounted outsider's speculation at that time: "They wondered if we could be profitable on a volume of just 100,000 cars each year." Wennlo's response to the dilemma was, "We have no choice but to find our niche in the business." As a result, division management was forced to rethink the future of Saab cars, and made the decision to implement a new business strategy in late 1979. The turbo project had served as a pilot for the new strategy which focused on providing better quality cars in upscale categories and a more aggressive marketing approach in Europe and the United States. Ödmann and the other members of management believed that, "Because of the size of the Swedish market (only 8 million people) and the high personal income taxes, the upscale end of the home market was not nearly large enough on its own for our new strategy." Saab introduced the 900 model to satisfy their newly defined target market.

The larger 900 model employed an innovative design, and was priced higher than the 99, Saab's only other car at that time. As Karlsson noted, "We tried to price the car so that we could keep those customers who had or would purchase the 99 model and so that we could compete against the other European specialist makers. One method we chose was market-adapted pricing, based on what our competitors were doing." The move into a higher class of car with the more expensive 900, however, meant that many of the old Saab customers could no longer afford to buy new Saabs. The division, therefore, had to make the decision to let part of the old customer group fade out. The 900 also represented a break with Saab tradition. Previously, technicians developed a car, and Saab set out to sell it. Now, strategy was being handed down to the technicians by senior management based on demands from the market place.

The new business strategy also meant that a stronger dealer network would have to be established. That process was somewhat more difficult in Europe than in the United States, because European dealers typically operated a single-franchise dealership and were unwilling to take on another manufacturer's car. In the United States, there were many multi-franchise dealers with a number of different brands under separate roofs. Ödmann noted that approximately 20 percent of U.S. Saab dealers in the 1980's were single-franchise dealers. In both the United States and Europe, those dealers who could sell cheaper models such as the 99 and 96, but were unwilling to expand with the new product line of the 900 were replaced. The result was a high degree of turnover among European Saab dealers. In the United States, the Saab dealer quickly evolved from the car enthusiast to a true businessperson or was replaced by a business-oriented dealer meeting these new criteria.

Another link to the strategy, known as "Project NGS," was the development of a New Generation of Saab, later known as the Saab 9000. The Saab 9000 was designed to compete in the luxury car market, a class above the 900 model. The company wanted a car that could compete with German luxury cars, both in Europe and the U.S. market. Though the first ideas for a larger car were sketched as early as 1973, the project had been forced to the sidelines by the oil crisis, and the launching activities surrounding the 900. However, after the new business strategy was decided upon in 1979, the go ahead was given to continue work on what was to become the 9000 model. By the end of 1984, the first production run of the 9000 began, and the car was introduced to the U.S. market in late 1985. Though Saab had experience introducing new models, the fact remained that, "the 900 was produced as a relatively quick and inexpensive means of developing a new model, by giving the old model 99 a facelift and equipping it with a series of greatly improved and modified engines."[1] Therefore, the development and introduction of the 9000 model was, in many ways, a new experience for Saab.

Saab and the Auto Business

The Saab Car Division was initially organized into three separate operating sectors: Development and Production, Marketing and After Marketing. Later, Development and Materials was split from Production. Each of the sectors was a separate organizational unit reporting to the general manager of the Car Division, who prior to April 1987, was Sten Wennlo, and since that time, Åke Norman.

Development and Materials

Saab's product development, especially since the late 1970s, was aimed at a high degree of product differentiation based on technological innovations. Beginning with Wennlo's testing of the turbo concept for the 99 model in 1977, Saab had successfully introduced a number of automotive features that later became standards for the industry. Starting in the early fifties, Saab was one of the earliest makers of a front-wheel-drive automobile, which was considered quite unorthodox for the time. Later innovations included Saab's diagonal braking system (composed of two independent systems designed to reduce front or rear lock-up), the headlight wiper-washer, five-mile-per-hour "self-repairing" bumpers, and daylight running lights—many of these and other innovations were subsequently adopted by other companies or became mandatory by legislation. The success of Saab's engine innovations was demonstrated in 1986 when Saab set the all-time world speed record for a production car.

Saab's product development philosophy in 1988 focused on two basic models, the 900 and the 9000. See Exhibit 4. The company produced a total of thirteen different versions of the two models, though each was fitted with a four cylinder, 16-valve engine. "Few competitors devoted such intensive efforts to engine development—an aspect which was of fundamental importance to Saab's philosophy."[2] Saab planned to continue to build volume for both models, while broadening the development of the 9000 program into the 1990s. As Public Relations Officer Peter Salzer noted, "Product enrichment will continue to be our tactic." In

[1]Bjorn-Eric Lindh, *The First Forty Years of Saab Cars.* (Stockholm: Forlagshuset Norden AB, 1987), p. 183.

[2]Lindh, p. 164.

Exhibit 4

Early Saab Aircraft & Saab 92

Saab 900 Turbo

1988, development costs represented 8.6 percent of total production-related costs. See Exhibit 5 for operating sector costs.

The production of both the 900 and 9000 models required the assembly of over 4,000 different parts. In 1988, costs for materials represented two-thirds of the total production costs for Saab cars. Both materials purchased from over 500 subcontractors and those materials produced in-house, primarily the engine and transmission, were included in those costs. S-Åke Aronsson, general manager of the production sector, remarked that, "One way of bringing down material costs would be to standardize and produce fewer body types than the 13 body types for the two models we make today. Another would be to increase volumes. Right now there are only two other car makers, Jaguar and Porsche, that produce such a high number of body types with such low volumes."

Exhibit 4   (Continued)

Saab 900 Cabriolet

Saab 9000 Turbo CD

Labor

The Saab Car Division employed 16,180 people in 1988, of which approximately 6,500 were production workers. Typically, Saab was the largest employer in the towns in which its plants were located. Saab's largest plant in Trollhättan was within 45 miles of two of competitor Volvo's car production facilities, resulting in a surplus of available jobs in the area. See Exhibit 6 for a map of Sweden. At Saab, blue collar and white collar labor costs represented 12.6 percent and 7.2 percent of total production costs, respectively. The average car production worker in Sweden cost manufacturers $12.75 per hour in 1987 compared with $19.98 in the United States, $16.91 in West Germany, and $11.97 in Japan.

The demographics of Saab's labor force had changed since the mid-1960s. At that time, fewer Swedish students were following the two-year

Exhibit 5   Comparative Car Production Costs

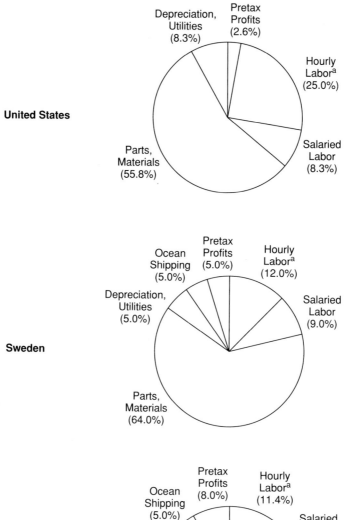

United States

Depreciation, Utilities (8.3%)
Pretax Profits (2.6%)
Hourly Labor[a] (25.0%)
Salaried Labor (8.3%)
Parts, Materials (55.8%)

Sweden

Ocean Shipping (5.0%)
Pretax Profits (5.0%)
Hourly Labor[a] (12.0%)
Depreciation, Utilities (5.0%)
Salaried Labor (9.0%)
Parts, Materials (64.0%)

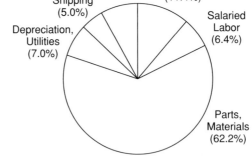

Japan

Ocean Shipping (5.0%)
Pretax Profits (8.0%)
Hourly Labor[a] (11.4%)
Depreciation, Utilities (7.0%)
Salaried Labor (6.4%)
Parts, Materials (62.2%)

[a]Hourly labor does not explicitly include benefits.

Source: Casewriter Estimates

Exhibit 6   Map of Sweden

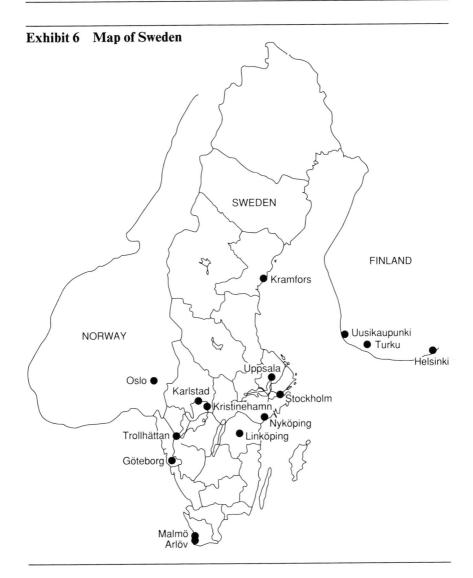

post high school track that led to university study, therefore providing a larger base of workers that would go on to production jobs at Saab. Vocational training was also integrated into a student's high school studies. By the mid-1970s, however, more students went on to follow the post high school track, lowering the number of students who would seek production jobs. In response, Saab began recruiting more women and immigrants. In the mid-1970s, one-third of Saab's employees were immigrants, with over 30 nations represented. By 1988, the percentage of immigrants had dropped to 17 percent, and Saab production workers were younger than their counterparts in the 1960s. Fifty-percent of workers were under 21 years old, and the average assembly line worker was 24 years old.

All of Saab's production workers were represented by a single union, the Metal Workers' Union of Sweden, which had over 460,000 members throughout the country. A framework for wage and benefit contracts was negotiated once each year on a national level in Sweden by the top representatives of all Swedish companies and the top union representatives. The largest union representative was the Swedish Trade Union Federation, (LO), which represented 24 unions and 2.5 million workers. The two largest unions among the 24 represented were the Municipal Workers' Union and The Metal Workers' Union. The largest company representative was the Swedish Employers' Federation (SAF), which represented 43,000 companies.

The wage and benefit contract negotiations covered all member Swedish companies and provided a floor agreement below which no individual company could settle. See Exhibit 7 for social welfare costs in Sweden and the United States. A company like Saab could, however, provide "add-ons" such as a subsidized cafeteria, free work clothes, and in-house physicians. Such additional benefits typically represented less than 7 percent of wages at Saab. Because of the wage floor negotiation system, wages were generally equal across all production jobs in a given category. Anders Svensson, manager of production development, explained another of Sweden's unique labor situations: "All employees in Sweden are in effect permanently employed. It is virtually impossible to fire a worker, and layoffs are allowed after negotiation only if production is scaled back. The only turnover we have, therefore, is the result of an employee's individual reasons." Turnover both in Sweden and for Saab averaged 21 percent among all production workers in 1988, nearly ten times higher than for other European car manufacturers.

Saab, like many other Swedish manufacturers, had a high degree of absenteeism among its production workers. On the average day in a typical Swedish firm and at Saab, between 20 percent and 22 percent of production workers were absent from work. Fifty-percent of the absent workers were on long-term leave (military, parental) and entitled to benefits equivalent to full wages. Those workers that were sick could also collect full wages and benefits for up to one week without a note from their physician. Saab employed between 1500 and 1600 more production workers than they needed to cover the high number of absentees. Absenteeism rates for other countries, such as Finland and Belgium, were between 20 percent and 30 percent less than for Sweden.

Production

When Saab began producing cars in 1946, the logical production site proved to be the company's military aircraft plant in Trollhättan, Sweden. Built in 1938, the plant was the largest employer in the town, and management hoped that "Project Small Car" could save the plant from closing due to a slowdown in military aircraft production following World War II. By 1988, the parent plant at Trollhättan was the largest of Saab's three car assembly and production facilities, and was completely dedicated to

Exhibit 7 Required Welfare Benefits Paid by the Employer in Sweden and the United States[a] S., 1988 (as a % of salary)

	Sweden[b]			United States	
	(1) Required Benefits for All Workers	(2) Cumulative Benefits for Hourly Workers	(3) Cumulative Benefits for Salaried Workers	(4) Required Benefits for All Workers	(5) Average Benefit Costs for All Workers
(1) Total pensions and savings	19.95%	23.13%	28.45%	7.51%	12.00%
Pension plans					3.79%
Savings and thrift plans					0.70%
Social security				7.51%	7.51%
National supplemental pension	10.00%	10.00%	10.00%		
National basic pension	9.45%	9.45%	9.45%		
Partial pension insurance	0.50%	0.50%	0.50%		
Supplementary pension		3.18%	8.50%		
(2) Total health insurance	9.30%	11.66%	9.65%		7.78%
Basic health insurance	9.30%	9.30%	9.30%		7.78%
Group health and disability insurance		1.40%			
Labor market no-fault liability insurance		0.42%	0.05%		
Occupational group life insurance		0.54%	0.30%		
(3) Total paid leave	12.00%	12.00%	12.00%		9.30%
Vacation pay	12.00%	12.00%	12.00%		4.80%
Holiday pay					3.29%
Sick leave pay					1.20%
(4) Total workers' compensation	0.60%	0.60%	0.60%	2.40%	2.40%
(5) Occupational safety	0.35%	0.35%	0.35%		

(Continued)

Exhibit 7   (Continued)

| | Sweden[b] | | | United States | |
	(1) Required Benefits for All Workers	(2) Cumulative Benefits for Hourly Workers	(3) Cumulative Benefits for Salaried Workers	(4) Required Benefits for All Workers	(5) Average Benefit Costs for All Workers
(6) Total job security	0.00%	0.32%	0.90%	1.50%	1.50%
Employment security fund		0.07%	0.90%		
Federal unemployment insurance				0.30%	0.30%
State unemployment insurance				1.20%	1.20%
Severance pay		0.20%			
Lay-off pay facility		0.05%			
(7) Total miscellaneous benefits	6.25%	6.25%	6.25%		3.32%
Labor market contribution	1.59%	1.59%	1.59%		
Premium pay					1.70%
Nonproduction bonuses					1.20%
Shift pay					0.40%
Adult education	0.26%	0.26%	0.26%		
Wage guarantee	0.20%	0.20%	0.20%		
Child care	2.20%	2.20%	2.20%		
General payroll tax	2.00%	2.00%	2.00%		
Other benefits					0.02%
Total required payments	48.45%	48.45%	48.45%	11.41%	11.41%
Total payments		54.31%	58.20%		36.26%

[a]Employees do not make contributions to welfare benefits in Sweden and employees in the United States are required to contribute 7.51 percent of salary to pensions only.

[b]Additional benefits are the result of collective agreements.

Source: Swedish Embassy Labor Department, U.S. Department of Labor, Bureau of Labor Statistics.

the manufacture of automobiles. The Trollhättan plant also housed the development and materials sectors.

In addition to the main production facility in Trollhättan, Saab produced and assembled cars in Arlov, Sweden, and Uusikaupunki, Finland. The Finnish plant was 50 percent owned by Saab and 50 percent owned by Finland. Wages and benefits for Finnish workers were much the same as those for Swedish workers. Saab also had smaller components production facilities in Kramfors, Kristinehamn, and Nyköping, all in Sweden. In 1988, potential capacity was approximately 55,000 cars at Trollhättan, 50,000 at Uusikaupunki, and 30,000 in Arlov. The Arlov plant would be phased out in 1989, and a new plant in Malmö, Sweden, capable of producing 60,000 cars, would be phased in. The new plant was built in Malmö because of the city's large labor force (due in part to the shut down of a shipyard there in 1986), and its location on a harbor.

The major stages involved in car production at Saab's Trollhättan plant were: pressing and stamping, body work, painting, and final assembly. See Exhibit 8 for a flowchart of the production process.

A. Pressing and Stamping. Car production began in the press shop. The press shop received several hundred pieces of metal which were pressed and stamped by workers to form the shape of the body of the car, whether a 900 or 9000 model. Workers in the press shop were typically among the highest skilled and had the longest service records of Saab's production workers. Press shop workers had lower than average absentee rates at 16 percent, of which 6 percent was the result of sickness. Turnover was among the lowest at 10 percent. "One finds more older male workers with families in the press shop," noted Aronsson. "Workers have more influence over their jobs and are generally better motivated here." The press shop operated three shifts at Trollhättan.

B. The Body Shop. After the structure of the body was pressed and stamped at the press shop, it continued on to the body shop, where all work on the body of the car was completed during two shifts. Work in the body shop had not been performed on an assembly line since 1978. Instead, workers formed teams of 8 to 10 people and carried out all work at fixed stations on stationary bodies. Body shop workers performed a series of tasks including roof work, side body, front end, and floor plan assembly, in a work area that was necessarily noisier and greasier than most others. There were nine workstations, each with its own team, for both the 900 and 9000 models at the Trollhättan plant. The teams allowed greater flexibility than an assembly line in that multiple models could be worked on at once. The team structure in the body shop made it unique among Saab's production areas. "The individual teams," Salzer said, "have a form of 'ownership' of their area, whether it be the floor plan or front assembly area. They are largely responsible for achieving the predetermined targets for volume and financial results, and they participate

Exhibit 8   Saab-Scania: The Car Division

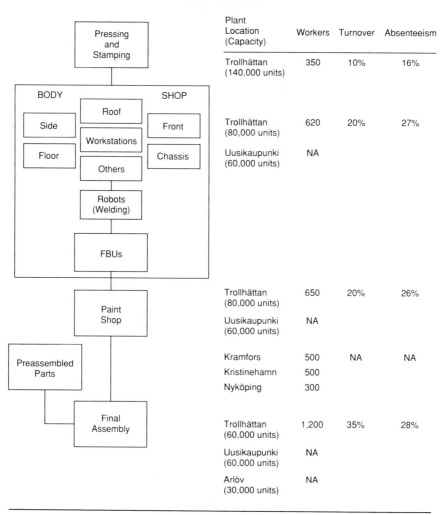

Plant Location (Capacity)	Workers	Turnover	Absenteeism
Trollhättan (140,000 units)	350	10%	16%
Trollhättan (80,000 units)	620	20%	27%
Uusikaupunki (60,000 units)	NA		
Trollhättan (80,000 units)	650	20%	26%
Uusikaupunki (60,000 units)	NA		
Kramfors	500	NA	NA
Kristinehamn	500		
Nyköping	300		
Trollhättan (60,000 units)	1,200	35%	28%
Uusikaupunki (60,000 units)	NA		
Arlöv (30,000 units)	NA		

in constructing their own budgets." Though not as good as the press shop, turnover in the body shop was still relatively low at 20 percent.

The work performed in the body shop after the cars left the team workstations was the most highly automated of all of the production stages. In this stage, robots performed over 80 percent of the spot welding required on each car. Gigantic welding robots automatically assembled and welded the complete body after being programmed for the specific car under construction. After leaving the teams of workers and the robots at the body shop, the cars were considered "fully-built-up (FBU) bodies." Both the Trollhättan and Uusikaupunki plants had body shops but virtually all stamping of body parts occurred at Trollhättan. The Arlov plant began its production process after it received 30,000 of the fully built-up bodies from the Trollhättan plant.

Salzer explained the reasoning behind Saab's decision to introduce the team concept to the initial portion and to automate the final phase of the body shop: "During the mid-1970s, we had difficulty recruiting and keeping workers on the assembly line in our body shops. The jobs were thought of as monotonous and undesirable." At that time, "turnover in the body shop was 78 percent. We needed to improve job content, worker motivation, and involvement," Aronsson added. The initial investment in reengineering the body shop's assembly line to include robots resulted in an increase in capital costs of 10 percent and a reduction in labor costs of 20 percent. However, in the pilot projects in 1976, Saab recouped its initial investment of $2.6 million in less than 3 years. The union was supportive of the automation effort because it meant better quality jobs for its members.

C. Painting. After the robots performed the welding function, the fully built-up units were sent to the paint shop to be painted. Here turnover was on par with the body shop at 20 percent and the absenteeism rate was 25 percent. The paint shop operated one shift, and was heavily automated. Aronsson remarked that, "Our paint shop is not as automated, however, as that of some of our competitors. We have very small production runs, and therefore cannot run off 100 identical green cars." After leaving the paint shop with one of the more than a dozen colors that Saab used, the cars headed for final assembly.

D. Final Assembly. In the final assembly stage, all inspected preassembled units not part of the body such as the chassis, engine, transmission, dashboard, lights, tires, and grille were either placed in or on the car. The final assembly area at Saab operated an assembly line with very little automation. Workers in final assembly had both the highest turnover and absenteeism rates among all of Saab's car workers. Turnover hovered at 34 percent and 28 percent of workers were absent on an average day. Aronsson noted that, "Often times there are 250 people less on Friday than there were the previous Monday." Bo Melander, vice president of the Metal Workers Union in Trollhättan said, "Job enrichment and job content is the only way to compete with other companies in Sweden for employees. It is very difficult to recruit employees to perform assembly line jobs." Saab had considered increasing the amount of automation in their production facilities. However, Svensson noted that, "The workers' costs for this type of operation are still lower than the cost of automating much of the manual work. Right now it would cost between $30 and $40 million to completely automate final assembly. Though automation brings flexibility, we must continue to be cost competitive."

Marketing

Saab's Sales and Marketing Sector, under the direction of Bengt Ödmann, had played an important role in shaping the new business direction that Saab took in 1979. The reworking of the Company's marketing policy to focus on the introduction of the turbo and the 900 model had been pivotal in maintaining Saab's profitability into the 1980s. Saab's market research had also evolved from the early days of building rally cars with aerodynamics that resembled those of an airplane to a solid foundation of research in the 1980s with computerized information systems, and demographic, lifestyle, purchasing habits, and competitor behavior studies. Karlsson explained that, "In 1980, we were not sure if the 900 model would make it to 1985; as it turned out, it was already a large success by 1983 and continues to be so even in the late 1980's. With that model, we learned the importance of looking at the market and producing what our customers wanted." Saab management viewed the average American Saab buyer as well-heeled, highly educated, and unlike many buyers of German luxury cars, unassuming. "Saab buyers are not show-offs," said Karlsson. Saab's advertising campaign focused on Saab as "the most intelligent cars ever built."

By 1988, Saab's marketing drive was focused on increasing sales in its largest market, the United States, while also trying to balance that effort with better sales in Europe and an expansion program into Japan and other Far Eastern markets including Australia. As Ödmann explained the approach: "We have three legs—the Nordic market, the U.S. market, and the European market. We wanted a fourth leg to stand on, and decided to try to penetrate the Japanese and other Pacific-rim markets." Ödmann believed that there were two main reasons for Saab's continued success in the United States: "The management at Saab-Scania of America, under the direction of President Robert Sinclair, has been exceptional. Also, American consumers and car dealers are much more willing to try a new make of car than their more conservative European counterparts." Saab continued its efforts to increase market penetration in the U.S., by seeking to appeal to drivers in the Western and Southern sections of the country. Traditionally thought of as a "snow-car," Saab was looking for ways to market its car in warmer climates. In addition, as part of their drive to increase sales in the luxury segment, Saab introduced the 9000 CD model in 1988. The CD was a sedan version of the 9000 that was targeted towards European and American drivers whose preference had traditionally leaned towards the sedan versions offered by Mercedes and BMW rather than towards the hatchback style of the basic 9000 model.

After Marketing

Saab depended heavily on the strength of its dealer network to build good dealer-customer relationships. It also relied on the dealer's service centers to take care of any minor quality problems that may have developed with its cars. For example, when the Turbo 99 model was first available to customers in 1978, a number of minor problems occurred due to the overheating of a fuel line adjacent to the turbo, Saab decided that the problems should be handled first at the dealer level and then solved at the factory. Ödmann stressed the dealer's importance to Saab's financial well-being, "To continue to earn more, we must continue to improve dealer performance as well as factory-dealer relations." As part of that effort, Saab had invested heavily in dealer and salesperson training centers.

Competitors

Saab Cars competed with a number of manufacturers domestically and internationally in the upscale car market. In the Nordic market (Denmark, Finland, Norway, and Sweden), Saab's closest competitors were Volvo and BMW. Karlsson believed that consumers in the Nordic market perceived Saab's market position to be "slightly above that of Volvo, but slightly below that of BMW." Throughout Europe and the United States, Saab viewed the 9000 and 900 Turbo's strongest competitors as Audi, BMW, Mercedes, and Volvo. The less expensive 900 models competed against a wider range of cars including some American and Japanese makes. In addition to the current list of competitors, Ödmann believed that the Japanese manufacturers, following the example of American Honda's Acura Division, posed a threat as they continued to enter the luxury car market with cars produced with lower labor and materials costs. For example, both Nissan and Toyota were planning to introduce their new luxury sedans, Infiniti and Lexus, in 1989 targeted towards the upscale car buyer.

In 1987, Volvo's total car sales across all markets were 418,600 units and $6.2 billion. Volvo sold 26 percent of its cars in the United States in 1987 for a total of $2.4 billion. Though Volvo was Saab's closest competitor, its strategy involved producing an entire range of cars. Its top-of-the-line model 780 was introduced in 1987 to appeal to its customers as they upgraded to new models. The thrust of Volvo's advertising campaign was safety and quality. Other competitors such as BMW and Mercedes stressed both luxury, and high performance features, but they also carried high price tags. Ödmann defended the uniqueness of Saab's strategy compared to that of its competitors, "We are a small car manufacturer with high costs and a short series of models. We're running a small shop, not a Macy's."

The U.S. market imported over 4 million cars from 23 manufacturers in 1987, making it the largest car importer in the world. Saab's unit market share of the U.S. import market was 1.12 percent in 1987, while Volvo's share was 2.65 percent, and BMW and Mercedes enjoyed shares of 2.19 percent and 2.24 percent, respectively. Japanese manufacturers dominated the U.S. import market with a 66.97 percent unit share. Saab cars enjoyed a unit share of 8.5 percent of their relevant market segment in the United States in 1987 and a 2.0 percent share in Western Europe. The 900 model alone had a segment market share of 1.5 percent in Western Europe in 1987. See Exhibit 9 for Saab's segment market share data of the U.S. import market.

Saab, like Volvo, took advantage of the depreciation of the Swedish

Exhibit 9   World Market Share Data of the Segment in Which Saab Competes

Share Percent	1987	1986	1985	1984	1983	1982	1981	1980	1979	1978
Sweden	16.6%	18.0%	15.8%	19.7%	19.8%	29.6%	29.0%	27.9%	25.6%	23.7%
Nordic countries excluding Sweden	6.5%	7.1%	7.4%	9.2%	9.6%	19.4%	19.7%	18.4%	17.9%	17.0%
Western Europe	2.1%	2.1%	1.8%	2.0%	1.9%	1.7%	1.6%	1.2%	1.0%	0.8%
United States[a]	8.5%	8.0%	8.1%	8.1%	7.2%	6.0%	5.3%	6.3%	7.1%	7.9%
TOTAL	5.1%	5.3%	4.7%	5.0%	4.7%	4.4%	3.8%	3.3%	3.1%	3.0%

[a]In 1987, Saab's relevant market segment in the United States was dominated by Volvo, which had a unit share of 18.2%. The BMW 300 and 500 series held the second largest share (12.8%), followed by the Toyota Supra and Cressida models (9.0%). Saab had the fourth largest share (8.5%), just ahead of Mazda's RX-7 and 929 (7.9%), and Audi (6.4%). Other players in the segment included the Acura Legend, Porsche 944, Peugeot 505, and the Maserati Biturbo.

Source: Company documents.

kronor from 1981 to 1985. Ödmann explained, "The favorable exchange rate helped us achieve the level of success that we did in the U.S. market." However, with the dollar's depreciation beginning in late 1985, Saab and the other European car manufacturers began losing market share as a result of their cars' higher prices. The U.S. tax reform bill and the stock-market crash in late 1987 reduced the number of upscale cars sold in the United States as well, as buyers turned to less expensive models.

Saab priced its cars based on the pricing policies of its competitors. The company began by looking at each of the markets its models competed in and selecting its main competitors. However, rather than pricing at their level, Saab focused on pricing slightly lower. "Unlike Mercedes, the leader in the luxury car market, which has an initial perception of their cars' market value and prices according to their cost increases, we must be cost competitive," said Karlsson. Saab's car prices had increased an average of 11.9 percent in 1987 and 7.8 percent in 1988 across all models, primarily as a result of exchange rate fluctuations and the addition of the new 16-valve engine to the 900 series.

The Saab car division had progressed from a limited producer of rally cars in the early 1940s to one of Sweden's largest exporters in 1988 and a top international car manufacturer. Saab had expanded rapidly in the period since 1979. Capital expenditures alone had grown at a compounded annual rate of 58 percent from 1982 to 1986. Two new products had been launched, a new plant at Malmö had been built, and the dealer network had been upgraded to match Saab's move into upscale markets. Saab's worldwide sales throughout the 1980s had grown at an average annual rate of 10 percent. As car buyers gradually changed over to the more expensive 9000 models, Saab believed its dollar car sales would continue to rise even more sharply. For 1988, Saab's total worldwide volume was 120,000 cars. With the addition of the Malmö plant, the company will gradually expand capacity to 180,000 units in the 1990s. The new capacity additions were needed to meet planned growth in Europe and the Far East, as well as North America.

The Swedish Economy in 1988

In 1988, the Swedish standard of living ranked among the highest in the world. Among the largest industrialized nations, gross national product (GNP) per capita in Sweden was surpassed by only three countries, one of which was the United States. The differential in personal incomes had been lowered by a steeply progressive income tax system and a wage policy that assigned priority to the lowest income groups. In 1988, income in the highest bracket was taxed at a federal rate of 72 percent, placing Sweden among the most highly taxed countries in the world. The average wage earner grossed $20,000 per year in 1988 and was taxed at a 50 percent rate. The average corporate tax rate was 52 percent. In addition to the high rate of federal income tax, the state income tax rate averaged 30.4 percent, and the value-added tax in Sweden was 23 percent.

Not only did Sweden have the highest income tax rates in the world, it also had a comprehensive social welfare benefit system that was the most generous in the world. Some of the social benefits that workers received were the result of collective bargaining agreements while others were the result of political decisions. In Sweden, 87 percent of the workforce (but 100 percent of blue collar workers) belonged to a union, compared to 20 percent in the United States, and 30 percent in West Germany. In 1988, the lowest level of non-wage social welfare benefits that companies were required to pay to all workers was 49.85 percent of a worker's pre-tax cash salary. However, the unions typically gained supplemental benefits for their workers, which raised that level to 56.05 percent. Salaried (white collar) workers received additional benefits that raised the level again to 59.60 percent. Swedish workers were not required to contribute any of their salary in benefits, though a portion of their income taxes funded the social welfare system. By comparison, the U.S. government required employers to pay 11.4 percent of a worker's annual pre-tax salary in social benefits and required employees to pay 7.5 percent. See Exhibit 10 for comparative social welfare costs in other countries. One of the largest problems Sweden faced in 1988 and the years ahead was the country's growing aging population. Retirement pensions were granted from the age of 65. In 1987, there were more than 1.5 million persons aged 65 and over (19 percent of the total population). This growing number of elderly people has led to increased public spending, especially on pensions and health care.

The social welfare system in Sweden was partially credited for the historically low unemployment rate in Sweden. Unemployment was 1.7 percent in Sweden in 1988, compared with nearly 9 percent in West Germany and under 6 percent in the United States. Because of the benefits each worker received and the virtual guarantee of lifetime employment, employee turnover was typically only the result of job dissatisfaction. In 1987, over half of Sweden's population of 8.4 million people were employed. However, with very slow population growth and prolonged life expectancy, those suited for employment (aged 16 to 64) constituted a declining percentage of the total population. Though there was a large inflow of immigrants into Sweden from the 1950s to the 1970s that increased the employable population, there had been a net outflow of immigrants from the labor pool in the 1980s.

Sweden's welfare system was the result of the policies of the Social Democratic government, which had ruled Sweden for all but six years from 1932 to 1988. The Social Democratic Party had the governing majority of the 349 seats in the Riksdag (legislature), which was the ultimate decision-making body. Presiding over the government was the Prime Minister, Ingvar Carlsson, who was assisted by 20 ministers. The ministers provided the basis for decision-making by preparing and submitting bills to the Riksdag for voting. Prime Minister Carlsson had been the

Exhibit 10   Employer and Employee Contributions to Average Welfare Benefits 1988 (as % of salary)

	Sweden		United States		W. Germany		Japan	
	Employer	Employee	Employer	Employee	Employer	Employee	Employer	Employee
Pensions	23.5%	0.0%	12.0%	7.5%	9.6%	9.6%	6.2%	6.2%
Health insurance	13.1%	0.0%	7.8%	0.0%	6.1%	6.1%	4.2%	4.2%
Unemployment	0.0%	0.0%	1.5%	0.0%	2.0%	2.0%	0.9%	0.6%
Workers' compensation	0.6%	0.0%	2.4%	0.0%	2.0%[b]	0.0%	7.0%[b]	0.0%
Paid leave	12.0%	0.0%	9.3%	0.0%	0.0%	0.0%	0.0%	0.0%
Occupational safety	0.4%	0.0%	0.0%	0.0%	0.0%	0.0%	0.0%	0.0%
Other benefits	6.3%	0.0%	3.3%	0.0%	0.0%	0.0%	0.0%	0.0%
Total average benefits	56.1%	0.0%	36.3%	7.5%	19.7%	17.7%	18.4%	11.0%
Total of employer and employee average contributions	56.1%		43.8%		37.4%		29.4%	

[a] 1986 data.

[b] Workers' compensation rates differ according to the risks of individual job categories. The rate shown is the average across all categories.

Source: Joseph A. Pechman, Comparative Tax Systems: Europe, Canada, and Japan. OECD, The Tax/Benefit Position of Production Workers 1986, Swedish Embassy, and the U.S. Department of Labor, Bureau of Labor Statistics.

successor to former Prime Minister Olof Palme, when Palme was assassinated in 1986.

In 1988, the government's economic policies focused on promoting an even distribution of real incomes, achieving price stability, and maintaining low unemployment. The stringent tax system, including a wealth tax levied on individuals whose income exceeded the equivalent of $65,000, helped smooth out real income distribution. Inflation in Sweden had followed the international upward trend in the 1960s and 1970s. The second oil price shock nearly doubled inflation from 7.2 percent in 1979 to 13.8 percent in 1980. By 1982, inflation had dropped to 8.6 percent on an annual basis, though following a devaluation later in that year, it climbed slightly to 8.9 percent. In 1988, inflation had been reduced to 6 percent, but was still ahead of most Western European countries. The Swedish government had, on several occasions since the 1970s, introduced price controls in the form of a general freeze on the price of goods and services.

Legislation in 1955 allowed companies to set aside up to 50 percent of pre-tax income as a reserve for future investment. This amount was also tax deductible for national income tax purposes. All of the income set aside had to be deposited in a special interest-free account with the Bank of Sweden. Control over the release of the funds was in the hands of the government. The government typically allowed companies to use its reserves for building construction, acquiring new machinery, and export promotion. When the government authorized the use of funds, the amount was not restored to taxable income. The investment reserve system was originally designed as a stabilization policy for Sweden, whereby the government would authorize the use of funds only during recessionary periods. However, by the mid-1970s, the system had evolved into a permanent investment stimulus for Swedish companies, with fund releases allowed each year, not just during recessions.

The Swedish economic environment, with its comparatively low unemployment, high tax rates, and generous social welfare benefits, appeared to provide a recipe for poor international competitiveness in the early 1970s. New technologies were spreading to countries with lower labor costs and then competing with Swedish exports. A series of currency devaluations in the late 1970s and early 1980s, permitted some recapture of the country's lost market share. However, much to the critics' surprise, by 1988, Sweden ran a trade surplus of $4.5 billion compared to the U.S. trade deficit of $160 billion. The Swedish trade performance in 1988 was largely a result of the expertise of companies in the transport equipment, electrical, telecommunications, chemical, and pharmaceutical industries. Saab-Scania, the fourth largest company in Sweden, was a major contributor to Sweden's export success. In 1987, the company's total exports would have accounted for virtually all of Sweden's trade surplus.

Questions

1. What is unique about the macroeconomic environment in which the SAAB Car division operates?
2. Describe the SAAB Car division's strategy. Evaluate their success in the international auto industry.
3. Will SAAB be able to maintain its competitiveness in the future? What are the major threats? What changes in strategy should SAAB management consider?

INDEX

ate Due